COVERED WITH NIGHT

COVERED
WITH
NIGHT

A Story of Murder and Indigenous
Justice in Early America

NICOLE EUSTACE

LIVERIGHT PUBLISHING CORPORATION

A DIVISION OF W. W. NORTON & COMPANY

Independent Publishers Since 1923

For information about permission to reproduce selections from this book, write to
Permissions, Liveright Publishing Corporation, a division of
W. W. Norton & Company, Inc., 500 Fifth Avenue, New York, NY 10110

For information about special discounts for bulk purchases, please contact
W. W. Norton Special Sales at specialsales@wwnorton.com or 800-233-4830

Manufacturing by LSC Communications, Harrisonburg
Production manager: Anna Oler

Library of Congress Cataloging-in-Publication Data

Names: Eustace, Nicole, author.
Title: Covered with night : a story of murder and indigenous justice in
early America / Nicole Eustace.
Description: First edition. | New York : Liveright Publishing Corporation, [2021] |
Includes bibliographical references and index.
Identifiers: LCCN 2020050130 | ISBN 9781631495878 (hardcover) |
ISBN 9781631495885 (epub)
Subjects: LCSH: Murder—United States—History—18th century. |
Criminal justice, Administration of—United States—History—18th century. |
Homicide investigation—United States—History—18th century.
Classification: LCC HV6524 .E78 2021 | DDC 364.152/30973—dc23
LC record available at https://lccn.loc.gov/2020050130

Liveright Publishing Corporation, 500 Fifth Avenue, New York, N.Y. 10110
www.wwnorton.com

W. W. Norton & Company Ltd., 15 Carlisle Street, London W1D 3BS

For

Alexander Thomas Eustace Klancnik

James Louis Eustace Klancnik

and

James Michael Klancnik, Jr.

This I would do if I found anyone burdened with grief
    even as I am.
I would console them for they would be covered with
    night and wrapped in darkness.
This would I lift with the words of condolence
and these strands of beads would become words with
    which I would address them.

—HIAWATHA, attributed by tradition,
The Constitution of the Five Nations or
the Iroquois Book of the Great Law

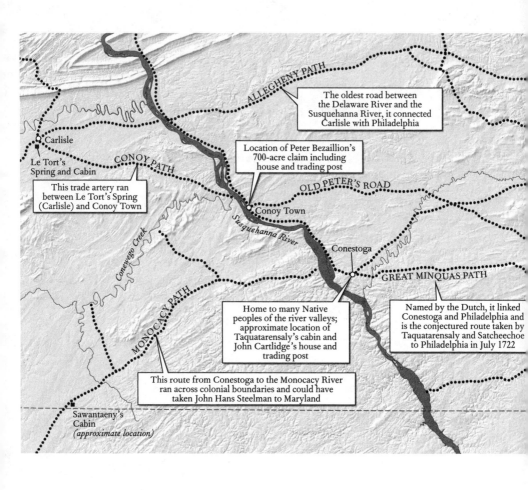

ALLEGHENY PATH

The oldest road between the Delaware River and the Susquehanna River, it connected Carlisle with Philadelphia

Carlisle

Le Tort's Spring and Cabin

CONOY PATH

Location of Peter Bezaillion's 700-acre claim including house and trading post

OLD PETER'S ROAD

This trade artery ran between Le Tort's Spring (Carlisle) and Conoy Town

Conewego Creek

Conoy Town

Susquehanna River

Conestoga

GREAT MINQUAS PATH

MONOCACY PATH

Home to many Native peoples of the river valleys; approximate location of Taquatarensaly's cabin and John Cartlidge's house and trading post

Named by the Dutch, it linked Conestoga and Philadelphia and is the conjectured route taken by Taquatarensaly and Satcheechoe to Philadelphia in July 1722

This route from Conestoga to the Monocacy River ran across colonial boundaries and could have taken John Hans Steelman to Maryland

Sawantaeny's Cabin
(approximate location)

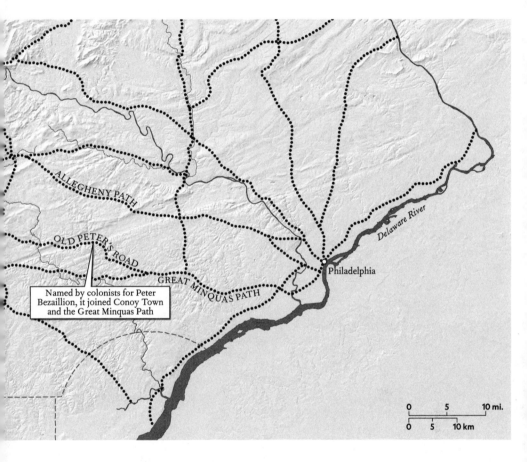

Named by colonists for Peter Bezaillion, it joined Conoy Town and the Great Minquas Path

ALLEGHENY PATH

OLD PETER'S ROAD

GREAT MINQUAS PATH

Delaware River

Philadelphia

0   5   10 mi.
0   5   10 km

"Indigenous Routes in the Susquehanna River Valley." Prepared for the author by Mapping Specialists. Based on a map from Paul A. W. Wallace, Indian Paths of Pennsylvania (Pennsylvania Historical & Museum Commission, 2018). Used with permission.

CONTENTS

COVERED WITH NIGHT

T OWARD THE END OF 1721, A QUAKER MAN NAMED ISAAC Norris discovered an alarming prediction in *The American Almanack for the Year of Christian Account, 1722*. A local magistrate, successful merchant, and gentleman farmer, Norris had stepped into the print-shop at the Sign of the Bible on Second Street in Philadelphia looking for weather predictions, not astrological speculations. More than a century after the first permanent English settlements were established in Jamestown and still half a century before a then-unimaginable break from the British Empire, colonists of Norris's era believed they were living in a new age of prosperity and rationality. Few could have expected that 1722 would usher in a crisis so severe that it would trans-fix the eastern seaboard from Native communities to colonial capitals and lead to debates that still echo today. But the pages of the 1722 *American Almanack* did provide certain clues about imminent events.[1]

Scanning the almanac pages in the weak December light, perhaps Norris felt no shiver of anticipation over its prediction of a "Total Eclipse of the Moon" sure to be "visible, if the Air be clear, on the 17th day of *June*." Illustrated with a woodcut of a dark-faced moon, the book warned that this celestial event "portends much evil." Specifi-cally, the author Titan Leeds claimed, the year would bring "*Consump-tions, Feavors, Fears, Exiles*." The list of coming catastrophes grew longer and ever more dire as Leeds predicted the "*Death of the Elder People*." Most ominous of all, Leeds called for the "*Murder* of some," adding, "and because the Eclipse falls in the *12th* house near the Drag-ons Tail i'll predict *Imprisonment* too." Isaac Norris, sensible Quaker, likely took little alarm at first. What he could not know, as he requested his own personal printing of the almanac—asking the shopkeeper and publisher Andrew Bradford to interleave his copy with blank pages on which he could jot personal notes and to bind the whole thing with a sturdy paperboard cover—was that every one of Leeds's predictions would soon come to pass.[2]

The book you now hold in your hands tells the story of that fateful year. Before another twelve months went by, the colony would be convulsed by a murder case involving two colonial fur traders and an Indian hunter. After a drunken night of bargaining beside a winter campfire in the woods near the Susquehanna River, two brothers named John and Edmund Cartlidge would assault a Seneca man named Sawantaeny and leave him for dead. Rival investigations by Indian leaders, including a Native spokesman known as "Captain Civility," and colonial officials, including Isaac Norris, resulted in fierce debates about the nature of true justice.

Many feared the attack might become just the first act of a full-scale war. The crisis created by the confrontation grew so grave that news of it reached the king's closest counselors on the British Board of Trade. It fueled urgent concern not only among the members of the Five Nations of the Haudenosaunee, including the Seneca Nation to which Sawantaeny belonged, but also among all the various Native peoples of the Susquehanna River valley, from Iroquois groups such as the Susquehannock (who were affiliates but not official members of the Five Nations) to Algonquian ones such as the Lenape and the Shawnee. Resolving the case required a region-wide treaty conference, including the governors of three colonies and the leaders of over a dozen Native nations. The Great Treaty of 1722, signed in Albany, New York, in September of that year, brought the case to a close, but it could not put to rest the questions about savagery, civility, and justice it raised.

Today, when people think of the founding documents of the United States, nothing from 1722 is likely to come to mind. Most people, of course, remember the Declaration of Independence and the Constitution of the United States. Those who have a longer arc of justice in view may think of the "Emancipation Proclamation" of 1863 or, perhaps, the related Civil War–era constitutional amendments that out-lawed slavery, guaranteed equal citizenship, and secured the right to vote regardless of race or previous freedom status. Perhaps some will cast their minds still further forward to the Nineteenth Amendment of 1920, granting women the right to vote. A small number may even call up the Indian Citizenship Act of 1924, which first offered Native people rights as citizens of the United States. But very few people will ever have found reason to stop to think of an obscure piece of parch-ment signed at Albany in 1722. Rare are those who have even heard of this agreement between members of the Five Nations of the Haudeno-saunee and representatives from the colonies of New York, Pennsylva-nia, and Virginia. Yet this is the oldest continuously recognized treaty in the history of the United States. Much more than a simple diplomatic instrument, the treaty records a foundational American debate over the nature of justice, one with guidance still left to give.[3]

THE GREAT TREATY OF 1722 entered into general obscurity almost as soon as it was written. The colonists who traveled to Albany for cross-cultural discussions that autumn believed they were averting a war, but they could not have known that they were enacting a key moment in American culture. Because they regarded the Native leaders they conferenced with as simple "savages," colonial magistrates could not imagine the possibility that the Indigenous ideas they were encounter-ing would endure for generations, dormant seeds awaiting the right moment for renewal.

Eighteenth-century Europeans and the settler colonists they sent to North America thought that the world could be neatly divided between savage peoples and civilized ones. As the French political phi-losopher Montesquieu summed things up in his masterwork, *The Spirit of Laws*, guiding legal principles arose from the character of the people who created them, "influenced by the climate, by the religion, by the laws, by the maxims of government, by precedents, morals, and cus-toms; from whence is formed a general spirit of nations." Montesquieu, in common with his European contemporaries, was quite sure that "nature and the climate rule almost alone over the savages." Assuring themselves that "savages" existed in a state of nature almost entirely removed from culture, European theorists gave little credence to the possibility of Native American philosophy.[4]

Yet the Pennsylvania murder case of 1722 contradicted such opinions; it led the Susquehannock man using the title "Captain Civility" to counsel colonial agents on the terms of true justice. John and Edmund Cartlidge violated both English and Indian norms of civilized behavior by attacking Sawantaeny. Brawling over a trade gone bad, the traders knocked the hunter unconscious, then fled the scene. By attacking Sawantaeny, the Cartlidges pitched all the peoples of the Susquehanna River valley into crisis. Because the Native man belonged to the Seneca Nation, one of the Five Nations of the Haudenosaunee, his death also drew concern from across Iroquoia, in Native communities from colonial Pennsylvania to colonial New York. Anxious to avert warfare, colonial leaders promised Native peoples that they would subject the accused killers to justice, even though a murder charge, if it were brought, could mean capital punishment for their own colonists.[5]

"Captain Civility" stepped forward to represent the Native peoples of the river valleys. Claiming the title by virtue of his unstinting efforts to bring people together in civil society, this diplomat tried to teach colonists the strength of the Indigenous commitment to building community. Native peoples sorrowing for Sawantaeny were "covered with night and wrapped in darkness," as generations of Iroquois storytellers would describe the feeling of grief. Dawn could come only when the mourners' grief was assuaged. On that new day, killers and survivors could become fully reconciled to one another. Following the loss of Sawantaeny, Captain Civility offered to welcome the traders back to Native villages, as soon as the colonists metaphorically "covered" the body of the slain man, by offering both ritual condolences and reparation payments. Native principles of civility stretched wide enough to embrace even the Cartlidge brothers, men accused of crimes so severe that the colonists believed that their actions might—pending an investigation of the precise circumstances of the killing—deserve a judicial sentence of death.[6]

Colonists were so unprepared for Native offers of clemency, a total inversion of their expectations, that they made little deliberate note of the philosophy that informed Native policy. Indigenous ideals entered the record made at Albany almost inadvertently, the by-product of colonial desires to document the land and trade agreements that would further Pennsylvania's prosperity and security. Still, colonists dutifully set down the speeches that Captain Civility and other Native speakers made to them. And in the process, they preserved Indigenous ideas on crime and punishment, violation and reconciliation. Today, we can learn more from the treaty than colonists were aware of recording. If we adopt Montesquieu's insight that laws offer a unique window into the spirit of a people—while rejecting his contention that some peoples could be cast as "savages" incapable of civility—we may realize how much we have left to learn from eighteenth-century Indigenous ideals of justice.[7]

To understand the spirit, we must tell the story. The essence of the Native approach to justice emerges not in any single piece of writing, authored by an acclaimed solitary genius and preserved for the ages in a magisterial tome. Rather, Indigenous understandings of civility were enacted again and again in countless small interactions and large diplomatic exchanges, in ritual traditions and customary practices passed down from one learned leader to another and shared with even the most ordinary members of society. In itself, the spare text of the Great Treaty of 1722 can only begin to suggest Indigenous attitudes; it gains full significance only when we witness the countless conversations and negotiations that led to its existence. If we step back into the time in which those ideas were recorded and fill in the details of who said what to whom and why, we can emerge with a fresh understanding. We can come to appreciate Indigenous history both for its own sake and for its integral, if too-long-overlooked, place in the history of the United States.[8]

IN MANY WAYS, NEITHER Isaac Norris nor anyone else should have been surprised by Titan Leeds's forecast of troubles to come. When the English boarded tall ships bound for America, they con-

sidered civility their most important cargo. The founding document
of Pennsylvania—the official charter granted by the English Crown
that first established William Penn's authority over the colony—had
declared in 1681 that Penn was acting "out of a commendable desire to
enlarge our English Empire and promote such useful commodities as
may be of benefit to us and our dominions as also to reduce the Savage Natives by Gentle and just manners to the Love of civill society
and Christian Religion." Colonists and Crown alike wanted to win
land and trade through overseas adventures. In return for these material rewards, they offered the original inhabitants of North America
what they regarded as the intangible riches of European culture and
religion. The English were certain that the value of "civil society" was
theirs to share with "savages." Civility, in this sense, was a synonym
for civilization, not mere good manners. But in any case, refined conduct had little to do with it. Those who called themselves "civill" were
frequently and extraordinarily violent.[9]

From the earliest days of the English Empire, its architects took
strength from classical theories that justified the seizure of alien lands
and peoples on the basis of the supposedly superior civilization of the
imperialists. In the sixteenth century, at a time when the Spanish were
establishing a significant empire on the other side of the Atlantic, the
English rehearsed for overseas expansion by invading Ireland. Sir
Thomas Smith, a professor and administrator at Cambridge University, opined in his 1549 *Discourse of the Commonweal of this Realm of
England* that "among all the nations of the world, they that be politic
and civil do master the rest." Civility guaranteed the right to mastery.
The very proof that the Irish were savage lay in England's success in
invading them. By the eighteenth century, as British thinkers began to
develop a new brand of ethics they called "moral philosophy," theorists such as Adam Smith relied on debased images of Native Americans as a key point of comparison with the elevated British. He told his
readers, "Among civilized nations, the virtues which are founded upon
humanity are more cultivated ... Among savages and barbarians, it
is quite otherwise." The rise of moral philosophy, with its high praise
for civility, did not merely coincide with the modern age of empire; it
actively helped underwrite it.[10]

By the time Norris picked up a copy of the Leeds almanac for 1722, the English had been sailing the Atlantic for over a century, seeking fortunes wherever they could. Land for planting, soil for stripping of minerals, forests for harvesting resources from fur to timber, sea lanes for commercial trading, and people for laboring were among the many sources of wealth eyed by English adventurers. And everything began to speed up after 1714, when, at last at peace with France and Spain after a protracted war, the British gained an exclusive contract from Spain to supply its empire with enslaved Africans along with the right to trade throughout the "South Sea," as the ocean around South America was then called. Courtiers and common folk across Britain invested heavily in the South Sea Company, only to lose everything when the bubble burst in 1720. Nothing but improved receipts from the colonies could repair the fortunes of Crown and country, and so the British began to keep a closer eye on North America than ever before. Maintaining smoother relations with Native peoples became key to these new efforts.[11]

The First Nations peoples of North America took immediate interest in trade with those arriving from over the water, and they had been interacting with various Europeans for close to two centuries before William Penn set sail. In the Susquehanna River region that would come to be called Pennsylvania, a Swedish minister created a one-hundred-word phrasebook of words in the Susquehannock language around 1640 that consisted entirely of nouns for food, tools, animals, and trade goods—from *Aanjooʒa*, "Linen, shirts" offered by the Swedes, to *Skajaano*, "valuables skins or furs, as sable etc." provided by Indians—and verb phrases relating to trade and exchange—from *Skaddanijnu*, "Will you sell or barter something?" to *Kassha schæænu*, "Give me that for nothing." As that last phrase hints, however, Native ideas about exchange differed in essential ways from European assumptions. The phrase supposedly meaning "Give me that for nothing" could better have been translated as "Please demonstrate your generosity and benevolent intentions with a gift." And indeed, words for friendship account for four of the seventy-six words or phrases included in the brief vocabulary list: *Generoo*, "Good friend"; *Agæn-deero*, "We are good friends"; *Chanooro hiss*, "I make much of you"; and

Jihadæœro, "My particularly good friend." Unlike the motives of personal profit and imperial power driving colonial settlers, Native peoples were interested in establishing relations of reciprocity that would expand their circles of community.[12]

The English were utterly mistaken in their belief that they alone understood the concept of living in "civil society" and that civility was a uniquely English achievement that Native peoples could appreciate only after being "reduced"—that is, conquered. While William Penn remained alive, this misunderstanding had few major ramifications. True, the English idea that trade goods should include enslaved human beings caused a certain level of unease in the Susquehanna region. Slavery grew quickly in the Pennsylvania colony, sometimes ensnaring Indigenous peoples as well as people of African origin, and local merchants profited significantly from human commerce. Still, so long as Pennsylvanians avoided systematically subjecting local Native peoples to the sufferings of slavery, they evaded trouble with them. William Penn's pacifist policies accorded closely enough with Native practices of comity and community that cross-cultural conflicts were easily contained. But when Penn died in 1718, his loss plunged both the future of his colony and its relations with the region's Indigenous inhabitants deeply into doubt.[13]

William Penn's death in 1718 set the stage for a different era in the colony. The British Crown, through its newly invigorated Board of Trade, was threatening to retake control from the Penn family. Meanwhile, William Penn's heirs were at odds with one another. His Quaker descendants by his first wife and his Anglican descendants by his second wife were vying for title to the proprietorship. A new Anglican governor by the name of William Keith, allied with the younger, Anglican members of the family, arrived in Pennsylvania promising stricter law and greater order. Local leaders in the colony, Provincial Council members like Isaac Norris and his friend and fellow Quaker James Logan, scrambled to figure out how and whether to work with him. James Logan was the official secretary for the colony, charged with taking detailed notes on all matters that came before the governor and his council. His loyalty was first to William Penn and then to his colony, but never to Keith.[14]

Relations between Governor Keith and local colonial leaders got off to a promising-enough start when Keith first entered the colony in 1718. Quaker members of the governor's council and the legislature joined him in pushing through a series of penal reforms increasing the variety of crimes that could be charged as capital offenses. Penn's original charter of 1682 had listed only two transgressions, murder and treason, as subject to the death penalty. However, by the time the legal revisions were finished in 1718, the colony's code listed more than a dozen crimes punishable by public execution, including robbery, burglary, witchcraft, and manslaughter. Still, members of the Quaker elite were never entirely enamored of Keith. They remained gravely concerned that the Anglican governor was displaying such extravagant greed for land that he would destabilize relations with Native people in the region while also, perhaps, cutting into their own profits.[15]

If the prosperity of men like Keith, Norris, and Logan could run aground on the shoals of violence, the fortunes of empire could founder almost as easily. British officials in London, like those in colonial capitals, knew how quickly a single act of aggression could ignite a region-wide conflict. Many of the deadliest colonial Indian wars to date had been sparked by a seemingly isolated murderous moment, from the crisis in Roanoke, Virginia, in 1586 to New England's Pequot War of 1634 to Massachusetts's King Philip's War in 1675 to the Anglo-Susquehannock Wars in Virginia that same year that touched off the general revolt known as Bacon's Rebellion. If colonists marked the year 1718 by the passing of William Penn, the Native peoples of the Susquehanna River valley defined it as the first year of peace following the end of a devastating regional conflict known as the Yamasee War, fought against South Carolina colonists who had been subjecting Native people to slavery. Large as the issues at stake were, like nearly every colonial British conflict with Indigenous peoples, the Yamasee War had begun as an effort to avenge a wrongful death. When the Cartlidge brothers attacked Sawantaeny, they not only committed a crime but set in motion a diplomatic crisis with the potential to imperil an empire.[16]

Confined thus far to a tight coastal territory between the Appalachian Mountains and the Atlantic Ocean, the British aimed at lay-

ing claim to the entire continent of North America. But nothing of
the kind could happen if they antagonized Native peoples beyond
endurance. Both Native and rival European powers stood between the
British and their ambitions. The French posed a particular problem.
Colonial French traders, slavers, soldiers, and priests had fanned out
through the seemingly endless forests. They had been busily twining
trade ties and strategic alliances with Native nations into a phantom
rope that the British felt around their necks. Colonists from New York
to Pennsylvania to Virginia were itching to snap the cordon by moving
westward into the broad Ohio River valley of the Great Lakes. Having
long watched France's actions in North America with a keen eye, the
British realized they would make more progress by keeping the Five
Nations beside them than by facing off against them.[17]

French pretensions aside, it was not they but the members of the
Five Nations of the Haudenosaunee who, along with other Native
groups, exercised control from Lake Champlain to the Chesapeake
Bay. From their base in Iroquoia (including the area colonists considered New York), the Five Nations were able to maintain influence
over a wide range of Native peoples and exert sway in the Susquehanna valley. As five separate nations, their most important relationships were with one another. Within their confederacy, different
factions placed greater or lesser emphasis on English versus French
alliances. But all had become expert at leveraging European rivalries
to strengthen themselves against other Native powers, most especially
against Algonquian groups in the Great Lakes basin. There were gains
to be made in war and trade by pitting the French against the British, or even simply by playing New York colonists against Pennsylvanians against Virginians. Well before Sawantaeny's death, the English
on both sides of the Atlantic already understood that they were living
within a Haudenosaunee axis of influence.[18]

"HEAVENLY OR AERIAL PRODIGIES," surprising and perplexing
objects in the night sky, "are too often the Forerunners of Misery and
Calamity unto mankind," Titan Leeds warned his fellow Pennsylva-

nians from the pages of his almanac in 1722. Leeds sensed correctly that the colony was at a tipping point. But he did not foresee that his fellow colonists' response to the assault on a Native man—their decision to arrest the suspects, jail them in the Philadelphia gaol, and investigate the crime while the men's lives hung in the balance—would in itself greatly offend Native peoples and contradict Indigenous ideas about justice. Even as the ink was still drying on Pennsylvania's severe update to its criminal code, Native peoples were advocating a diametrically opposed set of principles for addressing such crises. From Algonquian nations living on the Susquehanna to Haudenosaunee nations hundreds of miles off, Indigenous leaders in eastern North America supported neither execution nor incarceration as fair punishment for the killing. Rather, they sought emotional reconciliation and economic restitution for the resolution of crimes. At a postwar moment dedicated to cementing peace, Native peoples were far more interested in restoration than revenge. Sawantaeny's friends and countrymen in the Susquehanna region and beyond were now determined to counter death with life.[19]

This book uncovers much more than whether and why Sawantaeny died or if and how the Cartlidge brothers came to be punished. It recreates the daily life of the region to show what happened when colonists, who claimed that the aim of colonization was the expansion of civility yet subjected Indians to invasion and slavery, matched wits with Indians, whose reputation for ferocity belied their principled approach to resolving conflicts through ritual demonstrations of emotional reciprocity and material generosity. It tells the tales of Native people swept up in the case, from Sawantaeny's wife, Weenepeeweytah, who tended him as he lay dying, to a Cayuga hunter named Satcheechoe, who journeyed hundreds of miles carrying messages of great import between Haudenosaunee leaders and Pennsylvania magistrates, to a Conoy linguist known to colonists as "Smith the Ganawese," who translated at key encounters. It shares stories of ordinary days among the colonists—sowing cereal crops, shopping city stores for sundries, or bargaining at market fairs—interrupted by the crisis of the killing. From major figures such as the governor and his council members, including one named Jonathan Dickinson who liked to recount how he was once captured by cannibal Indians, to rival traders such as the French-American James Le Tort, who already had a murder in his family, many different colonists found themselves called to respond in some way to the killing. Even the lowest-ranking members of the colonial world—from John Cartlidge's indentured servant boy Jonathan Swindel, who was marched off to jail with his master and called to testify against him, to a condemned woman named Eleanor Moore, who swung from the scaffold during the summer the Cartlidges passed in jail—felt the impact of the attack on Sawantaeny. Throughout it all, the unwavering Indigenous emphasis on restorative healing for communities contrasted greatly with English stress on punitive measures for individual perpetrators.

Though the colonists' sometimes-benighted ideas threatened to eclipse Indigenous precepts, Native peoples stood fast in their beliefs. In the first decades of the eighteenth century, the Indigenous peoples of the mid-Atlantic region retained significant influence over the conduct of intermural justice. Captain Civility's call for the English to claim responsibility for Sawantaeny's loss and then apply Native norms of emotional and material justice was repeated again and again, until at last included in the rituals surrounding the Great Treaty of 1722.

The debates, ideas, and ideals that gave rise to the Great Treaty of 1722 together make up a founding American story that should be considered an essential element of the country's legacy. The leaders of the Five Nations certainly intended their message to endure. They told the colonists they met with at Albany, "We desire That the Peace and Tranquility that is now established between us, may be as clear as the Sun shining in its Lustre without any Cloud or Darkness and that the same may continue for ever." Far beyond the mere words that the treaty preserves, the history of how it came to be written deserves to be remembered. The tale of Sawantaeny and the Cartlidge brothers has long been waiting to be told.[20]

Chapter 1

TOMORROW'S DOOM

JULY 30–AUGUST 1, 1722

Seek Not to Know to Morrow's Doom
That is not ours which is to come.

—Titan Leeds, Verses for August,
The American Almanack for 1722

TRAPPED IN A BRICK PRISON ON THE CORNER OF HIGH AND Second Streets in Philadelphia, two fur traders named John and Edmund Cartlidge sit and hope for news about whether and when they will be put to trial for the death of a Seneca hunter named Sawantaeny. Beyond the building, odors of guts, dung, and offal waft with the smoke of the butchers' tobacco, the stink of fish, and the scent of the Delaware River. The noise of barking dogs and braying livestock swells with shouting voices, clopping hooves, ringing hammers, and the rolling casks that rattle over the wharves. Cut off within the prison, the Cartlidge brothers can only strain their senses and wish for a return to the world.[1]

Sunday is market day in colonial Philadelphia. On any other first day of the week, flush with funds from the sales of their furs, the Cartlidge brothers could blend in with the throngs browsing the thirty brick stalls laid out between the courthouse and the prison, join the chorus of complaints about all the riders who gallop and trot their horses even here in the busiest section of town, dodge the dung left piled on

This nineteenth-century engraving is based on eighteenth-century images and documents. Note the bell tower with clock that rises from the roof of the courthouse in the upper-left corner.

FIRST TOWN HALL AND COURT HOUSE, ENGRAVING IN FRANK M. ETTING, *AN HISTORICAL ACCOUNT OF THE OLD STATE HOUSE OF PENNSYLVANIA* (BOSTON: JAMES T. OSGOOD & CO., 1876), 8.

the paving stones, and protect their purchases from the interest of the countless unrestrained dogs marauding the streets. They could peer into the mouths of the sacks of meal and grain, required by law to be left open for inspection, or crush between their fingers a small pinch of one of the many kinds of herbs on offer. Instead, they pass this Sunday in late July 1722 waiting behind walls for some word of their fate.[2]

Neither trader has admitted to the killing. They concede that they came to blows with the hunter when he accused them of cheating him on a fair price for his furs, but they deny definite knowledge of his death. After the fight, they fled the scene, their victim bleeding but breathing. They have not seen him since. The brothers cannot say with certainty whether Sawantaeny is dead or alive. For all they know, he has recovered and returned to the woods. He may even, at this very

moment, be sighting game among the trees while they sweat out
another summer day in prison.[3]

The alleged crime occurred in February. Colony authorities first
arrested the Cartlidges in March. Still, as of late July, no trial has been
scheduled. Magistrates seem uncertain how to proceed. By now, the
brothers do not know whether to wish for a firm trial date; to hope that
the whole case may be dropped; or to live in dread of the penalty of
death. Almost anything might be an improvement over being held in
squalor and suspense.[4]

Native people have not wavered in their statements that Sawantaeny
was killed, whereas Pennsylvania's colonial leaders have equivocated.
In direct diplomatic communiqués, no colonial spokesman has dared
to directly contradict Indian assertions. Among themselves, however,
they maintain their uncertainty. The governor and his council lean in
different ways on different days. Officials sometimes insist that their
information is too incomplete to allow an immediate prosecution for
murder or even manslaughter; at other moments they proceed as if
Sawantaeny's death must be assumed as fact. Official inertia means the
Cartlidges could be detained without trial indefinitely.

ALTHOUGH THE CARTLIDGES CANNOT know it, an assorted group
of visitors is even now working its way toward Philadelphia to try to
free them. An Indian man, acting as messenger for the Five Nations of
the Haudenosaunee, popularly known as the Iroquois, approaches the
city from the west. He is traveling in the company of several friends
from his home community, Conestoga, along with a female ferry
keeper they have picked up along the way. The messenger brings with
him strong words sent by the leaders of the powerful league.[5]

The Haudenosaunee, whose territorial base covers much of what
colonists call New York, are dissatisfied with colonial conduct in
addressing the death of the Seneca man Sawantaeny. As the Senecas
are one of the five member nations of the Haudenosaunee Confederacy, they regard his death, even in distant Pennsylvania, as their direct

concern. They have tasked the messenger with making their objections heard.

The messenger, an Iroquoian-speaker named Satcheechoe, has made the long journey alone through the woods from Pennsylvania to New York's Iroquoia and back. But he has not gone directly from his meeting with Haudenosaunee leaders to meet with colonial officials in Philadelphia. Instead, he has first stopped at home near the Susquehanna River to summon a second man, one of his community's leaders. Satcheechoe has asked this man to help him solve a serious problem; he cannot communicate directly with the people of Philadelphia. Satcheechoe speaks little English. The few Pennsylvania colonists who manage to learn a Native language generally acquire only the rudiments of Delaware, an Algonquian tongue. But the Conestoga community does have a spokesman, a Susquehannock Indian named Taquatarensaly, who is fluent in Susquehannock, an Iroquoian language, as well as in Delaware, an Algonquian one.

As a pair, the two men can converse with the colonists—as long as a third intermediary can be found to span the final gulf from Delaware to English. Satcheechoe will speak in an Iroquoian tongue, which Taquatarensaly will translate into an Algonquian one, which a third person can then translate into English. Still, bridging language barriers does not guarantee closing comprehension gaps. No one can promise that the colonists will understand the Indians' concerns.[6]

A WIDE AUDIENCE IS watching this case on both sides of the Atlantic, wary of how a murder may roil relations with the powerful Iroquois. Few in London know the name Cartlidge and probably none know the name Sawantaeny. Leading Englishmen seldom trouble to refer to lesser men by name. In letters and notes about the case, authorities generally refer to them as "the traders" and "the hunter." Sawantaeny's name is written down only once, when a member of the Pennsylvania governor's council records it at the start of the colonial inquiry into the incident. But back in London, at the seat of the British Empire, there are men aware that violence on the Susquehanna could threaten British designs on North America.[7]

Although formally at peace with the French since 1713, the British have never let down their guard. They recognize the strategic importance of allying with the Haudenosaunee in order to buffer themselves against their European rivals. In 1715, the Council of Trade and Plantations in London wrote to James Stanhope, the king's secretary, asking him to inform His Majesty that "the five Nations of Indians lying on the back of New York, between the French of Canada, and our settlements, are the only barrier between the said French and their Indians, and H.M. Plantations as far as Virginia, and Maryland" and warning him that "they are capable, in great measure, of turning the European interest in those parts to which side soever they incline." In Pennsylvania, the colony's governor, Sir William Keith, echoed this assessment in his own report to the Lords of Trade in 1719, warning that although "the *Iroquese*, or five Nations have hitherto been preserved" as English allies, the French "daily continue to debauch them from the English." Keith had then offered a plan for preventing the French from "seducing" the Iroquois. Having positioned himself as a leading expert on Anglo-Indian relations, Keith knows British administrators will hold him to account if the crisis resulting from this killing can't be resolved.[8]

Now the Haudenosaunee are demanding that representatives from Pennsylvania travel to meet them at a treaty conference scheduled for August in Albany. Leaders of the Five Nations convene large reunions to refresh friendships and alliances amongst Native peoples on a regular basis. As colonists from New York have become significant trading partners, the Haudenosaunee have come to expect them to participate as well, but this is the first time they have extended an invitation to the settlers of Penn's colony. Once the Pennsylvanians arrive, the Haudenosaunee expect them to address the reported death of Sawantaeny, a man they recognize as a kinsman. They have sent the messenger Satcheechoe with a detailed list of their demands.

Gov. William Burnet of New York has convened the meeting in Albany with leaders of the Five Nations in order to strengthen alliances. The government of New York relies extensively on tax revenues generated by the fur trade, and so any incident that threatens the general peace of the region has the potential to create significant problems for New York. Burnet has no knowledge yet of the unfortunate episode in Pennsylvania, nor of the fact that Haudenosaunee leaders have designated his treaty meeting with them as the venue for addressing that crisis. He will be alarmed when he does discover these things. English administrators cannot tolerate even the possibility that their imperial ambitions could be downed by the suspicious disappearance of a single Indian man, even if he is, or was, a member of one of the continent's dominant Native powers.[9]

THE TWO INDIAN MESSENGERS, though different in background, now both hail from Conestoga, a hilltop community located near a spring, some sixty miles due west of Philadelphia. Conestoga means "people of the cabin pole," and by 1722, the residents of Conestoga, a mixed group of Indian families and a few English traders, all live in square-cornered cabins sided with board planks. Their houses sit scattered across a countryside dotted with fields and stippled with trees. Just to the north of Conestoga runs a watercourse known as "Indian Run" that branches into Conestoga Creek, which flows into the Susquehanna River. From time to time, the people move their settlement up or down in the river region, but they always keep near running water. In Conestoga's present location, refugees from many Native nations—fractured by warfare, slave raiding, and epidemic diseases—have been gathering to forge new lives since the 1690s. By the 1720s, it has become an important crossroads, a meeting place where people come together in complex thousand-layer combinations of family and friendship.[10]

Taquatarensaly carries many burdens with him as he helps Satcheechoe bear the Haudenosaunee message eastward. He has already survived decades of dislocation and death. Beginning with the first Swedish settlements in 1638, Europeans have upended Native lives. As the diplomatic representative of a small nation that has endured nearly a century of European invasions, and crosscutting incursions by rival Indigenous groups, Taquatarensaly has helped his community to weave and reweave a many-stranded web of relationships among multiple peoples.[11]

Words in many tongues echo across the Susquehanna valley. Two broad linguistic families, Algonquian and Iroquoian, categorize the major groups; from them branch many languages and peoples. The first groups to encounter William Penn included both the Algonquian Lenapes (or Delawares) and the Iroquoian Susquehannocks, now also called the Conestogas after the name of their main settlement. Though speakers of an Iroquoian language, the Susquehannocks were not members of the Haudenosaunee Confederacy and so remained subject to attack from their distant New York kin until the last quarter of the seventeenth century. As the Susquehannocks shrank, their villages were augmented by newly arriving peoples who soon became interconnected with them through trade and marriage. New Iroquoian additions include some members of the Seneca and Cayuga Nations. Other Algonquians in the region now include many Shawnee refugees from the Ohio River valley, along with Ganawese migrants from Maryland. Threatened from the north by peoples of the Great Lakes, menaced from the south by powerful Native groups from below the Potomac, and pushed westward by colonial aggressors everywhere, the peoples of the river valleys of Pennsylvania have built new lives together.[12]

This history flows through Taquatarensaly's veins. Confused by his multiethnic origins, Pennsylvanians report that he is "a descendant of the ancient Sasquehannah Indians the old settlers of these parts, but now reputed as of an Iroquois Descent." Often referred to as one of the "Conestoga," he is also sometimes called a "Cayuga." In fact, he has cultural and lineal connections to many groups. Now he needs to find out whether his diplomatic ties with the English can form a safety net for all of the peoples of the Susquehanna valley, and possibly even aid the cause of the Cartlidge brothers. He comes in peace, but he represents peoples hardened to war.[13]

NOT FAR FROM THE prison, another set of men gathers: Pennsylvania's governor, William Keith, Baronet, and the members of his council. They meet several times a week, perhaps over a steaming cup in a coffeehouse by the city's quay, in the chambers of the city courthouse, over a warm tankard in a tavern back room, or in the parlor of Edward Shippen's brick-built "Great House" on Second Street, which the governor has rented as his residence. The Cartlidge crisis figures regularly in their discussions, but so far they have found no easy response to the competing claims made by the case.[14]

Sir William strides the streets of Philadelphia satisfied to be the highest-ranking man in the colony. He is an English aristocrat who has just inherited his father's baronetcy—along with his father's seemingly bottomless debts and his long political conflict with the reigning British monarchy. Whatever his title, Keith's riches do not equal those of the most prosperous local merchants. As a non-Quaker, Keith is cut off from the religious fellowship that supports many a local political fortune. He has been at his post for fewer than four years: not enough time yet to recoup his father's lost wealth, but more than enough to arouse the animosity of Quaker members of his governing council. Many of them, like Sec. James Logan, enjoyed lifelong personal friendships with William Penn and think themselves far better guardians of his legacy and his property than Keith will ever be. Meanwhile, Keith's efforts to create an independent power base, by allying himself with the city's common folk, have only earned him the scorn of the ruling Quaker elite. With every step, Keith has to look over his shoulder, past the long, cascading black curls of his fashionable wig.[15]

The Quakers frown on fripperies such as wigs, and on "foolish pastimes" of all kinds. Cards, dice, and lotteries are all forbidden in the colony under penalty of law. But Keith is playing a still more dangerous game. Immediately after arriving in the colony, he rammed a legislative reform package through the colonial assembly in the hopes of ingratiating himself with the British Crown. He persuaded the legislature to dramatically tighten legal penalties used in the colony, rejecting many of William Penn's mild founding principles in favor of policies more closely aligned with the traditional British penal code. In particular, Keith stressed the importance of applying corporal and capital punishment. The revised sentencing guidelines make murder just one of dozens of crimes, from burglary to forgery, punishable by death. But what looked like a win for Keith in 1718 now looks more like a miscalculation.[16]

Keith's colleagues on the governing council have never fully trusted him, and the current criminal case concerning the Cartlidge brothers is straining colonial unity in new ways. Neither Keith nor the Quakers imagined that one of the first cases tried under the new penal code would weigh the lives of two English colonists against the claims of the continent's Native inhabitants. And if Keith's best protection against the shaky loyalty of the Quakers on his council lies in maintaining popularity with the common people of the colony, then executing one of their fellow colonists, all to settle the score with some Indians, looks like a highly risky option.

Keith can't afford to forget his other flank. He needs to keep peace with the Indians, the better to ensure security on 1,200 acres of land near Conestoga that he has recently claimed for himself. Quakers on the council question whether he has any right to take the land. The parcel is located in an area rumored to contain mineral deposits, where the Penn family may have a prior legal stake and where Native people may still have claims. But now British title disputes are the least of Keith's worries. A murder accusation in the region imperils everything. Unless delicately handled, an event like this could easily provoke Indian reprisals against nearby colonists. If that happens, all his dreams, of literally striking gold, will come to nothing.[17]

A pink-cheeked, soft-chinned, rosy-lipped man who, when the time comes to sit for an official portrait, chooses a suit of medieval armor topped with an ermine robe, Keith is to the manor born. Yet he has now been reduced to renting from another man, setting up house in the home of a commoner far richer than he is. Edward Shippen's city house and gardens are renowned for their beauty, but Keith wants to build a country property of his own, one that will return him to the sort of lifestyle to which he feels literally entitled. He has been imagining building a verdant estate near Conestoga complete with a country house to be called Fountain Low.[18]

The Indians must be satisfied. From the moment of colony founder

This anonymous nineteenth-century painting is believed to be based on an original painted in Philadelphia during William Keith's tenure. Sir William is pictured in medieval armor with an ermine stole. These are symbols of his knighthood, which, as the firstborn son of a baronet, he would have received at age twenty-one, even before inheriting his father's baronetcy. The finely worked white lace collar at his throat is a sign of eighteenth-century gentility, costly to produce and difficult to keep clean.

PORTRAIT OF SIR WILLIAM KEITH, CAPITAL PRESERVATION COMMITTEE, PENNSYLVANIA STATE ARCHIVES.

William Penn's first contact with the region's original inhabitants, every one of the colony's governors has promised equal justice for Native peoples. If the Five Nations demand their due, as is their right, that may mean capital punishment for the Cartlidges.[19]

COLONISTS CALL THE FOREST that the Indian men traverse "Pennsylvania," meaning Penn's Woods. Travelers' accounts report in detail on its sylvan glories: stands of oak, chestnut, hickory, walnut (both black and white), and beech; groves of maple, sugar maple, birch, sugar birch, hornbeam, cherry; spinneys of poplar, elm, linden, lotus, pine, and spruce. As he passes among the trees, Taquatarensaly knows that the English still want what Europeans have always wanted—trade, land, and power. The only question is how and whether the death of his neighbor Sawantaeny will shift the balance between the Indians and the British.[20]

The British seem to think that if they enact harsh enough punishments against the possible killers, from incarceration to execution, they can keep the peace in Pennsylvania. On the other hand, they keep quibbling over the strength of the evidence against the accused. Taquatarensaly has little doubt about what happened to Sawantaeny. He conducted his own investigation months ago. But he needs to make the English see how paltry even their most severe proposed punitive actions appear in Indian eyes.

As the people of Conestoga have long been telling colonists, "every mouse that ruffles the leaves" of the forest floor sounds to them like the footfall of a settler on some terrible errand. It has been a dozen years since Taquatarensaly translated to colonists his peoples' demand for "a cessation from murdering & taking them." Yet still, the Native peoples of Conestoga can ignore neither the never-ending English desire for more property nor the possibility that they themselves can be made into human property. Only in the last decade have the English promised to stop forcing Indians into slavery. Many Indigenous men, women, and children remain chained to lives of toil among the colonists, subject to being bought and sold for profit. Native peoples value freedom of movement above all else. If a visit from him can help his people's cause, and maybe free the Cartlidge brothers in the process, Taquatarensaly is ready and willing to walk.[21]

~

THE PRISON HOUSING THE Cartlidge brothers squats in the middle of the city's main market street, a fourteen-foot-long, twenty-foot-wide stack of brick, stone, lime, and sand. Forty years ago, people convicted of crimes were crated in a small open-sided cage on this same street. After a day or two of acute discomfort and embarrassment, stiff with confinement and soaked with their own bodily excretions, added to whatever combination of piss and rotted produce members of the public had aimed at them, such prisoners would have been released and left to get on with their lives. But the cage did not last. While city officials appreciated the way it allowed passersby to jeer at the humans being held like animals, they had found it too small to be practical for penning more than a few people for short periods. So the city council ordered a new, larger prison to be built of substantial materials.[22]

The newer, thick-walled prison containing the Cartlidges rises only one and a half stories aboveground, the first floor just six feet high—and the first four feet of that set below grade—with a second story of just seven feet more. City leaders, missing the old English tradition of public shaming, have adorned the area beside the prison with a few additional "public conveniences," as they call them. They have provided stocks, a pillory, a whipping post, and a branding iron, for the better entertainment of marketgoers and the greater pain of the condemned. And they have added a dunking stool for scolding drunken women. Days when the devices are in use, the street rings with cries and moans. On slow days, the empty equipment gapes silently at each person who passes.[23]

Now the Cartlidge brothers are lodged right under the prison roof, the hottest spot in the building. John Cartlidge could hardly have imagined that he would wind up like this. Back at home in Conestoga, when he wasn't traveling and trading for furs, he used to preside as a justice of the peace from a comfortable house graced with fine furnishings. There he could sit in his parlor and mark the passing of time with a look at the clock in its case or a glance at his watch. In his study, he could reach for six different guns. Now, stripped of his title and forced from his home, he is helpless to protect himself from whatever fate awaits him. He can keep time only by the sound of the courthouse bell.[24]

COME MONDAY MORNING, WILLIAM Pawlett opens the Philadelphia courthouse gates for the day and begins to sweep the public square. He earns just £8 a year for his work keeping the courthouse and its pavements clean. Still, great men come at his calling. It is he who heaves the ropes that ring the bell that will summon council members to the meeting the governor has called today with a visiting delegation of Indians.[25]

The scratch of his broom against the brick pavement as Pawlett passes beneath the stone arches of the courthouse blends into the clatter of the city morning. Gentlefolk in carriages, carters hauling cords of wood, draymen carrying brewers' barrels, and porters with their pipes of wine, their hogsheads of rum, sugar, or molasses are all forbidden to pass his gate. Though the courthouse sits directly atop the market stalls, all heavy deliveries must be made around back. No overweight load can be allowed to damage the carefully paved courtyard before the city's main public hall.[26]

Governor Keith would like nothing better than to keep himself above the dirt of the common thoroughfare, but the city's building owners are notoriously unreliable about keeping the ground in front of their establishments cobblestoned. The city mayor has appointed official Regulators of the Streets to conduct inspections and issue warnings to property owners who don't do their part to maintain the streets. Just two months ago, the city council had to pass a formal order to oblige the occupants of the governor's own street to pave the road before their doors. Reality always falls short of the regulations. If Keith allows his attention to wander for even a moment as he makes his way toward the courthouse, he is liable to arrive with his shoe buckles dusty or mucky, according to the dictates of the weather.[27]

TAQUATARENSALY AND SATCHEECHOE TRAVERSE mile after mile of forest on their journey to Philadelphia. They and their companions are following an Indian path stretched across the land like sinew. Years ago, skilled Susquehannocks (called Minquas by the Dutch and Mingos by the English) set the way for these men to walk, creating a straight and flat overland route from the Susquehanna to the Delaware, traversing many watercourses along the way, including the Brandywine and Schuylkill Rivers. The Dutch used to refer to the messengers' trail as the Great Minquas Path. The English at Philadelphia don't call it anything at all. They either do not know or will not acknowledge that the route is there.[28]

The mayor and the members of the Philadelphia City Council are not even sure whether any roads exist at all west of the Schuylkill. Planners hope that someday Philadelphia will be an expansive city that spans the distance between two rivers, from the Delaware to the Schuylkill. But as of 1722, Philadelphia's buildings have spread only a few blocks west from the Delaware. Despite the grand backwoods designs of a few would-be estate owners like William Keith, most Philadelphians have never so much as ventured over the Schuylkill. More and more traders and travelers from the west are crossing the Schuylkill at the point of High Street, then walking down its two-mile length to reach the city's market. Yet few city dwellers travel in the reverse direction.

Just two months ago, a confused city council ordered the mayor and his assistants to "inform themselves after the best manner they can . . . if any publick Road was lay'd out from ye west Side of the River Schulkill." Perhaps these officials are aware of an Indian path that they simply don't choose to dignify with the name "public road." But on the other hand, they also want to clarify exactly where the Philadelphia city line is, that is, "whether the Bounds of this City to the Westward

Extend over the River Schulkill." For the English, ambition and ignorance march in formation.[29]

The Conestoga messengers know the lay of the land. Indian paths
tie together far-flung people and places, allowing groups to gather
for hunting or disperse for farming, to meet for peace or scatter for
defense. Native peoples avoid building permanently settled towns,
with their quickly accumulating diseases and easily degrading soils.
Instead, they develop strong yet flexible societies that can expand or
contract according to need. For Indians, roads are the cords that con-
nect whole communities and cultures.[30]

Walking these routes, Taquatarensaly maintains contact with
peoples across the Susquehanna watershed. Still a young man, he has
been representing the interests of the Conestoga community for over
a decade, hosting colonial leaders from Philadelphia, Baltimore, and
Williamsburg at his cabin at Conestoga and visiting those colonial cities himself. He knew of the confrontation between Sawantaeny and the
Cartlidges weeks before anyone in Philadelphia got wind of it. And he
was among the first to investigate the facts of the crime and to ascertain
Iroquois opinions on it. Now he has an idea who may be able to forge
the last link in the language chain needed to bring the Haudenosaunee
message to English ears.[31]

Ordinarily, Taquatarensaly might have turned to John Cartlidge
as a translator. The trader learned a good deal of the Delaware tongue
in the course of living and working in the woods and has often been
used as an interpreter by Indians and colonists in both commercial and
diplomatic exchanges. Taquatarensaly is well acquainted with him. But
John can hardly be called on to act as an intermediary in the midst of
his own legal mess. Taquatarensaly will have to look elsewhere for
assistance. Fortunately, there is a good candidate right in his path.

Just more than halfway along its route from Conestoga to Philadelphia, the Great Minquas Path has to cross the Brandywine River. On
that waterway, a fifty-three-year-old woman named Alice Kirk, who
speaks the Delaware tongue well, owns and runs a busy ferry and inn
with her husband, Samuel. Ordinarily, married women in Pennsylvania don't own property, much less work in public as government translators. But Alice Kirk is no ordinary woman.[32]

Born to English colonists in Pennsylvania, Alice married a half-Swedish, half-Dutch man named William Vandever, who had been born in Manhattan in 1656, back when it was still New Amsterdam, and who later lived in Delaware as a river inn and ferry keeper. He died, childless, in 1718. Following Dutch property and inheritance law, William left all of his marital property to his wife, Alice, without restriction. William's procedure, all but impossible under English law, enabled Alice to remain a woman of independent means, even after taking a new husband. Though she married Samuel two years ago, Alice still retains full legal ownership of her property from her first marriage. She is one of a shrinking number of colonial women who has been able to pick the lock of English wedlock.[33]

Samuel, for his part, has only recently begun rising in the world, first being admitted as a taxpaying, voting freeman of Pennsylvania 1717, and then making a good match to the well-off widow Alice Smith Vandever in 1720. From Maryland to New Jersey, colonists have quickly come to know Samuel as "Mr. Samuel Kirk of Brandywine Ferry." People and money pass frequently across the threshold of the Kirks' inn. When bound servants run away from their labors, masters advertise in Philadelphia's daily paper the *American Weekly Mercury* advising anyone who "takes up" the runaways to notify Samuel Kirk, who can be trusted to hold the servants and pay the deliverers a cash reward. Bind or be bound is the way of this world, and Samuel and Alice have found their place in it.[34]

After living and working by an old Indian road at the Brandywine crossing point for some three decades, Alice Kirk has learned to speak Delaware and earned the recognition of men like Satcheechoe and Taquatarensaly. She can be ready in a moment if they call for her assistance. In inviting her to join their journey on Great Minquas Path, the two can't but hope that she will give them the means to transmit Indigenous ideas in English words.

⌐⌐⌐

MONDAYS, THE STREETS OUTSIDE the Philadelphia courthouse are noisier than ever. On that day of the week, the city sheriff takes to the shade of the courthouse to hold public auctions of property seized by the law. Readers of this week's *American Weekly Mercury*, the colony's first newspaper, are already anticipating the "Publick Vendue" advertised for next Monday at the courthouse, where they will have the chance to try for a nice price on "a very good Negro Woman and her Child" or perhaps to purchase "A Boy about 2 Years old, and a Mulatto Boy about 9 Years of Age." Their former masters have surrendered them to the sheriff for the satisfaction of debts. The erstwhile owners regard these human sales as preferable to the alternative of an extended stay in debtors' prison for themselves. And eager crowds will gather as the sheriff barks, to gawk at the shackled toddler and the others, even if they can't afford to bid.[35]

On this Monday morning, the thirtieth of July, after pushing his way through the throngs outside, the colony's official secretary, James Logan, dips his plume in ink and records the names of a dozen men and a single woman present for what he describes as "a public audience" appointed by the governor. The men in attendance, besides the governor, include four recently arrived Indians as well as four Quaker and four Anglican members of the council. Such religious balance means Keith can be confident he won't be outnumbered in the midst of this crucial meeting. The Indians include Satcheechoe and Taquatarensaly and two additional companions from Conestoga. The sole woman is the ferry keeper. Logan explains her presence by noting that Taquatarensaly is to interpret "from the Mingoe into the Delaware Indian tongue" and that Alice Kirk will translate "from that into English." Logan must scribble quickly, as Satcheechoe begins to speak.[36]

Almost immediately, the assembled Pennsylvania colonists can sense something wrong. Satcheechoe is addressing them without first presenting any gifts of wampum. He offers no intricately beaded belt of delicately drilled pieces of purple and white clamshell, not even a more ordinary string of beads threaded into a simple chain. Normally, Indian diplomats preface their official statements by offering ritual tokens of respect such as these, the better to signal the seriousness and sincerity of their communications. But Satcheechoe is plunging in without preamble.[37]

In omitting the formalities, Satcheechoe offers the Pennsylvanians a deliberate slight. If they listen carefully, they'll hear the explanation in the Indian's opening remark. He tells them that although he did succeed in meeting leaders of the Five Nations to discuss the apparent death, "the Chiefs had not time to meet & open the presents sent them by the Governour." Letting this sink in, he then adds that over the summer they had been too busy "getting vicytuals as fish out of the Rivers & some Venison from the woods" to bother much about the diplomatic offerings from Pennsylvania. Instead, they set them aside to be opened later along with gifts from the governors of other British colonies. Satcheechoe explains to the governor and council that he succeeded in arranging a meeting only with a leader of the Cayugas, one of the Five Nations of the Haudenosaunee. The other leaders claimed to be too busy to see him.[38]

At this, Satcheechoe advances a request. The governors of Virginia and New York are both planning to arrive in Albany to negotiate with the Five Nations next month, he says, and "they desire the Govr. and James Logan to come." The specificity of this invitation cannot be lost on the gathering. Before they can resolve the matter of Sawantaeny's death, the leaders of the Five Nations are demanding a personal appearance from the highest-ranking British government official of Pennsylvania, not mere messages shuttled by a Native envoy. And they also want a visit from Pennsylvania's most prominent Indian trader, James Logan. As a fur-trade aggregator, playing the middleman between individual fur traders and British merchants, Logan is uniquely well positioned to supply the Indians of the Five Nations with greater goods than the negligible colonial gifts they have so far scorned to notice.[39]

When a death occurs amongst the Haudenosaunee, the people mourn collectively, sharing in one another's sadness, then join together to rebuild broken social ties. In the last century, the Haudenosaunee fought many mourning wars in which they took captives from rival nations to adopt in place of their dead. But in more recent years, they have assumed a careful stance of armed neutrality, avoiding warfare and adapting their rituals in response to death. Now if a member of one of the Five Nations of the Haudenosaunee Confederacy suffers the loss of life, diplomacy, not warfare, usually results.[40]

Among the Haudenosaunee, people in grief are considered as being "covered with night." Assuaging the community's sadness requires addressing both the emotional and the material damage that results from a death, by making overtures of feeling along with more substantive reparations in the form of goods. The Haudenosaunee refer to this multistep process as "covering the dead" through the rituals of the "condolence ceremony." Pennsylvanians' half measures on both fronts—their hasty dispatches brought by a lone messenger bearing paltry gifts—have failed to meet with Indian expectations.[41]

Yet if Governor Keith thinks that the path out of Pennsylvania's predicament requires sacrificing the Cartlidges on the altar of English justice, Satcheechoe has more news for him. The Indians do not want to follow English precedents, and they most definitely do not want the Cartlidges to be executed. Satcheechoe tells the gathering that the one Cayuga leader with whom he was able to speak is, of course, "sorry for the Death of the Indian that was killed, for he was his own flesh and blood." But then Satcheechoe adds a significant twist.[42]

According to Kirk's translation from Taquatarensaly's gloss, "He desires that John Cartlidge may not be put to death for it." Though both brothers have been implicated in the crime, it seems that the Indians of the Five Nations have focused most closely on John; perhaps he, like James Logan, already has a reputation that reaches as far as New York's Iroquoia. Taking note of the stumbling way the Pennsylvanians have handled the case so far, Satcheechoe then anticipates and parries another potential feint. "Nor" will it be acceptable, he says, "that the Govr. should be angry and spare him for some time & put him to Death afterwards." It will not suffice for the governor merely to postpone punishment, only to impose it at a later date.[43]

Addressing the broader point of principle, Satcheechoe explains, "one life is enough to be lost, there should not two die." With these words, Satcheechoe does more than just announce the Haudenosaunee position on this particular case. He is articulating a broader worldview wholly at odds with English expectations. Emotion figures centrally in the Iroquois approach to justice: The sadness of the mourners, the remorse of the killers, the sympathies of the community all create the atmosphere necessary for successfully covering the dead by providing the grief-stricken with offerings of reparations. At the same time, the

Haudenosaunee believe it essential to avoid anger if further violence is to be prevented. Even killers can be forgiven and reintegrated into the community, as long as the emotional and material suffering they cause has been thoroughly redressed.[44]

The British, by contrast, view emotion as fundamentally out of place in the administration of law. William Keith has made himself clear on exactly this point. In rolling out his reform of the criminal code, he delivered and then published an address to the justices of the peace of Chester County in 1718 in which he specified exactly how judges should treat "prisoners indicted for murder." A key comment stands out among his instructions: "The Heart of Man being for the most part corrupted and defiled with the violence of his passions," Keith told his audience, true justice "commands . . . an impartial scrutiny be made." For Keith, emotion is corrupting and has no place in court. Whatever "confused mixture of Pity and Horror" may fill the minds of those charged with judging the accused, they must set all feeling aside "to discover the naked truth on which our Judgments, for or against one another, are simply to be founded." As the Cartlidges fester in prison, they know they should expect no sympathy from the authorities; after all, at the time of Keith's speech, John was one of the justices in the audience.[45]

So far, Satcheechoe is delivering an eyebrow-raising performance. His listeners on the governing council cannot have anticipated receiving Indian instruction on moral values. In this week's issue of the *American Weekly Mercury* they can read a long news item about Indians who "most barbarously murdered" colonists in New England. According to the story, survivors saw "Indians come firing through the woods after them, and heard them yell and howl in a most hideous manner." The report explains that the only reason a second wave of colonists escaped sharing the fate of the murdered ones was because they took warning from the "uncommon mirth" of the victors, correctly guessing "by their Behavior and the Manner of their Dancing and Rejoycing" that "the Indians had shed blood." Colonists describe paper Indians as people akin to animals, yowling creatures that delight in bloodshed. How then can the flesh-and-blood Indian appearing now before the council be lecturing the governor on avoiding anger and urging him against the mistake of taking life in response to death?[46]

⟋⟋

THE COLONISTS DO NOT know Satcheechoe well and they cannot tell what to make of his address. But they are better acquainted with his companion, Taquatarensaly, having held meetings with him for a dozen years before this. True, Taquatarensaly's name feels fat on English tongues. Colonists seldom write it the same way twice. But then again, English quills often waver over the spelling of words, even in their own language. James Logan, the council's official secretary, seems to lack confidence in the very name of the colony, recording it variously as Pennsilvania and Pennsylvania in government notes. Colonial writers raised in what remains largely an oral culture simply do their best to transcribe the letters that corresponded to the sounds they hear.[47]

Taquatarensaly, if that is his name, may have chosen or been given this name based on some outstanding personal trait or on his social role. As transliterated by Europeans, the two syllables that begin his name, "Taqua," share some similarity in sound with the old Susquehannock word "Atackqua," meaning "shoes." Considering how much shoe leather Taquatarensaly wears out walking between peoples and working out their differences, he easily could have taken the English name "Shoes."[48]

Faced with the challenge of Taquatarensaly's name, the colonists prefer using an English-language moniker. They call him "Captain Civility." English colonists like to impose humorous names on those they consider inferior. Enslaved people are often saddled with the names of writers and heroes of classical antiquity, from Cato to Hercules. Council member Isaac Norris, who has absented himself from this meeting to direct the draining and mowing of the meadows at his country manor, is currently overseeing the work of an enslaved man he calls "Caesar." Quite possibly, some colonial wit in a black frock coat and white silk stockings was showing off when he decided to solve the problem of a "savage" man's unpronounceable name by calling him "Civility."[49]

But no matter the ironic inflections the moniker may acquire in the mouths of Pennsylvania English-speakers, Civility's name also calls to mind more than half a century of Anglo-Indian relations. For generations, Susquehannocks have used "Civility" not as a personal name but as something more like a professional title for the person appointed as their ambassador to English colonists. In the 1660s, a Susquehannock man going by the name of "Civility" succeeded in such cordial negotiations with the governing council of Maryland that it supplied him with guns, lead, and shot. Later, in the 1690s, after a lapse in diplomatic relations, Maryland council members urged a new set of Susquehannock delegates that if they were "inclined to enter into a League with us," they should "make choice of some great man to preside over them as Civility formerly did." By now, the English name Civility has been used as the official title of one generation after another of Susquehannock diplomats to the English. In like manner, the Indians refer to every Pennsylvania governor as "Onas." An Iroquois word meaning "feather" or "quill," the honorific began as a pun on William Penn's name (as in quill pen) but is now used by area Indians as the generic title for whoever occupies the Pennsylvania governor's office. Even if the name "Civility" sparks thoughts of savagery among the colonists, for Indigenous peoples it evokes a long tradition of inclusive diplomacy.[50]

Moreover, Taquatarensaly commands enough respect from colonists to compel them to affix the honorific "Captain" in front of his name. He is not a governmental chief but a war captain, a man able to muster followers for military combat. To date, no colonial record has placed him on the battlefield, only on the council grounds, working tirelessly to negotiate peace for his people. But neither Keith nor the Quakers on his board nor the Cartlidges can know whether that is about to change. It seems almost impossible that the peaceable disposition of Captain Civility, much less the peaceful policies of the Five Nations, can endure the challenge of the apparent atrocity of the Cartlidge brothers.[51]

SATCHEECHOE TRIES TO LEAVE the governor and his council no
room to doubt what the Five Nations of the Haudenosaunee think must
be done. The time for temporizing has passed. Pressing his point, he
says again, "They desire John Cartlidge may not die for this. They
would not have him killed." The colonists have arrested both brothers,
but the Indians have concluded that John, the erstwhile justice of the
peace, is the main man responsible in the case. Nevertheless, they do
not want him to pay with his life or his liberty.[52]

To be sure that the Pennsylvanians understand this, Satcheechoe
adds, "John Cartlidge has been a long time Bound, and they desire he
may be bound no longer." Far from viewing the Cartlidges as inherent
and incorrigible criminals, the Haudenosaunee look at them more the
way the prisoners see themselves: as two men who, having once committed an error, have since lost too much time. The role they fill, as
traders and translators easing the exchange of Indian furs for English
trade goods, cannot be allowed to stand empty. Indians still regard the
Cartlidges as fit men to play this part so long as the damage they have
done—emotional, spiritual, and material—is first repaired.[53]

If the Pennsylvanians really want to resolve the situation,
Satcheechoe says, they should know that "all will be made up when
the Governor comes to Albany." Proposing the trip, Satcheechoe says
"when," not "if." "Now Squashes and Pompions are come they will be
able to travel," he insists, and Logan records. Time is ripe for a diplomatic harvest.[54]

The colonists listen quietly, following Indian protocol carefully
now. They are not participating in a conversation so much as attending
to an oration. They know they must allow Satcheechoe to deliver his
full speech without interruption, or they will cause him great offense.

"The Governor of New England," Satcheechoe goes on to explain,
has already sent the Five Nations "great Presents of Mach Coats, thirty
bundles of goods all tyed up." James Logan can well picture what
Satcheechoe means. Logan dispatches regular bulk purchase orders
to cloth merchants in England, detailing the precise style of coats he

needs in order to supply small-scale traders with goods that can tempt
Indian hunters into trading. With the Five Nations of New York able
to favor the soldiers and traders of different colonies according to the
enticements each one offers, Satcheechoe is reminding the Pennsylvanians of what they will need to present in order to compete.[55]

The leaders of the Five Nations expect the Pennsylvanians to pack
their bags, arrange their bundles, and head out for Albany. "Their
King," Satcheechoe tells his audience, "will come to Albany to see the
Govr. there, who he hopes will come in ten days. They desire that
Satcheechoe may come hither with the Governour." With these last
lines, Satcheechoe asserts his authority to issue the Pennsylvanians an
official summons. Logan lays down his pen and leaves no record of the
colonial response.[56]

IF ONLY THE CARTLIDGES, stuck up at the top of the High Street
Prison, could hear the council proceedings occurring a block away,
they might gain some relief from feeling the heat. Sawantaeny's nation
wants them freed. But as it is, the Cartlidges simply swelter through
another late July day in the prison attic.

The builders always intended the garret to "serve for a prison."
Colonists call the prison attic the "cock-loft" or "cockle-loft," because
in summer it grows so hot it resembles a "cockle," the furnace of a hop
or malt kiln. The four main rooms of the Philadelphia prison house are
reserved for the use of the gaoler, who lives and works there. He runs
a tavern from the ground floor, a sorry place that turns out plain meals
for those prisoners who can afford to pay. The barest possible rations
await those whose cost of care, calculated at two pence per day, falls to
the public. While the gaoler sloshes out steins of ale below, the prisoners roast like hops above.[57]

Just as well the Cartlidges never get comfortable. Regardless of
Satcheechoe's speeches on behalf of the Five Nations, many Quaker
council members still believe that Taquatarensaly and other members
of the local Conestoga community desire and deserve a trial. Despite
the Cartlidges' denials, magistrates have amassed substantial incrim-

inating evidence, the result of multiple interview sessions with varied witnesses, both Indian and British. They rather expect the Native people of Conestoga to form an official delegation to travel to Philadelphia to witness the judicial proceedings. And deeply suspicious of the governor's intentions, they intend to hold Keith to his promises to prosecute the case.[58]

Two days later, when Governor Keith once again convenes the council, one of the members moves "whether this might not be a proper occasion to consider the time of the Tryal of John and Edmund Cartlidge, that the Indians at Conestogoe may be Acquainted therewith with Civility at his Return home." The council calls for a consultation about setting a trial date with David Lloyd, the chief justice of Pennsylvania, and a Quaker of undoubted political as well as religious loyalty.[59]

How can Keith play for time? The last thing he wants now is a capital trial, just when it seems the Five Nations conveniently oppose such a proceeding. On the other hand, the opinion of the distant New York–based leaders of the Five Nations matters rather less for local security than the views maintained by people in the Susquehanna River region. Furthermore, none of the council members, regardless of their own differences of opinion, knows if they should accept Satcheechoe's description of the Five Nations' position, given that he has not authenticated it with any of the usual diplomatic tokens.[60]

Keith loosens himself from this tight corner by calling on the other two judges of his council, the Anglicans Anthony Palmer and William Assheton, and requesting that they withdraw to confer privately with Lloyd. He asks them if they "would please to give him & the Board their opinion, whether the offenders could be prosecuted effectually without a view first taken of the Body of the Indian supposed to be killed, by a Coroner's Inquest." How can they prosecute a murder if they can't find the cadaver? Keith knows how to turn legal technicality into political practicality.[61]

Taking the Anglican attorney general Andrew Hamilton with them for good measure, the three judges retire to a private chamber to deliberate. They soon return to offer the advice that, "where a view of the Body may be necessary for the information of the Jury (which 'tis presumed it may be in this Case) the same ought by no means to be neglected." Keith can let out his breath: no corpse, no case.[62]

The impromptu judicial panel continues, "It is therefore the opinion of the Judges that a view of the Body ought to be taken, and that the trial be deferr'd until the Govr. Return from Albany, in which opinion the Gov.r and the Board also agreed." The Cartlidges remain doomed to be left in limbo in prison for some time to come.[63]

WITH THAT, THE GOVERNOR calls back the Indians to make his final formal statement, and the group once again gathers in. One last time, Alice Kirk ferries the governor's words into Delaware; Taquatarensaly then translates this into Mingo and conveys the remarks to Satcheechoe. "My friend Satcheechoe," the governor says, "you have shown yourself a good Traveller and a Diligent Messenger." However dim his view of Satcheechoe's performance, Keith knows he has to deliver his own lines perfectly now.[64]

"I was surprised to see you bring no Credentials with you this last time," he tells Satcheechoe. By no credentials, of course, he means no wampum belts or strings. A man of William Keith's standing cannot allow a breach of decorum like this to pass without comment. But neither can he himself afford to offer any further slight. He is simply signaling that the Indian message of reproach has been received and understood. He hastens to add, "Yet I shall believe you have discharged your part well and that the occasion of your bringing no such thing is truly owing to the Cause you have assigned, that is that ye Chiefs could not meet then together." Better to save face and stick to the polite fiction that Satcheechoe has offered than to admit to having suffered an affront from the Iroquois in silence.[65]

Promising to make immediate plans to meet the Five Nations' demand to visit them along with Satcheechoe, Keith then turns to Taquatarensaly. "Civility," he tells him, "I desire you will inform all the Indians who are coming down to the Trial of John & Edmund Cartlidge, that the sd. Tryal is deferred until I return from Albany." With that, Keith presents Taquatarensaly and his traveling companions with what Logan calls, "some small tokens." These include provisions for their return journey to Conestoga, along with several "strouds," an English woven material popular with Indians.[66]

Strouds of stripe-edged red and blue woolen cloth, sometimes gifted but more often traded for deerskins, blanket Indian hunters up and down the eastern edge of the continent. They are so valued that the deceased are often buried wrapped in them. If the reports of Sawantaeny's death are true, such a piece of fabric may even now be serving him as a shroud.[67]

Chapter 2

TAQUATARENSALY
(CAPTAIN CIVILITY)

G OV. WILLIAM KEITH AND THE CONESTOGA MAN THE COL-onists call "Civility" met together for the first time in June of 1718, when the Indian journeyed with a large delegation to meet with the members of the Provincial Council in Philadelphia. His arrival per-plexed the city leaders. They were not sure who Taquatarensaly was, what he did, or why he wanted to speak with them. Using one of at least eight variant English spellings for Taquatarensaly's name, colony secretary James Logan noted the appearance in council of "Tagoto-lessa or Civility, the present Chief or Captain of the Conestogoe Indi-ans." In making this entry in the official minutes, Logan showed confidence neither in the man's name nor his title.[1]

In the early eighteenth-century colonial English world, knowing a man's calling tells you everything you need to know about his role in the community and his standing in society. Until you have identified a man's occupation, you can't place him as a person. The officials who draw up the city's tax lists pay close attention to such questions. Fine distinctions matter. A blacksmith heats his iron hotter than a white-smith warms his tin. Carpenters bang their hammers hard, while join-ers scrape softly with their planes. The uncured skins of the leather dresser cannot be mistaken for the smooth surface of the tanner's leather, the soft nap of the felter's wares, nor yet with the rich warmth of the currier's furs. Each of these trades is enumerated separately on the city's rolls, which include some 292 people engaged in some 68 different lines of work. Taquatarensaly fit none of these descriptions and James Logan did not know just how to describe him.[2]

Still, Pennsylvanian officials urgently needed to determine why the large assemblage of Native people, including members of the Conestoga, the Shawnee, the Ganawese, and the Delaware Nations, had collectively decided to "come from their respective habitations to pay a visit to" the Pennsylvania government. John Cartlidge was on hand in the city that day and Governor Keith requested that he serve as head translator. He ordered him to tell the gathering that he "had at their desire now called a council in order to hear what the Indians had to lay before them." Taquatarensaly did his best to explain, telling the governor, according to Logan's notes on Cartlidge's translation, that "they were come only on a friendly visit to see us and to renew the old League of friendship." Native peoples of the Susquehanna valley knew the importance of strengthening ties slowly over time. Visits in a time of calm could do much to build a cache of trust to draw on in times of crisis.[3]

Governor Keith had trouble accepting the Native man's words at face value. He "told them their visit was very acceptable, he hoped all was well with them, but desired them now to be free" in sharing their motives for visiting him. "If they had anything to complain of that wanted to be redressed," Keith wanted to hear it. Still new to Philadelphia and inexperienced in the ways of Indian diplomacy, he assumed that calling a meeting meant confronting a threat. In his eyes, every cross-cultural conversation involved negotiations over conflicting interests. What to make of the man standing before him claiming to be paying a simple social call, one he just happened to be conducting in the company of large numbers of strong young men? It would help if only Keith and the members of his council could figure out just what role the Native spokesman played among his own people. But even James Logan, the council member with the longest and most extensive trading ties among Indians, and, as secretary, the man responsible for all official records on the government's dealings with them, could offer at best partial assistance.[4]

The first time Taquatarensaly was mentioned in Logan's minutes, in 1710, he was identified simply as "Civility," without any modifier at all. But the next time Pennsylvania Council minutes made note of him, in 1712, they offered the information that they had been visited by "Civility, a War Captain & Chief." In 1713, they called him more simply "one of the chiefs of Conestogoe." He was then described as a "chief" twice more in 1715, as a "captain" accompanying another Indian identified as the Conestoga "chief" in 1716, and as one of multiple "chiefs of the Indians on Susquehanna" in 1717. Was he a chief or was he a war captain? Reflecting colonial incomprehension, on this day in 1718 Logan referenced him as "Civility, the present Chief or Captain of the Conestogoe Indians." Still, he had no doubt about Civility's military bona fides; that same note added that, "Civility said, that he with some of the young men had this last spring some inclination to go out to war."[5]

Pennsylvanians' uncertainty about how to describe Taquatarensaly's function reflects their basic unfamiliarity with Indian ways. As a descendent of the Susquehannock Indian Nation, also known as the "Mingos," Taquatarensaly is heir to a long tradition of Native American diplomacy. Native peoples of the American southeast have a specific title for a man who smooths relations between peoples by taking up membership in more than one society. Such a man acts simultaneously as a war captain who protects his people and as a spokesman able to intercede for both his own people and for any other peoples who formally adopted him as one of their own. They refer to such people by the title "Fanimingo."

English settlers have at least a glancing awareness of the term, mentioned in a letter written by a colonist named Thomas Nairne in 1708. According to Nairne, it is usual for a family in want of protection to choose "some growing man of esteem in the wars" and "claim him for the head or Chief of their family." The man so chosen is addressed thereafter as "chief" and honored with presents. In return, he is "to protect that family and take care of its concerns equally with those of his own." Nairne indicated that an analogous procedure could be used by "two nations at peace" who could designate a fanimingo to go between them. Each is to "chuse these protectors in the other" and, between them, these representatives are "to make up all Breaches between the 2 nations" should any occur. Such a go-between identifies equally with his family or nation of origin and with the one that ritually adopts him.[6]

Captain Civility's multiple memberships in the varied Native nations who claimed him; his role as spokesman for a diverse array of Susquehanna River valley peoples, including a range of Algonquian and Iroquoian groups; and his frequent contacts with European colonial leaders all stem from the role he performs in the tradition of the fanimingo. In fact, the word "Mingo" itself *means* chief. Local Algonquian groups call Iroquoian-speakers at Conestoga "Mingos" in recognition of the leadership positions that they have recently assumed in the region. Civility's prominent role as war captain, spokesperson, translator, and go-between for multiple regional peoples—all the duties expected of a "Fanni Mingo"—is one he is positioned to play not only by virtue of his own qualities but also by means of his nation's designation as "Mingos" or chiefs.[7]

Although Pennsylvania colonists have no direct familiarity with the precise term "fanimingo," when they call Taquatarensaly "Civility" they are using a word with much the same meaning. This old moniker from colonial Maryland may very well have originated as a rough translation for the Indian job title. When seventeenth-century Maryland colonists met such a diplomat and tried to understand the nature of his role, they would have searched for English words and concepts that could encapsulate the Susquehannock tradition of assigning a person to take up membership in multiple communities, serving as the living embodiment of civil society.[8]

The original English connotation of "civility" is of "senses relating to citizenship," including "a community of citizens regarded collectively." Seventeenth-century Susquehannock leaders given the title "Civility," who labored both to protect their own people and to create leagues with colonists, were doing nothing if not attempting to create a collective community—one that could encompass both Natives and newcomers. Far from conveying either a backhanded compliment to or a sarcastic critique of so-called savages, then, the title "Civility" may simply have been the best available early seventeenth-century English translation for a unique Native leadership position, one in which a designated protector used ritual relationships to unite disparate peoples.[9]

Taquatarensaly's words and actions at the June 1718 meeting that first brought him together with Logan, Keith, and Cartlidge contained many hints that he undertook the visit with the goal of furthering harmony among all of the peoples of the Susquehanna valley. Nothing signaled peaceful intentions like giving a gift. But even then, bridging cultural divides required teaching and learning on both sides. Taquatarensaly brought with him some deerskins for the governor and explained that he offered them in order to "to lay them under the Governor's feet to keep them & his house clean." He described this use of the skins because, unlike Native peoples who customarily lined their floors with skins and woven mats, colonists preferred to leave their floors bare and to place their rugs upon tables—where they could be more readily viewed and admired by guests seated in chairs. Native leaders from Conestoga remarked on this practice, as when one of their queens told another governor, in 1710, that she had brought him a bundle of furs and skins, "to make him a cover for his table, to be used in the same manner as the carpet then spread upon the council table." Perhaps observing that their skins had never been put to use as tablecloths, Taquatarensaly tried again, this time instructing the colonists on the skins' original purpose as floor cloths.[10]

Most important, he came to alert the governor and his council that although the people of Conestoga had recently suffered the death of their king, his passing had altered nothing in their commitment to good relations with the colonists. He told the governor, "tho their Last Good King is taken from them, they have one yet left who . . . has an English heart & a Great Love for the Christians." In Taquatarensaly's telling, the Indian king did more than just have English interests at heart; he had their very heart within his body. Such metaphors binding people bodily in mutual survival scarcely existed in the English diplomatic repertoire.[11]

Keith and his council found it easier to deal with the more concrete issues Civility raised that day: questions of war and trade. Pennsylvania colonists did not want the Native peoples of the Susquehanna River valley to fight against Indians to the south, for fear that such conflicts could easily affect colonial settlements. To their relief, Civility indicated that Indians would follow colonial directives. For their part, members of the Native community at Connestoga complained of the many unscrupulous traders in their midst who offered only liquor in exchange for furs. They reported that "there have been such quantities of that liquor carried of late amongst them, by loose persons who have no fixed settlements, that they are apprehensive of mischief [that] may arise from it." They could hardly have imagined then that the "mischief" might possibly amount to murder and that the future culprit stood among them even as they spoke.[12]

None of those assembled cast a second glance at John Cartlidge. Unlike "loose persons" with no fixed local ties, John was Taquatarensaly's neighbor, a welcome member of the greater Conestoga community. Far from considering him a threat, Native people approved when Governor Keith stated that John deserved the credit for maintaining Indian property boundaries and that colonists "had fenced their Corn Fields by John Cartlidges Care, who alone being placed within those Lines may be the more Capable of Looking after the tract and the Bounds of it." The English never came closer to honoring Indian ideals of cultural unity than when men like John Cartlidge fixed a home among them and used their local knowledge to safeguard Indian interests.[13]

Governor Keith was pleased with John Cartlidge's performance at the June 1718 meeting. His translations smoothed negotiations while his very presence enhanced cross-cultural relations. He and his council decided to reward John with an official position. The very next month, in July of 1718, when "the board proceeded to nominate persons to be added to the Commissions of Peace for the County of Philadelphia & Chester," among those appointed for Chester County was one John Cartlidge. Neither Civility nor anyone else present at his first joint meeting with Keith, Logan, and Cartlidge would ever have guessed that just four years later the newly appointed commissioner would stand accused of the most serious possible breach of the peace.[14]

Chapter 3

WHEN THINGS GO ILL

FEBRUARY 1722

When Things go ill, each Fool presumes t'advise,
And if more happy thinks himself more wise.

—Titan Leeds, Verses for February,
The American Almanack for 1722

"YOU OWE IT TO ME," SAYS SAWANTAENY. THE SENECA man is widely respected as a warrior and hunter. He stands his ground and gestures, a pot in his hand, toward the fur trader John Cartlidge.[1]

"You need not be angry," Sawantaeny tells him. They have been together for hours by the campfire already, talking and drinking and trying to come to terms. This is Sawantaeny's place, and John is his guest. His welcome is real, but he is beginning to wear it out.[2]

John and Sawantaeny confront each other on this cold dawn in the company of three other colonists, including John's brother, Edmund, as well as two white indentured servant lads whose names are William Wilkins and Jonathan Swindel. Multiple Native people are present as well. Some slip away from the fire and out of the historical record without leaving a trace. But several later serve as witnesses and have their names recorded by the Pennsylvania colonists. First of all, there is a man known to John and Edmund as "Ayaquachan, the Ganawese," whom they hired to lead them to Sawantaeny's cabin. Then there are two Shawnee youths named Aquannachke and Metheequeyta, who have joined the group hoping to take advantage of the chance to trade with John. And, of course, the Seneca Sawantaeny and his Shawnee wife, Weenepeeweytah, are there as well—though Weenepeeweytah has stayed in the cabin rather than join the rough group of men by the fire.

Thud. The clay pot hits the frozen ground. Ayaquachan is thirty years old, a member of the Conoy Nation with good local ties. Even the most experienced colonial traders rely on Native guides to steer them in the woods. Having directed the Cartlidge brothers on their journey yesterday and brought them straight to Sawantaeny and his wife, Ayaquachan regarded his job as complete and settled down to his reward—swallowing down John's supplies. Now he is facing the morning still "in liquor," half-dazed after a night of outdoor drinking, camped by the coals. Through bleary eyes, he watches the trader snatch the vessel from the hands of their host and hurl it down.[3]

JOHN DID NOT EXPECT to have this much trouble with Sawantaeny. He had simply planned to persuade Sawantaeny to give up his furs at low enough prices that he and his brother, Edmund, then James Logan the middleman, and then Logan's English merchant contacts could all reap the benefit. Deerskins always find a ready market, and raccoon is also selling well. Beaver pelts do not fetch as much now as they did a few years ago, but overall the trade is holding steady. Bearskins are so lucrative that James Logan, a man with an eye on many kinds of profit, likes to refer to himself with the exotic-sounding title "bearskin merchant." John was hoping to lubricate their negotiations with enough alcohol that Sawantaeny would be too content to desire anything more valuable than second-rate rum for his efforts, if not too compromised to demand a fair deal. Afterward, the Cartlidges' early offer of liquor is one thing all observers of the dispute agree upon. No sooner did the two brothers and a group of helpers land on Sawantaeny's doorstep than they toasted the Seneca man with a tot of rum to thank him for his hospitality.[4]

John and Edmund Cartlidge trotted into Monocasey Creek, located above a branch of the Potomac River, last night. They came in the company of the pair of English servant lads, whose contracts belong to John, along with the Conoy Indian guide they hired to help them find Sawantaeny. Along the way, their horse train picked up the two Shawnee boys in their late teens or early twenties. They have use for all five of these men; the Conoy (whom Pennsylvania colonists call the Ganawese) have long lived in the area and know the local land and people well. The English servants can lend critical muscle in loading and carrying furs and trade goods. The two Shawnee youths can do all of the above, plus help the Cartlidges converse with Sawantaeny through his wife, Weenepeeweytah, who is Shawnee as well.[5]

The men soon got busy piling up brush to create a bonfire big enough to burn till sunup, then tucked in beside it and started the spirits flowing. John Cartlidge passed out drinks in a "pott." Soon, the whole circle was "in liquor" and most of them stayed up all night, except for the two Shawnee boys who fell fast into a rum-assisted sleep. At a glance, the scene seemed ordinary enough. Colonists and Indians alike sip daily from redware jugs they make out of common local clay and red potsherds litter the ground at the nearest large settlement in Conestoga.[6]

But strictly speaking, John knew he had no business offering Sawantaeny liquor for his furs. At an Indian council held at John Cartlidge's own house at Conestoga just last summer, in July of 1721, representatives of the Five Nations complained to Pennsylvania's governor, William Keith, that "all their Disorders arose from the Use of Rum and Strong Spirits, which took away their sense and memory." Noting that "they had no such Liquors amongst themselves and were hurt with what [the colonists] furnished them," they added that they "desired that no more of that sort might be sent amongst them." Keith responded by assuring them, "I am sensible that Rum is very hurtful to Indians. We have made Laws that none should be carried among them, or if any were that it should be staved and thrown upon the Ground."[7]

Both Sawantaeny and John must know of this promise. Sawantaeny, as a leading member of the local Seneca community, itself one of the members of the Five Nations of the Iroquois, will be well aware of last summer's policy discussions. Meanwhile, John Cartlidge's ears must

be burning. Just a few years ago, in November of 1718, he was cited by
the Chester County Quarterly Court for the crime of "Selling liquor
by small measure." From traveling hunters to local neighbors, everyone seems to know that John Cartlidge's house at Conestoga offers a
good place to nip in for a quick drink.[8]

Yet neither John nor Edmund likes to let a little thing like the law
stand between them and profit or pleasure. Each of them already has
a long record of citations from Pennsylvania's Chester County Quarterly Court for engaging in offenses from "riot" (Edmund) to failure to
ensure "Conservation of Peace" (John) to "Diverse trespasses" (John
again), all aggravated by repeated notes that John "failed to appear"
to answer for his actions. Furthermore, John has been counting on the
fact that Governor Keith likes to talk out of both sides of his mouth.[9]

In the same 1721 speech in which he acknowledged the hurt caused
among Indians when Pennsylvania's colonial traders traffic in rum,
Governor Keith immediately shifted responsibility onto Indians,
claiming that "the Country is so wide, the woods are so dark and private, and so far out of my sight, that if the Indians themselves do not
prohibit their own People there is no way to prevent" rum sales from
occurring. In fact, Keith appreciates the money to be made in trading
Indian furs for English liquor and he has little intention of cutting off
this key source of capital. From rum to brandy, English alcohol helps
English colonists pour into Indian country.[10]

John Cartlidge has timed his trip north carefully for the tail end
of the winter season, after hunters like Sawantaeny have had months
to stockpile thick wintertime pelts, but before woodland trails become
clogged with spring mud. This should allow him to load up on the best
quality furs while reducing transportation costs and time. The key, of
course, is getting the lowest price on furs. As the Cartlidge brothers
plot how to get Sawantaeny's wares on the cheap, the words "dark,"
"private," and "out of sight" must sound just about right.

SAWANTAENY WILL NOT BACK DOWN. He is known to be a very civil
man, and a man of few words, but now he won't stop pressing John for

payment. He is valued as a chief among the Senecas and any goods he acquires will help him to provide for his people and to extend his influence among them. He does not think an evening's tippling can serve as fair compensation for the furs he has to offer.[11]

Sawantaeny has been sitting on a collection of pelts from animals he has labored many months in hunting and trapping. He has situated his cabin in an ideal locale. Even some two centuries into the colonial deerskin trade, the area remains so rich in game that, on a map made last year in Maryland, the surveyor indicated that Indians refer to a spot nearby as "Elks' Licking Place" because "great droves of those creatures" herd there to lick the salty soil. True, Sawantaeny took no offense when the traders arrived at his home yesterday and offered him a dram to help break the ice on a winter night. But he has no intention of trading away all his hard work in return for nothing more than a few pots of liquor.[12]

Caressing the pelts that he has gathered and his wife has dressed and cured, Sawantaeny and Weenepeeweytah could hardly have fathomed the columns of numbers swimming in the heads of the calculating Cartlidges. While English colonists clutch their goods in their fists, Native peoples pass their largesse freely from hand to hand. Like Sawantaeny, Weenepeeweytah enjoys a place of prominence among her own people. She claims Savannah, the chief of the Shawnees, as her cousin. As leading members of two of the many communities swept together on the waters of the Susquehanna, Sawantaeny and Weenepeeweytah understand the importance of gift exchange as a means of improving harmony among peoples.[13]

Leaders from the many nations living in and around Conestoga try to explain to colonists how broadly their people seek to distribute material riches, the better to create extensive bonds of benevolence between peoples. When asked at one treaty council how they liked the diplomatic gifts passed out by Pennsylvania officials, they replied that, "not only the Indians that were at Conestogoe . . . but likewise those of the whole Country, were pleased with what then passed, and that the Presents then delivered to them were divided into the smallest parts, that [they] might reach all the Indians everywhere & be read as a Letter." For Indians, gifting is a powerful means of communicating. They do everything they can to spread the word of friendship as widely as possible.[14]

Indians call on the analogy of the letter to try to show how sharing goods serves a larger purpose. According to Native principles, when two people—or two nations—exchange gifts, each offers the other a promise to work cooperatively for peace and plenty. Colonists ought to understand the analogy of the letter. After all, even in the English language, the word "correspondence" can signal more than simply a regular exchange of paper and ink. Mention of a close "correspondence" between two people or things can imply a strong similarity or equivalence between them. When they translate the Indian word as "letter," instead of using the more capacious term "correspondence," colonial interpreters obscure the fuller meaning of Native gifting. When Indians say that a gift can be "read as a letter" they mean not only that gifts can convey information but also, more important, that, like all "correspondence," they constitute "relations between persons or communities." This is, in fact, a primary definition of the word "correspondence" that has been very common in English since the seventeenth century. Yet most colonists hardly glance up from their leather-bound ledger books long enough to consider the Indian approach to gifting.[15]

Colonists' main interest in engaging in trade lies in buying and selling commodities in order to accumulate vast sums of money, not in allocating tokens of material and spiritual harmony as far and wide as possible. Even James Logan, the colony's preeminent fur trader, who at least perceives the difference in Indian versus English attitudes toward exchange, sees little reason to alter colonial practices. A decade ago at a treaty conference, he did make an effort to clear up confusion by countering Indian objections that traders were not generous enough by explaining "in relation to their Complaints of Trade, that they must Consider that the end that all Traders had in view by Buying and Selling was to gain something by it to themselves." Logan himself keeps a thick account book recording his personal "profits and losses." In the last year alone, he filled six eighteen-by-twenty-four-inch pages with his careful curling script, averaging an entry every two or three days for all of 1721. In line after line on alternating leaves, headed "Contra" for payments made "by" him and "Cash" for payments made "to"

him, he documented numerous transactions for "peltry" and "furs."
Against the mutual good of free distribution, Logan sets the individual
advantage of financial transactions.[16]

The English never waver in their devotion to the profit motive. At
last summer's 1721 conclave at Conestoga, when members of the Five
Nations, multiple peoples of the Susquehanna region, and representatives from colonial Pennsylvania all met, Governor Keith reprised
Logan's earlier comments. Keith told the assembled Indians, who
objected to the poor returns they received for their furs, "you must
take Care to make the best Bargain you can." After all, Keith asserted,
"every man must take care of himself." Individual opportunity drives
the ambitions of Pennsylvania colonists.[17]

At this same conference, colonists recorded, without truly regis-
tering, a request made by a representative of the Seneca Nation that,
"we may now be together as one people." The Senecas preceded this
request by presenting a "small parcel of dressed Skins" and followed
it by offering "a Bundle of Bear skins." By presenting ritual gifts
immediately before and after they spoke, the Seneca representatives
made their diplomatic message manifest. In pairing words and goods,
they were trying to make something ineffable—that is, the feelings
that came with unity—into something tangible. Through just such a
process of coming together, the members of the Five Nations of the
Haudenosaunee had managed to contain conflict among themselves
over the last century or more.[18]

But the assembled Pennsylvanians never considered the joining of
peoples that the Senecas proposed. Keith steadfastly insisted on stick-
ing to the colonial position, which viewed economic exchanges as a
form of competition between opposing groups. He informed the Indians repeatedly: "We believe, Those who go into the Woods and spend
all their time upon it [should] endeavour to make the best Bargains
they can for themselves." That small phrase, "we believe," signals
much about the Pennsylvania perspective. Colonists count themselves
as part of a collective "we" that does not include Native peoples. Their
sense of themselves as a separate people is defined by their belief system, one in which conducting commerce does not require merging
communities.[19]

It is not that Native peoples do not understand the colonial process of exchanging furs for currency or credit. To the contrary, many are quite as comfortable with cash as Logan himself is. On June 21, 1721, for example, on the same day that the treaty was signed at Conestoga, Logan registered a side payment on his "Contra" page with the note, "By Accot. of Peltry p[ai]d Civility for 6 ffall Deer." Logan recorded compensating Civility £1, 2 shillings for the skins. This payment was well below any officially calculated values for deerskins noted at other treaties and Logan, no doubt, congratulated himself on the business acumen he exercised in "gaining something" through the transaction. Still, Civility accepted Logan's payment without incident; neither he nor the other Native people present at the treaty could imagine removing societal implications from material exchanges. In Native eyes, trading connections always create communal ties.[20]

SOMETHING IN SAWANTAENY'S FACE as he stands up to John proves too much for the colonist. The Indian's very countenance gives umbrage. John shoves the hunter so hard that the Indian tumbles against a fallen tree. Struggling to his feet, Sawantaeny staggers dozens of yards over the frost-heaved ground to his cabin and seizes his gun. Weenepeeweytah shrieks out for him to stop, but she cannot prevent him from rushing off with it. She follows him back out the door and watches what comes next.[21]

William, the servant boy, runs up and tries to wrestle away Sawantaeny's gun but can't manage it. Then Edmund Cartlidge steps into the fray. Edmund is a big man, grown strong with the labor of the fur trade and stout with its profits. He jumps in where William the servant boy leaves off.[22]

Clap. The sound begins as a vibration on the top of Sawantaeny's head, like the snap of winter tree limbs broken by the weight of ice. *Thwack.* This is no splintering twig. This is Sawantaeny's own gun, striking hard against his shattering skull. *Crack.* The gun breaks clean in half with the third blow. Nearby, the bonfire hisses.[23]

Wood, brass, flint, and steel fashion many of life's ordinary objects, from buckets and kettles to houses and ships. Fastened together just so, they can combine to create a flintlock firearm. Afterward, if witnesses to the wilderness fight between the Seneca hunter Sawantaeny and the colonial fur traders John and Edmund Cartlidge agree on anything it is this: The fracas takes a turn when the Indian's own gun splinters across his head.[24]

Nearly every man at Conestoga owns a gun, the essential tool of hunters, the weapon of fighters, the treasured talisman tucked into the graves of the dead. Driven by the Iroquois, the Native peoples of the Susquehanna River region have been using European guns for a century now. Each escalation of the fur-trading, captive-taking complex has increased the distribution of arms in an ever-spiraling cycle with no end in sight.[25]

Some Native men of the Susquehanna region tote ordinary muskets, manufactured directly for the Indian trade. Others carry finely wrought specialty pieces, detailed with flourishes that can include serpentine brass side plates or butt plates with engraved finials. The flints, too, vary from gun to gun; the Senecas have long preferred wedge-shaped gunflints. These they make themselves by salvaging refuse English flint left in the Delaware Bay by colonial sea captains dumping their ballast. The people of Conestoga follow this preference as well, shunning North American and French flint in favor of hotter English sparks.[26]

Edmund's older brother watches him work, all the while stripping off his own clothes, readying to reenter the fight. Now, as the Indian sits dazed on the cold ground, blood running down his neck, the naked man moves in. John goes after Sawantaeny with fists and feet, punches and kicks—more branches broken in the wounded man's ribs.[27]

Sawantaeny's gun is little good to him just now. He is bleeding from his mouth, his nose, his head, his side. His throat rattles and he cannot speak. His wife comes to him and helps him back into their cabin. Has it been only moments since he dashed inside to find his weapon, then back out to struggle with the stingy English traders and their pack of young servants?[28]

ALREADY, JOHN IS DRESSING again, making up his bundles of goods. He directs William and Jonathan to help load up the packs, and then he and Edmund gallop away, their string of horses pounding behind them. Today, February 7, is Ash Wednesday, according to the almanac Titan Leeds published in Philadelphia. By the liturgical calendar of the Church of England, this is a day for atonement. But John, a Quaker, does not follow the ritual calendar of the Anglican Church and Edmund, his brother, has fallen away from Quakerism. The two Shawnee boys help Sawantaeny's wife get him back into the cabin, then follow after John and Edmund, catching up quickly. They are still half drunk on John's potent rum, but they yet hope to gain by John's skill at trading.[29]

The Cartlidges can't haul off from Monocasey fast enough. They intend to head straight back to Conestoga and proceed with their business affairs. Everything they have been working for is endangered by what they have just done. At best, Sawantaeny may survive to nurse an enormous grudge against them. At worst, he may actually die of his wounds, an event that could easily lead into all-out war between the Indians and the English.

Last year, when some English traders insulted some young Indian men they ran across in the woods by "using them with ill language, calling them dogs, &c.," word got back to the Iroquois, who brought the matter up at the treaty council held at John's house at Conestoga. The chiefs of the Five Nations said, "They take unkindly to this because Dogs have no sense or understanding: Whereas they are men and think that their Brothers should not compare them to such Creatures." The colonists managed to patch up that crisis and end last summer's conference with the Iroquois on a cordial note. But when the news spreads how the Cartlidges have gone well beyond insulting young men to the point of assaulting a recognized chief, the situation may grow grave. If the Cartlidges' attack on Sawantaeny has sabotaged the governor's diplomatic efforts, however unintentionally, there will be plenty of people ready to condemn them.[30]

Everyone knows about last summer's treaty because the governor's successful proceedings at the Conestoga conference were published in a widely distributed pamphlet. Heralded as the first English-language treaty between colonists and the Five Nations, it came out last July under the title *The Particulars of an Indian Treaty at Conestogoe, between his Excellency Sir William Keith, Bart. Governor of Pennsylvania, and the Deputies of the Five Nations. Published at the Request of the Gentlemen who Were Present and Waited upon the Governor in His Journey.* Keith is so keen to enhance his reputation as the man best positioned to steer the British Empire to fabulous wealth in American furs that he drew up this booklet to commemorate the accord—all the while protesting that he was publishing only at the insistence of his admiring gentlemen friends. Among other things, the pamphlet recounts how Keith, an Anglican, lectured Indians on principles of pacifism more often credited to Quakers. He demanded, "surely you cannot propose to get either Riches or Possessions by going . . . out to War: For when you kill a Deer you have the Flesh to eat and the Skin to sell, but when you return from War you bring nothing Home but the Scalp of a dead Man." Such words, no doubt, sounded nonsensical to the Iroquois— who never went to war in pursuit of riches and who resorted to fighting only when plunged in mourning. Still, Keith's stance resounded well with the English-speakers in his audience, both the "gentlemen present" when he gave it and the ones who read over his words back in the comfort of a Philadelphia coffeehouse.[31]

It will not look good when people find out that a Quaker instigated a backwoods brawl. Edmund's departure from the Society of Friends relates to his reputation for rioting. Now John could face disownment. John prizes his connections to the Society of Friends. Unlike most English colonists who open their letters with honorifics like "Dear sir" and close them, with false humility, "Your humble servant," John advertises his religious affiliation by using the simpler Quaker style of address. "Esteemed friend," he will greet his correspondent, signing off "thy true and loving friend." There is little room in love and pacifism for the sort of violent confrontation Cartlidge has just engaged in.[32]

Still, John Cartlidge's embarrassment will be nothing compared to the humiliation this could cause Governor Keith. An English publisher is even now reprinting Keith's literary efforts, proving the allure of accounts of Anglo-Iroquoian relations for transatlantic audiences. Readers in London will soon learn, if they don't know already, of "His Excellency the Governor's Care for the Publick Safety" of Pennsylvania, an effort that "plainly discovers itself in his Management of Affairs with the Indians in General and his late Toilsome Journey to . . . Conestogoe." (In fact, though no one knows it yet, the pamphlet will sell so well in London this year that it will be republished again in Dublin next year.) If all of Keith's toils end in a new Anglo-Indian war touched off by the Cartlidges' misjudgment at Monocasey, Keith is sure to subject John to an unpleasant reckoning. Indian talk of brotherhood may not survive such a crisis.[33]

BACK IN HIS CABIN, Sawantaeny lies as shattered as his gun. He is alone now, save for the faithful presence of Weenepeeweytah. The pieces of his broken weapon—trash now in the eyes of the English— still hold something of value in the eyes of Native people. The gun may no longer shoot but can still symbolize Sawantaeny's prowess as a hunter and the strength of his trade connections. Many a Native man at Conestoga has been proudly buried with his gun in perfect working condition, sent on his journey to the spirit world with arms of honor. And some men in the Susquehanna region have been buried along with the fragments of their flintlocks, the wood, stone, and steel useless as firearms, yet still able to evoke their worth as men.[34]

Witnesses say that Edmund Cartlidge drove the head of the steel cock of Sawantaeny's gun into his brain. "My friends have killed me," he tells his wife. He believes he is dying. She watches as his blood clots on the bearskin on which he lies. At least he has this, a pelt that he has won and that she has worked, something soft and warm to rest upon. Those are his only words to her. "His friends." This is how he thinks of John and Edmund Cartlidge, even now.[35]

THIS IS NOT HOW things were supposed to go. When John and Edmund Cartlidge tracked their way to Sawantaeny's cabin in the woods, ready to trade rum for furs, they were hoping to make a killing only in profits. John has his eye on some land that he hopes to purchase and Edmund is working to amass a fortune to equal his older brother's. John knows he stands to realize enormous gains if he can reach hunters like Sawantaeny and part them from their furs before any other traders arrive. The Cartlidges also know they have local rivals, not least in the form of a pair of Swedish settlers, a father and son named John Hans Steelman and John Hans Steelman Jr., who have been trading as much as £1,000 sterling at a time in English goods in exchange for furs.[36]

The senior Steelman was living and trading near Monocasey long before William Penn arrived to claim his trading territory as part of Pennsylvania. John Hans Steelman Jr., having grown up in the area, is now well connected with local people, Natives and newcomers alike. The Steelmans have hardly welcomed the encroachments of later-arriving traders, men like John and Edmund Cartlidge, who weave themselves into networks the Steelmans worked hard to create. For the Steelmans, this crisis may present an opportunity—not just to undermine rival traders but also to upend the entire upstart operation known as the Province of Pennsylvania. The moment the Cartlidges hurry back toward Conestoga, Steelman and some Native friends step over to Maryland to alert authorities there.[37]

"Sir," a man named Maj. John Bradford begins a letter to a correspondent, too rattled to remember to use any more polite salutation. He is writing to Col. Thomas Addison, the head of the colony of Maryland's militia, with critical intelligence. He ought to begin by explaining that he has key news to share. But he has no time to think about the craft of composition right now. "The Occasion of this Trouble," he plunges in without preamble, just as if he and Addison are in the middle of a conversation and Addison already knows there is trouble afoot, "is on the death of one of the chief men of the Sinicar Nation." Bradford, a junior officer in the Maryland militia, has just received this unwelcome news from John Hans Steelman Jr., who has arrived at Bradford's place in Maryland in the company of "some Indians" bearing tales of murder.[38]

As Bradford explains to Addison, a man "called Saroney" was "killed by two of the Conestogan Traders called John and Edmund Cartlidge who immediately fled on this Occasion." Bradford does not know the standard spelling of either Sawantaeny or the Seneca Nation, but he nonetheless nails the Cartlidge brothers. He warns that their crime may have region-wide repercussions. "The Consequence of this imprudent and base action seems very much to threaten this our province with an Indian war," he tells Addison. Bradford wrings his hands about the "unhappy accident" that led to an Indian's death and urges Addison, his superior officer in the militia, to persuade the governor to take immediate defensive action "to prevent shedding Innocent Blood" of colonists in Maryland.[39]

Addison writes back to Bradford and presses for further particulars. Bradford's first letter about the crisis, written in haste given the "emergent occasion," is too sparse to be useful. So Bradford returns to Steelman's combined group of colonial and Native witnesses to ask for further information. "The great Sinicar Indian by the best account I can have," Bradford tells Colonel Addison in a second letter, this one dated February 17, 1722, "was killed at Monocasey about ten days past by John Cartlidge of Conestogoe who was then in Company with his Brother Edmund Cartlidge." Getting into the gruesome details, he goes on: "the way he murdered him was by making a violent stroke at his head with the Indians own Gun and drove the head of the Cock into his Brains." By this account, John, not Edmund, drove Sawantaeny's gun into his head. Later, when Pennsylvania officials examine Native eyewitnesses at Conestoga, three different people will place the gun in Edmund's hand and a pair of colonial witnesses, interviewed separately but simultaneously in Philadelphia, will confirm this version. But Steelman and his group blame John alone. The discrepancy helps to account for the way the leaders of the Five Nations ultimately place their focus on John. It hints that the Haudenosaunee are getting information through their own communication networks, alerted by Native informants linked to the Steelmans.[40]

John Hans Steelman Jr. is well placed to know and communicate the views of Indians in the region. Raised in his father's log-cabin trading post, he is now visiting Maryland in the company of longtime Native friends and neighbors. A decade from now, Pennsylvania colonists will even record meeting with a man they identify as "John Hans, the Cayuga." While they won't mention whether this John Hans is a son born to John Hans Steelman Jr. and a Cayuga mother, or whether he is simply a Cayuga man who adopted Steelman's first and middle name as a means of symbolizing a strong bond of friendship, either possibility suggests how extensive Steelman Jr.'s connections among Native peoples are and will become.[41]

Steelman Jr. and his companions offer their own explanation of the Cartlidges' motives for assaulting Sawantaeny: "the reasons of this Fact were, because the said Indian would not buy of their Rum which they brought there to sell." Steelman Jr. is presenting an explanation for the Cartlidge killing that casts his rival fur traders in a very poor light. Even if the brothers harbored no intention to physically harm Sawantaeny when they set out to trade with him, Steelman is claiming that they did begin by deliberately skirting the law. If John and Edmund pushed rum on Sawantaeny in flagrant violation of last summer's signed treaty agreement, then their transgressions began as soon as they started to trade. According to English understandings of crime, the journey to perdition finishes with the first step into sin.[42]

Rum, despite its charms, imposes many harms. Native peoples have been saying as much for years. As a Delaware spokesman observed at a meeting in Philadelphia back in 1717, which included representatives of all the local nations and at which John Cartlidge served as translator, "young men" too easily become "generaly debauch with Rum, carried amongst them by strangers," so much so that they forsake all other goods until they lack even "all manner of Clothing & necessarys to go ahunting." When John Hans Steelman Jr. reports John Cartlidge for running rum, he is only raising a long-standing concern of many Susquehanna peoples.[43]

And so when John Hans Steelman Jr. tells John Bradford, "some Indians say that if the murtherer is brought to Justice the Sinicars will require no more," Bradford takes care to insert that information in the letter he is preparing for Addison to forward to Maryland's governor, Charles Calvert. "Use your endeavours with his Excellency," Bradford implores Addison, "that proper measures may be taken to preserve peace with the Indians on this unhappy occasion." When Bradford thinks about "proper measures," his mind strays to a supply of ammunition. "The Frontiers are in the greatest want of Powder and Ball to defend themselves," he says in his first letter. In his second he describes colonial settlers' "fear of the Indians," stressing again that "the Frontier Inhabitants are altogether uncapable of making any defence having neither Powder nor Ball." And yet, his letter holds out the hope that the Indians themselves may not be rushing toward war. If the murderers are brought to justice, Steelman and his companions claim, the Senecas will ask nothing more.[44]

Five days later, Gov. Charles Calvert of Maryland gathers his advisers in the council chamber in the city of Annapolis to consider what should be said and done in response to the alarming news that Col. Thomas Addison has just brought from up the Potomac. Everything about the letters spread before them offends their sense of order. These men are plantation owners, used to exercising tight control. Even the redbrick building in which they sit, though modest in size, boasts harmonious Palladian proportions. Constructed just four years ago, in 1718, it serves as a ballroom on gala evenings when the government is not in session. Plantation masters and mistresses, the sons and daughters of this tobacco colony, bow, curtsy, and twirl within it. But today, the sound of John Bradford's letters being read aloud in council drowns out any lingering echoes of dancers and fiddlers.[45]

Charles Calvert, the fifth Lord Baltimore, has been in full charge of his family's colony for less than a year. If there is one thing the new young lord does not want within the first months of his office, surely it is an Indian war. Maryland, like Pennsylvania, is owned and ruled by a single family. Charles's father, the fourth Lord Baltimore, died in 1715, when Charles was just sixteen years old. Now, having reached the age of majority as of his twenty-first birthday on September 29, 1721, Calvert has just taken over rule from his guardian and begun active administration of the government. Facing up to the crisis Colonel Addison has laid in his lap, he starts by writing instructions to send

back to John Bradford: "you are desired to be very Cautious in giving the Indians any Occasion of Coming to Blows." Surely Bradford
hardly needs to be told this. But when things go ill, each fool thinks
himself wise.[46]

Calvert immediately has several further thoughts on the crisis
unfolding on Monocasey Creek, which he soon conveys in his reply
to Bradford. First of all, he wants to be sure that Native peoples know
the violent men in question are not subjects of his colony and that the
territory on which the attack occurred is not in his jurisdiction. "By
all means possible," Calvert orders Bradford, "you contrive to let the
Indians know that the Murderers are under the Pennsylvania Government and that we are no ways Concern'd in it." If only crossing the case
off his books were as easy as crossing his *t*'s with aristocratic flourish.[47]

At the same time, Calvert—no doubt heeding the advice of more
seasoned members of his council—sees that there may be a peaceful
way out of this predicament. He tells Bradford to promise the Indians that "we shall write to the Governor of Pennsylvania that they
may have Reparation for the Injury done them, and that on our parts
we will always remain in perfect Friendship with them." Reparations,
rather than any other form of punishment, are understood by colonial
Marylanders to be the Five Nations' preferred means of redress.[48]

Still, Governor Calvert takes no chances. He adds a postscript to
his letter to Maj. John Bradford: "With this comes a Hundred weight
of Ball & a Note from Colo Addison for a Quarter Barrel of Powder at
his house." As the load of lead musket balls trundles westward, Colonel Addison stays behind, leaving it to Major Bradford to take charge
of defending the backcountry. Bradford is to take receipt of the shot,
then go to Addison's house and present his note permitting the release
of a supply of gunpowder. The colonel prefers to tarry awhile with the
fiddle players at Annapolis.[49]

Chapter 4

SAWANTAENY

WHAT DOES SAWANTAENY THINK AS HE LIES BLEEDING ON a bearskin inside his cabin on Monocasey Creek in February of 1722? What is he feeling as his wife, Weenepeeweytah, tends to him? Begin with the bearskin. Even after a great deal of trading with the Cartlidge brothers, Sawantaeny still retains that skin. Why?[1]

Bears hold a special place in Seneca religion and culture as "the most feared of magic beasts and one of the most frequent among them to enter into the fortunes of men." According to Seneca storytellers (who have maintained their nation's tales over many generations) the "monster bear" is called *Nia'gwai'he'gowa*. Seneca hunters have chased him "since the first people came" and his constellation can be seen in the stars.[2]

A good hunter lives in ritual communion with the animals whose lives support his. Before going after game, a careful hunter "always throws tobacco and asks ceremonial permission to kill game" and shows gratitude to the animals of the woods. The animals hold spiritual power in their bodies, referred to as "medicine," which they share willingly with those who treat them with reverence. As Sawantaeny stretches out upon his bearskin, he can take comfort from thoughts of the power flowing to him through the fur.[3]

It may be that Sawantaeny held back the bearskin when traders came to visit because it holds special meaning for him. In one old story, a Seneca hunter who was mortally wounded was restored to life again when animals gave their lives to prepare a "wonderful medicine for him." After a mixture of medicinal roots and animal medicine was poured down the huntsman's throat from the cup of an acorn, a bear "hugged him close in his hairy arms and kept him warm" until, at last, the man revived, pulled to his feet again by the bear. When he returned home, the hunter shared the medicine with all of his people. As the story taught, "it was true, the medicine healed the cuts and wounds made by the arrows and knives, and not one of the Iroquois was killed in their battle[s]." Sawantaeny may even hope that a little of the bear's medicine will aid him as he lies wounded.[4]

Yet before he collapsed, Sawantaeny told his wife that he had been killed. Whatever succor he might have hoped for from the bearskin, it seems he knew he would not rise to his feet again, at least in this world. So perhaps his thoughts now turn further back to the time before he was a hunter, to the days when he was a child and to stories where the bear was not monster but mother. On winter nights by smoky fires scented with tobacco, he, like many a Seneca youth before and after, could have heard tales of "the orphaned boy who lived with his wicked uncle." When the bad uncle buried his nephew alive in a foxhole, he was rescued and "cared for by a mother bear." Perhaps, as Sawantaeny slips away from life, he feels cradled in the mythical bear mother's embrace.[5]

THE SINGLE BEARSKIN THAT Sawantaeny valued for its personal comforts and spiritual cushion would bring John Cartlidge something less than 4 shillings if he were to resell it. When James Logan, acting as a fur-trade aggregator, sells 180 bearskins in a single transaction later this year, he will ask 4 shillings per skin, or £36 for his massive bundle. Could he have convinced Sawantaeny to part with his skin, Cartlidge, as the first link in a long chain of European commodity traders, would have gotten even less than 4 shillings for it (in order to leave room for profit at Logan's level). Yet with rum selling now for just about 2 shillings 4 pence per gallon (and assuming each gallon yields something like eighty-five drinks) every three drinks Cartlidge offered Sawantaeny cost him a penny. In other words, a bearskin is worth something like 144 shots of rum at fair prices. Sawantaeny would have to be drunk out of his senses entirely before he would agree to trade this pelt for more liquor than he could possibly consume. It defies logic to paint a picture of him as an angry, broken, drunken man, with so little left of value that he was reduced to begging John Cartlidge to pay him with an extra slurp of spirits for the few desirable skins he had—before he crawled off to die on his nearly worthless animal hide.[6]

Yet this is more or less the image that Governor Keith and his fellow members of the Pennsylvania Provincial Council maintain of Sawantaeny. Summing up their perspective on the case, council member Isaac Norris will soon inform the London merchant Henry Gouldney, in a long letter written in April of 1722, that "resentment" on Sawantaeny's face provoked the violent behavior displayed by the Cartlidges. Going still further, in an official review compiled for chiefs of the Five Nations, the council will declare that they "found that a Quarrel arose about Rum, between a Brother of the five nations who had hunted near Patowmeck and two of our Traders; the Indian man was angry, went hastily, and took his Gun to Kill the Englishmen, Whereupon in defence of themselves they seized him." Whereas Native people themselves reported to the Maryland authorities that Sawantaeny angered Cartlidge by refusing to take rum in trade for his skins—and that Cartlidge initiated the fight by shoving Sawantaeny so hard he landed against a fallen tree on the ground—Pennsylvania colonists will imply the reverse. By their account, Sawantaeny wanted more rum than Cartlidge would give and—in a moment of inebriated anger—he turned to violence.[7]

In reality, no direct observer of the events ever describes Sawantaeny as angry. To the contrary, Native witnesses say that Sawantaeny objected to the display of that very emotion in John Cartlidge, saying that "the Sinnekae told him he need not be angry at him." Nevertheless, Pennsylvania's officials want to tell a different tale.[8]

Colonists, too, have come to this encounter primed with old stories—and theirs say that savages are angry, always and everywhere. Virginia's governor, Alexander Spotswood, captured the prevailing colonial attitude in a letter he composed to the governor of New York in January of 1720 and copied to the governors of Maryland

and Pennsylvania. "The Indians are strangers to our refined notions of Honour & Justice," Spotswood asserted, adding that, "their Savage Nature will not bear reasoning upon their Conduct." According to such views, Indians are savages and savages are, by nature, inured to reason.[9]

Indeed, the British colonists involved in the Sawantaeny case bring with them assumptions that are deeply encoded in the language and literature of England—and that were in place long before any English colonist ever set foot in North America. As is true for William Keith, who claims that "the woods are so dark and private," from medieval times to now, the word "wood" has always conjured up both tree-filled landscapes and anger-crazed people.

Back in 1513, an English printer issued a book of verse that stated directly that savagery was the inevitable condition of people who lived in forests. It remained in print for some two centuries and, as late as 1709, London book buyers could still find the book for sale. In the verses, English readers learned of a mythical forest of classical Troy, where in "woods of plenteous thickness," there were "knights furious and wood." These verses employed "wood" both in its still-familiar sense as a noun meaning a forest dense with trees and in the now-archaic sense as an adjective meaning "out of one's mind, insane, lunatic . . . expressing fury or violence." While these two meanings for "wood," as sylvan realms or as crazed rage, derived from entirely separate Old English roots, their identical spellings closely gnarled their meanings.[10]

Because the two uses of the word "wood" were so often indistinguishable in English writing on savagery, English-speakers made strong associations between arboreal landscapes and anger, violence, animality, and savagery. According to the stories that colonists have been retelling for centuries, nothing could be less surprising than finding crazy, angry savages living deep among the trees. The woods, after all, drive people "wood."[11]

And yet, Sawantaeny is known among Native people not as a man given to anger but rather as one celebrated for being civil. His friend and fellow leader "Captain Civility" of Conestoga will describe him to colonial investigators as "a Warrior, a civil Man of very few Words."

Like "Captain Civility" himself, whose peaceable role is conveyed by his title—that of a leader charged with promoting unity among disparate peoples—Sawantaeny's reputation for being "civil" means much more than being appreciated as a pleasant and well-mannered person. Sawantaeny, like Civility, is a leader who has devoted his life to trying to bring the peoples of the Susquehanna region into communion.

SAWANTAENY LINGERS THROUGH THE night, with his wife keeping anxious watch. But come morning, she finds that he has breathed his last breath. Alone with his corpse, she flees the cabin, seeking help. It proves to be the last time she will ever see him. For when she returns, she finds his body has been taken, removed, and buried.[12]

"My friends have killed me" were Sawantaeny's last recorded words, an utterance that speaks volumes about the social world of the Senecas. Weenepeeweytah will remember those final words and do all she can to honor them. That single line says so much about who Sawantaeny was and what he hoped for: to be a leader who linked Indians and colonists together in friendship. Anglo-Pennsylvanians can scarcely imagine the sort of unified ties that Indians are striving for.[13]

Sawantaeny and Weenepeeweytah embodied this process, bringing together through their marriage an Iroquoian people (Sawantaeny's Seneca) with an Algonquian one (Weenepeeweytah's Shawnee). In these difficult days in the Susquehanna valley, Native nations are shuddering from encroaching stress on all sides, from raids by Native peoples to the north and south and from colonial wagons and pathogens rolling in from the east. In times like these, strategies and ceremonies of alliance matter as never before. In sharing their cabin, their lives, and their work, Sawantaeny and Weenepeeweytah exemplified how separate peoples could come together to provide for and protect one another. Like a Native hamper made of bark and bound with corded twine, Native marriages allow husbands and wives to remain members of different nations yet bring their lives and their peoples together. Wood and fiber combine to form a basket fit to carry many burdens.[14]

The designation of Cartlidge as a "friend" has formal diplomatic significance indicating that the Senecas should treat the conflict as an internal one between fellow participants in the Covenant Chain. The idea of the Covenant Chain is yet another powerful Iroquois metaphor for the ties of alliance they wished to draw between themselves and English colonists. A covenant is a voluntary mutual agreement, a shining chain the symbol of links between societies. Again and again, the Haudenosaunee call for accord with the English.[15]

Yet precisely because Sawantaeny was a member of the Five Nations of the Haudenosaunee—the confederacy that had gained power and prestige by fighting a series of seventeenth-century "mourning wars" in response to deaths in their community—his loss threatens grave danger. Unless all the peoples of the Susquehanna region agree that his death should be categorized as an accident among friends, it could touch off a new round of violence. Some loads are too great for even the sturdiest basket. Sawantaeny's wife and people may find the press of grief at his passing too heavy to bear. And they may seek to shift the weight of sorrow onto English colonists.[16]

As a warrior, Sawantaeny fought many battles, but as a civil leader he sought to spread peace within the League of the Five Nations and among their allies in the region. In essence, Sawantaeny's dying words—calling his killers his friends—offer a plea that he should not have lived a life of civility in vain.

Chapter 5

SORROW WILL COME FAST

MARCH 6, 1722

God send you joy, for sorrow will come fast enough.
— Titan Leeds, Verses for March,
The American Almanack for 1722

STANDING IN HIS LEATHER APRON IN HIS SHOP BENEATH the Sign of the Bible on Second Street, printer Andrew Bradford has idled his press and is biding his time. Even through closed windows, he can hear the moan of the wind. Titan Leeds's almanac predicted "Cloudy, or Wind and Snow or Rain" for the first week of March 1722 and now Bradford can confirm it. The gales roar with such force that no sloops from New York are sailing up the Delaware. Bradford wants to hold off on publishing this week's paper until the post arrives with shipping news and all the latest advices from New York.[1]

Customers who stagger over today from the gusty riverfront and stop into Bradford's store will find a small selection of books and pamphlets, and even a fascinating large-scale map of New York City that he is advertising: "A Curious Prospect of the City of New York, on Sheets of Royal Paper." They can buy barrels of molasses, whalebone for corset stays, and "also very good cork," so useful for stoppering any bottle you have. But they won't find a new copy of the *American Weekly Mercury*. When Bradford finally gives up waiting and goes to press, a full three days late, it will be without any news from New York and with only one ship "entered outward" to report—a vessel that sails from Philadelphia up toward the Susquehanna. Bradford will excuse himself to his readers by explaining, "We have these three days expected the New York Post and he is not yet arrived. It is suspected that the late strong winds have hindered his passage . . . for which reason we are obliged to publish the Weeks News without his Advices." But by then, the town's leaders will be too agitated by news brought down the Susquehanna to even notice the lack of tidings from New York.[2]

GOV. WILLIAM KEITH LEARNS the news on March 6, before anyone else on his council, when one Richard Langdon, a butcher from Conestoga, arrives and shatters his morning.

"Sundry persons of credit near Conestogoe," Langdon informs Keith, have told him of "the sudden death of an Indian at one of their Towns a considerable way above Conestogoe." Langdon may be claiming to speak for persons of credit, but he is hardly the sort of man Governor Keith generally prefers as a source of intelligence. In the colony's hierarchy, butchers rank low, scarcely above servants. Condemned as common swearers and drunkards by the city's upper sort, they trade in slaughter, doing the killing on which the city's life depends. Yet Keith knows that even men such as this can be useful. He cannot turn Langdon away without giving him a hearing.[3]

The butcher continues that the Indian's death was "occasioned (as it is said) by one or more blows given him by John or Edmund Cartlidge, or both of them." The governor starts with surprise. The man's claims are explosive, but then, what else would you really expect from a butcher? Just last year, city officials had to issue a 13 shilling, 4 pence fine to one who "blew up the meat of his calf, whereby the meat was made unwholesome to the human body." Now Keith is expected to accept the word of this tradesman that the well-connected John Cartlidge has potentially committed a capital crime?[4]

Keith knows John Cartlidge well. He spent a merry week talking, dining, and drinking with him in Cartlidge's large and comfortable house at Conestoga just last summer. He would never have credited that such a spacious home and bountiful table could exist so far out in the wilderness had he not visited it himself. But once they found each other, he and Cartlidge got on so well they even began talking about doing business together. Cartlidge is a man with his finger on the pulse of the province, alert to all the many ways that Penn's Woods may yield good fortunes.

Keith objects that Langdon may be misinformed. After all, he has "not received any certain Advice of the truth or circumstances of this unhappy accident by an Express Message from Conestogoe." Still, however "imperfect" Keith finds his relation of the facts, Langdon insists that he must listen to him.[5]

People of quality in the colonial community of Conestoga can talk of little else and, Langdon says stubbornly, he was "desired by some of them to give notice of it to the Governour." Keith doesn't want to believe Langdon, yet the man is not going away. When the governor challenges him to provide corroboration for these incredible claims, Langdon says that his neighbor David Robeson, a blacksmith, has come to town with him and can vouch for his story. With that, Keith bows to circumstance and orders Langdon and Robeson to "attend the board" at a meeting he will call for this afternoon. Now Keith needs to summon his council members to an emergency session. If the rumors are true, he will simply have to find a way to contain the situation.[6]

PHILADELPHIA PRESENTS A CURIOUS picture this morning. Down on the docks, where the barrels never stop rolling, the city still thrums. But out on the water, stalled seamen grow restless brooding over the muddy churn of the Delaware as they wait for more favorable weather. Someone drowned accidentally in these very waters just last week. Facing west from the decks, sailors can take in the sight of the town: a blocky cityscape of red and gray, brick walls topped by slate roofs. With some 4,883 people filling its houses, Philadelphia is already one of the larger port cities in British America. Yet the town is still much smaller than Boston, much less London, and a good deal more modest than many were led to expect.[7]

This mural is approximately 8 feet long and 1.5 feet wide. It features William Penn's coat of arms in the upper-left corner and the city of Philadelphia's coat of arms in the upper right. The city's arms depict characteristics that city residents wish to emphasize. Clockwise, beginning in the upper right, the quadrants show: a sheaf of wheat (hinting at the importance of land and agriculture); a ship (symbolizing commerce); a set of scales (symbolizing justice); and the shaking of hands (symbolizing peaceful accords). The view from the river of merchant ships flying British flags further emphasizes Atlantic trade. The numbered key at the bottom directs viewers to twenty-four important homes and public buildings, including: 3. Edward Shippen (whose house is being rented by Governor Keith); 6. Jonathan Dickinson; 17. Quak[e]r Meeting House; 18. The Court House; and 24. Penny Pott House.

PETER COOPER, *THE SOUTHEAST PROSPECT OF THE CITY OF PHILADELPHIA*, C. 1720, OIL ON CANVAS, THE LIBRARY COMPANY OF PHILADELPHIA.

Back in England, the main vision people have of the city is one sprung from the imagination of a young limner named Peter Cooper, who completed a commission to produce a view of "The Southeast Prospect of the City of Philadelphia" in 1720. With brushes and oils purchased from the merchant Isaac Norris, he painted a sort of dream version of the city, showing it not as it is, but as it could be. Charged with creating an enticing image to lure potential property investors, Cooper daubed his Philadelphia riverscape with many more buildings

than actually exist, dotted halls and houses with imaginary cornices and fanciful weathercocks, even topped the plain Quaker meetinghouse with a nonexistent steeple. Cooper's river is clogged with ships of every description, their red, white, and blue Union Jacks streaming from their jack staffs.[8]

Still, Cooper's perspective is not entirely invented. He has added an air of authenticity by noting prominent actual residences and public places, even providing a labeled and numbered key to help viewers identify the city's sights. Off to the right of the eight-foot-long painting, on the north end of the city, sits Number 24, Penny Pott House, so named because the tavern's patrons can purchase a good pot of ale there for only a penny. Sailors gather there today, waiting out the winds. On the south side of the prospect, at Number 6, Cooper has painted the imposing four-storied house of the Quaker merchant and Provincial Council member Jonathan Dickinson, whose redbrick manse is the single largest building in the city. Dickinson is setting out from that house right now, called forth by Governor Keith on some sort of urgent matter. Smack in the center of the painting's length sits the courthouse, its tall clock tower peering over the other roofs like a long-necked magistrate glaring down at the townsfolk.

INSIDE THE COURTHOUSE, THE governor's council members assemble: seven in all, four Quakers and three Anglicans. The governor serves as a fourth Anglican, equalizing power between the two factions. They are rich men all, united in the desire to maintain security and increase prosperity (most especially their own).

Keith opens the meeting by "acquaint[ing] the Board, that he had been surprised this morning with an imperfect relation from one Richard Langdon, a Butcher, lately come from Conestogoe, of the sudden death of an Indian." If Keith ever received a letter dated over two weeks ago from Maryland's Governor Calvert—if it was not lost on a river crossing or dropped from a saddlebag—he is telling no one. Instead, he claims not to have known of anything amiss at Conestoga until Langdon's arrival this morning. Keith would not wish to acknowledge such a letter; after all, both John Bradford in his first correspondence reporting the attack and Governor Calvert in his discussions with the Maryland council referred to the crime explicitly as a murder. Keith, by contrast, is already trying to downplay the death as an "unhappy Accident."[9]

Keith assures his council that he has lost no time alerting them. He knows, he says, that they "should be acquainted with the whole circumstances of this matter, as far as can yet be discovered here." He flatters them that his only desire is "that he might consult with them of the most proper measures to be taken on so extraordinary an occasion for preserving the Peace of the Province." He has to trust that this divided group will be able to reach some quick agreement on just what constitutes "proper measures." Explaining that Langdon has implicated John and Edmund Cartlidge in the crime, he adds that he has "some cause to fear the truth of what is now so confidently everywhere reported." It's the kind of news that leads to meaningful glances, discreet coughs, reddening faces.[10]

Four of these men, the Quakers Jonathan Dickinson, Richard Hill, and James Logan, along with Col. John French, an Anglican, stayed with Governor Keith at Cartlidge's house last summer when the Conestoga trader hosted them for a peace treaty with members of the Five Nations. Cartlidge proved such a gracious host, and the men enjoyed such a jolly time, that afterward one member of their party wrote a poem in Cartlidge's honor, "To J———n C———dge, Esq. on His Generous Entertainment of Sir William Keith, and his Company, at Conestogoe." Now, as the council members recall how "luxurious dishes graced the loaded board / With all bounties of rich nature stored," those languid summer days suddenly seem unreachably far away. None of them can have expected a turn of events such as this.[11]

They must decide what is to be done. To aid them in their assessment, Keith orders "the said Richard Langdon, and one David Robeson, a blacksmith . . . to attend the board at this time." The two men are "severally called," enter the chamber, are "examined upon oath," then find themselves summarily dismissed.[12]

The room soon swells to bursting with talk. Questions fly. Views are offered. Ideas multiply. Arguments are posed and opposed. Secretary Logan gives up taking notes and announces that he can't keep up. He satisfies himself with making an official record of "the difficulty in collecting the several opinions of the Members and putting their Resolutions in a proper Form and Method while the Council is sitting."[13]

The board is split between men of sense and men of wit. On one side, there are the Quakers. They weigh every event that occurs in the colony on the scale of morality (even if they sometimes have to place a discreet finger on the balance beam). Jonathan Dickinson, he of the four-story house, is the oldest, richest man on the council by far, and a man of wide experience. He sailed from Jamaica to Philadelphia over two decades ago by way of Florida, where he, his wife, and his son—and eleven enslaved people he claimed as his property—capsized and briefly faced Indian captivity in Spanish territory. Isaac Norris and Richard Hill are both slaveholding merchants and gentlemen farmers well on their way to amassing fortunes to rival Dickinson's. They are also brothers-in-law, each having married a daughter of Thomas Lloyd, a man who was one of William Penn's closest supporters and served as one of the colony's first governors. (Another Quaker member of the council, Samuel Preston, absent today, is married to a third Lloyd daughter, meaning that there are three brothers-in-law serving together.) Rounding out this tight-knit group is James Logan, who began his colonial career as Penn's personal secretary and now acts for the colony as provincial secretary—when he is not trading furs, trading rum, trading land, trading nearly anything at all that will augment his large and growing fortune.[14]

These four Quaker men regard themselves as part-time philosophers and constant men of faith. Dickinson has established his public reputation as a man of faith by publishing a memoir of his Florida adventure and painting it as a demonstration of the redeeming power of the Quaker god. Richard Hill has printed a memorial book of his daughter, Hannah's, religious meditations, following her untimely early death. Norris collects editions of Scottish moral philosophy and has them bound in sumptuous leather, beautifully tooled and embossed, and labeled with his own personal bookplate. Logan, meanwhile, not only maintains the largest private library anywhere in British America but also is hard at work writing his own would-be masterpiece of moral philosophy, a manuscript now growing to hundreds of pages. Age-old questions haunt Logan in new ways here in his new world: Are humans basically good or evil; is human nature the same everywhere; or are "civilized" people fundamentally different from "barbarous" people? Whatever they hear of the Cartlidge case, these four are bound to consider it a practical test of their ethical precepts.[15]

The Quaker men represent the establishment. William Keith needs to maneuver around, if not against, them. Now that Penn has died, and control of the colony has passed into the hands of Penn's Anglican sons from his second marriage, the season of Quaker rule may be ending. Even on this windy March morning, Keith can almost feel the thaw.

On Keith's side are the Anglican gentlemen he counts as his closest friends. They want their city to be known as a place of good taste and fine fashion, and they evaluate all the colony's happenings in terms of how events will add to, or detract from, the city's reputation for urbanity. They love nothing better than to gather of an evening to drink Jamaican rum, tell ribald stories, and compose naughty poems. Tales of their exploits are legend among the city's self-described better sort. One of the best involves a night of revelry back in 1703 when a bunch of them were arrested along with William Penn Jr. by a Quaker constable who objected to their noisy carousing. Council member Henry Brooke was a young man that night, but he has prospered so well collecting the king's customs duties that Keith offered him a seat on the council last year. Colonel French counts himself a close friend of these two and attends meetings of the same gentlemen's clubs that Keith and Brooke prefer. Of the Anglican group, Attorney General Andrew Hamilton is perhaps the most intellectually distinguished, having arrived in Pennsylvania by way of London's prestigious legal training ground, the Inns of Court, and rapidly established himself as one of the finest legal minds in the colonies. Still, gossips tease him as a ladies' man known for his skill at making widows merry.[16]

Like the Quakers, these four consider themselves sophisticated men of letters, but the kind of material they prefer reading and writing ranges from light verse to practical legal and economic tracts, not the kinds of moral and theological reflections that preoccupy their Quaker counterparts. Governor Keith lists poets and pamphleteers among his favorite drinking companions; the writer Aquila Rose, who composed the congratulatory rhyme for John Cartlidge last summer, traveled to Conestoga at Keith's invitation. Colonel French often tipples with Keith and friends, well liked as a man always ready with a bon mot. Henry Brooke, perpetual bachelor, prides himself on his way with words. His best-known ballad recounts the story of a young man named Michy, who was conceived when his parents "with tumbling together & heaven knows what, A thing on two legs called a Son [did] begot." No sooner had the baby Michy "wriggled his way from his Mothers right breast" than away he was "sent to ye Golden World, to trade." Michy prospered as a colonial merchant, but then squandered his riches on women-for-hire and returned home to Britain with nothing to show for his travels. Brooke's funny fable delivers a serious moral; in the colonies, fortunes come easy, but go quickly. Wise men don't squander the chances they get in this Golden World.[17]

After much discussion, none of it documented, resignation settles over the room where Keith presides. His board members agree that action must be taken and taken quickly. Whatever personal rivalries and cultural quarrels divide them must be set aside in light of this new crisis. Logan notes drily that "it appears to the board that there is just cause to believe that an Indian is actually dead."[18]

He presses forward. "And from the accounts the deponents give, there is Ground enough to suspect the said John or Edmund Cartlidge,

or both of them, have been some way or other instrumental or accessory to his death." They must consider the real possibility that John
Cartlidge has violated the foundational pacifism of his Quaker faith
and jeopardized the entire colony by killing an Indian. Logan adds
that "it is therefore the unanimous opinion of the Board that is of absolute necessity that some person or persons of Integrity, Reputation,
and Ability be forthwith dispatched to Conestogoe with full powers to
make Inquiry into this matter." Secretary Logan and Colonel French
answer the call. Even now, the government's representatives must be
evenly split between Quakers and Anglicans.[19]

Suddenly recovering the powers of his pen, Logan asserts that
the board will take whatever steps are necessary to ensure justice.
He knows that the notes he makes now may serve as a legal record in
the event that this crisis deepens and council members are called to
account by British authorities. Nowhere is any official record made of
the close connections between John Cartlidge and multiple members
of the board. To the contrary, Logan simply notes sternly that the officials sent to Conestoga will be empowered, "upon just Cause of Suspicion to commit any person or persons accessory to the death of the
said Indian." The Cartlidges may be committed to jail at the say-so of
French and Logan. An arrest is already in the offing, because nothing
matters more than making sure this isolated violent incident does not
ignite a larger conflict between Indians and colonists. Furthermore,
the delegation setting out for Conestoga is to be given wide latitude
"generally to dispatch such messages and take such measures as they
shall judge necessary to assure the publick Safety and Tranquility of
the Government."[20]

The board agrees that Logan and French should depart for Conestoga first thing in the morning. "It is ordered, that a Commission and
Instructions be prepared for the said Gentlemen, betwixt [now] and . . .
morning." But first, the governor agrees to present a personal petition
to the elected assembly of the colony "to move them by a Message, to
Pass a vote for making Provisions to defray the Charge of such unfore-
seen Negotiations with the Indians." Logan and French will give their
time, but not their money, to this errand. There are horses to bridle
and provisions to pack. Most important, there are gifts to select for pre-

sentation to the Indians at Conestoga, goods Logan will be more than happy to supply for a fair price. He makes a note explaining that such presents, "'tis conceived, will be the most effectual and Cheapest way to preserve their Friendship, and to quell any Disturbances which may hereafter possibly happen upon any such extraordinary events." Logan knows enough about Native customs to understand immediately that a death must be covered with material offerings. But he is greatly mistaken if he thinks that peace will come cheap.[21]

JONATHAN DICKINSON'S STATELY BRICK mansion stands warm and well lit, ready to welcome him back after today's council meeting. The house is there to remind him that whatever has happened to an Indian man somewhere in the wilds above the Susquehanna, he is safe within his own walls. Whereas once, after being nearly lost at sea, he was forced to share lodgings with Indians and "lie on a floor, swarming with abundance of many sorts of creeping things," now he shares ten rooms with two daughters, the last of his children still living at home. His wife, Mary, passed away three years ago, and so is not waiting there to hear the story of his day. But, otherwise, his house contains every possible comfort.

Dickinson's numberless possessions crowd together and jostle for his notice. In room after room, from the best parlor to the front parlor, from the green room to the red room, from the upper kitchen to the lower, from the best bedchamber to the one above the upper kitchen, all the way down to the cellar and all the way up to the north garret, feather beds, bolsters, pillows, and cushions, blue silk quilts and cinnamon-colored Persian ones lie ready to soften his cares. Everywhere, mahogany furniture shines in sunlight and shimmers in candlelight: couches and chairs and stools; clothes presses, seven chests of drawers, and ten tables. Wherever the eye rests, some smooth surface gleams: looking glasses, sconces, and candlesticks, yes, but also china teapots, teacups, and chocolate cups, glasses and tankards, marble mortars, copper porringers, brass kettles, silver spoons.[22]

Dickinson is so rich in mahogany, harvested from his own plantations, that he keeps loose boards of the precious wood lying unused in his storerooms. If any visitor to the house considers the deforestation that has remade Jamaica from a mahogany jungle into a series of clear-cut sugar plantations, they have only to look at the nearly inexhaustible immensity of Penn's Woods to distract themselves. True, mahogany does not grow in Pennsylvania, but oak and walnut are nearly as nice. Few if any take in the weight of all the dark wood displayed around Dickinson's home and think of the expert knowledge and heavy labor of enslaved Africans that was necessary to find and fell the trees, but many admire the way his daughters' smooth white hands look when poised over the polished wood.[23]

Anywhere Dickinson looks, he can catch a glimpse of his reflection and remind himself that he really is here, home in Philadelphia, not caught "in the cruelly devouring jaws of the inhuman cannibals of Florida," as his memoir describes the people he encountered after being shipwrecked on his way to Philadelphia. In reality, Dickinson saw no cannibalism in Florida, as evidenced by the complete absence of the topic anywhere within the pages of memoir. He included the sensational reference in the full title of his book simply to lure readers' attention and alert them that his story tells a tale of merciful Europeans besting cruel barbarians.[24]

Dickinson regards himself and his fellow Quaker merchants and planters as the epitome of civility. God's favor shows in the riches he enjoys, and he believes it his duty to maintain gratitude for his blessings at all times. As he tells readers in the preface to his memoir, explaining why he decided to tell the story of his deliverance from Indian captivity: "Ingratitude . . . after signal favors received is, amongst all civilized people, looked upon with just detestation . . . especially in time of such Light as now shineth." Dickinson lives in an age of Enlightenment and he knows it. Ships ply vast oceans and returning travelers bring to Europe evidence of wonders never seen before. God reveals new mysteries daily, and men of science—natural philosophers, as they call themselves—are unraveling these divine secrets in order to perfect human knowledge. The surest mark of their accomplishments is the steady accumulation of riches that an approving God bestows upon them. Meanwhile, moral philosophers are hard at work studying human nature itself, contrasting the customs of civilized and savage people in order to understand the course of human progress. In this time of light, everything seems possible.[25]

Dickinson's Indian adventure began in 1696, when he hired a captain and crew to sail him, his new wife, and their infant son, his namesake, Jonathan Dickinson Jr., from his Jamaica plantation to the city of Philadelphia, where he planned to set up shop as a merchant. He brought aboard with him twelve other people, all named in the introduction to his memoir: "Peter, London, Jack, Caesar, and Cujoe, a Child" were described as "Negroe-Men" while "Hagar, Sarah, Bella, Susanah, and Quensa" were marked down as "Negro Women" along with "Venus, an Indian Girle." All of these people were listed in brackets as "Belonging to Jonathan Dickinson." In other words, he counted them as his personal property; their cost, like their whimsical and classical names, offered further proof of Dickinson's wealth and sophistication.[26]

But Dickinson prides himself most of all on his claims to Christian civilization. He uses the story of his shipwreck on the Florida coast to inform educated readers of key points of difference between Europeans and the Native peoples of Florida. Perhaps the greatest factor in Dickinson's mind is the question of cruelty. Virtually synonymous with savagery, it is the very antithesis of Christian mercy and compassion. Overcoming Native cruelty proves to be Dickinson's greatest trial. And yet, he tells his readers, there's nothing so very curious in the fact "that they are thus cruel to Strangers, since they are unnatural to their own aged People; they having no more compassion on them than to make them Slaves to the younger." He senses no irony at all in criticizing Natives for their cruelty in practicing slavery in the same pages in which he documents his own fortune in slaves. After all, he would never enslave a fellow European, only peoples he regards as "unnatural" beings fundamentally different from himself. Nor does he perceive any paradox in fearing to be taken captive by Indians even as he claims ownership over the life of an "Indian Girle."[27]

Not all Quakers maintain such comfortable views of slavery. In fact, a vigorous segment of the very Quaker community that Dickinson set out to join had already denounced the practice as inherently immoral. Just three years before Dickinson sailed from Jamaica, the Monthly Meeting of Friends in Philadelphia (the formal organizational voice of Quakers in that city) published an address called *An Exhortation and Caution to Friends Concerning Buying or Keeping of Negroes.* The very first page of the address contradicted Dickinson's main rationalization for slavery, the idea that those under his sway were somehow unnatural. To the contrary, the official Quaker consensus stated: "*Negroes, Blacks,* and *Tawnies* are a real part of mankind, for whom Christ has shed his precious Blood and are capable of Salvation, as well as *White Men.*" In specifying that slavery was equally unacceptable for "Negroes, Blacks, and Tawnies," Quakers were opposing the enslavement of Africans, of African Americans, and of Native Americans alike.[28]

From the moment they first grasped the economic gains to be realized from slavery, Europeans began casting about for excuses to justify the practice. Nothing proved more useful to slaveholders in explaining how an autonomous *person* could be legally reclassified as an owned *object* than the claim that people of certain colors from certain continents differed in essential ways from the "real" members of mankind. Yet by 1693, key members of the Quaker faithful in Philadelphia recognized and rejected this fallacy.[29]

Members of the Philadelphia Monthly Meeting minced no words in denouncing the practice of slavery. They stated, "To buy Souls and Bodies of men for Money, to enslave them and their posterity to the end of the World, we judge is . . . [the] occasion of much War, Violence, Cruelty, and Oppression, and [is] Theft & Robbery of the highest Nature." Yet no sooner were their words printed than they were lost, as wealthy Quaker slaveholders rejected their arguments, accused them of unorthodoxy, and suppressed their cautionary pamphlet. The leader of the progressive Quakers, a man named George Keith—no relation whatsoever to the later Anglican governor William Keith—was essentially run out of town by Thomas Lloyd, James Logan, and other wealthy slaveholding Quakers determined not to be inconvenienced

SORROW WILL COME FAST   [83]

by his scruples. The antislavery statement George Keith helped bring to print would disappear from view, never to be republished and destined to be forgotten.[30]

In the meantime, Dickinson's memoir of his Florida adventure enjoys far greater success. Read and appreciated in Philadelphia today, it will go through seven more printings, the last one a century from now, in 1811. English readers, and Pennsylvania Germans who will eventually gain access to the work in translation, find Dickinson's reassurances of God's preference for Europeans too comforting to let go. Most Pennsylvanians do not own enslaved people and never will. But Dickinson's main concern, shoring up his own claims to be living a moral life as a devoted follower of Christ—even as he violates the terms in which Philadelphia Friends defined "the Fruits of the Spirit of Christ, which are *Love, Mercy, Goodness and Compassion* towards all in Misery"—will speak to the urgent anxieties of many as they seek to build an empire and then a new nation on Native land.[31]

Dickinson's story gains dramatic tension from the question of how a Christian, delivered into the very mouths of inhuman "cannibals," could emerge alive and unscathed. Dickinson gives God the ultimate credit. But the more immediate cause of his release carries important clues for the resolution of the current Cartlidge crisis.

Dickinson sets his tale's climax by telling his readers: "These *Maneater's* fury was at height, their knives in one hand and the poor shipwrecked People's heads in the other, their knees upon the other's shoulders and their looks dismal." Here they are, the always-angry savages, enacting just the sort of violent rage European expectations demand. But then, Dickinson twists the plot, claiming that "on a sudden the *Savages* were struck dumb and their countenances change[d], that they looked like another People." All at once, the anger left the Indians' faces and they dropped their knives to the ground. According to Dickinson, "God prevented further mischief." Yet he explained that it was the "*Caseeky's* Wife"—that is, the wife of the Indian's chief, or cacique—who, by divine will, was "made an instrument for their delivery, she and some others having something of tenderness of heart in them, though amongst such an inhumane crew." Dickinson credits

God with inspiring a Native woman to insist that the men set aside their savage anger.

Dickinson little understands that he has participated in a very common Native ceremony in which captive people are subjected to mock torture only to be dramatically released at the word of a woman and then offered food and fellowship. John Smith told just such a tale of his encounter with Pocahontas, a story that has been widely reprinted in England for over half a century already. Smith credited his personal magnetism for the Indians' shift in attitude; Dickinson thanks his God. Each thinks an individual woman has been uniquely overcome by feeling for him—by admiration, compassion or both—and persuaded a reluctant male leader to spare him. Neither man understands that, in Native societies, peace often comes in the form of a woman.[32]

Native peoples apportion leadership responsibilities between men and women, and they charge the latter with determining the fate of foreign captives. If a nation's women wish to see a man die, he will. But if, as is far more often the case, they wish to see him live, to become an ally and perhaps even a full member of their nation, then they will ritually "rescue" him from his mock torture. The power of the ceremony comes when the heightened emotions that captives experience in anticipation of violence are transformed into a still more powerful sense of catharsis when they are welcomed into the community.

If only Jonathan Dickinson understood the Native meaning of his short captivity, he might now advise the council to turn to Sawantaeny's wife for help in finding a way to respond to his death. But Dickinson does not know that Sawantaeny has a wife. He does not even know that Sawantaeny is a man with a name and a nation. Certainly, he cannot conceive that Sawantaeny, even in death, desires unity and peace. Dickinson cannot begin to comprehend how much he does not understand. He thinks that simply hearing that a savage has been killed tells him everything he needs to know. As he draws his damask bed curtains closed tonight and rests his head on his quilted silk head cloth patterned with a Holland stripe, Jonathan Dickinson will never guess that his own imagination draws pictures far bleaker than anything that may have run through Sawantaeny's mind as he lay bleeding on his bearskin.

A NEW DAY BRINGS new urgency to William Keith and the members of his council. Keith and company have dulled their quills with writing in the last twenty-four hours: a message to the members of the Pennsylvania House of Representatives to inform them of the new emergency, a legal commission for Secretary Logan and Colonel French authorizing them to act for the colony, a blank coroner's certificate in case they are able to find both the body and an expert to examine it, and, finally, detailed instructions for Logan and French to follow. All of these items have had to be discussed, debated, amended, approved, and fair copies made. Finally, the last drop of ink has been blotted, the final sheet of parchment rolled. The Great Seal of the Province adorns Logan and French's commission, the Lesser Seal their instructions.[33]

In Pennsylvania, when you want to awe someone with the full authority of English law, you attach the seal of the province to your document. Embossed seals are made by pressing a piece of parchment against an engraved metal plate to create a raised design in the surface of the paper. They can be cut out as needed and affixed to any plain piece of paper you wish to embellish. When a document is meant to look especially impressive, the seal can be scissored out with rococo curlicue edges or starburst triangular points. The seal itself is shaped like large medal, within which sits the Penn family crest, a basic shield with a crossbar embellished with a row of three discs. Clever folks will pun on Penn's name and note that the discs look like pennies. Above the shield, the word "mercy" appears, and beneath it the word "justice." Round about the circumference read the words "JOHN, THOMAS, AND RICHARD PENN, PROPRIETORS AND GOVERNORS OF PENNSYLVANIA." The promise of justice may give hope to the Native people of Conestoga. The Cartlidges will be praying for mercy. As for the governor and his council, their thoughts will continue to circle around pennies.[34]

Keith reports that the members of the House of Representatives have composed a message. In addition to thanking him for his immediate efforts to organize an official response to the crisis and urging him to work for its speedy resolution, they have promised that "this House

*This is the seal of William Penn, embossed on paper. It features his coat
of arms in the center with the words "Mercy" and "Justice" just above
and below it. It is circled by a band that reads "William Penn Proprietor
and Governor of Pennsylvania." After Penn's death in 1718, his sons
retain the seal but simply substitute their own names in the circular band
so that in 1722, the seal would read, "*JOHN, THOMAS, AND RICHARD
PENN, PROPRIETORS AND GOVERNORS OF PENNSYLVANIA."

SEAL OF THE PROVINCE OF PENNSYLVANIA IN LOGAN FAMILY PAPERS, OFFICIAL
LETTERS OF JAMES LOGAN, VOLUME 4, BOX 4, COLLECTION 379, AUTHOR'S
PHOTO FROM DOCUMENT AT THE HISTORICAL SOCIETY OF PENNSYLVANIA.

will cheerfully defray the necessary Charge that shall accrue." With
funding secure and the full backing of the government, there is no time
to lose. Logan and French set out that very day, bound for a confrontation at Conestoga that they can only hope will end in peace. Even in
this golden world, and at a time of such light, sorrow may come fast
unless they race to beat it.

Chapter 6

JOHN CARTLIDGE

J OHN CARTLIDGE HASTENS AWAY FROM MONOCASEY CREEK and heads straight for home. From the moment he threw down the empty pot Sawantaeny held in front of him, he has wanted to put the man from his mind. The Bible has a psalm that fits this occasion:

> *I am forgotten as a dead man, out of mind;*
> *I am like a broken vessel.*

John hardly slows long enough to order his thoughts, but his main wish is this: that everything may go on just as before, as if nothing had ever happened between him and Sawantaeny.[1]

ONCE SAFELY BACK IN his study at his substantial house in Conestoga, John can soothe himself by gazing out the window into the yard and watching his wealth pawing and prancing. His worldly goods amount to some £748, of which £168 is invested in horseflesh. While his net worth is only about one-third that of a city merchant like Jonathan Dickinson, it still adds up to a tidy sum. After all, a man wishing to qualify to serve as a justice of the peace need only prove that he is worth £20 per year. John keeps stud horses, broodmares, colts, and yearlings in every color: black, brown, sorrel, bay, gray, roan. In all, they number nearly four dozen: six studs, seventeen mares, and twenty-

three young ones. With every bray and snort, they chorus their con-
gratulations on his good fortune. Besides these, he has a dozen cows,
along with bulls, heifers, steers, and calves; nine sheep; and so many
hogs they can't be counted. Season after season, births compound his
herds, flocks, and droves.[2]

He and his wife, Elizabeth, are not nearly so fecund. So far they
have had only one living child, their baby Mary. Still, John maintains
many hopes for himself and Elizabeth, who was born to the Bartrams,
a locally prominent Quaker family. He is cultivating business schemes
along with wheat, barley, corn, and oats on the three hundred acres
he claims near Conestoga. Even of a February, he will have a dozen
acres sown with winter grain, shining green and gold against sparkling
snow on sunny days. Besides his livestock operation, he keeps a store
on his property where he has some £94 invested in "Indian goods" for
use in the fur trade. Resting there amongst the trade items is a bottle
chest, specially designed for transporting liquor over long distances,
along with some skins and tanned hides, all suddenly transformed into
talismans of his transgression.[3]

Cartlidge turns his mind firmly toward other business. He has been
scheming to go into mining. Rumor has it that mineral treasures are
buried in Pennsylvania's soil, just waiting for enterprising men to come
and dig their way to fabulous riches. Just this week, in the newspaper, a
New Jersey man named John Johnston is advertising for anyone "who
may have the appearance of Copper or other Mines on their Lands and
are not inclined to go on with the Work themselves." Johnston is offering to do the digging for the landowners and give them one-sixth of
any ore he finds on their lands. But John Cartlidge has an even better
idea. He wants to work with a surveyor to find promising land, then
quietly buy up as many more acres as possible.[4]

On February 17, some ten days after the incident up in Monocasey,
John Cartlidge writes a letter to one Isaac Taylor, one of the best
respected surveyors in Pennsylvania, to alert him that he has found
a hidden spot with a glittering secret: "I have viewed ye iron ore."
What he needs to figure out now is "ye most Easy way [to] Come at
ye Land." He tells Taylor, "if any old rights can be had I incline most
to make a purchase that way, however thy opinion in that matter is

what is desired by me." Half a century after William Penn founded the colony, most of the best lands are either owned by the proprietary family or still held by the region's Native inhabitants. Cartlidge is hoping against hope that he can find lands with absentee owners who will happily (ignorantly) transfer their titles to him for a bit of ready cash. And he wants to arrange a meeting with Taylor "for Conversing and Consulting ye best measures" to do this. He does not know that on the very same day he writes to the surveyor, Maj. John Bradford of Maryland is writing to Col. Thomas Addison with John Hans Steelman Jr.'s report of his violence against Sawantaeny. John Cartlidge may want to forget everything that happened upcountry and forge ahead with his business, but others in the Conestoga community remain deeply concerned.

⌐⌐⌐

JOHN'S ALTERCATION WITH SAWANTAENY has placed him in a difficult, but not impossible, position. He is a justice of the peace. He is the law here in Chester County and he is hardly going to act against himself. Even when the county court has seen fit to cite him for offenses, no one has ever succeeded in making him appear in court. Furthermore, Sawantaeny may not have been as bad off as he looked. He may have come out all right.

True, problems may come from gossip among his Euro-American neighbors. A man useful to Indians may prove a great nuisance to colonists. From time to time, John has had to tangle with settlers caught trespassing on Indian lands. Just last summer, when Indians complained to Governor Keith of "diverse abuses" committed by a man named John Grist, who had, "with diverse other persons, settled himself and Family and taken up Lands . . . without . . . any legal right to the same," Cartlidge had been drawn into the conflict.

Always alarmed at the possibility of upsetting the peaceful property relations on which the Penn family depends, Keith issued "a Warrant under his Hand and Seal, to direct John Cartlidge, Esqr., one of his Majestys Justices of the Peace, residing at Conestogoe, to warn and admonish the said John Grist." Cartlidge was ordered to inform Grist that unless he agreed to "relinquish the said lands," he, Cartlidge, was authorized to "raise the Possee Comitatus, and to burn and destroy their dwelling houses and Habitations." In the event, Grist had refused to comply. While John did not follow through on the threat to torch his home, Grist was duly arrested and imprisoned in Philadelphia. This is not the kind of move likely to make John popular with his fellow settlers. If serving as justice of the peace gives a man a certain stature, it also sets him up as a target of resentment—the more so if that man asserts Indian land rights when it suits the governor, but usurps them when it suits himself.

That brings the list of potential complications back to John's Indian neighbors. What are they likely to have to say about his fight with Sawantaeny? Nowadays, the Native peoples of the Susquehanna region have become increasingly assertive about maintaining their rights. They are making it clear that they will not tolerate excessive encroachments on their lands, by John Grist and his ilk or by anyone else. As the decades have piled up, Indians have become ever more concerned about the invasions of colonists—with their large households of children, servants, and slaves, and their ever-increasing numbers of livestock.

Farm animals are, after all, creatures of empire. As much as human colonists, their digging and scraping, their eating and eliminating are daily transforming the North American continent along with the lives of its Native peoples. Across British America, colonists like nothing better than turning their hogs loose to root for their food, leaving them to eat and breed in the wild and hunting them down again once a year. If the hogs get into a neighbor's cornfield, the legal fault lies with the farmer who fails to maintain good fences.[5]

Indians take a far less complimentary view of colonial pigs. Around Conestoga, Native people express concern about "great damages" done "by the keeping of Hogs" and complain to colonial officials that "they had often taken horses out of their Corn." They do their best to return stray hogs and horses to their owners. But they do not hesitate to shoot an animal they recognize as a repeat offender.[6]

Meanwhile, settler colonists regard animal droppings as the very basis of cultivation—in both the cultural and agricultural senses of the term. When a colonial farmer works manure into the soil, he sees himself civilizing the landscape, preparing the earth to produce European cereal crops. Indians see no sense in this. They need little added fertilizer because they cultivate strategic mixes of crops, such as corn, beans, and squash, that when planted together preserve soil fertility and optimize human nutrition. But here in Pennsylvania, English travelers admire the way the countryside is dotted with woods and well-manured farms.[7]

The English maintain their own theories about the worth of wheat and the use of animal waste. Sir Thomas Smith, a professor and administrator at Cambridge University, first opined on the topic in his 1549 *Discourse of the Commonweal of this Realm of England*. There, he listed the three essential things he thought were lacking in backward countries: "inhabitants, manurance, and pollicie," that is, colonists, animal dung, and imperial legal policy. Indians, on the other hand, are ever more wary of colonial inhabitants, have no use for animal excrement, and are not at all sure about the worth of colonial jurisprudence.[8]

So far, Native members of the Conestoga community have not gone on record against John Cartlidge and his teeming yard full of livestock, but that doesn't mean they can't. And now he has done something far more serious to offend them. The Indians may not come after him and demand justice for Sawantaeny, but then again, they may. True, the Shawnee boys were plenty ready to take off along with him, and others may take the same attitude. After all, Native peoples of the Susquehanna River valley have long claimed John Cartlidge as their friend. From his skill as a Delaware interpreter to his eagerness to trade, he has made himself a useful man to know. Around Conestoga, Native people have grown so accustomed to having his aid in their conversations with Philadelphia officials that, when he cannot be present for conferences, they lament that "they would have been glad if he would have come himself and given . . . an account of matters." He has mastered both woods lore and language skills and become a go-between par excellence. He will just have to hope his old reputation is enough to see him through this new crisis.[9]

JOHN SETS DOWN HIS pen, but he does not seal and send the letter to
surveyor Isaac Taylor. He needs a bit more time to mull things over and
make certain of his next moves. Doubts nag at him. Finally, he takes
up the letter again and squeezes in an extra sentence between the two
regularly spaced lines where he says he wishes "to know how wee shall
ye most Easy way Come att ye Land." He scrawls in miniature script:
"I have concluded to go on with business." The new insertion makes
no direct mention of his bloody confrontation with Sawantaeny and
it certainly offers no overt admission of guilt. If Taylor remains igno-
rant of John's recent actions, this letter will make him none the wiser.
But just in case Taylor has gotten some inkling of what transpired at
Monocasey, John wants to reassure him that his plans are unchanged
and his resolve is unshaken. After much thought, he has decided to go
on with business.[10]

Beneath his signature, "Jno. Cartlidge," he adds a long line of flourish, the better to underscore the strength of his conclusions. With that,
he folds up his letter and seals it with a neat red blob of sealing wax, a
confidential piece of correspondence from a confident man.[11]

UNFORTUNATELY FOR JOHN, HOWEVER, he will soon need every
ounce of his composure. Not everyone is impressed by his charade of
normalcy. Within days, "sundry persons of credit near Conestogoe"
will be able to talk of little besides "the sudden death of an Indian." At
this, John will swing into action again.

On March 6, 1722, the very day that the butcher Richard Langdon
and the blacksmith David Robeson reach Philadelphia carrying tales
about him, John Cartlidge calls a council at his house. He invites his
fellow local colonists, along with Captain Civility and many Native
community members, to gather for the occasion. He must try to get
this situation sorted out before any more senior members of the law
come to seek him.[12]

Chapter 7

WHAT CONTENT AND
DECENCY REQUIRE

MARCH 7–14, 1722

Superfluous Pomp and Wealth I not desire,
But what Content and Decency require.

—Titan Leeds, Verses for March,
The American Almanack for 1722

THE MOMENT THE INK DRIES ON THEIR COMMISSION, SEC. James Logan and Col. John French canter out of Philadelphia. They head west for the town of Chester, aiming straight for the house of the high sheriff. Logan and French are men more comfortable holding silver spoons than handling leg irons. They intend to put the arrest warrant directly into the sheriff's hands and let him get a good head start on them before they proceed to Conestoga. By the time they ride into the settlement, the Cartlidges should be safely under arrest.[1]

Logan and French arrive at Chester too late in the evening to meet with the sheriff. A bustling market town, full of fine houses of timber, brick, and stone, Chester boasts a courthouse, a Quaker meetinghouse, an Anglican church, and several taverns and inns, including the Boar's Head and the Pennsylvania Arms. The latter is the most modern and up-to-date establishment, but the former is more famous. The wooden sign of the boar's head has dangled from that inn's gabled eaves since the days when William Penn passed the winter there in 1683. Years later, candlelight still spills from its small leaded glass windows, while beneath its sixteen-foot-wide chimney, great logs blaze in the hearth. Fragrant woodsmoke drifts about with the promise of food and warmth.[2]

Once they find beds for the night, Logan and French send a servant with a note to the sheriff's house, requesting an appointment with him for first thing the following morning, March 8. The sheriff is exceedingly well known to them, and indeed to all the members of the council. Besides acting as an officer of the law, John Taylor serves Chester as a physician and as a sometime surveyor, a skill he learned from his father—the colony's most important surveyor, Isaac Taylor. If Sheriff John Taylor has been made privy to the contents of a certain letter his father, Surveyor Isaac Taylor, has just received from John Cartlidge— the one stating Cartlidge's determination "to go on with business"—it is fair to say that as of the morning of March 8, the high sheriff probably already knows more about the accused and his various actions and initiatives than anyone besides the man himself.[3]

"Apprehend the two brothers John and Edmund Cartlidge," Logan and French order Taylor, after explaining "the fact which occasioned our journey." They give the man his "proper warrant" and urge him to travel to Conestoga with "greater dispatch" than they intend to use. Arresting criminals is a job for young men and, at age twenty-seven, Sheriff Taylor should be good for it, even if it does mean taking a colleague into custody. Besides being a fellow man of the law, John Taylor and his father Isaac worked side by side with John Cartlidge to lay out a road from Conestoga to Brandywine just four years ago. Regardless, the younger Taylor knows he must now do the bidding of the Philadelphia officials. He makes haste for the Cartlidge house with Logan and French promising to follow in due course.[4]

WHILE SECRETARY LOGAN AND Colonel French rest and collect themselves, the investigation continues to gather speed in Philadelphia. More men are coming downriver with intelligence about the supposed murder. It is one thing to hear from a butcher and a blacksmith that a substantial man like John Cartlidge has committed a crime. But Governor Keith would prefer hearing from some of the "sundry persons of credit" who supposedly have knowledge of the situation. So when two New Jersey colonists named George Rescarrick and Richard Saltar Jr., who each styles himself as "gentleman," pay a visit to Philadelphia on March 10 and claim that they have just come from attending an emergency meeting of Indians and colonists called by John Cartlidge himself, they find a ready audience.[5]

George Rescarrick and Richard Saltar Jr. are both young men from substantial families in New Jersey. Rescarrick's widowed mother runs a tavern there in the town of Cranberry. Rescarrick himself has just come into an inheritance from his father, who left on his death a silver tankard, a dozen spoons, a cup—and a small fortune in the form of "7 slaves." Meanwhile, just twenty-three years old, on this March Saturday, Saltar is a newlywed, starting out in life with some help from his new wife Hannah's father, who, when he dies next month, will list "bonds due by Capt. Richard Saltar" among his £775 in assets. Hannah's father's estate also boasts £30 in silver plate, a Bible and other books, "3 negroes," valued at £150, and "2 white servants," listed at £21. Saltar will personally inventory his father-in-law's property for probate. He, like his friend Rescarrick and like all the Philadelphia officials interested in his testimony today, values fancy goods and knows how to price human life.[6]

Together, George Rescarrick and Richard Saltar Jr. tell a most interesting tale of John Cartlidge's actions. In sworn depositions, Rescarrick and Saltar state that "being at Conestoga" on the sixth of March, they were "present at a council held there by John and Edmund Cartlidge and other Christians there on the one part and one Captain Sevility an Ingen man who appeared for himself and many other Ingens present on ye other." Not bothering to prolong the fiction that Sawantaeny may still be breathing somewhere, they instead explain that Cartlidge called the session "to enquire into the cause and manner of the death of a certain Ingen man supposed to be killed by Edmund Carltidge etc." In this version of events, one of many that Philadelphia officials will have to sort through, John himself plays no part in the crime. He simply appears acting in his official capacity as justice of the peace, launching an inquiry into the conduct of his brother, Edmund.[7]

The scene, as Rescarrick and Saltar describe it, has Sawantaeny drinking, trading, and then demanding that "he would have more Rum or that he would shoot them." When Sawantaeny "went for his gun," Edmund followed, struggled to remove it from the Indian's hands, and, in so doing, "became entangled with the Indian" with the result that he "broke off the breech of the said gun" and struck the Indian with it "of which he died in a few days." By this account, the death appears to be the inadvertent consequence of understandable actions of self-defense.[8]

Saltar's deposition, taken first, lists several colonists as the interpreters at this meeting in the main statement. But at some point, the official who records the evidence adds a caret mark above the line and indicates that John Cartlidge also served as interpreter. Saltar initially omits that fact, perhaps deliberately. But it matters greatly; it means that Taquatarensaly and the other Indians present at that meeting literally could not say anything that John Cartlidge did not want to have heard.

Serving as an interpreter for the assembled Indians presented Cartlidge with the opportunity to put any words he wanted into their mouths. English colonists have a long history of playing ventriloquist for Native peoples. In Massachusetts Bay, in 1629, colonists created an official seal for the colony portraying a cartoon Indian with a speech bubble coming from his mouth saying, "Come over and help us." No one believed that the Native peoples of Massachusetts could actually quote from the Bible, Acts 16:9, but the notion that they called to colonists as Christian saviors fed settlers' vanity even as it salved their consciences. Cartlidge obviously found the practice of speaking for others equally convenient.[9]

Based on his knowledge of past negotiations between Pennsylvania colonists and the area's original inhabitants, Cartlidge already had a pretty good idea of what he wanted to have the Indians say. He could base his claims about their reaction to Sawantaeny's death on ones first made by the colony's founder. In his earliest days as proprietor, William Penn published an informational pamphlet about his new settlement painting an enticing picture of his colonial garden. In it, he also considered what would happen should violence hiss its way into his peaceful bower. Writing to his first group of investors, Penn took care to offer instruction about the response colonists could expect to receive from Indians in the case of blood crime. "The *Justice* they have is *Pecuniary*," Penn explained. "In case of any *Wrong* or *evil Fact*, be it *Murther* itself, they Attone by *Feasts* and *Presents* of their *Wampon*, which is proportioned to the quality of the *Offence* or *Person injured*." The membership of that initial investor group, called the Free Society of Traders, just happened to include one Edmund Cartlidge Sr., father to John and Edmund. Today, the Cartlidge brothers can only hope that monetary compensation—offers of feasts and presents—the standard requirement of Indian justice back in their father's first days as a colonist, still applies now, even to "murder itself."[10]

According to Richard Saltar, after Taquatarensaly, known to him as Captain Civility, listened to testimony about the assault on Sawantaeny, "the said Captain Sevillity on the part and behalf of the Indians said, that, at the first settlement of this country by the Christians, the Indians and they were two people, but after at the coming of William Penn he made the two people one flesh, and had so continued on the same chain of friendship ever since." Therefore, Civility assured those assembled, the Indians did not want the killing to disrupt Anglo-Indian relations. In fact, he went so far as to declare that, since Sawantaeny himself broke the peace by making the first violent move against the Cartlidges, he was at the least an "accessory" in his own death, perhaps even guilty of having "Murthered himself."[11]

Civility's apparently surprising speech actually reiterated—in closely matched language—the same urgent point he had made to colonists just two years before. In 1720, Civility had challenged Pennsylvania officials to regard themselves, as William Penn had, as being of "one Body, one Blood, one Heart, and one Head" with the colony's original inhabitants. Now he summed that up by saying that Penn "made the Two people one flesh." The Indians had the essentials of the story exactly right. The oral history Civility related in 1720 and reiterated in March of 1722 conforms closely to the written records of colonial Pennsylvanians. Colonists preserve a 1701 treaty, signed at Philadelphia with "Indians inhabiting upon and about the River Sasquehannah," in which Penn stated unequivocally that they should "forever hereafter be as one head & one heart & live in true Friendship & Amity as one people."[12]

The comments Saltar attributes to Civility show that for him, as for all Native peoples seeking close accord with colonial Pennsylvanians, the murder crisis presents opportunity as much as tragedy. Sawantaeny's death provides Indians with a dramatic occasion to affirm their commitment to uniting with colonial Pennsylvanians as one people. Whereas enemies can expect reciprocal violence when a killing occurs, friends and fellows can and should foreclose retaliation by making offers of reconciliation to the nation in grief.

"If the Christians were Satisfied, the Indians were so too," Saltar concludes. Hearing this evidence on March 10, just four days after the Cartlidge meeting took place, Philadelphia magistrates can almost convince themselves the crisis has been contained. George Rescarrick affirms that Saltar's "is a good and true deposition that reaches (if not the very words) the very sense of the said councils, according to the interpretation as this deponent understood." The recording official signs both documents "Jurat Coram me, B. Vining."[13]

B. Vining is the abbreviation of Benjamin Vining, a member of the Philadelphia city council, and a business associate of Aquila Rose— gentleman poet, close companion of William Keith, and ardent connoisseur of Cartlidge hospitality. In other words, Vining is just another member of the Church of England social circle surrounding William Keith. He conducts the interview with Rescarrick and Saltar by request and does his best to make it look as imposing as possible, adding the standard legalism "sworn before me" in Latin to attest to the gravity and accuracy of the document. He signs the document with swirling roundels and diamond gridwork so intricate that his name looks as much like a sketch for wrought-iron scrollwork as it does like a signature. Unfortunately, however, problems remain.[14]

The trouble is that Vining is creating an absurd transcription, copying down "the very words" Saltar attributes to Indians without having any true appreciation of the ideas the words propose. Whatever potential vision of cross-cultural unity William Penn may have embraced, John Cartlidge, William Keith, and the rest of their colonial contemporaries cannot imagine actually melding their interests with those of the Native peoples of North America. Yet this is the ideal that Native people are working so hard to convey. While colonists just wish the Cartlidge mess would end as soon as possible, Indians want Sawantaeny's death to provide a new beginning for Anglo-Indian relations. This incident is *not* going to be over in the space of a few days.[15]

The depositions prove to be worth little. For one thing, Governor Keith and at least a half a dozen other people already know that John, as well as Edmund, has been implicated in the attack. Since this is the case, what is John doing setting himself up as the investigator and adjudicator of his own crime? In actuality, Cartlidge's "council" may well correspond closely to Indian expectations that a murder should be countered with ritual feasting and gifts of mourning. But in the eyes of Pennsylvania colonists, Cartlidge's proceedings seem like an effort to mount a show trial to exonerate himself.[16]

The official minutes of the Provincial Council of Pennsylvania will contain no record that depositions were ever taken from Rescarrick and Saltar, and there will never be any public reference made to their testimony. Once the results of Logan and French's official inquiry start to circulate, no one will see any advantage in having knowledge of Cartlidge's personal conference made public. Because, even as Vining is interviewing the New Jersey gentlemen in Philadelphia, Logan and French are up the Susquehanna gathering detailed accounts of their own.

~~~

SHORTLY AFTER DAYBREAK ON March 9, James Logan and John French set out from Chester for Conestoga. Across the countryside, farmers are building fences this morning, mortising posts and hewing rails, readying their pastures for lambing and calving. Back at home, Logan's wife, Sarah, is expecting the fourth child of their eight years of marriage. Three months along, her mornings are beginning to ease. "Increase and multiply" commands the Christian Bible, and in the fertile lands of Pennsylvania, colonists do just that.[17]

Their day's journey poses little hardship, for the forests of Pennsylvania are so broad and open that a cart or a wain may roll through the middle of the woods. Colonists celebrate the "very delicate, pleas-

ant, and wholesome" airiness of Penn's Woods, lightened by so much
meadow ground that horses can go without being shod. Pennsylvania's colonists owe their enjoyment of these parklike conditions to the
active stewardship of Native peoples. Over many generations, Indians
have practiced controlled burning, setting small, quick-moving fires
to scorch away the forest underbrush and leave behind open clearings.
There, grasses regrow, game animals graze, and, as on this March day,
berry bushes burst into leaf.[18]

Colonists are sowing cover crops this morning: clover and trefoil
to return nutrients to ground made tired by growing English grains.
Soon the fields will be misted with green lobes growing in threes, the
regal purple of the clover mixing with the glorious gold of the poisonous trefoil, inedible to man and beast alike. Gentlemen farmers don't
dig the soil themselves, but they supervise those who do. The time of
leading men is taken by other kinds of cultivation.[19]

Logan and French have come to plant law in the wilderness. As
William Keith put it a few years ago, in the midst of urging Quakers
to acknowledge that the Crown of England, not the whims of William
Penn, are the true source of Pennsylvania law:

> These American Lands being new Discoveries of Tracts long Settled
> by their Native Inhabitants the Indians, who were under no subjection to nor had any knowledge of the Laws of England; those Laws
> whenever they come to reach these Lands, must by some regular
> method be extended to them, for they cannot be supposed of their
> own nature to accompany the people into these Tracts in America.

The Indians have no laws that colonists acknowledge as such. These
barren tracts of land, devoid of law, will not achieve legal order automatically. It is not enough for English people to settle the ground and
assume that the law will simply seed itself. No, the law must be deliberately laid down. The Quakers have given in and reformed their colony's laws to adhere to the strict standards of the English penal code.
Now Logan needs to make Indians understand what that means. Rake
and hoe, plow and harrow, cultivating civilization requires covering
the land with good English law.[20]

Yet Logan travels with more than English legal instruments in his saddlebags. He also carries with him an intricately beaded shell belt made of wampum, the sort of finely worked gift Indians regard as a mark of friendship and a measure of intent. Logan has been chosen for this mission as much for his familiarity with Native protocol as for his knowledge of English law. He was present ten years earlier at a ceremony held with members of the Lenape Nation in White Marsh, Pennsylvania, when the Lenapes conducted an exhibition of the condolence rituals they planned to perform for the Iroquois later that summer. Logan took his usual meticulous notes on that occasion, and the information he gleaned then will come in handy now. As much as Logan intends to assure the Indians at Conestoga that John and Edmund Cartlidge will be subjected to the full weight of English justice, he knows he will never head off Native retribution unless he follows the formal rituals that Indians expect.

Logan and French ride up to John Cartlidge's house in Conestoga late on the afternoon of March 9. Sheriff John Taylor has been expecting them and has placed John under house arrest. But even now, John does not fully grasp the gravity of his situation. Slippery as the horsehair couch he keeps in the main hall of his home, he is still hoping for an opportunity to slide off quietly. As far as he is concerned, his conference three days ago with Civility has effectively quelled the crisis. His brother, Edmund, is waiting right now on the other side of the Susquehanna with a string of horses, and John intends to join him and set off on a new trading venture across the Potomac just as soon as he can.[21]

This will not do. As soon as they learn of Edmund's whereabouts, Logan and French insist that he must return to Conestoga. "We have a necessity of seeing your brother," they inform John. He objects that nothing can be done so late in the day, a point Logan and French are forced to concede. But they have all evening to persuade him, as they have no better place to stay than in Cartlidge's own house.[22]

John is loath to give up his plans and call Edmund back to Conestoga. But weighing his options like so many coins balanced on the brass scale in his study, he can think of no better alternative than to obey. Logan and French know him and like him, facts that must be worth something. If he cooperates now, they may yet help him pass off the clipped coin of his March 6 council as a genuine exercise in justice.[23]

Logan congratulates himself on convincing John to order Edmund back, noting that "he was prevailed upon to send for him the next day." That morning, Logan and French also send word of their business to the chiefs of all the Native nations of Conestoga. "Have all those persons ready here who know anything of this matter," they instruct. "Fully inform us of every particular." They are determined to get to the bottom of the matter. But to do so, they must tackle the urgent issue of finding a reliable translator—they are not about to ignore John's conflict of interest and employ him as their interpreter, however much he may wish that they would.[24]

Logan knows the man they need, one Peter Bezaillion, formerly known as Pierre, an Indian trader and sometime translator who has lived in these parts since before they were claimed by William Penn. Logan respects Bezaillion's knowledge of Native languages and customs. It is partly thanks to a hand-drawn map of Indian territory that Pierre Bezaillion's brother Michel ("Michael") sketched for Logan on linen rag in 1718 that Logan has become aware of the rising strength and importance of the Iroquois. Most of Bezaillion's notes on the numbers and names of the Native peoples of eastern North America are in French, but along the Ohio River, in plain English, it says, "Ohio rises among ye Iroquois, 500 leagues." If anyone can help Logan now in his outreach to Indians, surely it is Bezaillion.[25]

The Philadelphia officials dispatch a messenger to fetch Bezaillion

OPPOSITE: *This map sketch, representing the fullest extent of colonial Pennsylvanians' knowledge of the interior of North America, shows the Mississippi River with three branching rivers we would now identify as the Wabash, the Ohio, and the Tennessee. Note that only the Ohio is named and that no scale of distance, compass orientation, or geographic coordinates are given. Nevertheless, Logan takes care to note that the "Ohio rises among ye Iroquois, 500 leagues," indicating colonial recognition of the influence and presence of the Haudenosaunee in eastern North America.*

"MINUTES TAKEN FROM MICHAEL BIZAILLON CONCERNING THE ROUTE FROM CANADA TO MECHASIPPI & THE INDIANS OF THOSE PLACES, 10BER 1718," LOGAN FAMILY PAPERS, VOLUME 11, BOX 11, COLLECTION 379, AUTHOR'S PHOTO FROM DOCUMENT AT THE HISTORICAL SOCIETY OF PENNSYLVANIA.

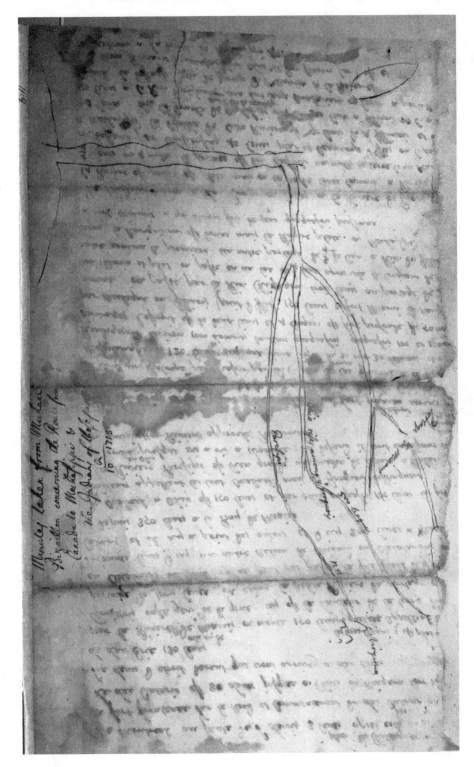

posthaste. Yet delays pile upon delays. Bezaillion lives thirty-six miles upriver, and it turns out that he has no horses at home. Had Logan and French known this in advance, they could have commandeered a steed from John Cartlidge and sent it up with the messenger. As it is, they can only sit and wait for the man to make his laborious way down on foot. Days pass and Edmund clops back from across the Susquehanna, trailing a long train of horses. Still there is no sign of Bezaillion.[26]

Whatever Logan talks about with Cartlidge during this holding period as he sits in Cartlidge's parlor, converses in his study, sleeps in the man's bed, or eats his victuals at Cartlidge's walnut table, he writes down none of it. Finally, four days later, on the afternoon of the thirteenth, Bezaillion at last arrives and ends their state of suspension. They have nearly reached the Ides of March and it is high time for John and Edmund to begin trying to settle their debts.[27]

THE LONG PAUSE HAS left ample time for word to spread that officials from Philadelphia have arrived in the neighborhood with a mandate to investigate the actions of the Cartlidge brothers. Several dozen Indians and colonists file in front of James Logan on Wednesday morning, March 14. Powdered wigs, white cravats, and woolen waistcoats adorn one group; black tattoos, red bead necklaces, and woolen matchcoats ornament the other. They face each other across a gray area of cultural conflict and confusion.[28]

Logan is a tall man, known for his "graceful yet grave demeanor." Readying himself, he notes that "Civility, Tannacharoe, Gunnebatorooja, and Toweena" are there along with "other old men of the Conestoga Indians." Joining them are "Savannah, Chief of the Shawanese, Winjack, Chief of the Gawanese, Tekaachroon, a Cayoogoe, and Oweeyekanowa, Noshtarghkamen, Delawares." There are also "present divers English & Indians." Multiple witnesses to the confrontation, colonist and Indian alike, have come to give evidence. Many more community members are here simply to supply an audience. Everyone who lives in and around Conestoga considers themselves connected to these events.[29]

Logan needs to project dignity now more than ever. He places a table between himself and the crowd and lays out the visual symbols of his authority right there on the board for inspection. Colonists won't accept his right to pass judgment on their justice of the peace unless they can read his commission from the governor and see that it has been issued under the Great Seal of the Province. Indians won't believe he speaks with sincerity and legitimacy unless he matches his words with the belt of wampum he has brought for this purpose.[30]

"Friends and brethren," Logan begins, "William Penn, our and your Father, when he first settled this country with English Subjects, made a firm League of Friendship and Brotherhood with all the Indians then in these parts and agreed that both you and his People should be all as one Flesh and Blood." He pauses then. His speech must be translated sentence by sentence. First Peter Bezaillion renders his words in Delaware. Then they are spoken again in "Shawanese" (Shawnee), "Ganawese" (Conoy), and "Mingo" (Iroquois). "Smith, the Ganawese, who excels in the skill of those Languages" takes charge of the task, along with "Civility."[31]

Taquatarensaly can't help but notice that Logan's opening words are close echoes of those he himself offered just one week earlier. Once again, Logan reminds Indians and English alike that they are to regard each other as members of "one flesh." Such repetition honors Indian expectations that alliances must be regularly refreshed and reaffirmed. Atoning for a death is not something that can be accomplished in one effort. Furthermore, Logan is invoking the very principle Indians wish to emphasize, that the crisis of death can be an opportunity for communal renewal as well as occasion of mourning.[32]

And yet, Logan has inserted another phrase, which, despite its apparent politeness, is likely to rankle the Indians assembled. He has claimed that they are brothers, and William Penn their common father. In saying so, Logan may seem to gesture in the direction of cross-cultural unity. But he actually stands firm in his belief in cultural hierarchy, one in which European leaders, such as Penn (and those leaders' designated representatives, such as himself) play the fathers while Indians and ordinary colonists play the sons. When Logan describes Penn as the father of the venerable men listening to him, he leaves open the interpretation that he regards all Indians as children.[33]

Native peoples are unlikely to overlook the implicit insult. They themselves greatly honor seniority; whereas young men are relied on in warfare, only older men are trusted to speak at diplomatic councils. The appearance of "old men" from Conestoga at this meeting is meant both to pay respect to Logan and to indicate the importance of this occasion. Logan ought to know how potentially offensive his words are because, less than two years earlier, in July of 1720, leaders from Conestoga told him explicitly "that when Governour Penn first held Councils with them, he promised them so much Love and Friendship that he would not call them Brothers, because Brothers might differ, nor Children, because these might offend and require Correction, but he would reckon them one Body, one Blood, one Heart, and one Head." Intentionally or not, Logan is being heavy-handed when he reasserts Penn's metaphorical fatherhood here today. He needs to get back on track quickly. The thing to do is to remind everyone present of the peaceful legacy left by William Penn.[34]

"Scarce any one injury has been done, nor any one complaint made on either side," he tells Indians and colonists alike, "except for the death of La Tour and his company, for near forty years past." His words blow into the ears of the crowd, a chill wind in the midst of spring sunshine. Everyone there will remember the story of Francis Latour, none with satisfaction. The man committed so many gross offenses against Indians, thieving their goods and stealing their children to sell into slavery, that one of them finally killed him. Then, after a cursory investigation yielded no suspects, Pennsylvania officials, who already regarded Latour as a dangerous nuisance—and a French one at that—decided to give up without prosecuting the crime. But Peter Bezaillion was Latour's neighbor, countryman, and fellow trader. Now he is the one who must square his shoulders and translate Logan's insinuation that his friend's fate should perhaps serve as a precedent for allowing Sawantaeny's killing to go unsolved and unpunished.[35]

Logan plunges on. "Your good friend, our Governor," he tells his audience, "sent us two, Colonel French and me, first to condole with you, which we now do very heartily, and next by the full Powers with which we are invested to inquire how the matter came to pass, that Justice may be done." Wampum belts and the Great Seal of the Province; Indian ways and English ones; Logan is doing his best to appease and impress at the same time. His offer of condolences, a ceremonial acknowledgment of the emotional pain of Sawantaeny's violent loss, adheres closely to Native protocols surrounding death and mourning. Yet he follows this concession to Indian practices with an immediate insistence on the power of English justice. Having delivered opening remarks designed to mollify Indian emotions without validating their ideas, Logan is ready to begin his real business: conducting an inquest into the death of Sawantaeny.[36]

Logan caps his formal preamble with one more pledge that delivers less than it seems to offer. "We will suffer no Injury to be done to any of you without punishing the offenders according to our Laws," he assures them. This sounds generous at first, a guarantee of legal equality. Yet, it reneges on the earliest commitments of William Penn, who announced his imminent arrival in North America in 1681 by sending a letter "to the Kings of the Indians in Pennsylvania" in which he promised that "in any thing that offends you or your People, you shall have a full and Speedy Satisfaction for the same by an equal number of just men on both sides." Logan is not offering to allow an equal number of Indians to sit beside colonists in judgment on the Cartlidges. His apparently fair proposal actually amounts to an effort to curtail Native influence.[37]

Logan knows he has a delicate task to accomplish. "We are now here to take . . . examinations, which we expect you will take care shall be given with truth and exactness, and without any partiality from resentment or favour," he tells his Indian listeners. What he means, most simply, is that the evidence they give should be as factual and as free of bias as possible. Yet at the same time, he is also advancing the broad proposition that, in order to be fair, they must set their emotions aside and ensure that no feelings of either anger (resentment) or affection (favor) distort their recollection of the facts. Logan's comments here echo the official position of William Keith who, following his successful push to strengthen the Pennsylvania penal code in 1718, cautioned against the corrupting influence of the passions in legal cases and urged, instead, "impartial scrutiny" for accused murderers. English colonists discount the Indian idea that emotions are an essential

element of the ritual redress of grief, viewing them primarily as potential impediments to the effective administration of justice.[38]

Logan reinforces this view by directing the collected chiefs to
charge their people "to speak the truth impartially without malice or
hatred, favor or affection on any account whatsoever." One by one,
under Logan's close questioning, witnesses offer testimony. The
Conoy guide named Ayaquachan, who had watched the attack while
still "in liquor"; the Shawnee youths who had joined the Cartlidges'
pack train; and John Cartlidge's two indentured servant lads, Wilkins
and Swindel, recount the events of that fateful morning: the fire, the
rum, the fight, the gun. They repeat Sawantaeny's words to John, saying that "the Sinnekae told him he need not be angry." They tell how
Edmund grabbed Sawantaeny's weapon and rained blows down on his
head, how John stripped off his clothes and delivered the kicks that
snapped Sawantaeny's ribs, and of how the rattling blood in Sawantaeny's nose and mouth drowned out his power of speech.[39]

Logan asks them, "When did Civility and the other Indians of
Conestogoe first hear of the death of the man, and by whom?"

"We heard it by several Indians, much about the same time the fact
was done," Civility answers.

"What was the Man's Name, his Nation, and Rank among his own
People?" Logan asks.

"His name was Sawantaeny of the Tsanondowaroons or Sinnekaes,
a warrior, a civil man of very few words," Civility says. He easily com-
prehends and answers Logan's questions regarding Sawantaeny's name
and Seneca nationality. But in response to Logan's question about
Sawantaeny's rank or social status, Civility answers instead with information about his public service as a warrior and a civil man. These, of
course, are the very roles that Civility himself fills, and British colonists have often referred to him as a "chief." In Maryland, Major Bradford declared that Sawantaeny was a "chief." But today the word is not
used. Perhaps Civility understands better than most that there simply
is no good English equivalent for the sort of contributions men like he
and Sawantaeny make to Native communities, the efforts they make to
harmonize relations among different societies.[40]

Logan presses forward with his questions, calling witnesses and examining each in turn. He conjures an English courtroom in the colonial woods. Peering out at the crowd from under his own heavy white headpiece, Logan communicates a great deal before he even opens his mouth. Wearing a wig signals that Logan stands near the top of a carefully ranked society in which each person knows their place. The elaborate curls have to be regularly waxed, shaped, and powdered, time-consuming tasks that only the wealthy have the servants to accomplish. Quakers who adhere closely to the teachings of society founder George Fox don't wear wigs; their devotion to Christian simplicity forbids it. But many a well-to-do Quaker, William Penn included, has chosen to wear one, despite the risk of being dismissed by more observant Quakers as mere "Perriwig Men." Logan takes his chances because, in wider English culture, the white wig silently but clearly indicates his high status.[41]

Taquatarensaly and the other Native leaders in attendance are also sending signals with the choices they make in their personal adornment. But the messages they convey are based on different cultural priorities. Polished red stone beads of catlinite are popular at Conestoga, sometimes honed into simple circles and squares, other times carved into the shape of faces or animals. Different beads can indicate clan memberships and carry spiritual meanings. At the same time, they showcase the far-flung alliances maintained by the peoples of Conestoga because catlinite originates not on the Susquehanna but on the Great Lakes. When Conestoga leaders wear these beads, they seek less to distinguish themselves above others than to demonstrate the wide reach of their community's spiritual and cultural connections.[42]

Logan complains afterward to his fellow council members that although "they were kept apart during the Examination," Native informants seemed to have collaborated ahead of time on their story, even to have agreed on which events each person would describe. When Logan tried to get them to elaborate on any point of evidence, "the Indians could not be prevailed with, alleging it was to no purpose to repeat what others had already declared." Indians want to ensure that Sawantaeny's story is told and that their collective injury is addressed. As Logan will explain later, "Great pains were taken and endeavors used to persuade these evidences to declare of themselves all that they particularly knew without considering what the others had said or were supposed by them to say." Calling the witnesses themselves "evidence," Logan wants to check and cross-check facts, the better to determine criminal culpability. The Native community members at Conestoga, on the other hand, care far more about bearing witness to Sawantaeny's suffering than giving evidence of the Cartlidges' crimes.[43]

Failing to draw out further testimony from any of the Indian men present on the night Sawantaeny was attacked, Logan turns next to interrogating Weenepeeweytah, his wife. She only repeats the same details as the others: the struggle for the gun, the strike on the head that broke the gun, the battering that broke two of her husband's ribs. Logan's frustration mounts and he declares, "they seem to have all agreed their story beforehand."[44]

Of Weenepeeweytah's crucial next words, Logan makes only the most perfunctory note. She tells him that Sawantaeny "said his friends had killed him." Logan does not press and question whether Sawantaeny actually spoke these words or whether his widow is offering a convenient invention. There is no way to know. What matters is the signal that these supposed words send about Native intentions. By claiming that Sawantaeny said this, Weenepeeweytah conveys the message that the Native inhabitants of Conestoga do not wish to treat this as a conflict between opposing peoples but rather as an unfortunate event in the history of a unified Anglo-Indian community. Logan certainly shares the Indians' desire to resolve the crisis without any further conflict, even if he doesn't embrace the full extent of Indian expectations. But he has limited, if any, comprehension of the formal role that Weenepeeweytah plays in diplomatic decision-making, despite his awareness that her cousin Savannah, present with her today, is a chief.[45]

Logan remains as concerned as ever about propitiating the leaders of the Five Nations. He picks up the wampum belt again, displaying it to the assembled Indians and telling them, "It was sent from the governor by us, to be forwarded with a message to the Sinneka Indians upon this unhappy accident." He then asks for a volunteer to go and deliver the belt to the Senecas. The colonists urgently need an emissary to intercede for them with the Five Nations. If Sawantaeny's closest neighbors on the Susquehanna will tell the Five Nations in New York that they regard the Pennsylvanians as friends, this may be enough to forestall any wider retaliation. But Logan's call goes unanswered. No one steps forward.[46]

Logan has no energy left to pursue the issue tonight. "Think by morning of a proper person to carry it," he tells them, couching his plea as an order. By now, Peter Bezaillion and the other interpreters are running dry on words. They have been eight hours in council and everyone is tired and hungry. John Cartlidge, on the other hand, has passed the day in silence. While once he could have stood side by side with Bezaillion, trading witticisms as they made their translations, today he sat sidelined in the shadows. Still, he does yet have a role to play. This is the moment to put into action William Penn's observation that pecuniary justice requires the offending party to host a feast. Native peoples have their own ideas about what content and decency require. Perhaps a generous apology in the form of food and drink will encourage someone among the Conestoga Indians to agree to Logan's request. John Cartlidge always has a good store of refreshments at the ready and so Logan orders him to supply meat and bread for the entire group, along with two gallons of rum to be made into punch. The true cost of John's refusal to serve Sawantaeny fairly is only beginning to sink in.[47]

Chapter 8

PETER BEZAILLION

SIXTY-YEAR-OLD TRANSLATOR PETER BEZAILLION READ-ies for bed at John Cartlidge's on the evening of March 14 no worse for wear after the three-day trek he made to get here. He established his trading post thirty-six miles upriver from Conestoga, but he knows this town and its inhabitants as well as any colonist does. The bridle path he hiked on his way here is one he wore down himself by traveling for decades on a course first set by the peoples of the river valleys. The path runs true over firm ground on an easterly course from Conoy Town, where he lives and trades, toward Philadelphia. It intersects Conestoga Creek at a convenient natural ford so that, even in March, a traveler need hardly worry about wet feet. Officially laid out by Pennsylvania surveyors in 1718 and dignified enough to be designated a "road" by then, the path is popularly known as "Peter's Road." After a lifetime of being repeatedly ordered before the Pennsylvania council on suspicion of wrongdoing—wanted for trespass, fined for trading without a license, even accused as a spy—Bezaillion has at last made a name for himself in the colony and even left his label on the land.[1]

Born in France, Pierre ("Peter") Bezaillion has lived and worked amongst the Native peoples of North America since migrating to Pennsylvania at the age of twenty-four. In some ways, Bezaillion practices the life of the *voyageur*, or traveler, a Franco-American colonist who crisscrosses the woods without stopping, never fully integrating into colonial society nor adopting all the trappings of Native life. In New

France, flamboyant voyageurs flaunt red woolen caps that mark their French origins and tattooed piercings that indicate their Indigenous connections. Yet here in Pennsylvania, Bezaillion has taken an English wife named Martha and made every effort to better blend in.[2]

Bezaillion has spent nearly four decades picking briars from his breeches, the souvenirs of a restless life of trading. Moving up and down the river valleys of the Susquehanna region, bartering with Native hunters for furs, he has grown fluent in the Delaware language and familiar with the seasonal shifts of Native communities. He himself was unable to settle down until at last, under a decade ago, he was finally granted an official license to trade and given legal recognition of his small land holdings from Pennsylvania officials. James Logan aided him in this process, a fact that doubtless adds to Bezaillion's willingness to provide his services as a translator now.[3]

Here in the colonies, there is no official position—or pay—for diplomatic interpreters. Often those living on the margins of the colony, people perched on the edge socially and geographically, pick up multiple languages as they go about their business. Then, when the need arises, they are simply expected to donate their time and linguistic talent in the service of peace and diplomacy. Colonists like Bezaillion accept such tasks as the cost of partial inclusion in Anglo-American colonial society. But Native interpreters expect to be compensated for their services, a point that may explain why James Logan and John French, having arrived at Conestoga with little in the way of goods or enticements, are having so much trouble finding any Native spokesman willing to act as their traveling messenger.[4]

Logan maintains extra leverage over Bezaillion because Bezaillion's life has been buffeted by strong religious and cultural crosscurrents. He migrated to North America in 1686, the year after the French King Louis XIV, aiming to rededicate France to Catholicism, revoked a policy known as the Edict of Nantes that had previously allowed toleration for Protestants. Thousands of endangered French Protestants, known as Huguenots, fled to avoid violent persecution, members of the Bezaillion family among them. Yet because competition between French Catholics and English Protestants on both sides of the Atlantic intensified greatly at the same time, English colonists reacted warily to the appearance of any French people in their midst, regardless of their religious outlook.⁵

Infantrymen in French blue faced off against British regulars in redcoats twice during Bezaillion's first decades in Pennsylvania, in the Nine Years' War (1688–1697) and again in the War of the Spanish Succession (1702–1713) and both conflicts reverberated across the seas. In North America, this rivalry meant that each side courted alliances with Native American groups that could help ensure the security of vulnerable colonies. Native peoples from the Great Lakes to the eastern seaboard benefited from colonists' constant anxiety. But the situation put a man like Peter Bezaillion—a Native French-speaker with close Indian ties making his way through woods newly claimed by the English—in a most ambiguous position.⁶

Bezaillion first came to the notice of Pennsylvania officials in 1693, the very year that the French began concerted attacks on the Haudenosaunee. The French raided the Five Nations less in an effort to defeat them than in an attempt to drive them into an alliance against the English. Much to English colonists' distress, the French largely succeeded with this tactic, with four of the five member nations of the Haudenosaunee Confederacy shifting from favoring the British to practicing neutrality by 1701. During this period, Bezaillion, apparently far from resigned to living under English rule, reportedly bragged to local Indians that the French would return to the Pennsylvania region soon. Just now, he explained "they could not be so kind to them because of the English," but once the French returned to power they would prove their worth as trading partners and military allies. He promised them "it would not be long ere they would buy their Land of them again"—that is, before the French would make further land payments to Native people.⁷

As if his boastful gossip weren't enough, Bezaillion further damned himself in the eyes of Pennsylvania officials when they heard that "several letters and powders" had been "sent to Canada by Peter Bisalion," along with a second "packet of letters," this one "sealed up in a blue linen cloth." Idle preening was one thing; directing intelligence and gunpowder to the enemy was another. In 1693, they hauled him before the council to explain himself. Lacking firm evidence to substantiate the rumors against him, they dropped the case without bringing any charges. But his troubles were only in remission. After five fragile years of peace, Britain and France went to war again in 1702, with the consequence that in June of 1703, Bezaillion found himself commanded to appear before the Pennsylvania council to face another inquiry into his loyalty, a directive that he "hold no Correspondence whatsoever with the Enemy," and a demand that he pay the hefty sum of £500 as "security" for his future good behavior.[8]

Bezaillion took this, too, in stride and continued about his business as if nothing had happened, with the perhaps predictable result that, by 1707, he landed once more in front of the council members. This time, they required that he answer a charge made by the Indians of Conestoga that that he, and half a dozen others, all of whom "spoke French, had seated themselves and built houses upon the branches of the Potomac" in an area claimed by the Pennsylvania proprietors. According to the Native people of Conestoga, the Frenchmen were squatting there in the belief that a lode of precious metal was located nearby, just awaiting men with wits and shovels sharp enough to find it.[9]

Mineral dreams fire the ambitions of many a European setting out for North America. The Spanish empire has reaped unimaginable wealth in gold and silver in its territories to the south, leaving the late-arriving English and French in desperate hopes of reproducing Spanish success. Books about the Americas routinely promise readers that the lands practically burst with bullion. A guidebook called the *Atlas Geographicus*, published in London in 1711, insists that, in Pennsylvania in particular, "the soil abounds with Mines, Samples of most sorts of Oar have been taken up here almost everywhere." If this book does not explicitly promise precious metal, it certainly implies that colonial Pennsylvanians have the right to hope for mineral riches. Indeed, in this age of alchemy, many educated men believe that, in the right conditions, the skillful can transform even iron pyrite into gold.[10]

But Peter Bezaillion, like all colonists dazzled by their own imaginations, stumbled over an inconvenient fact. Only extensive knowledge of the local land could yield clues about where to search for precious soil. And so, as they set out "in search of some Mineral or

Ore," Bezaillion and his French associates "pretended that in the Governor's name they . . . required the Indians of Conestoga to send some of their People with them to assist them, and be serviceable to them, for which the Governor would pay them." In the eyes of the members of the Provincial Council, Bezaillion practiced a double deception here, prospecting on land that belonged to the proprietors while trying to trick Indians into aiding him—all on the pretext that his efforts came at the behest of English authorities.[11]

Colonists across British America followed similar proceedings, mining the minds of Native peoples for information about the natural world. Newcomers tramped through the woods with possessive curiosity seeking to transform Native knowledge into profit, a process they likened to turning base metals into gold. Even when colonists acknowledged that they were benefiting from Native expertise, they credited Indians only with supplying the raw materials for finished European intellectual products.[12]

Unfortunately for Bezaillion, the Native peoples of Conestoga proved that they understood exactly what he was up to by reporting his schemes directly to the members of the Provincial Council of Pennsylvania. "The Queen and the principal men of Conestogoe" sent a messenger to the council saying that they did not think "these proceedings to be consistent with their past Treaties and Leagues of ffriendship." The queen, a woman named Canatowa, "desired to know whether the said persons were really sent by this Government and had thus seated themselves by their approbation and whether they had any order to desire the assistance of the said Indians, if not that they may be called home." James Logan and his fellow council members took a dim view of Bezaillion's efforts and "resolved that an Answer should be prepared to be sent to the Queen," thanking her for sending them notice of the mining scheme and advising her that the conspirators would be "required to repair to Philadelphia to give an Account" of their actions.[13]

Even on this occasion, Bezaillion tripped but did not fall. An unexpected ally stepped forward to catch him. Quaker members of the Provincial Council had taken the chance to send disciplinary orders for the Frenchmen, paired with their diplomatic message to the queen at Conestoga, at a moment when the colony's governor was out of the chamber. In those years, the colony's governor was not a co-religionist, but a Welshman named John Evans with little commitment to Quaker scruples. Once Evans returned to the council following day, he admitted to those assembled that he "found he had some Notion of Mines, and had his thoughts bent much that way" and even asserted that he had known of Bezaillion's plans in advance, "& had not discouraged him; that he had advised him to take some Indians with him." Brought up short, the council members were forced to allow Bezaillion, who had already paid a significant sum as security, to go back to business. Bezaillion, catlike, landed on his feet once again.[14]

Peter Bezaillion escaped punishment for his mining escapades because an Anglican governor at odds with Quaker magistrates—who were more loyal to Penn than to him—joined the Frenchman's desire to hunt down metal quarry. Unfortunately for Bezaillion, the rich lodes of his dreams evaded him then and have continued eluding him ever since. Still, in 1712, with French and British hostilities at last winding down, he applied to have his trading license renewed and met with a positive response from the council. France and Britain signed a formal peace treaty by 1713 and in June of that year, when Taquatarensaly visited Philadelphia with a message from the Cayugas and the Oneontas, two member nations of the Five Nations, council members "particularly acquainted" him "that our Queen had now made peace with the French." This proved to be a turning point both for Bazillion and for Taquatarensaly. Indians never complained about Bezaillion again and he grew prosperous through trading with them.[15]

Colonial Pennsylvanians and Native people alike eventually grew so used to having Bezaillion in their midst that, by 1717, the council began to employ him as an occasional interpreter. By 1718, Logan sought a personal consultation with him to learn what intelligence his brother in Canada could give him of the Iroquois. By 1720, Bezaillion would serve side by side with Taquatarensaly and John Cartlidge at the latter's home as the Pennsylvanians tried to puzzle out how their ancient alliances on the Susquehanna would hold up in an era of renewed strength for the Five Nations. On that occasion, the council notes reported how "Civility" took Logan aside and privately offered

the information that members of the Five Nations were expressing "dissatisfaction at the large settlements made by the English on
Susquehanna." In doing so, Taquatarensaly offered earnest proof of
his determination to act the part of the fanimingo, repairing breaches
between nations.[16]

Now, with Cartlidge under arrest, Peter Bezaillion and Taquatarensaly once again have key roles to play in determining whether, when,
and how to approach the Five Nations on behalf of Pennsylvania. For
Cartlidge himself, there are other paths forward, ones that Bezaillion
is well positioned to guess at. With rumors afoot that John Cartlidge
has actually succeeded in finding significant iron deposits, his quickest
route out of crisis may be marked with metal. What worked to ingratiate Bezaillion with Governor Evans may yet aid Cartlidge in gaining
favor with Governor Keith. Perhaps Cartlidge can escape his current
predicament via Peter's Road.

Chapter 9

TWO HEADS ARE
BETTER THAN ONE

MARCH 15–17, 1722

Two heads is better than one.

—Titan Leeds, Verses for March,
The American Almanack for 1722

J AMES LOGAN AND JOHN FRENCH RISE FROM THEIR NIGHT'S
rest to an uncertain new day. Yesterday evening seemed to end well
enough, with breaking bread, sharing meat, and passing rum punch
"among the company, which was large," as Logan noted. But problems
nag this morning: Why did no volunteers accept Logan's charge to
carry a conciliatory message from the colonists to the leaders of the
Five Nations? And what, precisely, should he and French say in their
missive? It is hard to know how best to depict the case.[1]

The matter of the rum poses a particular problem. Native witnesses
have given an inconsistent account of how much Sawantaeny drank
and of how alcohol figured in his argument with John. Some say John
and Sawantaeny argued because John pushed drink on him in place of
other payments. This is the tale John Hans Steelman took to Maryland.
Others claim the opposite: that conflict arose because John refused
Sawantaeny's demands for additional liquor. Aquannachke, the young
Shawnee man, claimed that "the Sinneka had Liquor over night and

was drunk with it." If this is the case, then Cartlidge is at fault for traf-
ficking in liquor instead of trading for goods, but Sawantaeny looks
blameworthy for imbibing to excess. On the other hand, the Ganawese
guide, Ayaquachan, stated that "John Cartlidge gave the Sennikae
some small Quantities of Punch and Rum three times that Night,"
leaving Sawantaeny demanding more in the morning. In this rendition of events, Sawantaeny told John, "he need not be angry at him for
asking more for he owed it to him." This account, if true, could exonerate John from any serious breach of the law against trading rum to
Indians, since it makes it seem that he never offered Sawantaeny more
than a sociable drop or two. But this version still convicts John of trying to cheat Sawantaeny. No matter what, this killing mounts a new
grievance atop the growing pile of Anglo-Indian disputes over liquor
and trade. And no matter what, Cartlidge's legal predicament has only
grown as a result of Logan's interrogation. Contrary to the pretenses
of John's prior conference, there can be no question now that John, as
well as Edmund, bears blame for Sawantaeny's death.[2]

This is the sort of situation that leads to uneasy rest. Logan's notes
make no mention of whether he and French are bunking in the front
chamber of the Cartlidge's house, usually preferred by John and his
wife Elizabeth—where the best bed is set up and where there is a
choice of chairs to sit on—or whether they have taken the back-facing
chamber over the parlor, which is supplied with only an ordinary bed.
Regardless, neither John nor Elizabeth can have passed a quiet night.[3]

～

LIQUOR POTS AND BOWLS and jugs. Goblets, glasses, cups, and
mugs. Match the shape of your receptacle to the type of your tipple.
When William Penn packed for his first transatlantic journey in 1682,
his personal equipment in silver plate alone included "one large tankard," "one caudle cup with three legs" (used for slurping caudle, the
gruel made of grain mixed with wine or beer), as well as "three tum-
blers, one large and two lesser," along with a "one handle cup" and
"two things for cruet tops." Pennsylvania colonists tip back vessels of

every kind in the course of drinking the equivalent of nearly seven ounces of hard alcohol per person per day.[4]

Indians, unfamiliar with alcohol before the arrival of Europeans, quickly learned the ways of liquor from them. In Pennsylvania, colonists' very first agreement with people of the Lenape Nation relied on liquid diplomacy. The same treaty in which Penn's agents promised that "if English or Indian should at any time abuse one the other Complaint might be made to their respective Governor . . . that satisfaction may be made according to their offence" offered an accompanying list of gifts that included numerous alcohol-related items: two hundred small glasses and twenty glass bottles, as well as "2 Anchors Rume, 1 Anchor Syder, 2 Anchors Beare." Just how much alcohol did an "anchor" of rum, cider, or beer amount to? Many years later, in 1701, council minutes noted that a trader brought to Indians "several anchors of Rum, to the quantity of about 140 gallons." However many gallons an "anchor" corresponded to, then, it certainly added up to a great deal of alcohol.[5]

Yet while alcohol anchored English relations with Native peoples from the moment of the colonists' first meeting with the Lenapes in 1682, Penn himself always worried about alcohol's effects on human relationships. In a farewell letter written to his own children that same summer, Penn warned them to "watch against anger, neither speak nor act in it, for, like drunkenness, it makes a man a beast and throws people into desperate inconveniences." Anger and alcohol course through this case. Sawantaeny's witnesses insist that he accused Cartlidge of being angry, whereas colonists are predisposed to blame Indians for anger. When Logan and French awaken this morning, they open their eyes to just the kind of "desperate inconveniences" that William Penn had long ago foreseen.[6]

The secretary and the colonel know their efforts so far have fallen short of Indian expectations, and they have had all night to wonder what and how much more they need to do. They decide to change tack. French will take the lead in addressing the Indians instead of Logan. The colonel's military bearing may convey an urgency that the city merchant's smooth blandishments have not. As soon as they are ready, the Pennsylvania officials head out to meet the Native leaders and resume their conversations. But this time they don't invite any extra onlookers to witness the proceedings.

"Friends and Brethren," French begins, "We informed you yesterday that we were sent by the Governour in very great Haste from Philadelphia upon the News of this unhappy Accident, which we have been enquiring into. We therefore, had not time to bring with us any Presents to make you." Taquatarensaly and the rest of the assembled Indians are listening, but they can hardly be pleased. The colonists' fixation on establishing minute facts is blinding them to the bigger picture; Native peoples want their collective grief to be assuaged emotionally and accounted for economically. Last night's supper was a move in the right direction, but the colonists still have far to travel if they want to reach peace.[7]

French can hardly bear to step to the Indians' drum. He antagonizes and apologizes in the same breath, blurting that, as for "presents . . . nor could we indeed believe they would be expected on this occasion. We thought however that if any should be wanted they might be easily had at Conestogoe, but find them very scarce." Three sentences in, the colonel is marching toward a cliff. He is supposed to be providing the Indians with satisfaction, but is instead criticizing them for seeking reparations. Meanwhile, he is calling attention to the fact that even though John Cartlidge was about to gallop off with Edmund on a new trading venture when the colonial officials arrived to arrest him, he has no supply of trade goods ready, only rum to offer.[8]

French gathers himself and continues: "We have however procured two Stroud Coats to be sent to our Brethren the Sinnekas, to cover our dead Friend." With his talk of covering the dead, French is at last acting in accordance with Native traditions, presenting physical objects that can serve as tangible signs of emotional and spiritual states.[9]

French lingers for a moment. They have also brought "this belt of wampum," he tells the Indians, holding it aloft to be admired, "to wipe away tears." His mention of tears is important to the Indians assembled. As they confront the crisis of murder, establishing the factual chain of cause and effect matters much less to them than addressing the embodied suffering that grief creates. They are waiting not for admissions of guilt but for declarations of remorse and expressions of grief. When Colonel French offers a belt of wampum as a ritual way to wipe away tears, he is trying to fall in line with Native practices. Up until now, Logan and French have been running the conference as a court of inquiry, whereas the assembled Native peoples are awaiting a show of sympathy.

Logan has some awareness of how far they have fallen short. He, after all, created Pennsylvania's first record of such rituals back in May of 1712 when a group of Lenapes on their way to visit the Five Nations met first with Pennsylvania officials and shared their plans for participating in Haudenosaunee-directed condolence ceremonies. On that occasion, the Lenapes described for members of the Pennsylvania Provincial Council a thirty-two-part message that they intended to deliver. Rehearsing their speeches point by point, they displayed the thirty-two coordinating belts of wampum to be given in confirmation of each statement. Declaration number thirty-one said that "they are sorry that their Children as well as theirs die; that their Eyes have been so shut up by it, that they could not see the Sun; Desire they may be opened & that all may be cheerful." For the Lenapes, who might otherwise be the subject of captive raiding by the Five Nations, maintaining their status as "friends" of the Haudenosaunee required engaging in rituals of condolence.[10]

Here was a tutorial, if the Pennsylvanians cared to learn, on how to mitigate the grief of death and initiate bonds of alliance by sharing tears and giving gifts. The goal of such ceremonies is to create an emotional climate of peace. Yet despite witnessing the Delaware demonstration of condolences in 1712, not until today, on the occasion of Sawantaeny's death, have Pennsylvania colonists officially recorded participating in a condolence ceremony themselves. Logan ought to know how to proceed here. But compared to the dozens of belts of wampum sent by the Lenapes to the Haudenosaunee, the Pennsylvania officials' offer of a single sash of wampum today hardly makes a strong diplomatic statement. To be effective, displays of goodwill need to be generous. French and Logan, acting on the council's orders to find the

*Logan recorded thirty-two declarations and sketched the unique
beaded patterns on thirty-two coordinating belts of wampum when
he met "the Delaware Indians according to appointment before they
Sett out on their Journey to ye Five Nations" in 1712. (Logan also
included two additional belts of wampum, numbers 33 and 34, given
by colonists to the Delawares, which they were invited to display,
but not give, to the Haudenosaunee.) This meeting is the first time
that colonial Pennsylvanians recorded information on the conduct of
Haudenosaunee condolence ceremonies. Pictured here are belts 31 to 34.*

"MINUTES OF THE PROVINCIAL COUNCIL OF PENNSYLVANIA, MAY 19, 1712, DETAIL WITH
WAMPUM BELT SKETCHES," MSS.974.8.P378, AMERICAN PHILOSOPHICAL SOCIETY.

"cheapest way to preserve their friendship" with the Indians, are bra-
zening out the day with one belt of wampum.[11]

Anyway, French is hurrying now. Without further ado, he reminds
them, "We yesterday recommended to you to think of a fit person to
carry the Message, which we hope you have done, and pitched upon
one accordingly." He words his plea as an offhand request, hoping
they have "pitched upon" someone to play the role of go between. But
this is a crucial moment of truth; the English need a Native intermediary to stake their claims with the Haudenosaunee.[12]

"The Indians answer," Logan records, "they had deferred the choice of a person till this meeting." In spite of Logan's parting charge that they think overnight about whom they might send with the colonists' message, the Indians won't be hustled. They have been waiting to see whether the colonists will commit time to the rituals of grief and do the crucial work of offering formal condolences. Though Logan, from the first moments of his speech yesterday, claimed that he and French came "to condole with you," only today, led by French, did the pair formally offer to cover the dead and wipe away tears by presenting stroud coats along with wampum and other gifts. He and French now have to hope their halting efforts are accepted as enough.[13]

At last, the Indians name "some one of them we much desired should be the Person" to intercede on their behalf. Logan and French know the name and readily agree, glad to accept the services of a person they believe they can rely on. If the Philadelphia officials have not yet satisfied Sawantaeny's community, they can at least hope that sending a formal emissary to the Five Nations now will put a final seal on the crisis. If the two extra stroud coats they offered this morning are enough to make amends, they are hardly going to complain about this minor cost. Logan and French have been reprieved. Or so they think.[14]

In the next moment, that much desired messenger "excuses himself" and refuses to serve the colonists. Logan does not write down who was asked, nor does he record why the decline came. There is still so much about Native ways that the colonists don't understand. Neither he nor French can know that months from now, in May, when their second-choice messenger, Satcheechoe, calls on the council in Philadelphia accompanied by Taquatarensaly, he will deliver only the scorn of the Haudenosaunee leaders unimpressed with their minor gifts and major failure to pay respects in person. The Pennsylvanians can't guess today that, by next August, after Satcheechoe has undertaken an equally ineffective return mission to Iroquoia, Governor Keith will find himself required to agree to journey to Haudenosaunee country to express grief directly, nor that he will then be forced to devote substantial funds toward making his condolences concrete. But Taquatarensaly can divine all of this right now. He knows how paltry the colonists' current offerings are in Native eyes, how little secondhand messages, two stroud cloths, and one belt of wampum will do to mend relations with the Haudenosaunee.[15]

For today, Logan mixes his worries with his ink. He updates his minutes with the information that "at length one Skatcheetchoo, a Cayoogoe of the ffive Nations, and of that next in situation to the Sinnekaes, who had for diverse years resided among our Indians was chosen." He is reassuring himself as he writes that Satcheechoe is up to the job, that as a member of the Cayuga Nation, he is especially close to those of the Seneca Nation and that as a longtime resident of Conestoga, he, like Taquatarensaly, has strong ties to the community here. Logan refers to local Native peoples collectively as "our Indians," meaning that they are allies, but also implying that colonists control them. This proves to be less than accurate; even as Logan is weighing Satcheechoe's qualifications, he in turn is evaluating Logan's terms.[16]

Satcheechoe wants some consideration for his troubles. He is not signing on as an errand runner simply to do the colonists' bidding. He tells the Philadelphians that he can "not leave his Family, who then wanted Bread" unless the colonists will provide for them while he is away. French meets his requirements, saying that "the next Day six Bushels of Corn should be brought to him for his family's support in his absence, and for his own journey he should have a stroud coat, a new gun, with three pounds of powder and six pounds of lead." Things seem to be looking up. Logan jots down the impression that "he seemed cheerfully to accept of" this offer. But no sooner does Logan congratulate himself than he realizes French has promised more than they can deliver. "A gun and lead we had from John Cartlidge," Logan explains, but Cartlidge has "no good Powder nor Strouds at home." Here is another damning detail. Cartlidge had no difficulty in supplying the condolence conference with two gallons of rum last night, at a cost of some five English shillings, according to the "Prices Currant at Philadelphia" listed in the American Weekly Mercury last week. But he does not have on hand many of the highly desirable imported goods Indians prefer.[17]

As a leading fur trader, James Logan maintains an ample supply of the most popular items and can easily trade £60 worth of products at a time. This coming fall, his shopping list will include yard after yard of strouds, blankets, duffels, half-thicks (the latter two fabrics bought in blue), gartering, and silk handkerchiefs. In addition to these cloth goods, Logan handles vermilion dye, useful in everything from pottery glazing to face painting, and a selection of cutlery including knives, awls, and steels. He stocks two gross of "iron harps" at a time, strong hooks useful for all sorts of work. He carries a range of decorative trinkets, including beads and a "gross"—a dozen dozen—of rings. And yes, he traffics powder and lead and rum. Still, he does not let munitions and liquor dominate his offerings the way John Cartlidge does. In one transaction, Logan records more money spent on ten and a half yards of "drugget," yet another kind of woolen cloth (£2, 9 shillings), than he does on ten gallons of rum (£1, 16 shillings, and 9 pence).[18]

Logan's customary ample assortment contrasts starkly with the meager offerings Cartlidge has on hand. What are Logan and French to do about Cartlidge's empty store now that they desperately need to offer payment in order to persuade Satcheechoe to aid their cause? They turn once more to Peter Bezaillion for a solution. He has both powder and strouds at his post upriver and promises that he will "deliver these to the messenger" if Satcheechoe will stop off at his place before proceeding further on his journey to the Iroquois.[19]

Logan is at last comfortable with their plan for proceeding, but the Indians still are not. They know that the leaders of the Five Nations will scoff at being sent nothing but two coats and one belt of wampum—on so grave an occasion as the killing of a man regarded as a chief. One of the elders present urges the wisdom of adding to the package being prepared for the Senecas a stroud and a string of wampum that John Cartlidge presented to the local community at Conestoga when he first met with them to discuss the killing nine days ago. For all his shortcomings, Cartlidge, it seems, acted astutely when he organized his meeting less as a court of inquest than as a ceremony of condolence. The people of Conestoga value the initial material and spiritual offerings Cartlidge made in the wake of Sawantaeny's death. And so the Native leaders gathered today "approve" of the suggestion to send Cartlidge's gifts on to the Senecas.[20]

Logan and French seek to press their advantage. Since the Indians are volunteering to pass onward to the Haudenosaunee the goods that Cartlidge originally intended for them, perhaps they will not mind also sending a message endorsing that of the colonists? Once again, the Philadelphians are misreading the situation. Just as the English Bible is regarded as holy because this physical book *is* the living word of the Lord, so the ritual objects that Indians pass from hand to hand carry sacred power because they substantiate—that is, give literal physical substance—to the messages they convey. "They gave us to understand," Logan tells the governor and other council members afterward, "that they could not join any words of theirs to our present, for no such thing was ever practiced by the Indians." A belt or string of wampum given as a token of condolence mingles the grief of giver and receiver; it holds value by making feelings palpable. There is no place in this process for a third party to interject with additional unsubstantiated messages.[21]

Still, the Indians assembled with French and Logan are committed to preserving the peace. After rejecting the absurd proposal that they add their words to Cartlidge's belt, they apologize that they have "no belt ready of their own, otherwise they would send it." For this, it turns out, Logan does have a solution. All along he has been holding a second wampum belt in reserve.[22]

"Civility was then privately informed that we had a belt also for them, (the Secretary having carried up two) which they might take as their own and send accordingly," Logan crowed later in his account to the council, adding, "he seemed much pleased with this." For Logan, official business conducted in private smacks of corrupt practices done in secret. Finding a way around the Indians' objections to endorsing the colonial position on Sawantaeny's death—and turning Civility to their way of thinking—amounts to a small triumph for Logan and French.[23]

Yet for Civility, this side offer of a second belt registers very differently. According to contemporary descriptions of the efforts expected of a fanimingo, if ever a go-between's efforts to preserve the peace fail, his duty then is to "send the people private intelligence to provide for their own safety." Well aware of the concerns of the assembled Native leaders that the colonists' offerings to the Five Nations are inadequate, Civility welcomes the chance to provide further quiet council to the

Philadelphia officials. In fact, he arranges with Smith and Logan that, after today's meeting ends, he will rejoin them later to continue their conversations. In ways that Logan and French simply do not appreciate, Civility is working even now to use the ceremonial resolution of this murder case as an opportunity to develop a deeper accord between the English and the Haudenosaunee.[24]

Logan, for his part, remains more concerned with discouraging aggression than encouraging communion. "We prepared to take our leaves," he recounted for his fellow council members, "but before we did this we judged it necessary to caution them." Logan and French want to emphasize that their commitment to equal justice means they will hold Indians as well as colonists to account for any crimes committed. They warn the Indians against taking revenge into their own hands. "As we would suffer none of our People to injure them without punishing the offenders," Logan intones, "so we could not receive injuries without requiring Satisfaction; And this we endeavored fully to impress upon them." Logan believes there is nothing left to say. He and French desire only to take "leave of them all, excepting Civility and the Messenger." Having said their final, formal farewells to everyone accept Taquatarensaly and Satcheechoe, the Philadelphians retire once more to their lodgings at John Cartlidge's.[25]

꙳

LOGAN AND FRENCH MAY be taking their ease at Cartlidge's house after another full day's meeting, but they are hardly taking his part. They have been at this business for ten days now and they are ready to return to their own firesides. It is time to bring things to a point. They must fashion words for the messenger to carry that will convey the seriousness of their intent to hold John to account while also restraining any Indian impulses toward revenge. They decide they are going to have to carry John back to Philadelphia under guard. They both know this turn of events will come as a shock to many, but no matter.

How different this stay is from the one they enjoyed here just last summer, back when the *American Weekly Mercury* reported to Philadelphia's reading public that "the Governor and all his Company were handsomely entertained and treated at the house of John Cartlidge, Esq., during their stay at Conestogoe." The newspaper explained that, "he went thither to meet the Heads of the Five Nations of Indians, who waited his coming to renew the treaties of peace and friendship with them." Nine months ago, leading men like Logan and French nodded approval when Aquila Rose burst into verse to praise "J———n C———dge, Esq. on his Generous Entertainment of Sir William Keith, and his Company at Conestogoe." As they chatted and plotted and boasted and teased, drinking round after round on those warm summer evenings, all were certain that John Cartlidge could be counted on to maintain ties with Indians and keep order among ordinary colonists, all while hosting the city's elite in comfortable style. From John's armchair to his good hair couch, they rested and raised their glasses. Rose celebrated how "in woods remote" city gentlemen "found . . . A House capacious and a fertile ground," a place where "flowing cups with sprightly liquor smiled / And pleasant talk the running hours beguiled." Now no one is smiling.[26]

When Taquatarensaly and Satcheechoe arrive at the Cartlidge house later that evening, Logan and French are prepared for them. Though Civility will not be traveling to Iroquoia on their behalf, he may still prove very helpful here at Conestoga, and so they are eager to have him as well as Satcheechoe consult with them about the speech they will send with Satcheechoe. Two heads, they believe, are better than one.

"Deliver this Belt from the Governor and Government of Pennsilvania to the King or Chief of the Sinnekaes," they tell Satcheechoe, and "say that the Words it brings are these."[27]

The two Pennsylvania men have selected their words for the Haudenosaunee like the savvy merchants they are. They begin with what they think the Senecas will want to hear: "William Penn made a firm Peace and League with the Indians in these parts nearly forty years agoe, which Leagues has often been renewed and never broken." Unbroken leagues sound something like the language of the Covenant Chain, the Five Nations' preferred metaphor for the links that unify distinct peoples.[28]

"An unhappy Accident has lately befallen us," they continue. "One of our Brethren and your People has lost his life by some of our People." Here they depict Sawantaeny as their own brother even as they also class him as one of the Five Nations' people. This, too, matches closely with Indian understandings that people can maintain memberships in multiple communities. Logan and French are weaving a blue thread here, dotting some vermilion there. But they certainly don't intend to get themselves up like Indians. The Philadelphians shift to telling the story on their own terms.

"Rum was the first cause of it," Logan and French explain. Their comment, making alcohol the agent and origin of the crisis, conveniently sidesteps the question of whether rum caused trouble because John tried to force it on an uninterested Sawantaeny or because Sawantaeny drank to excess and then demanded more.[29]

Either way, they continue, "he was warm and brought his Gun in Anger against them. They were afraid of his Gun, took it from him, wounded him, and he died." Canny Logan is definitely dealing falsely now, covertly switching the emotions of killer and victim. He himself has carefully recorded the eyewitness testimony that stated that Sawantaeny told John not to be angry. Yet when Logan retells the story, it is Sawantaeny's anger that threatens John and Edmund. The Indians have their own prohibitions on anger; Sawantaeny rebuked John for displaying any. By shifting the onus of anger onto Sawantaeny, Logan and French imply that he bears the responsibility for starting the confrontation that caused his death. Moreover, they blame the brothers for wounding Sawantaeny, but stop short of saying they deliberately killed him. These are the sorts of niceties that signal much in a British courtroom.[30]

In British eyes, even some forms of theft are sufficient grounds for execution, according to the strict new penal code of the colony. Last summer, just as Logan, French, and Keith paused to enjoy the "generous treat" at Cartlidge's house that led Aquila Rose to praise John and "his name repeat," a Black man in Philadelphia was put to death for committing a property crime. The same July issue of the *American Weekly Mercury* that documented Cartlidge's hospitality included another news item: "there was a special court called to try a Negroman for housebreaking." Likely John Cartlidge saw a copy of the issue of the paper in which his hospitality was immortalized and noted as well the news of the housebreaker's crime. The trial was convened in Philadelphia on July 7. By July 12, the accused "was found guilty, had the sentence of Death passed, and was accordingly executed." Five days from bench to grave. John and Edmund had better hope that their case proceeds more slowly and that they receive something *more* than equal justice.[31]

Even as Logan and French describe the case for leaders of the Five Nations in ways that may mitigate John's and Edmund's actions, they take care to assure the Indians that the men will face full legal consequences for their crime. "Our Governour, on the first news of it sent us two of his council to inquire into it," they tell Satcheechoe to tell the Senecas. "We have done it, and we are now taking the offenders to Philadia. to answer for their fault." Left unspoken is the assumption that John and Edmund may answer with their very lives. Logan and French invite Taquatarensaly and Satcheechoe to return to the Cartlidge house tomorrow to see everyone off. When they observe the Cartlidges being taken away by force, they will know that the men are being brought to justice.[32]

For now, Logan and French have only one thing left to add to their message. They repeat, in the formal cadences of Native condolences, "we send these strowds to cover our dead brother, and this belt to wipe away tears." Their emotional offering falls short of expressing any grief of their own, but at least they finally seem to have figured out how inadequate their material offerings are. The officials add, quickly, "when we know your mind, you shall have further reasonable satisfaction for your Loss."[33]

When the Pennsylvanians promise to give the Indians "satisfaction," they at last approach an understanding of the combined emotional and material compensation that Haudenosaunee expect in order to resolve a crisis of murder. The very word "satisfaction," defined as "the action of satisfying; the state or fact of being satisfied," has two major senses of meaning that, together, indicate the combination of words and actions the Five Nations require to redress a killing. The first major sense, "with reference to obligations," includes "the atoning *for* . . . an injury, offence, or fault by reparation, compensation, or the endurance of punishment." The second major sense, "with reference to desires or feelings," includes a "contented state of mind." The *Oxford English Dictionary* dates both senses of the word, still in use today, back to the early fifteenth century. And it includes a final definition, in use until at least the mid-seventeenth century, though starting to fade from common parlance by 1722: the "solution (of a difficulty)."[34]

The solution of a difficulty. The Haudenosaunee Confederacy itself had formed as the solution of a difficulty—the problem of how to limit bloodshed between groups. When Iroquoian peoples reacted to the grief of loss by seeking to replace their dead by conducting captive raids on rivals, they participated in a cycle of hostility that was difficult to contain. The formation of the Iroquois League of Peace united the Five Nations of the Haudenosaunee and replaced the violence of mourning among them with the serenity of condolences. While they could and did continue to wage war against outside groups, those within the League promised to comfort and protect one another, a guarantee of mutual support that only grew in importance under the stress of European diseases and military attacks. Their eventual coalescence into a more formalized Confederacy further consolidated these trends.[35]

These facts escape the full understanding of the Philadelphia officials. They are operating within their own assumptions about the fragility of justice and the vulnerability of alliances. When Logan and French present Civility with their spare belt of wampum, he "receives it privately," a point that seems to confirm the Philadelphia officials' hope that they have found an effective back channel through which to advance their own interests. But Civility indicates that he has no intention of keeping the second belt a secret. To the contrary, he tells them that he and Satcheechoe will "hold a Council the next day among themselves," gathering the leaders of the varied communities at Conestoga to develop a consensus on the further measures that will be needed to bridge remaining differences between Indians and English. The messengers promise Logan and French that "sending that belt in their own name, [they] would give an account by it of our governor's great care over them, and of all our proceedings in the matter." There's nothing to object to in that. Logan and French may at last have earned their evening's rest.[36]

ALL ACROSS THE COLONY at this hour, in taverns and ordinaries on city blocks and market squares, people are tipping back glasses and toasting the day's end. Some are quaffing home-brewed beer made of locally grown malt, others imported Madeira wine shipped from off the coast of Africa, still others rum, distilled from molasses produced by Africans enslaved in the Caribbean. In Philadelphia, the latest "prices current" listed in the paper show that brewers are shelling out 2 shillings and 6 pence for the ordinary "high colored" malt used for dark beers; 2 shillings and 9 pence for the "pale malt" needed for lighter ales. Rum is going for between 2 shillings and 4 pence and 2 shillings and 6 pence per gallon. Only gentry with good credit or a purse full of ready money can afford the Madeira on offer for £19 to £22 per pipe. But whatever and wherever they drink, English colonists view alcohol as a source of pleasure and profit, a reward to enjoy, a product to trade.[37]

To colonists, Native peoples appear to imbibe alcohol in the much same way that they do; from that first set of glasses gifted by William Penn's agent, the peoples of Conestoga have come to expect that strong beverages will be poured whenever they meet with Penn's colonists. But from the beginning, Native peoples have valued alcohol most of all as an element of the ceremonial exchanges and spiritual rites that help create bonds between communities. At Conestoga, even after goblets break and lose their function as drinking vessels, they can still serve as reminders of social ties with colonists. In Taquatarensaly's community, people chip clean the shattered ends of leftover wine stems and then go right on using them, now as decorative objects whose potent associations still remain sharp.[38]

Driven less by profit motives than by a desire to sacralize community connections, Native people remember the ideal of alcohol as anchor long after its deleterious effects threaten to leave them at sea. For decades now, Native people at Conestoga have complained about dishonest traders who try to use rum as a soporific to dampen their ability to demand fair deals. The colonist who brought "several anchors of rum, to the quantity of about 140 gallons" into a Shawnee settlement in 1701 did so with devious intent, the Indians complained then. "To induce them to receive it and to trade with him," he first "gave one cask as a present from him, upon which, being entreated to drink, they were afterwards much abused." John Cartlidge has tried just this tactic of gift and grab to disastrous effect.[39]

Before Logan and French can wrap up their work, they receive another dire piece of news: As Logan will recount, they are "the same Day credibly informed that the Five Nations had sent down a large belt of wampum, with the figure of a rundlet and a hatchet on it to the Indians settled upwards of the Sasquehannah, with orders to stave off all the Rum they met with." The beaded image of a barrel and an ax sends a message that needs no translation. A large belt speaks especially loudly. The Haudenosaunee have already heard the Native version of events that John Hans Steelman and his friends delivered in Maryland. Colonial Marylanders knew of Sawantaeny's death by February 17 and dated it to February 7. Satcheechoe estimates the travel time from Conestoga to Iroquoia at eight days. This means that, by today, leaders of the Five Nations have probably already known of Sawantaeny's death for a month and, even accounting for some eight days of return travel, have had three weeks to consider their message and have it woven into wampum.[40]

Information is power, and the Haudenosaunee have it. No words that Logan and French can pile up for Satcheechoe to carry will shake the Native knowledge that Sawantaeny was killed when he refused to accept alcohol in payment for his furs. Just as they demanded at the treaty conference last August, Haudenosaunee leaders want all rum barrels staved and broken, their liquid lies left to trickle away.[41]

Logan and French know that local colonists may object to this kind of property loss, but they must bring their own people into line and quickly. "We judged it necessary," Logan explains, "to send . . . a public order, under our hands and seals, to all our traders." The message they send is straightforward: "that as their carrying of Rum to the Indians was against Law, so the Indians staving it was no more than what from time to time they had been encouraged to do, and therefore they must take care not to cause any Riot or Breach of the Peace by making any Resistance." John Cartlidge has already breached Chester County's peace, perhaps irreparably. All Logan and French want now is a good night's sleep to brace themselves for morning, when they will cart off their justice of the peace to face justice himself.[42]

Chapter 10

WEENEPEEWEYTAH AND
ELIZABETH CARTLIDGE

A WOMAN'S WAILING FILLS THE MORNING AIR. STANDING in the Cartlidge yard, Logan and French try not to hear it. They are tying up their cinches with Civility and Satcheechoe, extracting a final promise that the pair will meet them again in Philadelphia some thirty days from now.[1]

"I hope to be with the Seneca in eight days," Satcheechoe tells them. Allowing ample time for the ceremonies of his visit and the preparation of return messages, he estimates that he will be back in Conestoga in a month's time. Civility agrees to join him on the last leg of his journey into Philadelphia "to give account . . . of the discharge of his message." A large delegation of Native elders from Conestoga is here to watch the final packing, girthing, and buckling, then give them a courteous send-off.[2]

Logan can hardly wait to set out, but now this woman's weeping is "causing some loss of time." He and French have just "then very much pressed John Cartlidge . . . to hasten to go along with us." John has no real choice now and he knows it. Logan and French have already bound his servant lad, Jonathan Swindel, having decided that his in-person testimony as an eyewitness will be wanted in Philadelphia. And Edmund has already been escorted under guard to his own house, the requirement to enter into custody softened by the privilege of a preliminary stop at home. John may resign himself, but Elizabeth is refusing to be parted from him. Her cries echo far and wide, snaring the attention of everyone within earshot and drawing concerned Native people to her door side.[3]

These two have been together since birth. In careful calligraphy, their names lie nestled together, John's resting just above Elizabeth's, in the lines of the local Quaker birth register. "John Cartlidge, the son of Edmund Cartlidge & Mary his wife was borne the 25th of the 3rd mon. 1684" reads the record of the Darby Monthly Meeting of the Society of Friends, followed immediately by another entry: "Elizabeth Bartram daughter of John Bartram And Elizabeth his wife was borne the 8th day of the 5th mon. 1684." Close to thirty-eight years ago, their two souls were embraced, one after the other, by the Quaker community in Chester County. They were raised side by side as neighbors and co-religionists, and their marriage united two of the founding families of the county. Elizabeth cannot accept their separation now.[4]

"His wife grieved almost to Distraction," Logan will tell the council. He means that she is nearly driving herself mad with crying. As for himself, he admits neither to any concern for his own sanity nor to any pangs of sympathy for Elizabeth. "She would force herself and her child with him," Logan says, "but was at length prevailed with to stay." He and French hold all the power here. If Elizabeth thinks they will respond to her feminine tears with a show of manly pity, she is much mistaken.[5]

Logan shuts his ears against Elizabeth's laments, but the Native people gathered there do not. "The woman's sorrows being loud," Logan says, "the Indians came to comfort her, and so we departed." His account ends there, sharp as the slap of a riding crop. If he has any curiosity about why the Indians respond as they do to Elizabeth, he keeps this to himself.[6]

BORN IN PENNSYLVANIA TO colonist parents, Elizabeth already knows well the horror and wonder of the lives they made here. At first, Pennsylvania seemed to them a heaven-sent asylum. Elizabeth's father, John, had been jailed in England for following his religious beliefs, and the wide-open skies of colony contrasted well with the stone cellars of

England. Yet, in 1711, nearly thirty years after the family first arrived, her brother William died after being captured by Tuscarora Indians when he tried to claim a large tract of their land in North Carolina. Her brother's widow and children survived to return to Pennsylvania with the harrowing tale. But even William's death did nothing to discourage his son John from appreciating the beauty of the American landscape. Elizabeth's nephew will write much of the Susquehanna region's attractions, of the "fine prospects" from its mountaintops, of its grounds well-watered by "large springs," and of the "rich vales" and "rich bottoms" that tempt with their fat soils. Meanwhile, until last month, she and her husband were doing well for themselves. Despite the demands of her position as mistress of one of the largest and best-provisioned homes in the Conestoga area, Elizabeth enjoys dressing in costly clothing and finds time for reading books of her own. Now, watching them haul John off to prison, she finds her family's fortunes reversed.[7]

Elizabeth is suddenly facing a sort of pseudo-widowhood. A colonial woman with an absent husband does her best to carry on his business as if it were her own. In cases like that of the Cartlidges, for whom running an inn is a shared venture, the wife may well already be acting, unofficially, as a business partner. Nevertheless, married women in Anglo-Pennsylvania do not legally own property beyond their personal effects. All of a family's wealth belongs to the husband, who also has sole power to enter into legal contracts, to appear in court as either a plaintiff or a defendant, and to vote or serve in office. Whatever happens, the husband always covers for the wife. The technical term for an Englishwoman's status is "feme covert," a phrase taken from French that literally means "covered wife." Though John's worldly goods amount to the tidy figure of £748, the sum total of Elizabeth's own personal holdings—her purse, her apparel, and her books—amounts to just £20. If she actually were to be widowed, Elizabeth would become a "feme sole"—that is, a solo woman—in which case she would be entitled to, at a minimum, a third of John's property, and possibly much more depending on the terms of his will. But with John alive but incarcerated, it is as if all their assets have been frozen. While a man languishes in jail, his wife and children live in peril.[8]

Occasionally, colonial magistrates acknowledge the hardship that a husband's imprisonment imposes on his wife and will even agree to release a man from custody on the grounds that his family's suffering is too great. When one Thomas Davis of Philadelphia was indicted, fined £5, and imprisoned in 1716 (for some unspecified crime apparently too minor to be recorded), the city council agreed that "he being very poor & his wife like to become a charge to ye Town if he should be kept in Goal," the sheriff should be ordered to "let him go at large." If Elizabeth and John are lucky, he may yet be shown this kind of clemency. But then again, Davis was arrested two years *before* the passage of the new 1718 criminal code, not four years after it. And of course, he wasn't arrested on suspicion of murder or manslaughter. For now, Elizabeth has nothing to lean on but the comfort being offered by the assembled Indians.⁹

TAQUATARENSALY, SATCHEECHOE, AND THE Native leaders ranged outside the Cartlidge house can only be disturbed by the abrupt turn of events that has resulted in John's being removed from his home while Elizabeth is left behind to grieve. They have just devoted the better part of two days to participating in condolence rituals, prodding and coaching the Pennsylvania colonists to play their parts appropriately. This meeting with Logan and French, coming on the heels of the one convened ten days ago by John Cartlidge, represented the second of what they hope will be a series of ceremonies. Step by step, they seek to repair the breach created by Sawantaeny's killing and leave the Anglo-Indian alliance stronger than ever. But now John Cartlidge has been taken away.

The colonists have departed without a backward glance, leaving it up to the Indians present to tend to the weeping woman. When women of the Five Nations mourn and cry over the loss of a community member, captured or killed by the enemy, their flow of tears sets off a cascade of consequences for the community. If the women remain disconsolate, the result may well be the start of a war aimed at taking captives to counterbalance the loss of the missing one. Only if the mourning women's grief can be assuaged can community calm be restored. Peace is much more likely to prevail in cases where a loss is the result of a misunderstanding between allied groups than when it comes as the manifestation of hostile rivalry. Either way, the decision rests with female elders; tranquility can only return if the ceremonies of condolence are carefully observed.[10]

What do the Native people consoling Elizabeth see when they look at this sobbing figure? Perhaps they could be forgiven for thinking that the sorrow of a pseudo-widow pales beside the anguish of Weenepeeweytah, forced to watch helplessly as her husband bled to death. But the Indians gathering around Elizabeth are taking the measure of her personal emotional turmoil as much out of concern for the state of Anglo-Indian relations as out of interest in her particular situation. They need to assess the political intentions and likely diplomatic impact of her demonstrations of dismay. For people of the Five Nations, a weeping female figure signals the threat of a society ready for war, whereas peace comes in the form of a woman. The Indians now offering to comfort Elizabeth can hardly comprehend how little power she has among her own people.[11]

⌇

WEENEPEEWEYTAH, GRANTED ONLY A few bare lines in Logan's notes on the meeting just concluded—and never mentioned before or again in the colonists' records—nonetheless holds the fate of John Cartlidge and his colony in her hands. If she were to cry as inconsolably as Elizabeth is doing, she would be sending an unmistakable signal in support of armed hostility. Weenepeeweytah is described as a Shawnee married to a Seneca, an Algonquian-speaking woman married to an Iroquoian-speaking man. For both groups, women's mourning can lead to warfare and compensatory captive-taking unless ritual condolences staunch the flow of grief.[12]

Well might Weenepeeweytah mourn. She told Logan and French that after tending her husband as he bled through the night and then finding him dead in the morning, she "was alone with the corpse." Rather than attempting to cope on her own, she left their cabin and "went to seek some help to bury him." She then passed over a week in the woods. Only as she was returning home again did she at last cross paths with a pair of her neighbors from Conestoga, who told her they had visited the cabin and, "finding the Man dead, buried him in the Cabin and were gone from thence before she returned." Weenepeeweytah repeated the point that "they had buried him in the ground," a detail that matters much to her. To ritually cover the dead, the body must first be respectfully interred in the earth.[13]

Weenepeeweytah gave no further details about the burial, but Logan and French called as witnesses the two people who actually performed the act. According to their testimony, Kannaannowch, a Cayuga man, first chanced on Sawantaeny's body and recognized the need to place him in the grave. Rather than take on the task himself, "he hired them to go bury him lest the Beasts or Fowls should eat him." Kannaannowch likely also conferred with his fellow Cayuga neighbors in Conestoga about the killing and either advised the envoys who went to Maryland in the company of John Hans or else traveled with them. John Hans, of course, had close ties to the Cayugas. The Cayugas were considered the younger brothers of the Senecas in the metaphorical longhouse that united the Five Nations of the Haudenosaunee. They thus took it as their special responsibility to see to it that the death of Sawantaeny was properly addressed.[14]

Logan identified those whom Kannaannowch chose to perform the burial only as the "wife to Passalty of Conestogoe" and as "the Hermaphrodite." It must be significant that Logan noted that the people who performed the duties for laying Sawantaeny to rest were "hired," meaning that "the Hermaphrodite" attended the burial in a professional capacity, recognized and respected in the local community. This third-gender person at ease moving between worlds likely appeared at the grave in a ceremonial role, offering Sawantaeny's soul a ritual introduction into the realm of the afterlife. Logan never mentioned such a person again. Likewise, he recorded neither the name nor the national affiliation of this caretaker. Still, as a two-spirit figure who joined masculine and feminine genders in one being, "the Hermaphrodite" stood as the literal embodiment of the ideal of unity and the rejection of polarities at the heart of Native practices of condolence, restitution, and reconciliation.[15]

According to Logan, "it was about seven Days after his Death that they went thither, for the Body then Stunk; They found three wounds in his Head, They washed away the Blood and the Brains appeared; that two of his Ribs were broke and his Side on that part was very black." Logan held his nose and recorded this forensic evidence without elaboration. Yet even his minimalist notes indicate that these two lavished care on Sawantaeny in death. They prepared Sawantaeny's body for the grave by bathing it and laid him to rest with ceremony.[16]

$$\backsim$$

NOW, EVEN AS MEMBERS of Weenepeeweytah's community continue to condole with her on the loss of her husband, they find themselves witnesses to a new round of feminine tears at a family rupture—this one afflicting the relations of a colonist. When Weenepeeweytah reported that Sawantaeny said his friends had killed him, she meant to indicate to the English colonists that no violent revenge should be sought. When Sawantaeny and Civility promised Logan and French that Sawantaeny would carry an extra belt in the name of the peoples of Conestoga to leaders of the Five Nations and use it to convey to the Haudenosaunee the appreciation that members of the Conestoga community felt for the governor's "great care over them," they reinforced the same message of peace and forbearance. But Native restraint appears not to have had the intended result. It seems that colonial officials are taking the very actions that Weenepeeweytah's words on friendship were intended to forestall. The have decided to bind John Cartlidge with chains, in effect to treat one of their own as captive—and they seem bent on bringing him face-to-face with death.

Chapter 11

FORGIVE ANYONE
SOONER THAN THYSELF

MARCH 21–26, 1722

Forgive anyone sooner than thy self.

—Titan Leeds, Verses for March,
The American Almanack for 1722

A JOURNEY DOWN FROM CONESTOGA GIVES A MAN A GOOD appetite. But no one offers to let Jonathan Swindel stop off at one of Philadelphia's many cookshops, where meat vendors are boiling and roasting beef and pork. Bakehouses across the city are sending forth their steaming scents of browning breads, rising cakes, and crisping tarts. That matters little. A growl from Swindel's stomach will impress no one, least of all the sheriff now waiting to take him into custody along with his master, John Cartlidge.[1]

Swindel is eighteen. Even caught up in the investigation of a possible murder, a servant lad will always try to peek at the city's wares as he passes through the streets. As the Cartlidge contingent makes its way east along High Street from the Schuylkill River to the Delaware, where the main marketplace keeps company with the courthouse and the jail, they can't help taking in the sights. Colorful painted placards festoon the city's storefronts, some of the only pictures Jonathan Swindel has ever seen. He can't so much as write his own name, and unlike his master and his master's wife, has had little opportunity in his life to look at books. Still, he can distract himself on his march to jail by snatching glimpses of the Sign of the Scales, where customers are pricing "haberdashery and sundry other European goods"; of the Sign of the Bible, where books, newspapers, and an ever-shifting variety of items is on offer, including molasses this week; or of the Sign of the Crown, where imported olives and capers can be found among the assorted goods.[2]

Jonathan Swindel has neither money nor opportunity to buy anything, but he himself is liable to being bought and sold. Indentured to John Cartlidge, he does have certain rights, set forth in a contract he cannot read, but they are strictly limited during his term of service. He is legally obligated to obey Cartlidge's every command and is subject to physical "correction" if he resists compliance. Years from now, once his term is finished, he will be allowed his "freedom dues," hopefully a set of farm implements and a new suit of clothes. For now, he lives day to day without a cent in his pocket, his life and labor valued at about £12, according to the inventory of his master's property, or about the price of two of Cartlidge's forty-four horses and colts. As long as he remains in service, he has no reason to expect more than a shirt, waistcoat, breeches, and coat made of the coarse cloth known as osnaburg, a rough fabric reserved for indentured and enslaved laborers that causes great discomfort to the body.[3]

Swindel has many causes for uneasiness as he itches and scratches his way toward incarceration. His status as a bound servant is deteriorating into a literal state of bondage. He is a material witness to a crime, perhaps even an accessory to a murder. He may very well be called to testify against the man who is the master of his fate. Now that he has seen firsthand how John's violence can turn lethal, he must be more cautious than ever. Whatever else he does as he takes in the city's sights, Swindel needs to gather his thoughts carefully.

TULIPS BLOOM IN ABUNDANCE outside the summerhouse that stands in the midst of the orchards and gardens of the Shippen mansion on

Second Street in Philadelphia. A procession of imported pinks, carnations, roses, and lilies, flanked by rows of transplanted local wildflowers, will nod to passersby as spring progresses into summer. But William Keith, who has taken up a lease on the house, is not here to see the first flowers of the season. After all the care that John French and James Logan took to manage the Conestoga matter with dispatch, they have returned to the city only to find that William Keith has left for the country.[4]

Logan would like to know exactly where the governor has gone and precisely what he is doing. He sends a note by messenger to alert Keith that he and French have reported back to town, and then he settles in to wait. He and his good friend Isaac Norris pass some time speculating about Keith. Not until the next day, on the morning of Wednesday, March 21, does the governor finally call his council to a meeting. "The Governour having been in the country at the time of the secretary and Colo. French's return from Conestogoe, upon notice of their arrival at Philadelphia came to town last night, and now expressed his satisfaction to see the said gentlemen returned from their Journey," Logan notes dryly in his official notes. He has more to say, but nothing he cares to commit to the council minutes.[5]

WILLIAM KEITH GAZES AROUND at the nine council members who have answered his summons this morning. There are six Quakers packing the bench, compared to three of his Anglican allies. Col. John French, Attorney General Andrew Hamilton, and good old Henry Brooke can probably be counted on to take his part whatever happens. But consider the other side. Secretary Logan is here, of course, flourishing nine large pages of notes set out in his best calligraphy. Joining him is Isaac Norris, who has brought both of his brothers-in-law: Richard Hill and Samuel Preston. Bolstering them are two more wealthy, aging Quaker merchants: Jonathan Dickinson and Thomas Masters, these latter two the owners of two of the city's most celebrated houses. Dickinson's mahogany-filled mansion is matched only by the Masters residence, a stately five-story pile that Logan calls "the most substantial fabric in town," conveniently located right across from the court-house. The two men are not rivals themselves, though, united as they are by the marriage of one of Thomas's sons with one of Jonathan's daughters. Keith's home comforts, borrowed not bought, can't compete with theirs.[6]

These closely connected Quaker grandees seem to think Keith's authority itself is on limited lease from the Penn family. Already, he has had trouble with many of the members of his council who see fit to question his commitment to keeping good order in the colony. Though Keith and his councilors united in creating a stiff new penal code for the colony just four years ago, they brought very different social assumptions with them in crafting the new laws and now have divergent expectations about how to apply them. Dickinson and Masters in particular, along with Hill, have been wielding their rapier pens against him.

These three are members of both the Provincial Council that governs the colony and the city council that administers Philadelphia. Last fall, in their capacity as city council members, they started a protracted paper skirmish with the governor over a drunken prank that they blew up into a major incident. It all started when a young ship master carousing at one of the taverns down on the docks "engaged in a very rude boyish action," as the Quakers described it, "in drawing a seat from under a youth then about to sit down." No sooner did the sailor yank the chair out from under his drinking companion than he was "reproved for the indecency of his action" by another tavern patron who had watched the whole scene unfold. At this rebuke, the sailor took offense and challenged the bystander to a duel. The two men met the next day and fought, each injuring the other. At that point, Keith stepped in to mediate between them. He ended their quarrel, but opted not to punish them for dueling.[7]

Keith has been playing the part of benevolent lord, setting himself up as a leader who can keep the public calm and offer clemency at the same time. As is the case in England, Pennsylvania's new statutes list crimes and chart corresponding sentences. Such justice appears objective, yet actually operates in ways that are highly subjective—because the law allows rulers wide latitude to adjust criminal consequences as they see fit. When a Black man is executed for a property crime, he receives no greater punishment than that decreed on parchment. But when English sailors play with death, Governor Keith can use his discretion to forgive their crime—an act of mercy that amounts to a show of power for him and an offering of racial privilege to them. The governor's legal prerogatives turn supposedly impartial justice into a form of patronage.[8]

Keith's approach follows standard practice among English aristocrats. But Philadelphia magistrates vehemently oppose the way Keith is using the performance of mercy. As men of merchant capital who lack aristocratic authority, members of the local Philadelphia elite wish to see the colony's laws employed for the protection of property and the promotion of security. Keith, a man lacking in fortune but favored with a high social position, is proffering leniency to petty criminals as a means to win the support of the people—and with it an alternate source of power. For that very reason, city leaders have pounced on his decision not to prosecute the dueling sailors and criticized him for trying to curry favor with rowdier elements of the populace.

"Here a penal law of the province was transgressed," charged the statement on the dueling incident that Hill, Dickinson, and Masters personally presented last fall to the governor on behalf of the city's aldermen. "A crime was committed," they insisted, "that the most civilized nations by the severest penalties guard against," and yet, they complained, the governor took no action whatsoever to hold the transgressors "to account for the breach of law." These colonial leaders believe that civilization rests on the invariable, swift, inflexible, and exact exercise of the law. In the absence of the gridiron offered by England's inherited social ranks, the colony's penal code is the only dam they have against a deluge of disorder. If tavern brawls are allowed to develop into duels, all efforts to govern the colony by the rule of law will go down to instant defeat.[9]

Hill, Dickinson, and Masters appealed to the governor to understand the unique dangers created by the colonial context. They explained that however insignificant the drinker's joke and subsequent duel may seem to Keith, in actuality it was a "crime that, in America, ought most carefully to be discouraged, where too many of the youth with as much heat of blood, regulated by as little education, affect the title of gentlemen upon as slender a foundation and in as wrong a manner as in any other part of the world." Fighting a duel has traditionally been regarded as the last resort of men of honor, and even for them such action is to be discouraged. The toleration of dueling among members of the lower orders invites chaos.[10]

Back in Britain, God himself anoints those who wear the crown. Blue-blooded men like William Keith are born with authority coursing through their veins. But everything is different here in the colonies, where no one carries a title and a white man's position is his own to make. The city's leaders are bound together by their friendships with one another and with William Penn, by their mercantile money, and by their tasteful displays of that wealth. They argue that they deserve their elevated social status because of their education and the ability it confers on them to control their emotions. A real gentleman does not grow hot-blooded. He earns the right to exercise power by learning to overpower his own passions, anger above all.[11]

However, having introduced the very penal code that these elite Quaker men are so keen to impose, Keith saw no need to listen to their lecture about the best way to deal with a drunken sailor. "I am, more immediately than any other magistrate, accountable to the king for the due preservation of his Majesty's peace in the colony," he reminded them. Quite simply, Keith is closest to the throne and bears the highest responsibility for maintaining the rule of law.[12]

Keith parried their criticism and lanced their dignity. "I must entreat you," he told them, "be so wise as to caution yourselves against such turbulent and ill minded spirits who . . . under a conceited independency dare to presume to oppose his Majesty's royal authority." Without quite calling the aldermen conceited and turbulent directly, he reminded them to beware of anyone who did display such "ill minded spirits." Keith left the aldermen sputtering that they were surprised to see him "deliver a speech to the corporation"—that is, to the city's governing council—"in so singular & unusual a manner." They responded, "We must acknowledge our surprise at the caution given us against 'such turbulent and ill minded spirits.' " However venerable these provincial leaders wish to appear, their grasp on status is vulnerable. Their local prominence stems from their riches and from their restraint of their negative emotions. Keith hit where it hurt when he warned them that antagonizing him amounted to trivializing themselves. Stinging from Keith's dismissal, they did their best to retreat to the high ground of legal theory, reminding Keith that "both the prerogative of the crown and the privileges of the people are, by the excellent and justly admired Constitution of England, secured by laws and known rules." In other words, Keith is not a law unto himself.[13]

As Keith and the Quakers on his council eye one another in the courthouse this morning, they all remain on high alert—for breaches of law, for breaks with deference. Logan plunges into a recital that will take him hours to complete. He delivers a copy of his report in writing, then proceeds to read the entire thing aloud for the consideration of the council. These literate men still live in an oral culture, and they would rather listen together to Logan's tale—adding in a comment here and a query there—than silently read it alone.[14]

Logan goes over everything that has occurred in the last two weeks, from his and French's arrival in Chester to their journey to Conestoga, their trouble finding a translator, the ceremonies they performed, the inquiry they conducted, the testimony they recorded, the negotiations they engaged in to find an emissary willing to travel to the Five Nations on their behalf, and their departure amidst the tears of Elizabeth Cartlidge. At last Logan concludes by telling the board that "we have brought John Cartlidge and Edmund Cartlidge prisoners to town, together with the lad Jonathan who was present at the fact, and have committed them to the custody of the High Sheriff of Philadelphia, where they now are." Narrations this long lead to sore backs and stiff legs, but the members of the council still need to sit tight.[15]

Despite the many facts spread before them, the governor and his council members are not sure what to think. Logan betrays his own fatigue by closely restating the last lines of his written comments. "The said Commissioners further reported," Logan records his own words while referring to himself in the third person, "that they had caused John and Edmund Cartlidge to be brought to Philadelphia, where they now remain in the sheriff's custody, by virtue of their warrant for suspicion in the killing of the Indian mentioned in this report." Just so. But what does this mean?[16]

"In our humble opinion," Logan clarifies, this is "the highest Cause of Commitment that the evidence taken . . . would admit of." He is treading as carefully as he can now. Arresting the Cartlidges for involvement in a suspicious death falls far short of a formal accusation of murder. But he and French have failed to obtain the evidence needed to support the higher charge. They have not verified the death by viewing Sawantaeny's remains.[17]

Here is a hint that the Quakers—though determined to stick closely to procedure—are searching for a way to mitigate the Cartlidges' crimes without resorting to anything so autocratic as a lordly pardon. John and Edmund Cartlidge are not ordinary colonists. They are sons of one of the colony's earliest settlers, connected to the colony's most prominent Quaker families, and regarded as useful men in their station. They deserve a measure of justice to be sure, but perhaps not a fatal dose. Though no one collects formal statistics on the social standing of accused criminals, purported victims, and the men who sit in judgment on them, everyone in Chester County recognizes that crimes committed by members of the lower sort against the so-called better sort are by far the most likely to come to court. The social inversion created by a case like this—when a man of the law has broken the law—is something many leading men would prefer to remove from the public eye as quickly as possible.[18]

"The Body of the Indian supposed to be killed had been buried about six weeks before" their arrival at Conestoga, Logan defends his and French's conduct to the council. They could hardly have found it "in a solitary uninhabited wilderness, three Days Journey from thence." He asks them to imagine the trek he and French would have had to undertake, liable to lose their way, maybe even their lives, deep in the woods. "It was not only out of time to have a satisfactory view taken of the same," Logan tells them, "but also it was impractical." If an Indian falls in a forest but no colonist is there to see it, can a death be said to have occurred?[19]

There is more. Logan objects as well that "it was impractical from them to get such a number of Christians to undertake that journey as would constitute a legal Jury." Here is a key point. Far from maintaining William Penn's promise that if a crime is committed by a colonist against an Indian, the matter will be judged "by an equal number of just men on both sides," Logan insists that only Christians can decide legal matters involving colonists. In this, at least, he marches in perfect time with William Keith.[20]

When Keith introduced the new penal code of 1718 with instructions to the colony's justices of the peace, he declared in a speech that he then published as a printed pamphlet that "the Law will not permit that any *Christian* shall incur the Penalty of his Life, except upon the full and plain Testimony of Men openly professing their Belief of the same Faith in our Blessed Saviour Christ." Keith offered common Christian faith as the guarantor of fair jurisprudence; pious people can be relied on never to pervert justice lest they draw divine punishment down on themselves. He did not necessarily impose the policy as a matter of deliberate prejudice against Native peoples. Nevertheless, this insistence on Christianity effectively disqualifies Indians from participating in the adjudication of capital crimes. Christianity tops the list of traits Europeans have begun to use to define themselves as a people apart.[21]

As Logan raises the problems of the impossibility of finding the body and the impracticality of seating a Christian jury, tensions lower all around the room. "Hereupon it was the unanimous Opinion of the Board," Logan congratulates himself, "that the commissioners had faithfully and diligently executed the trust reposed in them." None of these men wants to see the Cartlidges executed for killing an Indian; yet at the same time they cannot be seen to be undermining the rule of law that they themselves insist upon. So they fall back on "reasoning upon the most legal as well as prudential methods, that in this uncommon and extraordinary Case could be taken for a more clear Discovery of the Truth in order to bring the offenders to Justice." Having claimed that civility is brittle enough to break over a tavern tussle, they cannot treat the Cartlidges' crimes as less than earth-shattering. They settle on the useful device of pairing official statements of severity with protracted bureaucratic delays.[22]

In spite of the extensive evidence already in hand—Logan's lengthy official report, along with various sworn statements and official depositions—the members of the council ask for more. They call in David Evans, the deputy sheriff, and order him: "Keep the said prisoners, John and Edmund Cartlidge, in safe custody, by virtue of the commissioners' warrant whereby they stand already committed." Jail remains the most secure place for the Cartlidges, their incarceration the safest course for the colony. Meanwhile, the council has a new order for the sheriff: "Produce Jonathan Swindel, John Cartlidge's servant, before this Board tomorrow at three in the afternoon," they tell him. The commissioners want to hear from an eyewitness of colonial origin. They have heard much from the Native peoples of many nations who gave evidence at Conestoga. They have had secondhand accounts from a number of interested settlers reporting on rumors or commenting on actions the Cartlidges took after the fact. But they have yet to hear a description of events from an English colonist actually present at the attack. For that, they need Jonathan Swindel.[23]

SHORTLY BEFORE THREE P.M. on Thursday, March 22, the city sheriff marches Jonathan Swindel past the Philadelphia town clock and into his audience with the governor and his council. The great timepiece invites the wonder of all who pass beneath it. Peter Stretch, the city's first official clock master, keeps its marvelous brass mechanisms in good working condition. Wealthy men consider the town clock to be an instrument of discipline, its mechanical hands urging working folk to order their lives with precision. But they rely on it far less themselves, since in addition to carrying pocket watches, they can commission Stretch to build them smaller-scale clocks for use in their homes. For his genteel customers, Stretch supplies tall clocks in cases made of every wood from pine to oak to walnut and mahogany, the faces and movements fashioned from combinations of iron, steel, brass, bronze, and sometimes silver. Stretch can add detail to dial, tympanum, or frieze: cast-metal cherubs blushing under their curls or winged death heads flying in the fretwork. Tempus fugit. All the same, colonists of every rank admire the town clock as evidence of the city's civility. It serves as a free gift to the public, allowing poor lads like Jonathan Swindel their own chance to mark the time.[24]

Governor Keith admits Swindel to the council chamber with due pomp, requiring him to swear "upon ye holy Evangelists of Almighty God" before his testimony can be heard. His Christian bona fides established, Swindel launches into his account. Once again, the council members hear of the rum and the furs, the gun and the blows. Swindel does add in a few key new details.[25]

"Cartlidge dealt with the Indian for a quantity of skins, about 50," he says he "supposes." Until today, council members had no sense of the scale of the Cartlidges' transaction with Sawantaeny. They now know how unlikely it is that the Cartlidges could possibly have soaked Sawantaeny with enough liquor overnight to make for a fair trade for fifty skins.[26]

All eyes are on Swindel. Such intense official scrutiny would be enough to make anyone feel prickly, even if not wearing osnaburg. Swindel tries to think. None of the men gathered before him seem terribly impressed by what he has to tell them. He dredges his memory for something of value and hits on the question of clothing. After John Cartlidge first pushed Sawantaeny to the ground, and just before the Indian ran to his cabin to get his gun, Swindel says he saw Sawantaeny "hastily casting his blanket from about his shoulders." This detail offers an interesting inversion of the evidence of three different Native witnesses, each examined separately by Logan and French. A Ganawese witness said that he "saw John Cartlidge stripping off his clothes near the fire." A Shawnee man said that "John Cartlidge being at the Fire there stripped off his Clothes." And Weenepeeweytah, Sawantaeny's wife, stated "that John Cartlidge stript off his Clothes." None of the Indian descriptions of the fight mentioned the hunter removing his clothing, only that John disrobed.[27]

In the sometimes wordless communications of colonial encounters, nothing signals an intent to do bodily harm like stripping off one's clothes—the better to avoid damage to one of the most valuable material possessions most people own. At this very moment, somewhere outside the courthouse windows, a runaway named John Lee is skulking around the city wearing many layers of stolen clothing over his servant's-issue osnaburg shirt. Lee sports three different jackets at once: a camblet coat, on top of a dark drugget with a red lining, over a striped Holland lined with checked linen, all over his original osnaburg. For boys like this runaway, three extra layers of clothing mean at least three opportunities to strike a valuable bargain. Swindel would be only too happy to escape likewise. But here inside the courthouse, he can't evade the supervision of the sheriff. And he knows he has only this one chance to say something, anything, that may win favor from and for his master. He forces himself to continue.[28]

If, as Swindel is now claiming, Sawantaeny undressed first, this would imply that the Cartlidges' later violence came in self-defense in response to his symbolic threats. Swindel rushes to offer the governor and council more details that might support this version of events. He turns to describing the Indian's gun. "Powder fell out of ye pan of ye gun," he tells them. In case they don't understand the significance of this, he adds that he "believed the gun was loaded." If this is true, it adds to the possibility that the Cartlidges can claim to have acted to protect their own lives. No one else has mentioned anything about whether the gun was loaded until now.[29]

An official is writing down everything Swindel says, elegant streams of ink flowing into lines the young man himself cannot begin to decode. This is the first and last time in his life that anyone will bother to preserve his words. Then, suddenly, it is all over and he is dismissed, led out once more by the sheriff. "And further this deponent saith not," the magistrates note.[30]

Logan takes little interest in Swindel's testimony. No sooner has the servant been sent out of the chamber than Logan pronounces that "his deposition or evidence not appearing to warrant any higher cause of commitment than what the Commissioners at Conestogoe had already made, viz: the suspicion of killing, it was not thought proper to alter the commitment of the prisoners, but leave them in the hands of the law." The Cartlidges are to be left to languish in prison.[31]

Swindel's testimony amounts to nothing. He has not hurt the Cartlidges' case, nor has he helped it. Although officials transcribe the servant's testimony in detail, Logan leaves these notes on Swindel out of the formal minutes kept for the council. Perhaps the secretary prefers not to take up the implication that the Cartlidges could be innocent by reason of self-defense. Or perhaps he does not wish to record the likelihood that Cartlidge cheated Sawantaeny. Either way, Swindel's evidence will only survive separately, left on loose sheets that could easily be lost to history.[32]

THE AFTERNOON IS WEARING on. Feathered sculls swoop over clock dials, frightening the cherubs. The hours chime. Life is timorous and death ambitious here in the colonies, where any given day may be your last. At the end of every month, the city paper, the *American Weekly Mercury*, tallies how many souls have come and gone over the last thirty days. It lists the births and deaths of European colonists according to religious persuasion: Quakers, Presbyterians, and members of the Church of England. This month, 8 babies were christened for the Church of England and 4 people interred; 6 Presbyterians born and 3 buried; 29 new Quakers welcomed and just 6 bid farewell. You can see the Quakers' prosperity in their low mortality. The paper does not track the births of "Negroes," but does record their deaths and their final resting place in "the Strangers Burying Ground." People of African origin do not count as "Christians," no matter their religious beliefs, and no denomination gives them a Christian burial. Even those who become followers of Christ can't shed the taint of being hereditary heathens, always regarded as less than fully Christian and thus available to be enslaved. The same is true of Indians, though no colonist even tries to keep count of the deaths of indigenous people, unfathomable as they are now that settler colonists' wars and diseases decimate their numbers. Sawantaeny's loss adds nothing to the *Mercury*'s fatality figures for March.[33]

Cramped in their prison confine, the Cartlidge brothers can only wonder how soon they may be added to the paper's death count. With John's servant called to testify today, they know that officials have not dropped the case. John's ceremonial efforts with Indians have in no way aided his legal status with colonists. Already this is his and Edmund's seventh day away from home. Spring is the time for planting seeds, for calving, foaling, and farrowing, not for sitting locked away. A whole year's gains may be lost with one season in jail. John turns now to his knowledge of the law. He is a justice of the peace and he understands his rights. He and Edmund may petition the council to have their confinement ended. They decide to do just that.

SITTING HIGH ON THE second floor of the courthouse as afternoon turns to evening, Keith and his council can gaze through the many large windows into the fading spring light, their view framed by grids of wooden mullions. Just so, they must order the world into quadrants, the high and the low, the pardoned and the condemned.

"There are two vacancies in the standing commission of Oyer and Terminer," the council members remind Governor Keith. *Oyer* and *terminer.* To hear and determine: This is the court charged with adjudicating cases of murder.[34]

"Perhaps the circumstances of this affair might require a special commission," says one of the company. Logan declines to record who makes this ominous point, only that "it was observed."[35]

"Produce a copy of the last Commission of Oyer & Terminer for the Tryal of Capital Crimes and Felonies of Death," Keith orders. Logan complies, fetching the necessary legal papers and reading them aloud. Attorney General Andrew Hamilton gives his opinion that all vacancies on the commission should be filled.[36]

"It would answer this as well as other cases of the like nature," the council agrees.[37]

Another messenger bows his way into the room. The governor and the Church of England men will doff their hats, while the Quakers only stiffly incline their heads. "A Petition from John & Edmd. Cartlidge was presented to the Board, and read," Logan notes.[38]

He reports that the two men declare themselves to be "heartily sorry for the death of the Indian (if he be really dead) on suspicion whereof they now stand committed." No tanner, skiver in hand, could split a hide more finely than these fur traders have shaved their apology. They are sorry. Heartily so. But only if "the Indian"—they do not use their trading partner Sawantaeny's name—"be really dead." If he is, in fact, alive and well, then they have been arrested under false pretenses. Indeed, Logan indicates that the accused hasten to add, "Nor can they believe that what was done on their part by reason of the amazing Surprize they were in can be the occasion of the said Indian's Death." Their assault on Sawantaeny occurred "by surprise" and without premeditation. They do not think they hurt him severely enough to have killed him. The Cartlidges are peeling back the charges against them from every edge, hoping to separate themselves from the crime.[39]

English common law guarantees certain rights to the accused. John knows exactly what they are. He follows up his half apology with a full demand to exercise his legal prerogatives, telling the board that he and Edmund "earnestly pray for a speedy trial (if this board finds a trial necessary) or otherwise that they may be admitted to bail, which they conceive to be a Privilege due to them by the Law of the Land." Even now, John technically *is* the law in Chester County and he is determined to demand his due. The brothers beg no one's pardon as they seek to exonerate themselves.[40]

"After some reasoning upon the subject of this petition," Logan reports, "the Question was put, Whether the Petitioners ought to be admitted to Bail or not?" The chamber fills again with the rustle of paper and the quelling of coughs. Here is yet another moment of decision. But first the council members have a vote to take.[41]

"It carried in the affirmative," Logan reports. The two prisoners are to be summoned to appear publicly before the governor and his council on Saturday, there to post bail before being set free to await a possible trial.[42]

Before that can happen, though, they decide they must strip John of his title. They can hardly impress the public with the strength of law if the law arrives at court in irons. "It was moved," Logan notes, "that John Cartlidge's name be struck out of the commission of Justice of the Peace for Chester County." Divided as the governor and his council may be, this much they can unite on. The proposal, Logan says, was "readily agreed by the Governor." The council members may secretly be prepared to forgive the Cartlidges for a possible killing, but they can't ignore the clear and present threat John poses to the public peace.[43]

SEATED AT HIS TABLE, William Keith warms the bottom of a stick of vermilion sealing wax. He feels the heat but will take care not to burn his fingers. In a quiet room, a dollop of wax makes a soft splotch as it hits paper, round and red as a drop of blood. Keith lets the wax cool a moment from liquid to paste, then presses smartly with his seal to emboss the wax with an intricate pattern of scrolls. Surveyor Isaac Taylor will recognize this as the governor's own authentic design.[44]

It has been two days since John and Edmund posted bail at an official public hearing in the courthouse square. Each man has had to put up £500, supplied by wealthy city dwellers with the money to act as surety. Keith has personally sworn John to return to appear before the council again on April 20, "there to make answer to such matters as on his Majesty's behalf shall be objected against him concerning the Death of Sawanteenee." In the meantime, Keith has instructed him not to travel over the Susquehanna to trade.[45]

Now Keith can turn back to his other concerns, most especially to investigating certain intriguing land prospects. He has gotten wind of John Cartlidge's mining scheme and he is very definitely interested in learning more. Rather inconveniently, Logan and French made it back to Philadelphia before Keith himself returned from his scouting expedition. The secretary registered his annoyance by remarking upon the governor's absence in the colony's official records. But, no matter. Logan cannot know just where the governor has been, nor with whom he has been speaking. He will not know that Keith is now asking Isaac Taylor to act on his behalf.

A gentleman correspondent likes to keep a variety of stationery supplies easy to hand. He may have paper by the ream or quire, parchment, blank books for accounts and copybooks for letters, ink powder, quills, pens, inkhorns and penknives, sealing wax and wafers. Such are the tools of the trade of a man of letters.[46]

"Sir," Keith addresses Taylor in his long, lean, steeply slanted script, "things being now ripe for the affair we talked of, I entreat that upon receipt of this, you will take ye horse and come up to me." Keith is too clever to put down in writing just what he wants to finish discussing with Taylor. Even a letter neatly sealed can be broken open by prying fingers. And after all, he has no need to repeat himself. The surveyor can hardly have forgotten their conversation of just a few days ago. "There is need for dispatch," Keith clarifies, in case his haste is not already clear. "This will very much oblige," he promises.[47]

John Cartlidge's violence may have antagonized Indians to the point of imperiling the governor's plans for land acquisition. On the other hand, the intelligence John has gathered from Native informants about the possibilities of metal ore, located on lands only nominally owned by the proprietary family, may more than make up for his violent missteps. Much will now depend on how quickly Surveyor Taylor can saddle up his horse and stake land claims for Keith and Cartlidge. And of course it will be crucial to keep the Quakers in the dark. Keith snuffs out his candle and greets the night.

Chapter 12

ISAAC NORRIS

ISAAC NORRIS IS DREAMING OF LANDSCAPES—NOT OF THE fields and fences surrounding his Pennsylvania plantation, an estate he calls Fairhill, nor of the woods and mountainsides that rise to the west, but rather of the verdant English countryside. It is the second week of April and his son and namesake, Isaac Norris Jr., twenty-one years old this year, is just setting sail on a trip to England. Now that he has come of age, Norris Jr. plans to try his hand as an Atlantic merchant for the first time. While he is at it, his father is entrusting him with another important task: paying calls on his English contacts, discreetly delivering letters that contain exact information on the recent murder crisis in the colony. So long as Norris Jr. is there, his father also asks him to take the opportunity to purchase household items for the family, the sorts of genteel decorative goods that distinguish a colonial gentleman. In particular, Norris Sr. wants his son to see about acquiring a nice set of paintings. He is hoping for "a Good Landscape or Two, ye prospect Geometrically Extended—Well and beautifully shaded." Nothing symbolizes English civilization like a lovely landscape executed in oils.[1]

To correspondents in London, Norris Sr. describes himself and his Philadelphia friends as "we Indians, plain simple fellows of America." His protestations belie his ambitions. Norris Sr. has every confidence that he can leverage the profits of the Americas into a lifestyle comparable to that of an English lord. Only the actual Indigenous peoples of America stand in the way of his establishing a new lineage of landed heirs. Until now, William Penn's policies of peace have allowed settlers

*This drawing of Isaac Norris's country seat, built in 1717, gives some idea
of the grandeur in which he lives. Here the large central house is shown with
projecting side wings, flanked by smaller dependent buildings that help to
exaggerate the size of the main structure. Surrounded by symmetrical gardens,
the house is approached via a central promenade lined with fruit trees that
makes for a grand entrance as a visitor prepares to mount the broad steps up to
the elevated front door. All is designed to display Norris's claims to mastery.*

to smoothly convert Native lands into colonial property titles. But the
Cartlidge mess has imperiled this process for everyone.[2]

Members of the proprietary family will want to know whom to
blame for the debacle on the Susquehanna. Norris Sr. and James Logan
have been engaging in close conversation about the case for weeks now,
deciding how best to inform the Penns about the deadly crime. More
particularly, they have been strategizing about how to undermine the
governor's standing with the Penn family. Penn's widow, Hannah, was
his second wife and does not share his Quaker faith; she and her children selected William Keith to be the colony's new governor in part
because he, like they, is not Quaker. For Logan and Norris Sr. it is bad

enough that just four years after William Penn's passing, his pacifist vision for the colony has been threatened by violence. That the crime should be committed by a colonist, and by a Quaker justice of the peace at that, calls into question their management capabilities. On the other hand, Norris Sr. and Logan know enough about William Keith's own aspirations to guess that, in a pinch, he will always put himself before the proprietary family. This knowledge may prove essential now.

Norris Sr. and Logan have settled on a two-pronged strategy. Logan, who is an official executor of William Penn's estate as well as the colony's provincial secretary, will write directly to Widow Hannah Penn. He will not put before her eyes all the sordid details of the Cartlidge case, but he will allude to his suspicions regarding the recent activities of the governor. Norris Sr., meanwhile, will spill all the details about the grisly attack in a letter of his own to the London merchant Henry Gouldney, one of William Penn's English executors and thus trusted equally by James Logan and Hannah Penn.

"Honoured Mistress," Logan addresses Widow Penn in a letter dated April 12, "the Governor is a very able Gentleman, excellently well qualified for a public post." Best to begin by flattering her discernment in choosing the man who administers her government. But then Logan slides sideways to begin a stealth attack on the governor's character. "His failings," Logan says, "have mostly been to his own loss and of those who have trusted money matters to him." Logan well knows that Hannah Penn is among those who have trusted Keith with financial matters; quietly he is warning her that her trust would be better placed in him. Knowing he will have her attention now, he adds, "But something further has happened within this fortnight in which I am by no means satisfied, viz, his taking up what is reputed to be a copper mine beyond Susquehanna." Now he has come out with it. Keith may think he has put one past Logan, but the secretary has never been bested yet.[3]

Coyly, Logan declines to provide Widow Penn with details about Keith's scheming, referring her instead to a letter written by "Isaac Norris, who has much more leisure than me" to write "an account of all his proceedings that were then known." Likewise, Logan refers only obliquely to the murder investigation, telling her, "I have had my hands full of late." He complains that "this business" (meaning Keith's surreptitious efforts to establish new land claims for himself) "falling out soon after my journey to Conestoga with Colonel French about that of the Cartlidges, related at length by Isaac Norris in his letter to Henry Gouldney, I have been very much straightened." Logan avoids giving possible offense to Widow Penn by discussing the gory details of the investigation into Sawantaeny's killing, but makes it clear where she can direct her inquiries if she wishes to hear more.

NORRIS IS MORE PREOCCUPIED with cares than Logan admits to Widow Penn. He only has extensive time to devote to correspondence because he is laid up with sickness. "Ye gout took me in left foot," he confides in his daybook for April, complaining of "great pain," the foot being "much swelled," leaving him "disabled from walking." Fine dining, hard drinking, and high living have sapped his strength, but they have not stilled his pen. "Thus being confined from other employ-ments by a fit of etc., do I swell my letters," Norris Sr. jokes to Henry Gouldney in the crucial letter referenced by Logan.[4]

But nothing quells Norris for long. There's too much juicy news to share. He does not mention the possible murder case at first. Instead, he starts with other more general news. "Ye people here are bending their thoughts (these poor times) to get suddenly rich," he says. "Mines, ore, gold, silver, copper are full in everybody's mouth." So much salivating over hopes of easy wealth. Norris is not the only man to have his appe-tites awakened by colonial possibilities.

Excited as others may be, however, Norris takes a dim view of the prospect for reasons he is eager to share with Gouldney. "I say, if this should be more than chimerical, I fear it will create as yet more trou-ble." Greedy men inside and outside Pennsylvania will stop at noth-ing to try to make the precious metal theirs. First Norris warns that rumors of the discovery will likely reinvigorate a never-resolved bor-der dispute with Maryland, with each colony seeking to lay claim to as much potential mining territory as possible. "I think ye Proprietor of Maryland is now of age," Norris calculates. He knows full well that

Charles Calvert, the fifth Lord Baltimore, is now the same age as his son, twenty-one years old, and in full control of the Maryland government. If he also knows of Calvert's letter to Keith concerning the Cartlidge murder case, he says nothing on that score.[5]

Yet the killing is the very next topic to which Norris's restless mind turns. "There is a case lately happened which may, 'tis feared, prove dangerous to ye peace of the province," he says. Norris spares no details, giving Gouldney two pages of description of the progress of the Cartlidge case to date, including the inquiry at Conestoga; the Cartlidges' arrest; their release on bail; and the as-yet-unanswered diplomatic message sent to the Five Nations. But he then brings discussion back round to the mines. "The discovery on Susquehannah," he speculates, was "ye inducement to ye Governor to journey thither." Revelation of the mine rumors, he adds, "I presume has been chiefly made to him by this John Cartlidge." The plot twists. Norris and Logan have figured out two crucial things: that John was working on a secret mining scheme with Isaac Taylor before his inconvenient arrest, *and* that John has quietly let the governor in on the secret in the hopes of ingratiating himself with the man whose pardon could save his life. "I hear," Norris tells Gouldney, "that John Cartlidge was taken into ye Governor's company to ye place—whence 'tis feared there is danger of too much easiness in ye case." In other words, Norris warns, Governor Keith may go easy on the Cartlidge prosecution, even extend John an offer of noble mercy, all because the fur trader has bribed him with a hot financial tip. The illegal land grab the two are planning will come at the expense of both the proprietary family's property rights and the rule of law in the colony. "But," Norris sniffs, "I hope better."[6]

⁓

WHILE KEITH AND CARTLIDGE have been angling for mineral riches, Norris has been staking his fortune in more ordinary fashion, spending the last month overseeing spring preparations on the plantation. Weeks have been devoted to the never-ending work of converting forests into fences and land into property.[7]

As Norris elevates his gouty leg and elongates his letters, outside his study window men he holds in slavery strew the ground with new seeds. Cuffee, Dick, and Caesar have finished sowing cover crops and (with the help of several extra hands hired by the day) have moved on to planting oats. Cuffee has been sent out alone with four bushels of oats, some 128 pounds to shoulder. The man's name suggests his long journey to Norris's fields. It derives from an Asante name, Kofi, meaning Friday, a popular man's name among the Akan people of Ghana. In Jamaica, this traditional name has changed subtly from Kofi to Cuffee. Since Isaac Norris came to Philadelphia from Jamaica in 1692, there is every possibility that he forced Cuffee to migrate with him at that time.[8]

Cuffee may have arrived in Philadelphia with little besides his name, but that alone carries a powerful tradition. Across the British Caribbean and American colonies, free and enslaved people alike keep alive an image of the Akan people as formidable warriors who control one of the most powerful armies in their gold-rich region of Africa. A man named Cuffee drew on this military expertise when he led a conspiracy against slavery in Barbados in 1675. That Cuffee was summarily executed before he could realize his vision of freedom, but another man named "Cuffy" led an armed rising of 185 men in Jamaica in 1685.[9]

However much control Norris attempts to exert over the enslaved man called Cuffee who works his land, however much toil he tries to extract, Cuffee manages to sow seeds of defiance where Norris has been hoping to see oats. Norris grouses to his journal that "Cuffee, by blunder, sowed 4 bushels on the east side of ye barn on little more than an acre." Norris can do nothing to recover the seed grain wasted by the man's mistake. He describes it merely as a "blunder," an error due to stupidity. He does not allow himself to consider that the man's action may not have been an accident but an act of everyday resistance against him. Such an admission of vulnerability cannot be tolerated, especially at a moment when Norris's pose of mastery is compromised by physical immobility.[10]

"Knaves and lawless rogues too much increase upon us," Norris tells his correspondent Henry Gouldney, "we shall dress up a man of

rags if he has but impudence enough to attempt mighty things." The
fallen justice of the peace is just one prime example of a larger problem. Unworthy men throughout the colony may try on the clothing
of men of real authority, but they can never match their inner quality.
In a show of reverse snobbery, Norris warns his son to guard against
"ye fluttering, gaudy colors or show which ye empty and weak heads
appear in." Sober clothes signal strong minds.[11]

To prove and improve his own refinement, Norris prefers not to
adorn his body but to furnish his mind, like his house, with English
ornaments. In his letter to Isaac Jr., he instructs his son to buy multiple
copies of "school books for ye boys"—that is, for Isaac Jr.'s younger
brothers. He requests twenty-four different titles, including *Bright-
land's Useful Companion and English Grammar*, Greek grammar books,
a Latin dictionary, and texts by the best-known classical authors: Cato,
Cicero, Virgil, and Horace. "Let all be good editions, well and true
printed & good paper," he says.[12]

Norris likes his books custom bound in supple leather, the front
covers tooled with delicate filigree designs, the spines marked with
short titles embossed in gold. When these books reach Fairhill,
Norris will mark them as his own by pasting inside his personal
bookplate—featuring the Norris family crest. This pacifist Quaker,
this self-described "plain simple fellow of America," claims links to
medieval English heraldry. His shield is divided by a chevron—set
with a star at the apex—with a sable falcon head in each of the three
resulting segments. No Norris of today hunts anything but a fortune.
Still, claiming links to a chivalric past soothes some of the pain of sitting still with a propped-up foot while watching his laborers outside
prepare his plantation for its most productive season. He has not come
to America to live like an Indian, but rather like the English lord he
wishes he were.[13]

He may have to send overseas for his books, but Norris is determined
to master both classical wisdom and modern advances. In one recently
published philosophical volume he keeps with him at Fairhill, Anthony
Ashley Cooper, Earl of Shaftesbury, proposes to analyze the *Characteristicks of Men, Manners, Opinions, Times*. Shaftesbury declares:

they who have no help from learning to observe the wider periods or
revolutions of human kind, the alterations which happen in manners,
and the flux and reflux of politeness, wit, and art; are apt at every turn
to make the present age their standard and imagine nothing barbarous or savage but what is contrary to the manners of their own time.

This is the crux of everything for Norris and his fellow colonial leaders. If they read widely and learn well, they will be able to rise above
the distractions of passing fashions. They will not fall for the comforting fallacy that their current culture has set the standard of civility for
all time. Shaftesbury continues:

> To a just *Naturalist* or *Humanist*, who knows the creature man, and
> judges of his growth and improvement in society, it appears evidently
> that we *British* men were ... barbarous and unciviliz'd in respect of
> the *Romans*.

Shaftesbury is arguing that human accomplishments are ever increasing and that the British, justly proud though they may be of their current achievements, must recognize that their civilization was brought to
them by conquering Romans. If this implies criticism of early Britain,
the thought that the British of today are like the Romans of yesteryear
soothes away the sting. Now the British can congratulate themselves on
being the ones to bring civility to the Native peoples of North America.[14]

Shaftesbury, himself an investor in the colony of Carolina, has a
vested interest in drawing such flattering parallels between ancient
Rome and modern Britain. Norris wants to make Shaftesbury's ideas
his own. Not for him the blundering stupidity he claims to see in
"empty and weak heads" and enslaved men. Norris and his fellow colonists embrace the idea that their arrival in North America replicates
the ancient Roman invasion of England—their thefts of land and labor
actually gifts of superior civilization.

Transforming the American forests, first into Penn's Woods and
then into English gardens, infuses the environment itself with English
ideals. And so Norris wishes most of all for paintings of the English
countryside. "If you should meet with by accident a cheap and good

landscape or two," he tells Isaac Jr. with elaborate casualness, "I did not care if thou bought them for my garden closet, as thou remembers my begun designs on my chimney piece there." His closet is his private study, a place for writing letters, reading books, and contemplating the elaborate formal gardens he cultivates with the help of the same laborers who work the rest of his plantation. He plans to hang his English pictures over his American mantel, visible proof that he is keeping up civilization in the colonies.[15]

The Cartlidge crisis represents an urgent threat to Norris's well-regulated world. As he scrolls out his account to Henry Gouldney, he can't contain his sense of foreboding. "Ye peace of the province" he tells his English correspondent, is "deeply concerned" in the outcome of the case. The situation seems to be spiraling dangerously. The first priority is to satisfy Native people that justice will be done. Next, Pennsylvania's leaders must consider how their management of the colony, and of this case, will be judged by the proprietary family. For the Quaker merchants on the Provincial Council, another key problem remains how to constrain the governor's more grandiose impulses toward setting himself up as the single face of justice. He may well offer to personally pardon the Cartlidges. And yet, not even the Quaker members of the council truly wish to prosecute the Cartlidges to the full extent of the law. They keep turning to the legal technicalities that may leave them room to maneuver.[16]

Norris justifies the council's conduct as best he can in the account he provides to Gouldney. So far, he says, the inquiry has uncovered nothing but "Indian evidence" and, crucially, not "ye body." Council members did try to interview white witnesses, he explains, but there were no reliable men available. The best they could do was interrogate servants and, the Cartlidges' "servants being suspected to favor their masters in ye narrative, murder could not be directly charged upon them, only suspicion then for manslaughter." Such lines could be read as an expression of regret at the weakness of the indictment. Or they could be recognized as a carefully worded excuse for finessing the law ever so slightly in the Cartlidges' favor. After all, Logan himself has so far recommended against bringing murder charges.[17]

Still, Norris does not know how or when the crisis will end. He is counting the days until the Cartlidges, now out on bail, are required to "appear at Philadelphia the 20th instant, about which time, ye messenger from ye Sinekaas is expected to return." On the twentieth instant: On the twentieth day of this very month they will know how the Senecas are reacting to the killing of one of their own by a colonist. For Norris and Logan, everything is on hold until then. Yet Governor Keith, sights set on claiming as many acres of mineral earth as he can, seems determined to wait for no one and nothing.[18]

Chapter 13

HE WILL GO TO LAW

APRIL 4–7, 1722

He will go to law.

—Titan Leeds, Verses for April,
The American Almanack for 1722

D ANCERS BEGIN TO CIRCLE AS DARKNESS FALLS ON CON-
estoga. Taquatarensaly watches and listens as the young men of his
community raise their iron hatchets and lift their voices, urging one
another to action. In the world of Native men, spring and summer
are the time for warfare. Hunting slows for the season as game animals, grown sinewy through the long winter, shed their cold-weather
coats and whelp their young. By autumn, fawns and cubs and kits
will be fat and grown, ready for the chase again. But for today,
Native men are targeting enemies. Word has traveled through the
woods that the leaders of the Five Nations expect their allies on the
Susquehanna to take up arms and prove their loyalty. Taquatarensaly is a war captain. But now he is not certain that fighting beside
the Five Nations is the best course for the peoples of the river valleys. Long after twilight has deepened into night, he is still considering what should be done.[1]

DAYBREAK BRINGS BIRDSONG ALONG with fresh problems and possibilities. English travelers in Pennsylvania report that the countryside
is flocked with birds, "especially upon that Great and Famous River
Suskahanah, which runs right down through the heart of the country."
There, fowlers can find "geese, divers, brands, curlew, eagles and tur-
keys, pheasants, partridges, pigeons, heath-birds, black birds." Tur-
keys make the best eating of all, easily reaching forty or fifty pounds
in weight. But perhaps most intriguing is "that strange and remarkable
Fowl, call'd (in these Parts) the Mocking Bird, that imitates all sorts
of Birds in their various notes." As Taquatarensaly starts his day, still
mulling what may come of last night's ceremonies, the cacophony in
the trees echoes his contending thoughts.[2]

Civility's role as a sort of "fanimingo," one who works to weave
together many peoples, requires him to consider multiple issues when
trying to help plan policy. Whatever actions the people of Conestoga
take will be decided by consensus, with councils of male and female
elders acting as advisers. The question is just what guidance Civility
should contribute. The polyglot peoples of Conestoga, bound together
by common experiences of disease and violent dislocation as well as
by shared social and cultural traditions, maintain flexible alliances
with many polities. Algonquian groups enduring demographic stress,
including Lenapes, Shawnees, and Conoys, live alongside equally vulnerable Iroquoian ones like the Susquehannock; all of these smaller
peoples strive to maintain good relations with the larger and far more
powerful collection of Iroquoian groups formally allied as the Five
Nations of the Haudenosaunee. The protection of the Five Nations has
proven important against enemy rivals, and yet it also brings a burden of responsibility: that the men of the Susquehanna region will
rise up at their bidding. In this situation, the colonists of Pennsylvania, like the settlers of New France, have sometimes provided a useful
counterweight.[3]

From the first moment that William Penn offered friendship to the
peoples of the river valleys, they have carefully preserved records of
their ties to the newcomers. At Conestoga, one highly skilled carver
has taken an antler, cut and split it with a sandstone saw, then carefully
chiseled the resultant slab of calcified bone into an exquisitely delicate

This comb, measuring 4.75 inches high, was found at Conestoga Town during archaeological excavations conducted by the Pennsylvania Historical Commission. It reflects traditional Susquehannock techniques.

ANTLER COMB FROM CONESTOGA TOWN, AUTHOR'S PHOTO
FROM THE METROPOLITAN MUSEUM OF ART.

hair comb. The comb features the full-length figures of two men facing each other: a Native man on one side and a colonist—costumed
in the distinctive Quaker three-cornered hat—on the other. Each
man stands strong inside his own symmetrical rectangular frame, one
hand on his outer hip. Yet each man's inner hand stretches out across
the frame to link with the other's. On the Conestoga comb, Indian
and Englishman join in solidarity even as each retains a separate section of space. They achieve unity *and* keep autonomy. With a decorative accessory like this on his head, a man can never have peace far
from mind.[4]

Before Taquatarensaly can arrive at any decisions about whether
to take up the hatchet on behalf of the Haudenosaunee, his ears pick
up a new sound: pounding hooves vibrating over the ground. A small
group of visitors is arriving on horseback, their flashing buckles and
buttons advertising their city origins. William Keith, baronet, governor of Pennsylvania, sits high in the saddle, riding along with Isaac
Taylor, surveyor general of the province, and none other than John
Cartlidge, stripped of all titles yet out on bail—and back in the good
graces of the governor.[5]

Today is April 5, as the colonists reckon the date, twelve days
since Cartlidge was freed and ten since the governor wrote to Taylor
to demand his assistance with a certain "affair." The three wasted no
time heading north up the Susquehanna to the very spot of ground
where Cartlidge identified potential ore deposits. Taylor went to work
measuring and marking the land and now Keith has come to test the
reaction of the people of Conestoga to his sudden incursion into their
neighborhood.[6]

As the men greet one another, Keith continues his comfortable calculations about the land he has just claimed. But his happy expectations are interrupted by some most unwelcome news. As he will later
recount, "I was certainly informed that the Young Men of that Town
had made a famous War Dance the night before and were preparing
immediately to go out to War." Keith's worst fears about the possible impact of the Cartlidges' murderous actions now seem about to
be realized. "I thought it absolutely necessary," Keith explains later to
officials in Philadelphia, "to hold a Council with the Indians in Cap-

tain Civility's cabin next morning." Keith intended only to pay a quick visit to Conestoga, stopping just long enough to make casual mention of his doings. He has been hoping that a cursory reference to his land grab will be enough to prove that he has given Natives legal notice of his actions—without drawing enough scrutiny to generate objections. But now he must hold a formal council, broaching again the dangerous topic of Sawantaeny's death—this time with a direct threat of war hanging over the proceedings.[7]

SLOWLY BUT SURELY, INDIANS are drawing colonists deeper into the woods. After two conferences held at John Cartlidge's cabin this spring, the first called by Cartlidge himself and the second convened by James Logan and John French, Anglo-Pennsylvanians are now meeting Indians to formally discuss Sawantaeny's death yet again—this time at a site controlled by a Native leader. Keith evidentially deems Cartlidge's house an unsuitable location for a meeting, now that the man has been formally arrested in connection with a suspicious death. Yet the change of venue also marks an achievement for the Indians. According to Native protocols, the host of any gathering enjoys the higher status. Whereas Keith has come in pomp to purloin property, Taquatarensaly receives him as a supplicant.

As a small company of Native leaders files into Taquatarensaly's cabin to meet with Keith on the morning of April 6, the governor gathers his thoughts; Indian war dances, like Indian guns, have a way of focusing the mind. He has spent the last day preparing his remarks carefully and has enlisted translators to interpret "from the English into the Delaware Tongue" and "from that into the Mingo and Shawanois Language." There are no Lenapes or Delawares present at this meeting; the Native leaders in attendance include "the Chiefs of the Mingoes, the Shawanoise & the Ganway Indians"—that is, the Susquehannocks, the Shawnees, and the Conoys. But since John Cartlidge is the only English colonist present with knowledge of a Native language, and since Delaware is the only Native language he knows, Delaware is to be the first step in a long game of linguistic hopscotch.

Keith does enlist a German colonist along with a Native man he refers to as "Ganaway Tom" to cross-check Cartlidge's interpretations. But he does not try to make do without Cartlidge. He has more faith in an Englishman accused of murder than in an innocent German or Indian. Of course, Keith cannot know, much less control, how "Captain Civility" and "Ganaway Tom" will translate from Lenape to "the Mingoe and Shawanois Languages" respectively. Still, he is determined to make the best of it.[8]

"Friends and Brothers," Keith begins addressing the group in affectionate terms, "I hope you have not forgot the treaty which I made last summer with the Five Nations in your hearing & presence at this place." Best to remind everyone that he, Keith, has his own relations with the Five Nations. But he then offers his listeners pride of place. "I then talked to them as our very good friends and allies," Keith says. "But when I speak to you, I think I speak to my own flesh and blood." Here, at last, are sentiments that at least approach the kind of declaration that Taquatarensaly has long been waiting to hear: English colonists and the people of Conestoga are so closely united as to comprise a single family, perhaps even a single body.[9]

Flesh and blood. Of a scant one hundred words and phrases ever translated from Susquehannock into English and recorded in a pocket glossary for the use of colonial traders, one of those words is flesh: *orocguae*. For that one moment, the governor's attitude seems to accord closely with that of the Indians.[10]

But as Keith continues, he makes it clear that he has a very particular type of flesh-and-blood relationship in mind: "I expect," he tells them, that you will "look upon me even as a child would respect and obey the words of a tender father." There it is. Keith wants to position the Indian leaders in front of him as his subordinates. He takes for granted that they will accept this role. Fathers rule in Keith's world, and he would have it no other way. The governor's view that the authority of the state grows naturally from the absolute law of fathers over sons is already over twenty years out of date in England. John Locke has long since dismantled Sir Robert Filmer's praise of *Patriarchia* point by point. But Keith has every reason to cling to Filmer's ideas; his own position as baronet is one he enjoys by virtue of the simple accident of being his father's firstborn son. Meanwhile, he is centuries ahead of his time in applying literal patriarchy to relations between Europeans and Natives. Long after Britain has ceded North America to an (as-yet-unimaginable) nation called the United States, whites will continue to set themselves up as fathers to Indians, taking their land while claiming merely to be managing their minors' property.[11]

Keith suffers not a pang of doubt about his right to mastery. And so he can afford to adopt an ingratiating tone with the Indians he has called to assembly. He decides to draw on Indian use of emotion in oratory: "Consider then, my Children," he adds, "how I have expressed my love to you in all the councils we have held together." Love between rulers and the ruled is not an unknown concept in English governance. Just last fall, Governor Keith boasted to the members of the Pennsylvania Assembly, "I meet with such hearty welcome and kind entertainment wheresoever I happen to go in the country that I think I may depend on the love and affections of the people." Yet that mention of the love of the people is the only officially recorded reference Keith ever makes to such an emotional link between himself and Euro-Pennsylvanians in eight years of rule in the colony. By contrast, he celebrates "love" between Indians and colonists some three dozen times in the same period. Indians rely on emotional exchanges to foster voluntary bonds, whereas the English only bother to invoke emotion when they want to cloak the imposition of power. The British king whose might backs Keith's authority over Indians is too far distant to be of any practical assistance, and he has behind him only a paper army of Quaker pacifists. Since he can't easily threaten Indians with force, his best strategy is to sway them with sentiment. Keith may not know a word of any Native language, but he is still doing his best to talk like an Indian.[12]

≈

OUTSIDE CIVILITY'S CABIN, WOMEN hoe the black April earth into mounds around the houses. Iron hoes scrape over sedimentary rocks—limestone, sandstone, shale—setting a Native rhythm of renewal. Whereas the English view farming as a man's occupation,

Native peoples across the Americas rely on women as crop producers. Into each small hillock, women and girls place several grains of
seed corn. They will need only to step into their dooryards to weed
their plants or chase away squawking birds and marauding colonial
livestock. In the next few weeks, they will do a second sowing of bean
and squash seeds, so that the vining plants can stake themselves on the
growing cornstalks and all can prosper together. Even as Taquatarensaly listens and waits his turn to speak, his female kin and neighbors
work the soil, willing seedlings to spring from the dirt.[13]

Keith is still only warming up. "Remember," he asks, "the message
I have sent to neighboring governments in your behalf?" Here he is
referring to efforts he made last summer, following the meeting with
the Five Nations held at Conestoga, to help establish bilateral relations
with the colonies of Maryland and Virginia. "Remember also," he continues, "how at your request I removed one John Grist from a settlement which he had made on the other side Susquehanna because you
complained he disturbed you?" Keith has not chosen this example of his
"paternal" care for his Native "children" at random. On the contrary,
Grist is the man whose home John Cartlidge threatened, on Keith's
orders, to set ablaze unless he stopped squatting on Indian lands. By
bringing up this episode now, Keith reminds the people of Conestoga
of both his own previous efforts to protect them and of Cartlidge's role
in interceding for the community. Could men who proved themselves
so careful of Native land rights just last summer pose any threat to
them this spring?[14]

"Consider likewise," Keith persists, "with what expedition I lately
sent up two Counselors, James Logan and Colonel French, to inquire
after the report that was spread of an Indian's being killed in the
woods?" What effort must it take for John Cartlidge to translate these
words impassively, as if he, too, were simply the recipient of unsubstantiated reports of a murky episode concerning an unknown man.
"A message was immediately dispatched to the Sinnekaes," Keith tells
them, heedless of the fact that Taquatarensaly himself closely consulted
on the content of that communication. "And the parties suspected were
in the meantime carried Prisoners to Philadelphia where they were
bound in great sums of money to appear." An echo of jangling chains

rattles the woods with these words. Yet Keith proceeds quite as if the "prisoner" in question were not standing free before them all, translating his words.[15]

"They are to be tried by the English laws so soon as the messenger from the Sinnakaes returns, or any other proof can be had that the Indian is dead or was actually killed by them." Keith believes so strongly in the gift he is giving the Indians in granting them the privileges of English law, that he never considers how the assembled Shawnee leaders may react to the casual implication that the eyewitness testimony of Sawantaeny's wife, a member of their nation, as well as that of three Native men, two Shawnee and one Conoy, fails to meet English standards of proof. Still, the surest way to keep the Cartlidges alive may be to continue to cast doubt on the reality of Sawantaeny's death.[16]

TRIED BY THE ENGLISH LAWS. Keith himself defined what this should mean when he introduced a reformed penal code into the colony in 1718: "Be it enacted by William Keith, Esquire, by and with the King's royal approbation," his proclamation began, that "petty treason, misprisions of treason, murder, manslaughter, homicides, and all other such crimes and misprisions . . . shall be made capital or felonies of death." By this definition, either murder or manslaughter may merit execution. Council members have been working to frame the attack as a case of manslaughter, but, by the terms of the 1718 penal code, either crime can constitute a felony. True, even a felony charge does not necessitate death; the code specifies that "challenges are allowed" and that defendants may have the ancient English right to "benefit of clergy," whereby a penalty can be reduced for a first-time offense. Still, the Cartlidges don't yet know precisely how they will be charged, much less how those charges will be handled.[17]

The literal meaning of "felony" in old English was "anger," a connotation that still shadows the legal classification of violent misdeeds. Determining whether a man acted in malice when he took the life of another remains key to defining the legal charges against a killer. In other words, Pennsylvanians mean more than they say when they claim that Sawantaeny and not John was angry. According to a popular English legal treatise, *Conductor Generalis, . . . Collected Out of All the books Hitherto Written . . . on Common or Statute-law*—a conduct guide for officers of the law first printed in London in 1674 that will just happen to appear in Pennsylvania this year—anger plays an important part in mitigating accountability for crimes. According to that manual, "if angry words pass between two Persons, and then one pulls the other by the Nose or fillips him with his Finger, and the Person thus assaulted kills the other with a Sword, this is but Manslaughter because the Peace was broken by the Deceased." By the traditions of English law, if the hunter's anger can be proven, the trader's guilt can be reduced.[18]

When John Cartlidge and Taquatarensaly met together in conference in early March, weeks before any Philadelphia official had yet gotten news of the fight, they reportedly discussed the altercation in just these sorts of terms. According to George Rescarrick and Richard Saltar Jr., the young gentlemen slaveholders from New Jersey who traveled from Conestoga to Philadelphia to testify on March 10, "the Sd Capt. Sevillity on ye part and behalf of the Indians" took the position that since Natives and colonists had been bound by a "chain of friendship" since the first coming of William Penn:

> that as the S[ai]d Indian had first Attempted to Brake that Chane Soe longe Continued, the S[ai]d Sevility answered for himself and the Indians, That he looked upon it yt neither the Christians Kill'd him [n]or yt ye Indians Kill'd him, but yt he lookt upon the s[ai]d Indian to be Accessory or Rather had Kill'd and Murthered himself.

Could Captain Civility possibly have invoked an English legal concept such as "accessory"? Perhaps the suspicion that John personally crafted this canny legal argument is what led Logan to redact the Saltar deposition from the official record. Still, this may also be evidence that, in the aftermath of the attack on Sawantaeny, Native people are seeking ways to mitigate the damage. Whether, metaphorically, Sawantaeny broke the chain of friendship or pulled John by the nose, the point is simply that members of the polyglot community at Conestoga, Indigenous peoples and colonists alike, have been hoping from the beginning that closer bilateral relations may grow out of this crisis.[19]

Still, Pennsylvania officials remain unsure how to achieve amity while observing every legal nicety. Keith now leans toward treating Sawantaeny's fate as the case of a missing person. Doing so risks offending Native peoples. However, this way of framing the case could allow him to champion the law and still spare the Cartlidges, all without needing to resort to either a reduced sentence in the event of a manslaughter conviction or, still more controversial, a public pardon in the event of the brothers being found guilty of murder. Not only would Keith's official interference on behalf of the Cartlidges further annoy the members of his council, but it might also call unwelcome attention to the depth and nature of his connections with John.

Keith may appear to be opposing John with his talk of prisoners and trials, but partners always face each other when playing whist. "I have done these things," Keith assures his audience, "to show the English as well as the Indians, That if any one hurts an Indian, He will be tried and punished in the same manner as if he had done it to an English man." The governor shuffles and cuts the deck.[20]

He has finished trying to ingratiate himself. He is done mollifying and apologizing. He needs to stop these people from forming a war party with little but the force of his personality. "I find myself sick and my head aches," Keith says now, "for I hear bad news." No one listening can have any doubt as to what he wishes to discuss.[21]

"Here I make a vow," Keith warns the assembled Indians, "that if any of you shall dare or presume to go out to war at this time, I will immediately cause all trade with you to cease: So that you shall want powder and lead, nay even clothing to cover your nakedness." In theory, colonists ought to be able to prevent Native people from using guns against them simply by controlling Indian access to arms. Yet the reality is far more complicated. Traders and merchants want the furs that can be supplied in much greater numbers by expert Indian gunmen than by old-fashioned archers and trappers. Each British colony contends with the others for favorable trade terms with Native nations; if one colony refuses to supply Indians with arms and ammunition, a rival colony is likely to fill the gap. And then, too, there is the ever-present peril of imperial competition from the French, who are only too willing to provide weapons whenever their English rivals falter. But the threat to cut off Indian access to ammunition and all other trade goods is the only weapon Keith has ready to hand.[22]

"I expect your answer tomorrow morning," Keith proclaims, adding: "Take care how you provoke me to be angry with you for your follies." In the end, his own unwavering conviction of his right to rule may be the strongest card Keith holds.[23]

"IF I TAKE THE wings of morning, and dwell in the uttermost parts of the sea; Even there shall thy hand lead me, and thy right hand shall hold me." John Cartlidge, lukewarm Quaker, may not often appeal to God. But now he has no option left but to hope, as the Bible puts it, that "the darkness and the light are both alike to thee." He has caused a man's death. He has kept his wits. He has offered ceremonial condolences to the Indians whose lives he ruptured with his violent acts. He has cooperated with authority and apologized with alacrity, all while avoiding any outright admission of guilt. He has done what he can to make himself indispensable to the governor, the one man who may, if so inclined, waive legal proceedings against him in a show of noblesse oblige. But now the Native community at Conestoga is threatening war. As dawn breaks, Cartlidge can only wait to see what will fly in on the wings of morning.[24]

Taquatarensaly clutches a piece of dried animal skin as he greets the governor early on April 7. Decades old, the folded parchment offered to Indians long ago by William Penn has begun to stiffen and yellow. Taquatarensaly, a skilled linguist, has not learned the language inked on the scroll in his hands. Still, he has taken care to preserve this token of peace. The peoples of the river valleys intend no direct threat to Pennsylvania; if their war parties do make a sortie it will be in Virginia and not against colonists there but against Native rivals.[25]

English is useful for communicating with colonists, but most of

Taquatarensaly's efforts at advancing civility are aimed at Native men and women, working to align the predominantly Algonquian-speakers of the Delaware valley with the Iroquoian-speakers from the Hudson region to the Ohio valley. While Governor Keith in Pennsylvania, like his fellow governors in Virginia and New York, regards relations between the Five Nations and the English colonies as the single most important diplomatic relationship in the Northeastern woodlands, the peoples of the river valleys consider their complex ties with the Five Nations to be the defining relationship of their world. As a "Mingo"-speaker of an Iroquoian language, Susquehannock, Taquatarensaly has a key role to play. The many small Native polities based in and around Conestoga look to the "Mingos" generally, and to Taquatarensaly particularly, to mediate relations with the Five Nations.

As of today, the Five Nations are not calling for the peoples of Conestoga to go and make war on colonists. To the contrary, they are targeting rival nations based south of the Potomac. Far from simply reacting to Sawantaeny's death—which has only just occurred—the Haudenosaunee are instead responding to a prior tragedy that greatly damaged the ranks of their leadership. Governor Keith has just been boasting of his mission to Virginia last summer to try to strengthen ties between that tidewater colony and the Five Nations. He thinks Taquatarensaly and his people will be ready to congratulate him on his rousing success. He remains oblivious to the fact that Native peoples regard that meeting as a catastrophe. Of the five important Haudenosaunee leaders who journeyed to Virginia last summer, only one came back alive; the other four died under suspicious circumstances.[26]

These gaping losses must be reversed. Last winter, even as John Cartlidge was aiming kicks at Sawantaeny, deputies from the Five Nations were traveling to Albany with a message demanding that the colony of Virginia should "deliver up to them four boys as satisfaction for the loss of their four Great Men." Each missing leader has left behind a hollow that can only be filled by replacing the lost members of the Haudenosaunnee population one for one. According to a March report from the Virginia governor to his council, the representatives of the Five Nations who addressed New York's governor at Albany were "threatening in the case of refusal to revenge themselves on the inhabitants of Virginia." Now in April, already tired of waiting for Virginians to respond, the Five Nations are eager to move forward by sending their allies on the Susquehanna on a captive-taking raid among the Siouan-speaking peoples of the southeast, members of nations with few ties to the north.[27]

Keith and Cartlidge are deeply worried that Sawantaeny's death could touch off a regionwide conflict, but the fact is that his death is only one among countless griefs Native peoples have had to contend with in recent years. And the Five Nations' most urgent concern remains the loss of their own leaders. As Virginia's governor tells his council, the surviving rulers of the Five Nations are convinced that the dead men were all deliberately "poisoned [t]here by Indians tributary to Virginia"—that is, by Siouan-speaking peoples, such as Creeks and Catawbas, over whom the Virginia colony claimed control. It is on this basis that the Haudenosaunee are demanding that Virginia settlers compensate them for their losses. But since the colonists have so far failed to comply, the Five Nations is calling on the peoples of Conestoga to solve the problem by raiding Native enemies to the south.[28]

The Virginians don't share the Indians' belief that the deaths resulted from ingesting lethal substances. They note of the sick Indians that "their distemper appearing to be only a common intermitting fever, no other regard was had here to that Suspicion of theirs." Virginians may discount the poisoning theory and disclaim all responsibility for the leaders' deaths, but that has done little to quiet the drums of Conestoga.[29]

Neither Natives nor colonists understand what causes "intermittent fevers," and each group applies its own explanatory system to confronting the unknown. The English note a seasonal pattern to bouts of "fever and ague," believing that the illness, to which they also fall victim, is caused by hot climates and stagnant air. Indians, for their part, attribute illness to spiritual malice, blaming cases of sickness on dissatisfied gods and the humans and animals who make malign use of cosmological powers. Many Native herbalists have extensive horticultural knowledge, including familiarity with noxious plants, making poisoning a true possibility. But neither Englishmen nor Indians imagine that the noisome mosquitos that buzz about the English slave ships arriving regularly from Africa by way of the Caribbean are to blame for their suffering. Keith is threatening to cut off colonial trade if Taquatarensaly and his neighbors go after war captives; if only Indigenous peoples could instead stop the exchange of disease they would have less reason to go to war in the first place.[30]

AS TAQUATARENSALY CONSIDERS THE options—the obligations of the peoples of Conestoga to the Five Nations versus the perils they will face if they go on a raid for captives, not to mention the complications such actions could create with colonists—he sees this meeting as a useful opportunity. From the first moment that William Penn met with area Natives to assert property rights in their territory, he promised that the colonial presence in the region would offer an important counterweight to the influence of the Five Nations. If Taquatarensaly can remind Keith of these obligations today, the peoples of Conestoga may avoid a risky raiding mission while still receiving the benefits of alliance and trade. The English have many interesting small goods to offer: beads of glass or porcelain or brass, and silver objects from bracelets, pendants, and rings to snuff boxes. Native consumers at Conestoga enjoy selecting from this variety of items as well as the rum, guns, and cloth that make up the bulk of colonists' wares.[31]

With the new day's birds chittering outside his doorway, Taquatarensaly uses the same tactics with William Keith that the governor used with him. He opens this morning's council by addressing the governor in exactly the terms the colonist wishes to hear. He tells him that the peoples of Conestoga "are willing and content to follow his advice. For that they know the Governor to be Absolute Ruler and it becomes them to submit." How easily, it seems, Keith has brought the Indians to heel. Absolutism may be on the wane in England, but Keith appears to be enforcing it here on the Susquehanna. Even better, Taquatarensaly continues by saying that, "these were but young men who desired now to go to war, and since the governor disapproved of it, they would stop them from going out at this time." Taquatarensaly's words are as soft as ermine, as shiny as plate armor. They seem to trumpet the governor's power.[32]

Keith does not pause to consider that mirrors are very common trade items at Conestoga, rectangular glasses fitted into molded wooden frames. Most are quite plain, but they can be elaborately carved. Perhaps he should have. Like a looking glass that reverses the image it appears to reproduce, Taquatarensaly begins to offer just the kind of qualifications, protestations, and emendations to his apparent declaration of submission that the governor engaged in after speaking of the peoples of Conestoga as his own flesh and blood.[33]

"Since they have resolved to stop their young men from going to war," Taquatarensaly says on behalf of the community's leaders, "they desire the Governor would give directions that the Christians in their neighborhood may not beat or ill use their young people." In other words, Taquatarensaly wants the governor to assure a total armistice in the region. If Native young men don't go to war, they also should not be subject to colonial attack. The governor is to forbid the many Pennsylvania colonists who are not Quaker pacifists from assaulting Indians while leaning on the government of Maryland as well. And that is not all; he also wants an explicit assurance from the governor that if the people of Conestoga agree to ignore the urgings of the Five Nations, Keith will honor the promises of William Penn made to act as a regional counterweight to their northern neighbors.

"When the proprietor William Penn came into the country forty years ago," Taquatarensaly tells Keith, "he got some person at New York to purchase the lands on Susquehanna from the Five Nations who pretended a right to them having conquered the people formerly settled there." The Five Nations *pretended* a right to land in Pennsylvania. This key word comes through clearly even in translation. The peoples of the river valleys did not recognize any right on the part of the Five Nations to dispose of their lands. Not only did Native peoples lack traditions of individual land ownership, but they also lacked any conception of war as territorial conquest. Even if the Five Nations had "conquered" the peoples of Conestoga, they had gained thereby

only a right to demand tribute in goods and labor—including, potentially, military service. They had not won the authority to alienate the
property rights of those who claimed the Susquehanna region as their
Native ground.[34]

Yet Penn's pretentions, based in part on those of the Iroquois, had
not led to conflict at Conestoga because he purchased those lands only
to then reconfirm the rights of the peoples of the river valleys. Taquatarensaly recounts that when "the Conestogoes understood he had
bought their land, they were very sorry, upon which William Penn
took the Parchment and laid it down upon the Ground, saying to them
that it should be in common amongst them, viz the English and the
Indians." Taquatarensaly has taken command of their collective imaginations now, asking them to picture the scene of Penn putting down
his parchment as a man might lay down his arms.[35]

"When William Penn had after that manner given them the same
privilege of the land as his own people," Taquatarensaly continues,
"he told them he would not do as the Marylanders did by calling them
children or brothers only. For often parents would be apt to whip their
children too severely and brothers sometimes differ." For all that he
initially seemed to accept Keith's claims to absolute authority, Civility
now explicitly rejects Keith's darling vision of himself as the English
father of Indian children. This, he is claiming, is contrary to the spirit
of Penn's promises to the Native inhabitants of his new colony.[36]

"Neither would he compare the Friendship between him and the
Sasquehanna Indians to a Chain," Taquatarensaly continued, here
claiming that Penn explicitly rejected the symbol of alliance that had
come into common use to describe relations between the English and
the Five Nations at Albany, "for the rain might sometimes rust it; or
a tree fall and break it." In dismissing the defining diplomatic metaphor of the Five Nations as flawed, Taquatarensaly again announced
his own distinct vision of cross-cultural relations. His model relies not
on linking people across great distances, but on melding lives.[37]

Still paraphrasing William Penn, he tells Keith, "He said he should
be esteemed by him and his people as the same flesh and blood with the
Christians, and the same as if one man's body was to be divided in two

parts." Here it is again. Taquatarensaly is insisting that only the concept of shared flesh can capture the right relationship between Natives and newcomers in Pennsylvania.[38]

What does Taquatarensaly mean when he speaks of the "same flesh"? The phrase has strong Christian overtones. The book of Genesis uses the notion of flesh to describe the perfect union of husband and wife, commanding, "therefore shall a man leave his father and his mother, and shall cleave unto his wife: and they shall be one flesh." Taquatarensaly may well be correct in claiming that William Penn used the phrase in speaking with Native peoples. Nevertheless, Penn never wrote the phrase down in any of the tens of thousands of pages of writing he produced in his lifetime, nor did Pennsylvania's rulers, from the governor and his council to city magistrates, ever turn to the phrase. Yet Taquatarensaly uses it regularly, seemingly appropriating this Christian symbol for his own purposes. Significantly, leaders of the Five Nations of the Haudenosaunee have relied on conjugal metaphors, including direct references to sexual intercourse, as a means of describing the basis of their desired alliances with Europeans for nearly a century by this time. Whatever the overlap between Penn's and Civility's thinking, conjugal union as a conceptual model for alliance has a long Iroquois tradition.[39]

In focusing attention on the concept of two people/one flesh, Taquatarensaly communicates clearly that he does not wish to relate to colonists as a putative child, but rather as an effective partner. In turning to a conjugal metaphor for a diplomatic relationship he is exactly paralleling the political philosophy of the great English theorist John Locke. Not only does Locke utterly reject the validity of the hereditary father/son relationship as a model for governance, he promotes instead the marital relationship of husband and wife as a fundamental example of the emerging principles of contract. Just as both parties must agree to a marriage proposal, Locke argues, so government should be by consent. Taquatarensaly may cater to Keith's expectations by addressing him as "Absolute Ruler," but everything he subsequently says reveals the phrase to be empty diplomatic flattery from a skilled negotiator and nuanced thinker.[40]

Taquatarensaly brandishes the parchment he has been holding and dramatically declares it to be the very same one that Penn gave the peoples of Conestoga many years ago. "He presented to the Governor the Parchment in his hand to be read." Once again, Taquatarensaly is mirroring the colonists; where Penn once cast parchment down, he invites Keith to take his parchment up.[41]

He is essentially daring William Keith to deny that he, Taquatarensaly, has accurately represented the terms of Penn's relations with his people. Promising "never to be hasty in going out to war," he explains that the friendship between colonists and Indians requires that when "any accidental difference" occurs, "the party wronged should, as it were, embrace or lay hold of the other's head, endeavoring to put it in a firm and steady posture." If the Cartlidges temporarily went off their heads in attacking Sawantaeny, Native people are prepared to be sure they now have their heads back on straight. But on no account do the Indians of Conestoga wish to see them decapitated by the demands of English justice.[42]

Now Taquatarensaly once again returns to the problem of rum and the traders who offer liquor for the land itself, reminding the governor that Penn promised to stop a practice that led to so many varied losses among Native peoples. "They observe with satisfaction how that the Christians have got money and grown rich by holding lands and selling them to one another," Taquatarensaly observes, adding that "they (viz. the Indians) could live contentedly and also grow rich if it was not for the quantities of rum that is suffered to come amongst them." Keith has followed protocol and listened without interrupting as Taquatarensaly has ranged over a variety of topics. But with the Native man's mention of land he at last sees an opening to broach the subject that brought him to Conestoga in the first place: his hopes to stake a claim to mineral mines.[43]

Keith reports that he "bid Civility ask all the Indians present if they were well pleased to understand that the Governor had taken up a small tract of land so near them on the other side of the Susquehanna River." To the governor's immense satisfaction, he reports "they answered that they liked it rather well." Everything seems to be falling into place exactly as Keith and Cartlidge have hoped. No one at Conestoga is calling for the Cartlidges' heads, and Keith can assure himself that his new land acquisition won't be interpreted as an act of hostile aggression.[44]

—

KEITH TAKES A REST to collect himself. He wishes to make a closing statement to the assembled Indians, one in which he will offer them vague promises of support in return for concrete assurances that they won't go to war and that he is welcome to their land. He wants to get the wording right. By that evening, he has drafted his remarks:

> I will rejoice as often as it is in my power to do you any good. And as you very rightly say that the Christians and the Indians here are but one flesh, it must therefore be true that what is good for the one will also be good for the other. So that when, like wise men, we take time to think, most certainly our councils will ever perfectly agree, and then our thoughts as well as our bodies will still be united together.

What is good for one is good for the other. In his eagerness to end their meeting on amicable terms, Keith nearly chants the nursery rhyme: What is sauce for the goose is sauce for the gander. He is repeating again Taquatarensaly's key phrase: that the colonists and Indians are as "one flesh," nodding toward the idea of a metaphoric marriage between Native peoples and English settlers. Taquatarensaly could be forgiven for thinking he has last extended the principles of civility to the English.[45]

And yet Keith has little intention of honoring the meaning of the Indian words he mouths. Among Native Americans, marriages are not only entered into by choice but also easily exited at will. When a man and woman join in marriage, men move to live with the families of their new wives and women retain their property rights. Marriages may be lifelong, but only if both partners remain satisfied with the union; parting is a simple matter of mutual agreement. Among Indians, both spouses maintain their original clan identity when they enter matrimony, and their union functions as a true partnership.[46]

These are not the terms of English marriages, nor is equality on

Keith's mind as negotiates with the people of Conestoga. In the remainder of his speech, he modifies many of Taquatarensaly's positions even as he mimes agreement with them. He denies that the Five Nations are at odds with Indians to the south, asserting instead that even now the Virginia governor is making arrangements to "send an ambassador very speedily to Albany in order to make peace between the Five Nations and all the Southern Indians on that side of the Great Lakes." He can't deny that Penn promised that he and the people of Conestoga would hold lands in common, but he transforms the meaning of that agreement by saying, "He was so good to tell your people that . . . the lands should still be in common between his people and them but you answered that a very little land would serve you and thereupon you fully confirmed his right by your own consent." Then, for good measure, he adds a complaint that Indians are allowing their dogs to attack colonists' livestock—never mind that these confrontations occur where dogs guard Native crops. Only at the very end does Keith offer any concession to Taquatarensaly, assuring him that given their successful conference, "I shall forget what is past . . . and the trade shall be free and open as formerly." He likewise promises to "endeavor" to prevent "such quantities" of rum from being sold to Indians and offers a "present" of three casks of biscuit "to help your wives and families until the new crop of corn comes in." He makes no detailed promises of security and offers nothing but his goodwill in exchange for his new property. All in all, Keith has gained much and given little.[47]

WHEN KEITH AFFIRMS THAT Indians consented to the land transfers initiated by William Penn, he transforms the symbolic import of the "one flesh" model of cross-cultural relations. To do so he need only to lean on English understandings of marriage. Locke believes, in accordance with the traditions of English common law, that once a woman gives her consent to marriage, she is bound in wedlock and obligated to obey her husband. Likewise, in Locke's model of governance, the new reliance on contract does not eliminate the role of the monarch; it only ensures that the king must consult the people as he governs the realm.

Far from initiating a relationship between equal partners, in Keith's usage, the marriage metaphor only reaffirms the subordinate position of Native peoples, much as English wives must always defer to their husbands.[48]

Colonial Pennsylvanians rarely use the phrase "one flesh" among themselves. But the one example of usage that enters the public record in the first forty years of the colony's existence tells a damning tale. As the *Minutes of the Provincial Council* relate, in 1700, one William Smith was jailed on suspicion of having raped a young woman named Elizabeth Henbury. But Smith and his family, fearing for his fate, successfully pressured Henbury into agreeing to secretly marry her rapist while he remained behind bars. As a result, Smith's father won his son's release from prison on the grounds that "he having clandestinely married the woman in prison he committed the rape on, & as they were now one flesh, she could give no evidence against her husband." Even if Henbury was raped before marriage, testifying to that fact after she and her husband had become "one flesh" would have amounted to a form of self-incrimination. When an Englishwoman becomes one with a man in marriage, she loses her legal personhood and any independent rights. Keith is well aware of this legal precept as he accommodates Taquatarensaly and tells him that "Christians and Indians are but one flesh."[49]

Keith will ride away first thing in the morning, trusting to Cartlidge to follow him back to Philadelphia in time for his looming court date. Once back in council, Keith will have much to discuss with his board. Certain members are unlikely to approve of his proceedings. Cartlidge must still go to law. And of course they have to await the return of the messenger from the Senecas. Yet everything now looks very promising. Keith is ever more confident that he can shape the colony to his will.

By this late in the day, all but one kind of bird has ceased its calling. Only the mockingbird sings at night. It sounds so much like so many others and yet all its noises signify nothing. Those who travel the forests in this region quickly learn to beware its false notes. As one contemporary visitor observes in a memoir of a Pennsylvania journey, "the Mocking Bird is . . . of an odd nature. He is called so for his incessant noise like the barking of a dog, and often occasions the unwary traveler to mistake his way." Chattering, imitating, nattering away, the mockingbird disorients all who harken to it. "I was once lost in the woods by hearing one of them," the memoirist continues, "sometimes it was before me, then behind, that I was five hours before I could find the way home."[50]

Chapter 14

SATCHEECHOE

A S HE WORKS HIS WAY BACK FROM HIS MEETING WITH THE Five Nations, Satcheechoe follows a trail that runs straight and true. Winter gives way to spring as he travels south, leaving April and entering May, the surrounding woods awakening with his every step. He is both departing home and going home. Born into the Cayuga Nation, he has just spent weeks in the river community of his birth and is now trekking once more toward Conestoga, where he has made a new life near the Susquehanna. The colonists who sent him off as their messenger—carrying two stroud coats and three belts of wampum to present to the "King or Chief of the Sinnekaes"—have the fullest hope those items will go far to "cover the dead" and "wipe away tears." But his Cayuga kin, who call the dead man, Sawantaeny, one of their own, have sent Satcheechoe back again burdened with the demand that colonists make better "Satisfaction for the loss of their brother." Steering between the colonists and the Five Nations of the Haudenosaunee, he must walk a careful course. Hugging the low ridges that buckle up along the floor of the region's valleys, he attempts to avoid both the frost-melt mud that mires low-lying areas and the ice patches that still dot the flinty mountainsides.[1]

Native peoples have crosshatched the northeastern woodlands with a convenient variety of these valley-ridge paths, finding the hidden mountain gaps that allow them to set their courses dry, level, and direct. For matters of great urgency, they depend on relay runners to convey messages rapidly across great distances. These paths link

Native communities together for trade and for treaties. If needed, small war parties can travel from Iroquoia in the north to Cherokee country in the south in about five days. In allowing himself eight days to reach the Five Nations from Conestoga, Satcheechoe proposed a comparatively quick pace for himself. His plan for a thirty-day round-trip journey suggests that he meant to spend about two weeks among members of the Five Nations, leaving ample time for both formal ceremonies and informal visits.[2]

Exactly where within Haudenosaunee country Satcheechoe travels is something colonists don't record and likely don't know. Though the Pennsylvania colonists will write on his return that Satcheechoe visited the "river where he was born," watercourses abound in Iroquoia, making this, too, an uncertain reference. If he headed for Cayuga Lake, he would have had to go almost due north, a distance of some 175 miles through mountainous terrain. Alternatively, he might have ranged a far longer distance, as much as 250 miles, skirting northeast along the edge of the Appalachian Mountains until he hit the great artery running between the western Seneca and the eastern Mohawk known as the "Iroquois Trail." Either way, such distances would require him to cover some twenty or thirty miles a day, perhaps an excessive expectation in early spring.[3]

Logan's notes on Satcheechoe's plans say only that he had "hoped to be with the Sinnekaes in Eight Days." His goal was less to arrive at a particular geographic position than to make contact with a specific set of people. Native communities are mobile ones made up of flexible ties between groups, not fixed physical boundaries. Only lived experience and local knowledge can imbue landscapes with meaning, creating a felt sense of place that transcends any empirically measured space. Satcheechoe needed less to journey to any concrete location than to make a key human connection, and in this he has succeeded.[4]

Colonists are waiting urgently for the news he carries now. Regardless of his exact route, having left Conestoga on the seventeenth of March and promised to be gone for thirty days, he has been looked for in Philadelphia since about the seventeenth of April. But he has not arrived as expected. He is still in the midst of his journey as April cedes to May, and so he hurries southward over the greening ground.

SATCHEECHOE MOVES THROUGH A landscape that pulses with meaning, the earth and its animals offering him both practical support and spiritual sustenance. Shouldering his gun as he walks, he scans his surroundings for signs of game. He has insisted on a new firearm as part of the price of this journey, in order to be sure he can provide for and protect himself. While awaiting his safe return, his family back in Conestoga will be living in part on the bushels of corn he negotiated from colonists and hoping he manages to land some game, even this early in the season.[5]

The most common animals of the woods and waters of the Northeast—the bear and the wolf, the deer and the beaver, the eel and the turtle, the duck, the heron, and hawk—do more than simply supply the meat for spits and stewpots, the fur and skins for clothing and shelter, the characters for fireside stories. They lend their names to the family clans that make up each of the Five Nations of the Haudenosaunee and each can share its spiritual power with humans. More than that, the rocks, trees, and even the winds of Iroquoia have divine aid to offer to those who know how to reciprocate with thanks and respect. On streams and rivers throughout the Susquehanna region from which Satcheechoe has traveled and to which he now returns, a keen eye can discern figures and patterns chiseled into the river rocks by Native peoples. Beside and beneath the running waters, circles and lines, human forms and animal shapes adorn the massive stones, marks of deeper understanding etched into the landscape.[6]

Colonists know comparatively little about the ground they have begun to take from beneath the feet of Native people. Try as they may to learn the lay of the land, to create amateur maps using local informants as James Logan does, to collect elegant published editions as Isaac Norris does, or even to commission surveys in the service of land claims as William Keith is doing, they succeed in overcoming their geographic ignorance in only the most limited ways. Whereas other European powers, most notably the Portuguese and the Spanish, developed sophisticated mathematical methods of calculating longitude and latitude based on precise astronomical measurements some two centuries ago, English mapmakers are still relying more on landmarks, qualitative descriptions of major landscape features, than on any precise geometric calculations. In the midst of expanding colonial property claims in North America, this leads to a great deal of confusion and disagreement, not only between colonists and Indians but also between and within colonies themselves.[7]

Another quarter century from now, when Lewis Evans, a London cartographer, makes a map of *Pennsylvania, New-Jersey, New York, and the Three Delaware Counties* he will still know very little of the land Satcheechoe travels now. Ironically, Evans will add a note of thanks to Isaac Norris for allowing him the use of his map collections, "which were of singular service to me, containing variety of draughts not to be met with elsewhere." Yet Lewis can draw little of the terrain west of what he labels the "Endless Mountains" (to be called the Appalachians by later generations). "To fill those parts where our settlements and discoveries have not yet extended to," he apologizes from the empty place on his page, "I have introduced sev[era]l useful remarks." In other words, he fills up the blank space in his knowledge with his own musings on the American landscape.[8]

The English, like Indians, are sure that the Earth carries the marks of the divine. "These mountains," Evans tells map viewers, "furnish endless Funds for Systems and Theories of the World." He is especially keen to seek out evidence of "the Deluge"—that is, the biblical flood of Noah—noting that as far as thirty miles inland from the sea, "vast Beds of Shells of all sorts in Pairs" have been found. For the English as for Indians, the soil itself shelters spiritual revelations.[9]

SATCHEECHOE MAY HAVE LITTLE need of imparting sacred truths to colonists, but he must find a way to impress upon them the importance of Native protocols. The colonists clearly think that sending two of their representatives on the short trip from Philadelphia to Conestoga and then charging a lone Native messenger to deliver remarks of regret to the leaders of the Haudenosaunee demonstrates serious con-

cern for the death of Sawantaeny. But Satcheechoe has been instructed
to explain to them that "two persons were not sufficient to make it up
and answer for the whole country." The Five Nations have faced many
deaths in the last year, as Satcheechoe, Taquatarensaly, and the rest of
the Conestoga community know all too well, and they are determined
to be properly compensated. No one has asked Satcheechoe to demand
an English captive to compensate for losing Sawantaeny, much less
instructed him to threaten war against colonists. But the Five Nations
have charged him to declare that "they are now making war" against
their traditional Southern enemies and that "they may make peace
with those people and so have peace with all the main" only if they
first receive proper attention, in the form of visiting dignitaries laden
with gifts, from Pennsylvania's leaders.[10]

The Haudenosaunee are pursuing a strategy of balance, making
demands for trade and alliance on the governors of the largest English
colonies in their region—New York, Pennsylvania, and Virginia—
while continuing to conduct captive raids on longtime Native antago-
nists to the south. This spring they have set out against a Southern
nation whose name the Pennsylvanians will record as "Cheekaragoes"
when they hear it from Satcheechoe's mouth. This phonetic spelling,
never used before or after, leaves unclear whether the Haudenosaunee
sorties are going against Cherokees (speakers of an Iroquoian language, but not members of the Five Nations) or perhaps against Chickasaws or Choctaws (speakers of Muskogean languages), or then again
perhaps against Creeks or Catawbas (speakers of Siouan languages).
Ultimately, colonists understand the political geography of the Native
world as little as they understand the topography of Native land. Yet
Satcheechoe must find a way to wring diplomatic concessions from
colonial incomprehension. As he works his way back toward Philadelphia, he knows his task will be to make colonists understand something
more about Native ways of assuaging grief and countering death.[11]

The boundary lines that most concern colonists are the ones they
draw themselves. Whatever route Satcheechoe takes as he retraces his
steps through lands already claimed by English settlers, he is liable to
see English symbols carved or burned deep into the trunks of trees.
He may catch sight of a "spruce tree with the letter P at the foot of a

mountain" or a "white oak marked with the letter *P* standing by the Indian path." William Penn began branding the forest with his initials shortly after he started marketing his colony with his family name. The *P* tree brands are described in the first land deed signed between William Penn and the land's original inhabitants, and they mark the moment Pennsylvania's colonists began teaching Indigenous peoples about English ways of life. The *P* stands for Penn, but it might as easily stand for "private property" or for "primer"—that is, for an English schoolchild's alphabet book. Despite all the empty areas on their maps, colonists seldom question the superiority of their knowledge. And most of all, they pride themselves on English law. In one of the "useful remarks" he adds as filler to cover terra incognita, cartographer Lewis Evans informs the viewers of his map that Pennsylvania "is a Country of Liberty & good Laws, where Justice is administered without rigor." As Satcheechoe travels the blank territory of Lewis's parchment, he can only wonder if and how he will ever persuade colonists to meet him on the terrain of Native justice.[12]

Chapter 15

STARK NAUGHT

MAY 4–11, 1722

From little Good to stark naught.

—Titan Leeds, Verses for May,
The American Almanack for 1722

FIRE FLICKERS ON THE WATERS OF THE DELAWARE AND smoke smudges the city as Governor Keith convenes the members of his board. Down south of Dock Street, ships careen beside the river, undersides exposed to the air. Beneath them, shoremen wave burning faggots, passing purifying flames over the ooze of seaweed, mud, and seashells that clings to the vessels' hulls. Then they scrape away the charred remains with brooms and rakes. The tall-mast ships that carry the city's commerce must be breamed like this on a regular basis. But cleaning the ships means clogging the air. Governor Keith and his councilors all concur that the colony itself needs a good breaming. But they have not agreed which bottoms ought to be scorched.[1]

They sit uneasy in their chairs. As the morning's business begins on May 3, the governor has pushed Satcheechoe and his journey to the back of his mind. He and his council are considering new legislative measures to combat crime in the colony. Last week's paper brought news of a sensational murder in neighboring New Castle, Delaware, a Pennsylvania county also under Penn family ownership. A woman there, Eleanor Moore, "received Sentence of Death upon ... being convicted of the Murther of a Bastard Child born of the Body of the said Eleanor Moore." Disorderly women fit the image that leading men maintain of the origins of crime. Having founded the Quaker colony on strictly virtuous principles, they are certain that hordes of lower-class English servants arriving on their shores are the main vector of the moral contamination that creates sin and crime alike.[2]

Already suspected of cultivating popular favor by taking a light attitude toward tavern misdemeanors, Keith is also under scrutiny for his treatment of the Cartlidges, the accused Indian killers. This new case of infanticide cannot simply be allowed to slip past quickly. Keith knows he needs to make a show of severity. This morning in the council meeting, "some Amendments" are "proposed by the Governour, with the Advice of the Council, to the Bill entituled An Act for imposing a Duty on Persons convicted of heinous Crimes, imported into this Province as Servants or otherwise." Leading men believe the colony cannot function without the labor of servants, but allowing the vicious poor into the colony—barnacles on the ship of fortune—carries risks to the wealthy.[3]

Those who lack property are widely believed to lack probity as well. In principle, the governor and his councilors are devoted to the administration of equal justice, but in practice they regard the lower sort of people as especially prone to crime. They think that, if they can bar criminals of the servant class from coming to the colony, they will contain the spread of lawlessness. Council members have not forgotten Keith's jibes about their "conceited independency" and are more determined than ever to ensure that he will set and enforce laws to curb disorder among the lower sort.[4]

While the city buzzes about the Moore case, men of letters are winking at one another about a certain saucy book that has just been published in London called *The Misfortunes of the Famous Moll Flanders*, who "was Twelve Years a Whore, five times a Wife (wherof once to her own Brother) Twelve Years a Thief, eight years a transported felon in Virginia, at last grew rich, lived honest, and died a Penitent." By next week, Andrew Bradford will publish a notice about the *Flanders* book in the *Weekly Mercury* so that every common taverngoer listening as the paper is read aloud will know about the story. The novel, written by the famous Daniel Defoe as a follow-up to his best-selling novel *Robinson Crusoe*, immediately touches a nerve in Philadelphia. The idea that "transported felons" are ruining the English colonies raises sharp concerns for the city's elite and the view that women, as daughters of Eve, are especially prone to sin has survived Quaker efforts to promote spiritual parity between women and men.[5]

IT HAS BEEN TWO weeks since Keith reported back to the board on his actions up the Susquehanna, and nothing has been the same since. Back on April 16, Keith informed the board of his mapmaking expedition near Conestoga, skipping lightly over the news that he had "the Surveyor General of this Province along with me in Company" and that "after a little Consideration, I ordered him to Locate and survey some part of the Right I possessed viz: only five hundred acres upon that Spot on the other Side Sasquehannah." He carefully made no mention of the fact that John Cartlidge had also been with him or of his hopes that the land in question harbored a potential fortune in mineral wealth. These were minor details. After all, what are five hundred acres, more or less, among the sloping hills of rolled banknotes that dot Pennsylvania's terrain? Every man here has come seeking his fortune. And so what if he, the colony's chief magistrate, is consorting with an accused killer, if that man holds knowledge that may provide the key to riches?[6]

Instead, the governor lingered on his own heroic response to being "very much surprised with a certain account that the young men of Conestogoe had made a famous War dance the night before, and that they were all going out to War immediately." Hoping to arrest council members' attention with a story of his firm and capable management of an Indian threat, he proudly produced "the minutes which I carefully took myself of all that passed between me and the Indians." But Secretary Logan never bothered to insert those notes into the official records of the colony. Logan was too incensed by his private knowledge of Keith's other secret dealings to take seriously the supposed gravity of the Indian threat Keith claimed to have contained.[7]

Logan never had any intention of keeping Keith's secrets for him. He informed on the governor in his April 12 letter to his "Honored Mistress," Hannah Penn, saying that he was "by no means satisfied" with the conduct of Governor Keith, "viz. his taking up what is reputed a Copper Mine beyond Susquehannah." Logan recounted to her a direct confrontation he had with Keith upon the latter's return to Philadelphia from his surveying trip, confiding: "I spent some hours with him upon it, sometimes roughly enough and sometimes smoother Upon all which my Opinion is that he resolves as far as possible to have the thing in his own power and then will claim a merit in making terms with you upon shares." Rake firmly in hand, sometimes roughly and sometimes smoothly, Logan labored to loosen every cracked shell and clod of dirt from Keith's keel. Not only has this ambitious newcomer to the colony been plotting to seize a mining fortune that rightfully belongs to the proprietary family, but he has also been audacious enough to plan to offer a portion of his stolen lucre back as a gift. "I have taken so much pains to leave as little of it as may be in his power," Logan assured Hannah Penn, "that he is disobliged with me at present." Yet, somehow, the disobliged governor, his distrustful secretary, and the disgruntled Quakers on his council must continue to conduct the colony's business.[8]

Determined not to be outflanked, Keith immediately launched countercharges against Logan and the council, claiming that Logan and his friends were themselves quietly trying to grab up land. On April 16, "directing his discourse to Richard Hill, Isaac Norris, and James Logan, Proprietary Agents" as Logan described it in the minutes, Keith "complained that James Steel," the manager of the official Pennsylvania Land Office, had "without paying due regard to the Governour's Authority . . . pretended to Survey Land over the River Sasquehannah." Keith asserted that this "action, as it appeared, a Contempt of the Governor's authority," was more than a personal affront to him. He claimed that it "might be of unhappy Consequence with the Indians, as being contrary to what the Governr. in his Treaty two or three days before had stipulated with them." In other words, no sooner had Keith arrived back in Philadelphia than news had leaked of his actions in the backcountry. His council members took immediate steps to block his land claims with counterclaims of their own. Suddenly the conference Keith conducted with the people of Conestoga matters more than ever. He is hoping that their acquiescence to his property claim can serve to authenticate his title, while any challenge to his holdings can be cast as dangerous to regional diplomacy. Coming to the crux of the matter, "the Governour desired to know if James Steel had any directions from the said Agents or Commissioners for his proceeding herein." As an aristocratic but impoverished governor and the wealthy but socially insecure men of his council engage in a colonial land race, they are risking inciting conflicts with the region's Native inhabitants that could imperil the stability of the British Empire in America.[9]

⁓

NOW, WEEKS LATER, AS Keith peers out from under the heavy curtain of his wig, many of the gazes that meet his are far from friendly. Meeting attendance is light this morning. Present are only the governor himself, James Logan, the three Quaker brothers-in-law (Samuel Preston, Richard Hill, and Isaac Norris), and the bon vivant Henry Brooke. Of this group, few openly admit to being fans of *Moll Flanders*; the governor can count only Henry Brooke as a clear ally.[10]

In this uneasy atmosphere of scraping rakes and burning reeds, the council members suddenly find their deliberations interrupted by the surprise arrival of a long-awaited delegation. Logan records "the Messenger sent by the Secretary to Colo French, from Conestogoe to the Five Nations, being returned with Civility, and some other Indians from Conestogoe along with him." All talk of taxing English criminals who enter the colony is immediately suspended. Keith and council must set aside their own squabbles and confront the renewed emergency in front of them.[11]

Governor Keith invites Satcheechoe, Taquatarensaly, and the rest of their party to attend a hastily convened council meeting first thing tomorrow morning and orders that "that the Assembly now sitting have notice by a Message from the Governour, to be present at Council if they think fit." John and Edmund, having duly "appeared before the

Governour in Council and desired their appearance might be Entered in Discharge of the Condition of their Recognizance" back on April 20 have been allowed to post bail a second time and resume their lives as freemen. However, with attention to their case mounting daily, their liberty may be once again in jeopardy.[12]

Brick by brick, the crisis has mounted faster and higher than a city wall crawling with masons. John Cartlidge once hoped that all memory of the incident would be lost somewhere safely up Monocasey Creek. Instead, word has spread down the Susquehanna and across the Northeast. Native leaders at Conestoga are in communication with chiefs of the Five Nations. And now the governor and his council are inviting assembly members from across the colony to consider the affair.

A SIZABLE CROWD FILES into the Philadelphia courthouse on Friday morning, the fourth of May. Besides the governor and the council members present yesterday when the Indians first arrived in town, Attorney General Andrew Hamilton and recently appointed board member Anthony Palmer join the proceedings. Their attendance returns the council to an uneasy balance between Quakers and Anglicans. Logan doesn't note who among the members of the assembly joins the throng, but does record the presence of "Tacuttelence, als Civility, Satcheechoa, the Messenger sent to the five Nations, now returned," along with two other Indians never mentioned before or again in the colonial minutes, Tiollhanse and Collhageherad. As usual, Civility is to act as "Interpreter from the Minguay into the Delaware Language." On hand today to translate "from the Delaware into English" is one Edward Farmer. Farmer, a known "gentleman" of Philadelphia County, just happens to have long familiarity with this case; he attended the Cartlidge brothers' first appearance at the courthouse back in March and put up £250 toward John's £500 bail. Though John himself will have no chance to shape or shade Civility's words today, his trusted friend Edward Farmer may.[13]

Satcheechoe, "the Messenger . . . now returned," hardly looks the part of a courier in the eyes of most colonists. When they imagine a messenger, they are more apt to picture the woodcut figures that flank the masthead of their city paper. The winged god Mercury, clad in a Roman helmet, soars each week over the landscape on the left side of the page, promising to carry news from near and far. To the right side of the *American Weekly Mercury* masthead, a colonist in a tricornered hat gallops on horseback blasting tidings with a bugle. Nowhere pictured in the paper is an Indian herald, his long hair held back with a thick coil of brass wire as he treads skillfully over ancient pathways, confident that information is power. Yet events now hinge on the words of just such a missing figure.[14]

As the governor and Civility exchange preliminary pleasantries— Keith declares that he and his council "are here to receive the Words of their great friends and Allies the five Nations," while Taquatarensaly makes apologies for members of the Conestoga community unable to be present today—Satcheechoe readies himself to speak. On arriving home from Iroquoia, he took time to stop at Conestoga to visit his family and to pick up a few companions before proceeding to Philadelphia.

Satcheechoe and Taquatarensaly have made a deliberate choice in traveling with just two other men today; a larger delegation would offer colonists the honor of something more like a state visit. The Five

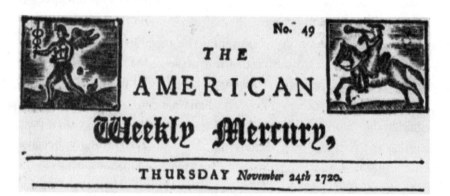

The masthead features two woodcut illustrations. On the left flies Mercury, the winged-foot Roman messenger to the gods, holding aloft a scroll. On the right a colonist rides on horseback blowing a bugle to advertise the arrival of the news. The overstuffed saddlebag holds newspapers and letters. As the only British colonial newspaper then published outside of Boston, Bradford's paper had some claim to serving "America" and not just Pennsylvania.

MASTHEAD, THE AMERICAN WEEKLY MERCURY.

Nations want to create no such impression. To the contrary, they have sent him to rebuke the English for their failures to observe proper diplomatic protocols. Any throat clearing dies down rapidly as Keith invites Satcheechoe to "deliver what they had to say to him & his Council."[15]

The messenger begins by recounting that "James Logan came up to Conestogoe from the Govr. On the News of one of their Cousins being killed." He acknowledges that the colonists expressed "great sorrow for the unhappy accident and had delivered a Belt of Wampum to wipe away their Tears." This much, the Five Nations approve. They expect condolences to include first the open expression of emotion and then an offer of wampum to set an official seal on the sentiments.[16]

Satcheechoe assures the governor "they had received that Belt and now returned another also to wipe away" the tears of the colonists. With that, he holds up a belt of wampum, its tubular shell beads polished to a sheen, its smooth weight supple in his hands. The soft luster of sacred shells reflects the glimmer of glistening tears, a play of light meant to banish the shadows of sorrow. Logan watches and records the action: "he delivers another Belt of Wampum and says That they are thus far well pleased with what is done." As Keith receives the gifts of blue and white beads woven into intricate patterns of opalescence, he may mistake this for a shining moment in his governorship.[17]

But then Satcheechoe tells the assembled colonists that the chiefs of the Five Nations "hope the Bones of the Dead man will be taken care of and kept in memory & that they desire a good understanding may be preserved between them & us." Satcheechoe is teaching the colonists a pattern of call and response, but colonists can't voice their part. They can't reply that they have cared for Sawantaeny's bones, because they have done nothing at all to offer his body sacred respects. To the contrary, they are still clinging to the faint possibility that there *is* no body to be found because Sawantaeny is not really dead. The news that peaceful relations with the Five Nations now hinge on the issue of whether or not Sawantaeny's bones have been cared for is enough to send a tremor of unease through the council.[18]

Taquatarensaly and Satcheechoe understand that "the Hermaphrodite" who appeared at the grave acted there in a spiritual capacity, hired to conduct the proper ceremonies over Sawantaeny. Burials at

Conestoga follow an important set of ceremonies. The departed are laid in the grave lying on their backs with their heads facing west/northwest toward the setting sun. Workaday items are placed with the dead, most often brass kettles and iron knives—ordinary implements of interrupted lives, offered now as an aid to starting anew in the afterlife. The Seneca, in particular, sometimes add sacred objects to burial sites, such as small "false face" effigies finely carved in red catlinite, placed there to act as personal guardian spirits. As a leading man, Sawantaeny likely received an especially careful burial, perhaps was even given a catlinite ornament. The problem is that the colonists simply have no information about any of this. They have done nothing to locate Sawantaeny's body, much less to ceremonially lay his bones to rest. Satcheechoe knows that only his Native neighbors at Conestoga, not English colonists, have tended to Sawantaeny.[19]

And he has more to reproach them with. He goes on to note that although the leaders of the Five Nations "have received also from the Govr. Two Strouds which they will keep as long as they live . . . [they] do not receive them as any satisfaction for the Loss of their Brother." Logan promised that the colonists would do more to recompense the Indians than simply sending two strouds; Satcheechoe is here to tell Keith that the Indians are determined to hold them to this. The next message is still more strident. Satcheechoe tells them that the Five Nations accept Logan's message that "no heartburning should be left," but first they insist that they must "agree upon what satisfaction should be made to them for the Loss of their Relation." He presents a third belt of wampum at this point, to impress upon the colonists the seriousness of his demands.[20]

With his next words Satcheechoe offers up yet another flash of white and blue:

He presents another Belt from the Chief of all the Five Nations, who says, This Governmt sent up two members of the Council to Conestogoe upon this Business, but two persons were not sufficient to make it up and answer for a whole Country. They expect a greater number of People & now send this Belt to require the Governour to go up to

him, For as the offence was committed by the English, it is the Govrs.
Duty to go up to them, and not theirs to come to us.

Here is a heavy hint that when Captain Civility apologized for the small number of Native people in his delegation today, he was tactfully calling attention to a matter of deliberate diplomatic symbolism. The Five Nations may say they "desire a good understanding may be preserved" with the colonists, but an offense has been committed. There is nothing deferential in the declaration that the leaders of the Five Nations "require" the governor of Pennsylvania to travel in person to meet with them.[21]

Satcheechoe continues by explaining, "This Belt is to shew the Governour that He may come safely to them." In effect, he is instructing the governor to use this wampum belt as a sort of visitor's pass for travel through Iroquoia. Keith is being ordered to pay court to the leaders of the Five Nations in their own land. Satcheechoe adds, "they are now making War with the Cheekaragoes, but on the Goverour's coming they may make Peace with those People & so have Peace with all the Main." Cold comfort for the governor to have this outside confirmation of the imminent peril of war that he has been trying to describe to the members of his council.[22]

Satcheechoe still has one final point left to make. Presenting four threads of wampum beads, he says, "These are sent as a string to draw away the Governour as by the arm immediately, even this day without any Loss of Time that so all may be friends together." The Governor may wish to treat the Indians as suppliants at his court, but they have quite another view of this meeting. Taquatarensaly and Satcheechoe together have wrapped their words around his arm like a lariat and are leading him off by a string. Yes, the Five Nations are offering friendship, asking for bonds of alliance. Beaded strings often feature in Native diplomacy, offered to punctuate secondary points in the major messages commemorated by larger, more elaborately beaded belts. Yet this deliberate, explicit use of strings to pull the governor by the arm toward the Five Nations stands out. For, when Indian groups take captives, they routinely make use of beaded halters and strings. The chiefs of the Five Nations may be metaphorically positioning the Pennsylvania governor himself as their bondsman, captive to their commands.[23]

Governor Keith understands that he is being asked to undertake a diplomatic mission, but he does not yet fully fathom the force of the invitation. With the hour for a midday meal upon them, council members are unconcerned with making immediate travel plans. Keith adjourns his council until four o'clock. When the council reconvenes privately without the Indians late that afternoon, members focus not on the wide-open possibility of diplomatic catastrophe, but rather on the narrower question of how best to manage an inconvenient crime.[24]

The "Cartlidge's Committee" offers the council an update on the case and, as a result, it is "resolved that John & Edmund Cartlidge be delivered into the hands of the proper Magistrates in order to be prosecuted according to Law." The brothers' brief interlude of freedom is coming to a quick close. With any luck, by now they have finished sowing their spring crops and ordered their affairs. The council commands "that they continue in the Custody of the Sheriff of Philadelphia, by virtue of the Governrs Commitment." The governor, who cannot imagine himself in shackles, does nothing to stop the chaining of the Cartlidges again, only hoping this move will both put an end to carping about his management of the colony and set the course for improved relations with the Five Nations.[25]

AS LOGAN AND THE rest of the council members file into the courthouse chamber the next morning, May 5, they have many matters on their minds. Governor Keith wants to move forward with coordinating an official response to the message received from the Five Nations yesterday. He presents drafts of two proposed addresses, one to be sent to the Five Nations, the other "to be delivered to our own Indians." But though the speeches are "laid before the board" without delay, the council members decline to render any definite opinion on their contents. "The subject matter of both," Logan notes dryly, was "further discoursed." But though voices rise and fall, the Quakers refuse to approve the governor's message. In a sure sign that Logan himself does not endorse the governor's position, he omits Keith's drafts from the council minutes. He notes only that the issue is "referr'd to the next meeting of the Council." That meeting itself is not scheduled.[26]

Rather than focusing on Satcheechoe, Taquatarensaly, and their demands, Logan and the others want to keep their sights trained on the legislation regarding "Persons convicted of Heinous Crimes and imported into this Province." If the governor thought the Indians' sudden arrival could provide a distraction from Logan and company's efforts to further tighten the merchant elite's control over the common people of the colony, his council stands ready to forcibly redirect his attention.[27]

Keith's board is refusing to "take any Cognizance" of Indian demands this morning. While the governor suddenly wants to curry favor with Indians—the better to back up his new land claims—his councilmen are more concerned with reinforcing their own authority over the lower classes in the colony. They are determined to get Keith's signature on a new criminal bill, charging a "duty," or tax, on all convicts transported into the colony. Tacking a government fee onto the price of servants drawn from England's convict class may help lower the number of such people arriving at the port of Philadelphia. Keith agrees to the plan; Logan notes with satisfaction that "the Govr. Gave his Assent and passed it into Law of this Province, and ordered the same to be sealed & published forthwith." James Logan can hang up his broom and scraper for the day. He has kept iron control over the council agenda. As for the Indian matter, he is not about to allow the governor to rush the diplomatic process.[28]

THE COUNCIL REMAINS OUT of session for four more days, until Wednesday May 9. In the interim, James Logan tends to his household affairs. Having purchased posts last Wednesday and rails last Thursday, he has on hand all the materials needed for the never-ending work of claiming and fencing ground. Ever busy, today he also records purchasing "a wig etc.," and so he arrives for the afternoon meeting of the council with a freshly pomaded and powdered coif of curls. It is now two months to the day since Secretary Logan and Colonel French first rode into Conestoga to begin a formal inquiry into the reported killing. Meanwhile, five full days have passed since Satcheechoe's arrival in Philadelphia; the gravity of the Indians' demands has had ample time to penetrate the wig wax and sink into the minds of the governor and his council.[29]

Keith presents to the board a memorandum that he intends to send to the assembly, setting out the current state of affairs and the steps needed to address it. For once, all seem ready to act with one accord. Keith tells the assembly members that "with due Regard to the publick Justice of this Government & to what you recommend" as well as "by advice of the Council," the accused have been imprisoned again this week and plans made for "prosecuting John and Edmund Cartlidge according to the common Course of the Laws." Keith aims to present himself in the best possible light as a man of the law.[30]

And yet, Keith explains, it seems that Satcheechoe and Taquatarensaly expect much more than the simple reincarceration of the suspects. Keith warns the legislature, "I still find that all our just expectations in the Issue of that affair, as well as in accommodating matters with the Indians to Content, are in danger of being frustrated." After at least three formal conferences between Indians and English—the meeting convened by John Cartlidge with the aid of Captain Civility, the investigation initiated by Logan and French, and the agreement to avert warfare engineered at Captain Civility's cabin by Governor Keith—it seems that Satcheechoe and the captain have at last succeeded in educating colonial officials about Indian protocols.[31]

As Keith lays down a three-step strategy for the assembly to consider, much boils down to money. First of all, the governor confides that he intends to "promise to meet the Sachims of the Five Nations at Albany this Summer, as it seems they expect." Reluctant as he is to undertake such a long journey, Keith has finally come to understand that only his personal appearance before the leaders of the Five Nations will suffice to demonstrate the ritual sorrow and remorse of the colonists for the death of Sawantaeny. In the Native view, there is simply no substitute for face-to-face relationships. He warns, however, that he cannot possibly embark on such a journey unless the assembly is willing to fully finance the venture, not only to cover the charges he and his retinue are bound to run up in the course of travel, but also to pay for "the Presents that must be there made to the Indians upon renewing all our former Treaties of Friendship with them." For Native peoples, gifts and greetings go together, each a key element in repairing the pain of grief.[32]

Second of all, the governor asks that "the House will please immediately issue an order upon the Provincial Treasurer to pay in Course what the Governour & Council thinks proper to be given to the Indians at their Departure, and to confirm what the Governour has now to say to the Sachims of the Five Nations by the Return of the same Messenger." Keith realizes that Satcheechoe and Taquatarensaly have every intention of remaining in the city until they receive some compensation for the trouble they have taken in running messages for the colonists. Furthermore, Keith is not ready to depart Philadelphia instantly. He wants Satcheechoe to return to Iroquoia without him and stall for time, not drag him off by the arm "immediately" as the leaders of the Five Nations instructed. But if he intends to send Satcheechoe back again alone, he certainly cannot risk sending him back empty-handed.[33]

EVEN AS THE COUNCIL sits in session, Eleanor Moore, the woman condemned to death for committing infanticide, is making a speech in New Castle at the place of her execution. Confessing her crime and begging forgiveness, on May 9, Eleanor reportedly says, "I pray that this public Satisfaction which I am now to pay to Justice, may be a Caution to those who now surround me." A mob of onlookers mills about beneath the gibbet, straining to hear her final words. "All others who may come to Knowledge of my grievous Sin and fearful Punishment," Eleanor advises, should "apply themselves in their youth to remember their Creator, and to avoid loose Company and Sabbath-breaking, which by sad Experience I now find must needs end in Sorrow and Disgrace." In another few minutes Eleanor's life is snuffed out, her death attributed to nothing more than her own sinfulness. Her words confirming her own moral culpability will be reprinted in the next week's paper, serving notice to one and all that—whatever the outcome of the Cartlidge case—the colony's magistrates are fully prepared to implement the new stronger penal code whenever they see fit.[34]

Keith will never admit that the belief prevalent amongst gentlemen—that members of the lower orders are not merely materially disadvantaged but also morally degenerate—means that legal standards are not applied in the same way to people at all levels of society. As the aristocratic English moral philosopher, the Earl of Shaftesbury, only recently observed, in his *Characteristics of Man, Manners, Opinions, Times*, published in London in 1714, "the mere Vulgar of Mankind often stand in need of such a rectifying Object as *the Gallows*." For all that the Quaker sect began with promises to renounce excess material possessions along with artificial social distinctions, by 1722 the buckled and bewigged gentry of Pennsylvania has come to regard financial success as the just reward of spiritual and moral progress.[35]

"THE LAWS OF OUR Great King," Keith tells Taquatarensaly and Satcheechoe when he finally offers them a formal reply on May 11, fully a week after their arrival in town, "must be strictly kept and obeyed without making any difference or distinction between the greatest and the poorest man amongst us. I say all these things to you that you may . . . tell them to your People & your children." Keith wants word of English law to spread to Indians for "then they will know us to be just and good men." Keith has made the most of the long interim between meetings by writing up the remarks he intends to deliver, taking into account all he has learned about the affairs of the Five Nations, from their concern over the deaths of their leaders who traveled to Virginia last summer, to their rebukes over his handling of the death of Sawantaeny. He plans to bandage up the diplomatic damage with a sumptuous offering of English fabrics. With him in the courtroom today, he has calico and silk, shirts and stockings, goods of Asia for the people of North America. Most of all, he strokes his sheepskins, the parchment pages on which he has recorded his coming pronouncements on the topic of criminal law.[36]

"Tell my great Brother & good Friend," Keith begins, directing Satcheechoe what to say to "Saccumcheuts, and the other Chiefs of the Five Nations," that "we joyfully accept the four Belts & Strings of Wampum which they sent to us by him." Keith is determined to go through his paces methodically. "My heart was indeed filled with sorrow for the loss of our Brother who is dead," he says of his reaction to the loss of Sawantaeny. He adds that, since "the rest of the Brethren desire us to wipe away our tears, we will dry them, but our Grief still remains." Here is the required ritual declaration of sadness. Keith invokes the bodily signs of wet eyes and daubing hands essential for beginning the ceremonial repair of social ties.[37]

Keith moves then to address the first of the Five Nations' many objections to his proceedings to date. "Our message from Conestogoe," he says, "was only sent to Express our sorrow & not to offer any satisfaction for our Brothers death." With this, he counters the Five Nations' complaints that the minor quantity of wampum sent so far will not serve "as any satisfaction" for Sawantaeny's death. On the contrary, he assures them, "We have already taken & shall continue to pursue the same measures with the offenders as if an Englishman had lost his Life." Ignoring the fact that Satcheechoe requested condolences and reparations, not penal corrections and reprisals, Keith turns the discussion to questions of crime and punishment and promises to follow English legal protocols. Keith offers up the prize of equal justice for the Indians' inspection, saying that the Cartlidge brothers "must be judged by the Laws of our Great King." Even as Keith seems to adhere to the highest ideals of cross-cultural conflict resolution, he is actually breaking the promise of William Penn to try cases before an "equal number of just men on both sides."[38]

Keith hastens to smooth away any offense caused by the condescending assumption that leaders of the Five Nations should come and pay court to the colonists if they wish to further discuss Sawantaeny's death. "I do not find in the written words of the Message sent from Conestogoe, by Sacheechoe," Keith declares, "that we desired any of the Chiefs of the great Five Nations to come to us just now." Keith denies ever having demanded that the Indians dance attendance on him. At the same time, he hastens to avoid any implication that the leaders of the Five Nations are not welcome in Philadelphia. "When I have done what the Laws of our great King directs to be done, for punishing those who have caused us this Grief, then I shall be pleased to see any great men that the Brethren will please to send, either to Conestogoe or this place." Keith sticks closely to his main point: promoting the merits of English justice.[39]

After adding a few more formal remarks, promising to make preparations for a voyage to New York later in the summer, and presenting his planned gifts for "the Sachims of the Five Nations," Keith turns to address his "Friends & Brothers of Conestogoe" and returns once more to his preferred theme: the primacy of English jurisprudence. "If any of our people commit a wicked & foolish action, our Laws will punish him for it," Keith boasts to Taquatarensaly and the rest of the Conestoga community that "he cannot escape or buy it off with any Ransom. Our Laws are all written down, and it is the will of our Great King that We obey them." Keith derides the offer of reparations as the payment of a ransom. He speaks as if English law were a timeless thing. And yet, of course, he well knows that the ink has hardly dried on the new penal code recently approved in Pennsylvania.[40]

In glossy black iron gall ink, colonists enumerated a greatly expanded number of capital crimes. The complete list of capital crimes now includes: "high treason, misprision of treason, murder (including petit treason), manslaughter, sodomy, buggery, rape, robbery, infanticide (including concealing the death of an infant or encouraging the mother to do so), maiming (including accessories), witchcraft, burglary, and arson (house, barn, stable, or outhouse)." Had the Cartlidges committed manslaughter thirty years ago, the crime would not have counted as a felony. Now, all of a sudden, it does. Iron inks are prone to fading to rust, of course, depending on whether rainwater, vinegar, white wine, or even ale is used as the solvent. Yet the script on these statutes has not yet had time to brown.[41]

Rather than making any reference to just how recently the colonial laws he intends to enforce were adopted, Keith turns back again to his critique of Indian traditions of justice. "We have heard that it is a Custom amongst you," Keith notes, "when an Indian happens to be Killed, that his Relations often demand & expect Money or Goods for satisfaction. But the Laws of our Great King will not suffer any such thing to be done amongst us." Quite as if he has not just requested and received approval for substantial payments to Indians, Keith makes a great show of the fact that, under English law, people cannot buy their way out of culpability for crime. This is the basis of impartial justice as the English understand it.[42]

Keith emphasizes that among the English, the cost of murder can only be repaid with the life of the perpetrator, telling them that "such a man by our Laws must die." Still, Keith directs this threat as much toward Native people—to deter them from planning retaliation—as toward the Cartlidges themselves. If the Cartlidges are charged with manslaughter but not murder, the governor will have new options at his disposal. Keith hastens to elaborate:

> if we understand that the man who was killed had provoked the other
> by doing any act whereby he intended to hurt him, so that he sud-
> denly killed the man in his Passion without having time to consider
> or think upon it. Our Law will not put such a man to death the first
> time he commits that fault.

The crux of the question, as the colonists see it, is this: Did Sawantaeny first grow angry with John, who then, acting in self-defense, inadvertently committed manslaughter? Or did John first grow angry with Sawantaeny, who then, defending himself against unwarranted aggression, became a victim of murder?[43]

Always, the case pivots on the fulcrum of anger. And here the Cartlidges do have a problem. Ayaquachan, the Conoy guide who testified to Logan and French at Conestoga, stated that it was John who first turned to violence, seizing Sawantaeny's pot and shattering it on the ground when the hunter demanded more rum. He said explicitly that Sawantaeny had responded by telling John "he need not be angry at him." And when Sawantaeny "still pressed him to give it; that John then pushed the Indian down who fell with his Neck cross a faln tree, where he lay for some time, and then rising walk'd up to his Cabin." According to this eyewitness, whose account was confirmed and reconfirmed by the other Native participants whom Logan examined, Sawantaeny went for his gun only after John had struck him to the ground. John, not Sawantaeny, initiated the physical violence. Keith and company may want to classify the crime as manslaughter, not murder, but the case refuses to neatly fit the criteria unless they discount key elements of "the evidences" that Logan so meticulously collected.[44]

Keith, of course, does not rehearse the scene of the killing aloud at this meeting. Instead, he confines himself to lecturing in the abstract on how well the "laws must be strictly kept and obeyed." With this message, Keith sends no beaded belts at all. For now, the governor is offering the leaders of the Five Nations only English texts and English textiles: disquisitions on the merits of England's written legal codes along with formal offerings of "Five of the finest Calico Shirts, five pair of fine Silk Stockings, five pair of Silk Garters, and, five Silk Handkerchiefs." Satcheechoe will have to carry the governor's gifts back to Iroquoia knowing that his work at alliance-building is unlikely to succeed without wampum and in the absence of a personal journey by the governor. The Cartlidge brothers will have to lie awake at night breathing the stale, faintly smoky air of the jail and hoping they, unlike Eleanor Moore, may yet escape feeling the rough cord of a hempen noose about their necks.[45]

Chapter 16

WILLIAM KEITH

Gov. William Keith clicks open the clasp of his folding knife and runs the hardened shear steel along the shaft of a quill. He is sharpening his thoughts as well as his pen. He has agreed with members of the colonial assembly on a new package of laws for the better governance of the colony—more codes to regulate high crimes and reduce the traffic in liquor. Now he plans a formal address to members of the Pennsylvania Assembly to mark the occasion. Having chosen the topic of "impartial justice," he intends to portray himself in the best possible light. Not for nothing does the baronet sit for his official portrait wearing plate armor studded with gold. He is now in something close to open battle with the members of his council.[1]

May blossoms as the Cartlidges stare at the bare brick walls of their prison confine. Crops grow, gnats hatch, plots ripen. When John Cartlidge confided his hopes of mineral wealth to Keith back in March, he intended to make himself too valuable to the governor to be prosecuted for murder. However, now that Keith has been shown the lands and has surveyed them in his own name, Cartlidge has become more than expendable. His continued existence is actually objectionable if it gives offense to the Native peoples whose cooperation Keith needs to realize his own dreams of fortune. Keith simply cannot allow the Cartlidge brothers' attack on an Indian—and on a member of the strategically essential Five Nations, no less—to undermine all that he has been working to achieve. As Keith sees it, persuading the Indians to accept the gift of English justice will, in a single stroke, resolve the murder crisis, enhance his own growing property interests, and cement his transatlantic reputation as an able colonial administrator.

In his meeting with the Indians just over a week ago, Keith did his best to explain the English position in terms that would persuade Captain Civility and Satcheechoe to preserve peace and cede property. Now that the Cartlidge brothers are once again being held in prison, he has been able to assure the Indians, "we have already taken & shall continue to pursue the same measures with the offenders as if an Englishman had lost his Life." Again and again, he holds up the potential of a capital prosecution as the ultimate sign of colonial goodwill toward Indians.[2]

Keith would prefer not to antagonize the Native peoples slated to be near neighbors in his mining operation, but neither is he willing to invest large amounts of time maintaining relations. Shrugging off the string of wampum Satcheechoe and Civility wrapped round his arm, he told them, "I would go with pleasure a great way" to see leaders of the Five Nations "at their own habitations." But not now. "I cannot travel unless it be upon a Horse or in a Ship," he explained, offering Satcheechoe a backward compliment for the strength and endurance he has displayed on his recent round-trip foot journey, "and I am just now very busie with my Assembly making Laws to hinder the Christians from carrying Rum out into the Woods to hurt the Indians." There is at least truth to this claim.[3]

Keith is prepared to cooperate with Quakers on new legislation to limit the sale of rum in the colony. But condemning the Cartlidges for trading liquor to Indians neither redresses the fundamental complaint of the peoples of Conestoga that they are regularly forced to purchase English goods at inflated rates, nor does anything to advance the goals of unification at the heart of Civility's efforts. Willfully blind to Civility's desire to bring their peoples together, Keith instead emphasizes the impartial and impersonal nature of colonial law.

Keith never wavers for a moment in his belief in the ability of English courts to arrive at unbiased judgments on the basis of reasoned analysis. It is not that emotion has no role at all to play in the administration of English justice. As Keith tells the Indians, "the Laws of our Great King" draw "a difference between the case of a man Killed in a Quarrel through heat of Blood, and when the Design is form'd in the mind beforehand to destroy or kill a man." One of the many keys to adjudicating between murder and manslaughter comes in measuring the mind of the killer, assessing the emotions of the accused in order to analyze the motivation for crime. Yet, in the English system, once charged, an accused person loses any right to emotional attention. As Keith has summed it up for the colony's justices of the peace, no "confused mixture of pity and horror"—for either the criminal defendant or for the victim—should cloud the judgment of judge and jury on questions of guilt or innocence. The Native approach contrasts strongly with English procedures, elevating feelings alongside facts. When faced with a killing within their communities, Native peoples subsume issues of guilt and punishment beneath efforts to redress the anguish of victims, acknowledge the remorse of perpetrators, and above all reestablish communal bonds.[4]

PRECISELY FIVE YEARS HAVE passed since Keith rode up to Philadelphia in a dust cloud of intrigue in May of 1717. Keith was tasked that day with the wicked pleasure of announcing to the sitting governor, Charles Gookin, that he was to be replaced, immediately, by Keith himself. Logan and the rest of the Quaker grandees on the governor's council cooperated eagerly with Keith on that occasion. They had come into conflict with Gookin because that gentleman, an Anglican, had recently announced a new policy forbidding anyone to hold office who would not first swear to perform the duties of the position. Quaker faith demanded that followers adhere to truth in all things; observant Quakers thus refused to swear oaths on the grounds that doing so implied that in any other circumstance they might speak less than the truth. Both sides dug in during the oaths controversy, and the business of government effectively ground to a halt. Though Quakers attempted to continue the work of the courts and the legislature, Gookin declined to legitimate any actions they took on the grounds that, without a proper swearing-in, they were not actually officeholders at all.[5]

In the midst of this imbroglio, William Penn suffered a debilitating stroke. At that point his wife, Hannah, acting in her husband's stead, nominated Keith to take over the governorship from the beleaguered Gookin, hoping thereby to restore order in the colony. At first, the shakeup worked as intended. Keith and Logan struck up a mutually convenient alliance and collaborated on the 1718 penal reforms that strengthened the severity of the law in the colony, yet allowed new lenience for Quakers who could now simply "affirm" that they would perform the duties of public office without the need to "swear" their promises.[6]

But William Penn died within the year—before the Board of Trade could approve and confirm the proprietary family's appointment of Keith as Governor. Meanwhile, the Penn family's very ownership of the colony came into doubt because William Penn, deeply in debt when he died in 1718, had been negotiating to return his proprietary right to the Crown in exchange for a payment of £12,000. At the time of his passing, he had received a preliminary payment of £1,000, meaning that neither his heirs nor the people of Pennsylvania could know for certain *who* had the authority to appoint the colony's governor. As a result, almost from the beginning, Keith felt his own hold on office to be deeply insecure.[7]

The new governor tried to shore up his standing by tripling his efforts: working to make himself acceptable to William Penn's heirs, to leading Pennsylvania Quakers, and to the British Board of Trade. In his first days in Philadelphia, Keith leaned heavily on the advice and authority of James Logan. He busied himself sussing out the particulars of local politics, all the while sniffing out possibilities for enhancing his own fortune. It did not take Keith long to notice that Logan was reaping huge profits in the fur trade nor to realize that if he could establish himself as a key intermediary between English colonists and the Native inhabitants of the continent, he would be well positioned both to serve the security interests of the Crown and to skim off fur-trade profits for himself.

Keith fell to work with gusto in his first year in Philadelphia, establishing his presence with performances like his speech to the justices of the peace about how to set aside their passions in order to fairly adjudicate crime. Meanwhile, he tried to improve his profile on the other side of the Atlantic by preparing a lengthy report for the information of the Board of Trade that he titled "A State of the Indian Nations." Keith regarded the members of the Five Nations as the most important Native figures in the mid-Atlantic region: the dominant trade power and the key to English military security against the French. He called for the establishment of "four forts" scattered across the Ohio valley, on the "back side" of the English colonies. These posts would serve equally as military garrisons and trading centers, allowing both for defense and for the development of Indian commerce. Superintending such a system would give Pennsylvania preeminence over rival colonies with longer traditions of Indian trading, including Maryland and New York.[8]

Keith was carefully cultivating a transatlantic audience for his Indian policy, setting himself up as the hero of the play and the Five Nations as key actors in the chorus. Yet Keith's 1718 trade report also created the first rumblings of conflict with Logan. Observing that the fur trade "will enrich particulars in proportion to the quantity they deal in and the profit it brings, which in late years has been so considerable," Keith took a position that argued, without ever saying so directly, that Logan's near total domination of the Pennsylvania fur trade ought to be curtailed. Phrasing his oblique attack on Logan's wealth as a principled point of patriotism, the governor cautioned the members of the Board of Trade:

> lest it should at any time be represented to your Lordships, that in imitation of the French, a Society may be incorporated, and a Company erected for carrying on the trade upon this Continent wt. the Indians, I must beg leave to observe these Colonies . . . from the taste they have of English liberty, are naturally averse to all monopolies.

Keith cast all of his actions in light of transatlantic politics. Events in the Pennsylvania backcountry could affect not only the balance of trade but also the very balance of imperial power. Left unstated was the point of greatest importance to Keith—that a gentleman such as himself could not compete for Logan's profits if the Board of Trade were to create an official license for Logan to engross everything himself.[9]

Keith submitted his letter to the Board of Trade on February 16, 1719, providing James Logan with a copy and inviting him to offer "observations upon it with the greatest freedom." He implied that he was ready to edit his report in response to any comments or corrections Logan cared to make. From the moment he read it, Logan grasped that—useful as Keith's arrival had been in bringing about Gookin's ouster and an end to the odious insistence on oath-taking—the man's appearance on the scene posed a new set of problems. Logan prepared a lengthy set of notes to guide Keith in making revisions to his report. In the process, he did his best to cajole the new governor out of views he knew would be greatly to his own disadvantage as well as detrimental to the pacifist traditions established by William Penn. Logan began by contesting Keith's claims about the value of the fur trade:

> Thy Report . . . will I doubt [not] give a notion that the Indian Trade in these British Colonies is a considerable thing, when as upon a reasonable computation I believe the whole of it will not be found to amount to 40,000 Sterling which is scarce so much as some one merchant in divers parts of Europe will pass thro his hands in a year.

Logan claimed that the profits of the fur trade were far too paltry for the British Board of Trade to concern itself with, certainly nothing needing closer oversight from the Crown, and nothing tempting enough to draw competitors into his sphere of action. Yet Logan made his suggestions on April 8, 1719, more than two months *after* the dateline of the governor's letter to the board. He protested both too much and too late. Keith had already vaulted ahead with his own version of events and his account was the one received and officially recorded in London.[10]

~

IF KEITH HAS NEVER truly aligned himself with Logan, recent conflicts have accentuated their differences. With Logan challenging him directly over his surveying exploits and writing tattling letters to Hannah Penn about his activities, Keith needs to regroup. John Cartlidge's actions this year—from his discovery of potential mining lands in Native territory to his near simultaneous killing of a Native man—have brought many long-simmering issues to a boil. If Keith can manage these multiple crises adroitly, the governorship will become a true seat of grandeur: allowing him to act as the dominant player in the fur trade, the director of mining operations in the region, the master of Native diplomacy, and the giver of law in the colony. The situation requires a new surface display of cooperation with Quakers, and so he has agreed to collaborate with them on the legislation they have been pushing to restrict migration to the colony for people with prior criminal records in England while also limiting the sale of hard alcohol to Indians. Disorderly spirits come in many forms, and Keith will not waste any more time quarreling with Quaker efforts to tamp down unruly elements in the colony.

Keith knows he needs to do something dramatic to improve the health of his relations with Pennsylvania's leading colonists. He is planning a formal speech to mark the signing of the new legislation package into law; he intends to use the occasion to underscore the efforts he has made to nurse peace and prosperity in the colony. Whenever the humors of the human body require rebalancing, efforts must be made to drain off excess fluids: black bile, yellow bile, blood, and phlegm. According to the best medical theory of the day, illness results from unbalanced fluid levels, and bloodletting is one widely recognized therapeutic technique for bringing them back into harmony. As Keith contemplates the remarks he intends to make, he prepares to draw a bit of blood.[11]

A gentleman keeps many blades in his private collection. In addition to tools like his penknife, he will also have his own personal set of lancets, fine-honed scalpels with which to let blood. Lancet cases can be purchased in many luxury materials: sharkskin, shagreen, tortoiseshell or mother-of-pearl, steel, brass, or silver-gilt. Often, they are engraved with initials or a family crest.[12]

"Gentlem[e]n of the Assembly," Keith begins his speech on May 22 with the usual courteous honorifics, "when we reflect upon the Accidents and Difficulties that have occurr'd to us, we must be convinced . . . that Justice . . . cannot be upheld . . . without . . . Confidence between me and the Representatives of the People." Murderous crimes threaten to mount into a calamitous war. The colony has been injured, and all those in leading roles must care for and support one another.[13]

Mentally, Keith fingers his lancet case. "The safest and most satisfactory Way, to promote and secure the Peace and Happiness of the good People of Pennsylvania," he says, "will be to administer impartial Justice in all Cases whatsoever, according to the known and established Laws of the Land." Who could object to such an entirely conventional prescription?[14]

But now Keith flashes steel. Adherence to the principles of "impartial justice," he says, "will be our best and surest Defense against the Outrages of the Wicked." Just who does Keith have in mind when he refers to the wicked? The legislators assembled before him may at first assume this is just another reference to the criminal Cartlidge brothers. But then Keith makes his cut, saying, "so this excellent plain Rule will, one time or other, most certainly bring to Light and overcome the hidden Projects and mistaken Wisdom of ill-designing Men, if there be any such amongst us." Keith has moved so swiftly it may be that few will notice his nicks on the provincial secretary. Still, Logan has to feel the smart. As if to rub salt in the wound, Keith enlists William Bradford to reprint his speech in this week's *Mercury*, where all can consider his insinuations.[15]

On May 24, Keith writes a new letter to the Council of Trade:

Having heard that . . . others at London intend to apply . . . for a grant of the Royal Mines in these parts, and having reason to believe from some experiments which I have lately made, that some very useful discoveries of that nature may be made in many places of this Province, *proposes* that Governors be ordered to report to H.M. [His Majesty] the particular discoveries that have been already made in their Governments, before H.M. grant away any such royalties.

Keith is so excited as he crafts this letter that he shifts within a single sentence from the first person, "experiments which *I* have lately made," to the third, "[he] *proposes* that Governors be ordered to report to

H.M." When it comes down to it, Keith would rather take his chances reporting directly to the Crown and reaping the rewards of being a royal agent than continue to compete with Logan to be the Penn family's best-trusted proxy. If Logan thinks he can preempt Keith's claims to a potential copper fortune by informing against him to Hannah Penn, Keith decides to go over the heads of the colony's proprietors by bringing the possibility of mining wealth directly to the attention of the Board of Trade.[16]

Lancets can only be used a few times before they grow bent or dull and should be discarded. Fortunately, purchasing new ones is a simple matter. Just this week for example, in the very same issue of the *Weekly Mercury* that carries a copy of "The Speech of His Excellency Sir William Keith, Bart. Governor of the Province of Pennsylvania &c. to the General Assembly of the Said Province, after Passing Several Bills, May the 22, 1722," there is also an advertisement for medical supplies. "There are to be sold . . . at Mr. Oliver Galtree's in High Street near the Prison in Philadelphia All Sorts of Medicine, Drugs, &c. for ready Money, and any Person may be there supplied with Lancets for Bleeding, at very Reasonable Rates. They are very choice and lately come from London." Keith cannot help but hope that many more "choice" blades may soon arrive from London—in the form of fresh favorable orders from the Board of Trade.[17]

Chapter 17

TAKE HIM NOW

JUNE 15–JULY 2, 1722

Take him now.

—Titan Leeds, Verses for June,
The American Almanack for 1722

SOMEONE HAS SET THE STARS SPINNING ON SECOND STREET. Inside his print shop, beneath the Sign of the Bible, Andrew Bradford is demonstrating the use of some globes he has advertised for sale. This June he is offering buyers "a Pair of Globes Nine Inches Diameter, with their Appurtenances." Globes are usually sold in sets to the lucky few with the means to purchase them and the education to appreciate them. One orb is terrestrial, the other celestial, promising new understandings of the Earth and its heavens. The globes come equipped with stands and are suspended inside an assemblage of wooden hoops. For the world's globe, these hoops trace the earth's circles of latitude and longitude, inscribed with words that sound like incantations: Equator and Prime Meridian, Capricorn and Cancer. Around the sphere of the sky, painted and gilded stars glint, showing the constellations with their pagan names. You can run your fingers across the smooth surface of the globe and gently roll it forward to send the stars rotating in their courses.[1]

These are the tools of a new science, but they carry more than a whiff of magic. Across the colony, people are waiting anxiously for the eclipse that has been foretold by local almanac writer Titan Leeds. Studying the globes may help the public better understand the coming event, predicted to occur just a few days from now. But it will do little to stop the worries wheeling in people's minds. Leeds has warned his readers that "Aerial Prodigies are too often the Forerunners of Misery and Calamity unto mankind." And already, his predictions of "murther" and "imprisonment too" have all too clearly come to pass.[2]

Bradford sees a lot through the windows of his shop and hears still more in conversation with his customers. He keeps tabs on events and tailors his inventory to meet the needs of the moment. This week, in addition to offering astronomical instruments in anticipation of the eclipse, he is also advertising in his weekly newspaper a new book he has just put into print: *Conductor Generalis or the Office, Duty and Authority of Justices of the Peace*. He believes there is enough demand for this key legal reference book to make it worthwhile for him to create his own reprint of the English original and offer it for sale to the reading public. People are looking for detailed legal guidance, and Bradford, ever the entrepreneur, is eager to serve. His advertisement crows that the publication has been "long expected," by which he means eagerly anticipated.[3]

Across the colony people are already talking about the Cartlidge case. Besides the many officials who will need to consult the *Conductor Generalis*, with its detailed lists of crimes, punishments, and procedures, there is a still-wider potential customer base made up of the curious. Anyone can easily master the book's information, Bradford's newspaper advertisement assures, because he has "alphabetically digested" the material for readers under different section titles and included "a Table directing to the ready finding out the proper Matter under those Titles." Common people eager to consider every angle on the question of just what to do about the brothers John and Edmund— still incarcerated just a few doors down on Second Street—have only to stop into Bradford's shop to pick up a book copy along with the latest gossip. While they are there, they may even be able to persuade the proprietor to let them give the world a whirl.[4]

Only about ten books and pamphlets were printed in Philadelphia in the year 1722. Each was produced by Andrew Bradford. Of these, only Conductor Generalis *was a reprint of an English title; apparently colonists needed the book too urgently to wait for a British import.*

"M," CONDUCTOR GENERALIS, TABLE OF CONTENTS, DETAIL.

GOVERNOR KEITH SWEATS AND frets as dusk shades into darkness on the evening of June 18. The moon rose and set without incident last night. Titan Leeds has obviously missed the mark. Even if the eclipse comes tonight, Keith will have little energy left for searching the skies over Conestoga. He has been tramping the swamps near the Maryland border for days in the company of a surveyor and a justice of the peace. As if he did not have vexations enough, what with the fractious colonists of Pennsylvania and the restive Native peoples of the Susquehanna, now it seems that colonial Marylanders are determined to revive old border disputes with their Pennsylvania neighbors. The mining rumors have made it to Maryland. Squatters and rogue surveyors are everywhere. A man who can't get a property title recognized by one colony thinks nothing of filing an application for the same land with the other. It will take the lawyers years to sort it all out, and by the time the Board of Trade makes any final determinations, false claimants may have stripped all the ore from the ground. Meanwhile, the latest Lord Calvert has designs on lands that Penn family members believe they can prove to be theirs—that is, unless the Board of Trade ultimately decrees that the Penn family has lost its claim on the colony entirely and that ownership has reverted to the Crown.[5]

Indeed, Lord Calvert is so very irked with the Pennsylvania colonists that he has just sent a Maryland sheriff to surprise their official surveyor—Isaac Taylor—in the woods, seize him, and place him under arrest. Summarily hauled back to Annapolis, Taylor is now being held without bail on the pretext that he has violated Maryland sovereignty by surveying for Pennsylvania. Serious as this is as a breach of intercolonial decorum, Baltimore's action is also highly inconvenient to Keith personally. Keith, of course, has been working closely with Taylor on a certain "affair" ripe for action ever since hearing rumors of ore deposits upriver from Conestoga. Now his private schemes to claim this property are becoming hopelessly tangled up in a larger border dispute between the two proprietary families of Pennsylvania and Maryland. Still, William Keith is nothing if not resourceful.[6]

Keith is lodging now with Francis Worley near Conestoga. Sworn in as a justice of the peace for Chester County in the same year as John Cartlidge, Worley has seamlessly absorbed his former colleague's judicial work and, conveniently for Keith, also boasts excellent skills as a surveyor. Indeed, Worley can provide Keith with most every service Cartlidge used to offer, including a place to sleep. Keith prefers lodging in Worley's house to taking a bed at William Barns's nearby "Publick House for ye accommodation of Man and Horse." Barns just opened his inn this year in a bid to take advantage of the business opportunity created by the "great concourse of Travellers along ye Road . . . to

Maryland and likewise to Conestoga." But Keith would rather take his ease in private at Worley's than sit with all and sundry in the poplar-paneled tavern hall at Barns's.[7]

Tonight, however, comfort proves elusive. Insects swarm incessantly as Keith tosses in his bed, oppressed by heat and tormented by whining. Travelers' accounts warn that all the lands near the Pennsylvania/Maryland border "are very unhealthy being swampy Ground and Fevers raging continually." No one is sure exactly why ague so often sets into the bones of those who sleep near damp ground, but most believe it has something to do with the fetid air. Only the insects seem to thrive there, happily adding to the overall misery of the people. Smoky fires set to ward off mosquitos burn before houses all across the countryside, but they help only a bit.[8]

Keith has just sent off a letter to his council members, dated "From Francis Worley's near Conestogoe, June 18th, 1722," informing them about conditions in the backcountry. "Finding the Indians, since I came last here, to be very much alarm'd with the noise of an intended Survey from Mary Land, upon the banks of the Susquehanna, I held a Council with them at Conestogoe," he writes. Casting himself as an advocate for Indians vulnerable to illegal encroachments from Maryland settlers, Keith has promised that he will protect them from "unjust practices." In fact, he has told the peoples of Conestoga, "if you approve my thoughts, I will immediately take up a large tract of land on the other side of the Sasquehanna for the Grandson of William Penn." Keith puts little effort into the pretense that Indians' interests are his main concern. He does not even record details about those with whom he held this conversation. He simply claims vaguely in his notes that "present" at the meeting were "the Chiefs of the Conestoga, Shawana, and Ganaway Indians," without naming any names. Still, the governor does mention making use of two interpreters: one James Le Tort, a well-known fur trader who has often worked as an interpreter alongside John Cartlidge at prior meetings, and the second, "Smith, the Ganaway," a member of the Conoy nation whose linguistic gifts are highly regarded in the Conestoga community. John Cartlidge, then, is little missed.[9]

Keith tells the Indians he addresses on June 15 that he intends to claim the land for William Penn's grandson, "for when his name is marked upon the Trees, it will keep off the Mary Landers." Afterward, Keith promises, "he bearing the same kind heart to the Indians which his grandfather did, will be glad to give you any part of his Land for your own use and Convenience, but if other people take it up they will make settlements upon it, and then it will not be in his power to give it to you." Logical absurdities abound here. Keith is asking the Indians for permission to claim their land for Pennsylvania in order to protect them from having it taken by Maryland. The Native peoples of Conestoga could be forgiven for seeing this as a distinction without a difference. But it all makes sense when viewed Keith's way. He intends to mine the Native countryside, then retreat back to the city. Once he has raked the soil's riches into his own corner, he will leave Native peoples to make the best they can of the denuded, perhaps desacralized, ground.[10]

The man who delivers an answer from the assembled Native people the next day, June 16, is listed in Keith's notes as "Tawenea." The name is never mentioned before or after in colonial records; surely it does not belong to anyone with the authority to authorize Keith's desired actions. In any case, "Tawenea" tells the interpreters, and Keith duly records, that "they very much approve what the Govr. Spoke, and like his Council to them very well, but they are not willing to discourse particularly on the Business of Land lest the five Nations may reproach or blame them." These community representatives are making it clear that they will neither override the Five Nations nor make any agreement in the absence of Taquatarensaly and Satcheechoe. Everyone at Conestoga knows that these two have already informed Keith that he has been ordered to Albany. It is past time for him to begin making definite travel arrangements. Tawenea tells him that "the Cayugoes are always claiming some Right to Lands on Sasquehannah, even where they themselves now live; wherefore they think it will be a very proper time when the Gov.r goes to Albany to settle that matter with the Cayugoes and then all parties will be satisfied." Mention of the Cayuga Nation is significant here. Often the peoples of Conestoga reference their obligations to the Senecas, but now Tawenea invokes the Cayugas—the nation with which both Taquatarensaly and Satcheechoe are most closely linked. If Keith thinks he can move past Sawantaeny's death and avoid a long trip to New York by going behind the backs of Taquatarensaly and Satcheechoe while they are away from Conestoga—occupied acting as his emissaries, no less—his hopes are bound to be disappointed. No ceremonial delegations, no territorial concessions.[11]

Still Keith, as always, hears only what he wants to hear. Composing his letter to the council today, he has simply claimed that, on being informed of his plans to survey lands for the Penns, the Indians have responded that "they were all exceedingly pleased with this proposition." After consulting with Colonel French, whom he has brought along on this trip, Keith tells the council that he has taken a "Resolution to go over the Susquehannah and see the above Survey made and run out directly, and I purpose to begin it tomorrow morning." By the time his letter reaches Philadelphia, he will have new initials carved in the tree trunks. By then, nothing the council can say will be able to cancel his actions. Everything would be to Keith's satisfaction, if only his head would stop throbbing.

Keith set out to mark his new land claim with the gleam of metal ore glinting in his mind's eye. All across Pennsylvania and Maryland this summer, rival surveyors are marching to do the bidding of competing colonial leaders. English mapmakers commonly use what they call a Gunter's chain to take the measure of the land. Made of brass, such chains are always 66 feet long, which amounts to 4 poles (a standard Old English measure equal to 16.5 feet). One hundred oval links, each connected by a smaller round ring, form the chain. Working their cables over rocks and around trees, these woodsmen make little use of refined mathematics. Mercator projections have existed since the 1560s, while the French began experimenting with the metric system in the 1670s. But in 1720s Pennsylvania, colonists brazen their way across the landscape in 16.5-foot increments. On horseback or on foot, in fair weather and foul, surveyors string their way westward toward the heart of the continent, stretching their chains over the ground as if taking the land itself captive.[12]

Five days later, on June 23, Keith celebrates that the deed is done. John French and Francis Worley have completed their work, marking a plot from a "Red Oak" upon the Susquehanna River "West South West Ten miles to a Chestnut." They make no measurements of longitude or latitude, gauging their progress only by presence of the trees. "From thence" they report going "North West and by North to a Black Oak" and "from thence to Sir William Keith's western Corner Tree." They trudge along from signal trunk to signal trunk, marking letters in the bark. Not bothering with mathematics, they trust that the colony's property claims will be amply substantiated by the testimony of the trees.[13]

Governor Keith marks the occasion by writing a sharply worded letter to Charles Calvert, 5th Lord Baltimore, new governor of Maryland, describing the actions he has taken to stake Pennsylvania's claims to the disputed territory. Claiming that Calvert's colonists "justly bear the title of Land Pirates," Keith smugly informs him that "I now did, at the earnest Request of the Indians, order a Survey to be forwith made upon the Banks of Susquehanna." Seldom has William Keith felt cooler or more collected.[14]

He closes his letter on a personal note, as if to suggest that no private ill will has motivated his public actions. "My fatigue in the Woods has brought a small Fever upon me, which an ounce of Bark has pretty much abated," Keith confides. He still has no idea of what made him sick or why quinine aided in his recovery. Keith's medical complaint won't receive the name "malaria" for another two decades. Even when the English do finally adopt a seemingly scientific term for the disease, they will simply adopt the Italian words for bad ("mal") air ("aria") uncritically, giving a new name to an old idea. For now, Keith cares only that his health is improving and his land prospects are again looking promising. "Tomorrow I shall return home by slow Journeys directly to Philadelphia, where I should rejoice to see you once more," he tells Calvert. In other words, Maryland's lord is always welcome to pay court to him in Philadelphia. What sort of reception he himself will receive when he once more calls his council into session, he does not hazard to guess.[15]

ISAAC NORRIS CRADLES THE crisp pages of his almanac in his hands, smooths open the book, turns it sideways, and writes the words "a Long Drought" along the margin of the page, stretching the phrase in easy script from the eighteenth of June back toward the eighth. Printed perpendicular to his note in a serif font is Titan Leeds's prediction: "Full Moon the 17th day & at Night, Moon Eclipsed." Despite the clear skies, Norris sees nothing unusual on the 17th. On the 18th, however, outside his chamber window at Fairhill, a deep shadow passes over the grounds, darkening his carefully cultivated view of flowers, shrubs, and fruit trees elegantly arranged along geometrical paths. The rainless skies over Philadelphia that night mean that whoever purchased the pair of globes from Andrew Bradford last week—the advertisement for the instruments has disappeared from this week's paper, indicating a successful sale—has likely enjoyed a spectacular celestial show.[16]

Norris may be too preoccupied with events on the ground to set his gaze on the sky tonight. A new grave has been dug in the Quaker burying-ground. "Our friend Jona. Dickinson after a long wasting Sickness Dy'd [on the] 16th," he explains in a letter to his "beloved son" Isaac Jr., who is, he hopes, now safely seeing sights, paying calls, and tending to business in London. In the pages of his almanac, Norris records a short stark summary: "16 J.D. dy'd bury'd ye 18." There are no published memorials to Jonathan Dickinson, that great merchant of mahogany and men, that chronicler of Florida captivity among "inhuman cannibals," but surely his is one of the number of "Males Buried, 6" of the "People called Quakers" counted up in the June total of "Births, Burials, and Casualties in the City of Philadelphia" printed in the newspaper at the end of the month.[17]

Jonathan Dickinson has died secure in the belief in his own sophistication and civility. He breathed his last on a feather bed and bolster in the "best room" of his four-story house, far from the filthy floor he reported sleeping on during his brief time among the Native peoples of Florida. And yet many of the colonists he has left behind—with their interest in astrology stronger than their knowledge of astronomy, with their efforts to claim land more reliant on describing trees than measuring distance—are far less advanced than they like to think. Coming on the same day as the eclipse, his burial may provoke some mourners to reflect on how their world now teeters between revelation and reason. But most pass by such thoughts in complacent ignorance.[18]

Of the few colonists who have ever paused to dwell on the relation between religion, science, and true civility, many have found themselves unwelcome to live in Pennsylvania. George Keith—the Quaker minister who tried and failed to persuade leading Philadelphians like Dickinson, Norris, and Logan not to hold humans as property back in the 1690s—had once earned his living in Pennsylvania as a surveyor. But after the controversies created by his social activism forced him to leave the colony, he returned to England, changed professions, and took orders as an Anglican priest. He never ceased searching for progress, scientific as well as social and spiritual. In the last years of his life, he devoted himself to the linked disciplines of astronomy and geography. But his former Quaker coreligionists in Philadelphia have accepted few if any of his findings.[19]

In 1709, George Keith, now called Reverend Keith, published a final book, *Geography and Navigation Compleated: Being a New Theory and Method Whereby the True Longitude of Any Place in the World May be Found*, in which he laid out the mathematical formulas needed for determining locations on land or sea. Though Reverend Keith recommended using a "Celestial orb" as an instrument of calculation, he made no reference whatsoever to the divine and never conflated the sky with heaven. But none of Reverend Keith's former friends in Philadelphia has deigned to acquire his treatise on navigation any more than they took to his *An Exhortation and Caution to Friends Concerning Buying or Keeping of Negroes*. Isaac Norris enjoys the lingering drama of astrology offered by Titan Leeds, while James Logan contents himself with purchasing works that affirm that when "a mighty blazing *Comet* appears" in the night sky, "what miserable effects of War, Ruine, and Devastation, in the most parts of the known World, follow . . . the heels of this stupendious Harbinger is obvious to all." No Pennsylvania book collectors ever import George Keith's work on astronomy.[20]

Pennsylvanians also prefer to forget another crucial aspect of George Keith's teachings: his testimony against corporal punishment and imprisonment. Starting from the Society of Friends' principled opposition to armed warfare, Keith extended his analysis to critique

bodily coercion of all kinds. His teachings were memorialized in England by a publicity pamphlet about Penn's colony published in London
in 1698. The author of that pamphlet, Gabriel Thomas, summed up
Keith's teachings by saying that he warned Quakers:

> that they should not be concern'd in the compelling part of the
> Worldly Government, and that they should set their *Negroes* at Lib-
> erty after some reasonable time of Service; likewise, they should not
> take the Advantage of the Law against one another, as to procure
> them any Corporeal Punishment.

So much has changed since George Keith left the colony. Today, Quakers have become more involved in the "compelling part of government" than ever and support the imposition of a vastly expanded list
of capital crimes in the new penal code. They continue to profit handsomely from holding humans in perpetual bondage. And now they
are most definitely engaged in taking "advantage of the law against
one another" in holding the Quaker John Cartlidge and his younger
brother, Edmund, for a capital crime. Meanwhile, Reverend Keith's
mathematics have had equally little effect on the rustic surveyors of
colonial Pennsylvania, still tramping the woods and dragging their
chains through the timber.[21]

AS THE JUNE DAYS lengthen, the Cartlidges' time in confinement
stretches before them indefinitely. No date has been set yet for a trial,
and no new word on their case has arrived from the Five Nations.
John's position as interpreter has been eclipsed by James Le Tort, his
land and legal interests overtaken by the efforts of Francis Worley. The
fur trade, too, goes on without them. From April to June, James Logan
records transactions with six different trappers and traders in which
he purchases: "77 racoons, 1 Catt, 37 fall D[ee]r;" £3, 13 shillings,
and 6 and a half pence worth of "skins." He also twice notes "Sundry
accounts paid for furs" and makes an entry for payment for "a bundle
of Deer Skins." On June 18, the day of John Dickinson's burial, Logan

buys "a Bear skin." It seems the Cartlidge brothers are fallen and forgotten men, their absence little noted and less lamented.[22]

Then, on June 22, Logan adds an unexpected entry into the "Contra" column of his expense ledger. Easy to overlook among the purchases of pelts inked onto the broad cream pages is an item of extra significance: "By John Cartlidge paid . . . on John's note." The amount of interest Logan pays, £1 and 15 shillings, is negligible, but the value is incalculable. John may be a pawn, but he is not altogether without remaining social ties. Just when Governor Keith seems to have discovered the convenience of keeping the Cartlidges incarcerated, John has found another connection to the outside. Keith seems determined to claim title on the mineral lands that he, John Cartlidge, found first. Cartlidge reacts by renewing his ties with his old patron, James Logan, a man more than a little interested in learning all the details of Keith's doings upriver.[23]

With Jonathan Dickinson gone to his grave, Gov. William Keith returns home to the news that death has eliminated one of his staunchest adversaries. Now perhaps he can avoid being drawn into debates about when and whether to exercise the full severity of the law, in cases of tavern foolery—or even in instances of cross-cultural killing. Buoyed by the success of his latest meeting with members of the Native community at Conestoga, his subsequent extra surveying expedition on the Susquehanna, his assertion of prerogative over the young lord of Maryland, not to mention the relief brought on by taking a good dose of quinine bark, Keith has every reason to feel that he is managing beautifully on many fronts.

Still, a burr prickles the governor's seat as he rides his horse back toward the city; the members of his council have refused his request for supplies for the Native community at Conestoga. While still at Francis Worley's, Keith had written to his board: "there being no bread Corn to be had in these parts, I desire you will concur with me in directing the Provincial Treasurer to hire a Waggon &. Send up directly 1000 weight of bread, 3 bushels of Salt, & 40 Gallons of the best Rum, with Sugar proportionable." He had hoped to spend public funds fulfilling the private promise he made to the Indians made in April that he would "rejoice as often as it is in my power to do you any good." How better to ensure that his new land claims in their neighborhood remain unopposed than by providing them with a handsome treat of salt, corn bread, and rum punch? But the council members coolly rejected his request, replying, "We are troubled to hear of the Scarcity of Provisions there, but seeing the Govr. has not mentioned to what publick use" the desired items would be put, they have declared that, "with submission" to his authority, they decline to "concern themselves in ordering it." William Keith may conduct his affairs with one eye cast to the west for his Indian observers and the other scanning the eastern horizon for his audiences on the Board of Trade and the Penn family. But the council members at the center of the action have no intention of applauding his performance. They are keeping their own gaze carefully pinned on the colony's purse strings.[24]

No sooner does Governor Keith call his council back into session on July 2 than his subordinates begin to question his right to survey lands on the Susquehanna. How can Keith make the assertion that he is claiming the lands for the Penn family when no one knows when or whether the Board of Trade will confirm their right to remain as proprietors? The council calls Colonel French to testify about the surveying trip. To Keith's relief, French backs him without reservation, saying "he was humbly of opinion that the Govr. had acted with great Prudence and Caution in pursuing the only effectual measure which the present situation of affairs would allow, for quieting the minds of the Indians and preserving the public peace." French, like Keith, believes Indian affairs remain poised precariously on the brink of disaster. Furthermore, he adds, "whatsoever turn the affairs of [the Penn] family might take" he does not see "how the Governs. having caused these lands to be surveyed . . . could be interpreted to the prejudice of a Family for whose service it was so plainly meant and intended." By blurring the boundary between his own land claims and those he is staking on behalf of the Penns, Keith once more slips just out of the council members' grasp.[25]

Effectively quelled for the moment, the council members present a more pressing order of business; John and Edmund Cartlidge have sent in a new plea for action on their case. Logan records that "a petition from John & Edmund Cartlidge, Prisoners in Philada. Gaol was read, praying that in regard of their long Confinement, and now that all Lawful Evidences of the Fact, for which they stand Committed, may upon notice given them be ready to appear, they may therefore be admitted to a Tryal." John demands that they take him now to face justice. Edmund asks the same. They prefer anything to languishing any longer in jail. There can be no further fact-finding needed. Whatever evidence they have in their own defense can be produced anytime the court calls for it.[26]

As the *Conductor Generalis* makes clear, their best defense under English law is the fact, agreed upon by all, that they sought out Sawantaeny for purposes of peaceful trade, not with any prior intent to do him injury. According to the handbook on justice that Andrew Bradford has just published, what makes the difference between murder and manslaughter is that in the latter case, when a homicidal attack occurs, "there must be no deliberate Act, but the falling out must be sudden." Under English law, the timing of thoughts and feelings matter.[27]

The English pay close attention to the temporal dimensions of crime. In order to mitigate the crime of killing, the person who perpetrates the violence must be transported by anger in the moment of committing the act, yet not have had any previous ill will toward the person attacked. In this regard, there is a certain convergence between the English approach and the Native one. For the Indians what matters most is also the nature of the prior relationship, that Sawantaeny, through his wife, maintained that he had been killed by his friends. These are the points on which the Cartlidges' best hopes rest, with both their English and their Indian judges.[28]

Members of council coalesce around the idea that the case should now proceed to trial without delay. Even with Jonathan Dickinson gone, the colony's merchant magistrates remain determined to insist that Governor Keith follow the straight road of the rule of law to the end of the Cartlidge case, not the winding paths of aristocratic whim and favor. Andrew Bradford has kept the issue front and center in their minds. Not only has he reprinted the manual *Conductor Generalis* in full, which clearly lays out the procedures for adjudicating crimes according to the norms of English liberty, but he has also been publishing republican political essays in his *Weekly Mercury* all month.[29]

Winking broadly at his readers by printing a disclaimer that "I can't but be sorry that a piece leveled at particular Vice and Humour among the General, and published in *Great Britain*, should be imagined as a Reflection on Particular Men in these Parts of the World," Bradford then reprinted an essay under the headline "Cato's Letters," in which the classical statesman spoke out against the dictatorship of Julius Caesar. Cato warned from Bradford's pages: "the World is governed by Men, and Men by their Passions; which being boundless and insatiable, are always terrible when they are not controlled: Who was ever satiated with Riches or surfeited with Power or tired with Honors?" If any of Bradford's readers apply these warnings about the insatiability of power to the administration of William Keith, Bradford denies responsibility. Nevertheless, James Logan clearly appreciates the printer's efforts because, not many years after this, he sets about producing his own original translation of Cato's letters, *Cato's Moral Distiches Englished in Couplets*, a political treatise in verse that will be published in Philadelphia in 1735.[30]

The pressure to uphold law and liberty takes immediate effect in the Cartlidge case. "It was recommended," James Logan notes crisply in the colony's official minutes for July 2, "to fix a day sometime this month for the Tryal of the petitioners." At last it seems there may be an end in sight to the Cartlidges' ordeal. If their hopes for a quick pardon from Keith seem unlikely to be realized, their right to a jury trial has at last been affirmed. For now, John and Edmund will have to remain quietly confined, but one day soon they may find release. In the meantime, Keith turns briskly back to his main interest: ingratiating himself with the Five Nations, the better to secure his own new property claims and those of the proprietary colony at large.[31]

He has at last resigned himself to the thought of more "fatigue" in the woods and has begun to prepare himself for a journey north. "Having promised, by the Advice of the Assembly and this Board, to meet the Chiefs of the Five Nations at Albany, it is absolutely necessary that a suitable present be provided for the Indians on that occasion," Keith informs his council. If he is going to fulfill Iroquois demands for a face-to-face meeting on their terms, he knows he cannot arrive empty-handed. And yet his council members have just rejected a similar request to offer food supplies to their nearest Native neighbors at Conestoga. Hoping there is yet a way to work around the council, Keith is now "pleased to declare his Intention of calling the Assembly together immediately after Harvest" to request the legislature's financial support. Somehow or other he must gather the money and the moral authority needed to resolve this crisis once and for all. Harvest, of course, remains many months off.[32]

In the meantime, the stars will revolve in their courses and with them the fortunes of men. Astronomy and geography are the twin sciences of this new century. The celestial and the terrestrial are linked not only by myth and magic but also by the practical techniques of the newest mathematics. Unlike the Gunter's chain, whose clumsy method of measuring remains in use by Governor Keith and company, pairs of globes that precisely model the span of the sky and the shape of the Earth offer unprecedented precision to those eager to claim land. They allow surveyors to coordinate observations of the heavens with gauges of the ground in order to pinpoint geographic locations.

Far more than the eclipse alone marks this as a momentous week. Globes, it turns out, are instruments of empire. Bradford's sale of a pair of them has sent the colony one turn closer to the future.[33]

Chapter 18

OUSEWAYTEICHKS
(SMITH THE GANAWESE)

THE ECLIPSE HAS PASSED, YET ALL ACROSS THE SUSQUE-hanna River valley this summer, people remain "covered with night and wrapped in darkness," in the words of the traditional Haudeno-saunee description of grief. Sawantaeny has been gone five months and still his death has not been correctly covered by the colonists. In Conoy Town, an Algonquian community of sapling-and-bark oblong oval houses set together a couple of dozen miles upriver from Conestoga, people of many Native nations begin to gather in mid-July. They are readying themselves for a long journey to Albany, answering the call of the Five Nations to meet with them beneath the Great Tree of Peace. Leaders from Conestoga have journeyed north to Conoy Town to meet with the people there, known to Pennsylvanians as the "Ganawese."[1]

The "Ganawese," or Conoys, have been plunged in metaphorical darkness for decades now. Originally residents of lands now claimed by Virginia and Delaware, they have suffered dislocation, violence, and disease on a catastrophic scale. Yet they keep traveling toward light. Since 1705, when they first arrived here as refugees, they have lived peacefully on the Susquehanna, thanks to an agreement from the Delaware that "they might settle amongst them." Today, the local Conoys and their visiting Conestoga neighbors are greeting a travel-ing delegation of Nanticokes, another Algonquian people on their way north to Iroquoia from Maryland. Collectively, these allied groups intend to plan their ceremonial approach to the Five Nations.[2]

Many of those massing at Conoy Town have come to seek assistance in strengthening their ties with the powerful Haudenosaunee. They look for help to a prominent local man named Ousewayteichks, known to Anglo-Pennsylvanians as Captain Smith, or "Smith, the Ganawese." In the midst of stress and chaos, Captain Smith has emerged as a singular figure, a diplomat and interpreter of unmatched resourcefulness. Almost alone amongst the people of the river valleys, Smith, it is reported by Pennsylvania colonists, "is said to speak all the several languages, viz. his own or the Ganawese, the Mingoe, the Shawanese, & Delaware to perfection." At the same time, he is an exemplary figure, well versed in a wide-ranging Algonquian tradition of long-distance diplomacy.[3]

The Nanticokes, in particular, are hoping that Smith will serve as their intermediary when they arrive in Iroquoia. Eager to "have the best Interpreter they could find in the Conoy town, which they find is Capt. Smith," they press him to act on their behalf. But there is a problem with their plan. Captain Smith has already committed to accompanying an entirely different delegation to Albany; Gov. William Keith is counting on his aid.[4]

Not directly linked to any of the people principally involved in Sawantaeny's death, Captain Smith nevertheless has such dense community connections he can't escape involvement in the case. He served beside Captain Civility in the March meeting between Sec. James Logan, Col. John French, and the peoples of Conestoga concerning the killing. On that occasion, Logan noted that "he excels in the skill of languages." He is personally well acquainted with John Cartlidge, having acted alongside him as a translator at meetings before the murder crisis began. Last month, he gained close knowledge of Governor Keith's latest projects when he translated Keith's request to the local community for permission to survey lands close to Conoy Town ahead of squatters from Maryland. Keith was so pleased with Smith's aid on that occasion that he has now asked him to accompany him to Albany as his official translator.[5]

In the northeastern woodlands, the forest winds whisper in Algonquian. Algonquian peoples are legendary linguists, known for carrying communications across great expanses, able to create complex
community networks by weaving linguistic connections. Speakers of
varied Algonquian languages crisscross the region, their footfalls packing down paths marked with tree carvings, branch piles, stone heaps,
and rock paintings, road signs rich with meaning for those with local
knowledge. Native messengers read the land as literature, a repository
of stories easily understood by those who have eyes to see. Messengers bring vital information—and disinformation—about everything
from the migrations of game animals to the machinations of men. Living in the river valleys that have cradled so many new Native alliances,
Captain Smith exceeds even most other Algonquians in his mastery of
multilingual diplomacy.[6]

Captain Smith's main network is a Native one. Perfectly fluent in
four different languages from the separate Algonquian and Iroquoian
language families, he has not troubled to learn English. Yet he is savvy
enough to adopt an English name and title. Two years ago, in July of
1720, when Pennsylvanians first took notice of him in their official colony records, Logan recorded meeting "a Ganawese Indian who called
him Captm. Smith." Logan implied that "Captain Smith" was a name
that Ousewayteichks chose for himself. If so, Ousewayteichks must
have some relationship to a colonial man named Smith that he considers significant enough to honor by using the Englishman's name in
diplomatic contexts.[7]

No one records when or why Smith the Ganawese took on that
name, much less mentions which colonist inspired his choice. Still,
they do leave certain clues. A colonial surveyor from New Kent
County, Virginia, a man by the name of "Captain Christopher Smith,"
travels extensively in this region. Like many a colonial surveyor, he is
more closely acquainted with the Native landscape and its people than
ordinary colonists are. In fact, this Captain Smith negotiates actively
with the Haudenosaunee. Just five years ago, in 1717, he traveled to
Iroquoia on behalf of Virginia's governor, Alexander Spotswood, to
address regional tensions between rival Native groups. On his way
home from that trip, he stopped off in Conestoga, where he was met by

Pennsylvania's newly arrived Gov. William Keith, along with assorted unnamed "Chiefs, & others of the Conestogoe or Mingo Indians, the Delawares, the Shawanois and the Gunawoise, all Inhabitants upon or near the Banks of the River Susquehannah." In all likelihood, the man who soon came to be known as "Smith the Ganawese" was among the gathered "Gunawoise" who conversed that day with the Virginia translator and surveyor, Capt. Christopher Smith. Indeed, whether or not the pair did talk on that particular occasion in 1717, the two Smiths clearly worked in overlapping worlds.[8]

When Governor Keith arrived among the Conoys last month hoping to survey Native lands, "Captain Smith the Ganwese" understood his intentions and helped him accomplish his desires. He both provided Keith with essential translation services and offered him crucial intelligence. In particular, Captain Smith's translation of the speaker Tawenea's claim that it was the "Cayuga" who were currently objecting to Pennsylvania's land claims on the Susquehanna was important. Certainly, it helps explain why Governor Keith is now so eager to make use of Smith's linguistic expertise as he plans his own trip north to meet leaders of the Five Nations of the Haudenosaunee. By turning to the able Captain Smith as translator, Keith can end his reliance on the combined services of the two Cayuga men, Captain Civility and Satcheechoe, whose interests seem to be rapidly diverging from his own.[9]

"Smith the Ganawese's" lack of English indicates how peripheral the colonists remain in his view, despite the impact of their many forms of incursion. Yet the Cartlidge case has drawn him into its vortex, demanding that he place new stress on the work of building cross-cultural relations. Now the Nanticokes' overture to him presents an acute dilemma: Should he act principally on behalf of Native people or consent to speak in the service of the colonists? Which course will ultimately allow him to best advance the needs and concerns of his own Conoy community? Undecided how to respond to these competing requests, Captain Smith sends word to Philadelphia to find out whether Governor Keith is willing to release him from his commitment.

He may not know how to speak or write English, but Captain Smith

knows exactly how to contact someone who does. He brings his predicament to a nearby justice of the peace, one James Mitchell. Writing
from the "township of Donnegall, bounded by the Susquehanna, July
12th" (a colonial community close to Conoy Town), Justice Mitchell
scrawls out a hurried message. Sending his letter "by express," Mitchell
informs the governor that he may be about to lose Smith's assistance to
the needs of the Nanticokes. "He tells them he has promised to go with
Yr Excelly," Mitchell says, too hurried to spell out "your excellency,"
and assures Keith "that without your leave he will not alter from his
promise." Captain Smith is a man of his word. Still, Keith is clearly both
being asked to reaffirm his arrangement with Smith and being put on
notice that he will need to take steps to retain the translator's services.[10]

Justice Mitchell's letter contains another crucial piece of intelligence, if Governor Keith only has the wit to appreciate it. Unable to
ignore the waves of people assembling at Conoy Town, Mitchell has
made inquiries into their motivations. "The Reason of their going they
say," Mitchell tells Keith, "is to renew former friendship and strengthen
it in unity for time to come." They have decided that a group approach
to the Five Nations from the various peoples of the Susquehanna valley will be the best way to ensure a successful council. "And for that
end they carry alongst with them 32 Belts of Wampum & four long
strings of the same, to give as a Present, and delivers a Speech with
them severally." This is precisely the same number of belts, thirty-
two, that the peoples of the river valleys presented collectively to the
leaders of the Five Nations exactly a decade ago in 1712 when James
Logan made his sketches of each unique geometric design. Here, then,
is a significant clue that the Indigenous peoples of the Pennsylvania
region are reenacting important rituals at regular intervals, adhering
to essential requirements of calendar and culture that colonists scarcely
notice. Once more, the Indians attempt to offer instruction to recalci-
trant colonial students. In a time of darkness and sadness, the light that
shimmers along the surface of strings and belts of wampum has unique
spiritual power to renew ties among people. There simply can be no
diplomacy without the personal presentation of wampum, offered as
the material substance of ritual feelings.[11]

Native tradition holds that the Great Law of Peace of the Five Nations itself began when the spirit Hayonwhatha, plunged in mourning, picked strands of rushes and strung them with shells, saying, "This I would do if I found anyone burdened with grief as I am. I would console them for they would be covered with night and wrapped in darkness. This would I lift with the words of condolence and these strands of beads would become words with which I would address them." When the Haudenosaunee followed this teaching, peace began to grow among them. By the first decades of the eighteenth century, Native people across the Northeast, Algonquian as well as Iroquois, have learned the fundamental importance of pairing words and beads, offering ritual condolences for death along with beautifully worked belts of wampum, whenever they seek to smooth away conflicts or build connections. Emotions must be addressed before politics; emotional exchanges are the very basis of national formation and diplomatic negotiation. And binding cords of wampum embody the emotional and spiritual bonds between peoples. When offered along with ritual speeches, wampum does many things. It ties together the work of the colonial government seal that authenticates, of the colonial Christian cross that consecrates, and of the colonial book that commemorates— all in one gleaming belt.[12]

When Pennsylvania colonists continue to grumble about Native demands for "presents," sometimes going so far as to mistake wampum simply as a Native form of money, they entirely miss the central importance of *presence* in the Native world. Wampum holds memories and messages more effectively than paper and parchment for the simple reason that it acquires full meaning only when held aloft in the hands of knowledgeable speakers. So much of colonial life relies on anonymous exchanges, from printed texts that circulate without authors ever meeting readers to manufactured products bought by consumers who never meet the producers. Knowledge grows and markets multiply in the colonists' mobile transatlantic world, but personal relationships and communal responsibilities are being lost along the way. For Captain Smith, who has devoted himself to learning the languages that allow him to draw people together, plotting a journey without planning words of condolence and preparing belts of wampum would be obvious folly. Yet Governor Keith has hardly a glimmer of true understanding of Native ways.[13]

Instead, Keith keys into the last line of Mitchell's message from Conoy Town. The assembled Indians think it "their Duty to have their Intentions made Known to Yr. Ecellcy & Honoble Council & will wait your approbation, but in hast[e] because they are straitned for Provisions." The people have packed food sufficient for a journey to Iroquoia, but waiting too long for the governor to issue his approval of their trip will force them to eat away their limited stores. This is Keith's kind of conundrum. He scrolls off a reply "To my friend Winjack, King of the Ganawese" and sends it back in care of the same express messenger who delivered Mitchell's missive. He tells the Native leader, "I have heard that your friends the Nanticokes . . . want Capt. Smith for their interpreter, but you know he is engaged to go with me to Albany and I desire you will send him down to me at Philada." Keith thinks nothing of commanding a Native "king" to yield one of his most effective diplomats to him. He believes his directive will be accepted because he accompanies his demand with an offering, saying, "I have ordered Justice Mitchell to give you some flour and bread to entertain your friends the Nanticokes." Keith is following his plan to use presents to induce the peoples of the upper Susquehanna to let him prospect for mineral wealth on their property. He simply does not realize that if and when Captain Smith accepts his demand to join him in Philadelphia, it will be because the Algonquian interpreter is fully committed to assisting in the project of cross-cultural alliance-building begun by Civility and Satcheechoe. Captain Smith is acting in concert with his Conestoga neighbors to enhance relations with colonists, not seeking to enrich himself at the expense of others.[14]

Chapter 19

MONEY AND GOOD MEN

AUGUST 3–15, 1722

Money and good men are scarce.

—Titan Leeds, Verses for August,
The American Almanack for 1722

AS AUGUST SWEATS, SARAH LOGAN STEWS. IT IS THE TIME of the rising of the apron. She is great with child, yet her mind dwells not on birth but on death. She has been having strange forebodings. James Logan, Indian trader, governor's secretary, the Penn family's dependable man in the colony, goes before his fellow council members and tells them that, whatever the Indians say, he cannot go to Albany. His young wife is "ready to lie down" he tells them. "If I went," he explains, she worries that "she should not live to see me again."[1]

Thirty years old this year, Sarah is eighteen years younger than her husband. She has three living children: Sarah, her firstborn, named after her, is going on eight years old and starting to take on a motherly role with her two younger siblings, William age four, and Hannah age two. The secret of Sarah's swollen sadness comes in the nearly four-year gap between Sarah and William. Baby James once burbled in that space, a firstborn son named in honor of his father. For a brief moment after his birth, they were a family of four, two Sarahs and two Jameses—English migrants who had managed to reproduce themselves and their culture in a new colonial world. But wee James died five years ago this July, when he was only six months old.[2]

They call it a staircase family, when the children are born every two years, because you can line them all up in a row in age order and skip your hand down the smooth steps of their gleaming heads. But Sarah has lost her footing on a missing stair and now she cannot steady herself. For most, summer marks the time to begin gathering in the fruits of the year. "Began to Reap ye New Field Wheat," Isaac Norris notes in his diary in July this year, near the fifth anniversary of James's death. Sarah is less sure of her harvest.[3]

GOV. WILLIAM KEITH SURVEYS the council members assembled before him in the courthouse chamber on the third day of August. Itchy weather for wigs, this. Down on Water Street, at the Sign of the Scales, they have been flogging "several Sorts of Shalloons, Tammies, Broad Cloths, Druggets, Threads, with Haberdashery and sundry other European Goods" all summer. Not much call for English wovens in this American heat. Tempers are apt to rise with the temperature and you will have to look far to find the man who isn't chafing in his cravat today.[4]

Yet here is James Logan, pen poised pertly as ever, quite as if he has not just offered to inconvenience the governor. What is that man plotting now? Having resigned himself to swatting horseflies all the way to Albany, Keith invited Logan to accompany him. After all, the leaders of the Five Nations asked for the colony's secretary by name. Better to keep Logan saddled beside him than to leave him at home to scheme behind his back. Keith followed formalities and notified the legislature of the personnel he planned to bring with him, indicating that he expected the company of Richard Hill and James Logan along with that of a French fur trader named James Le Tort, whom he called upon to act as his translator. Not Smith the Ganawese. In the end, the Native interpreter has withdrawn his offer to serve and left Keith scrambling to find a qualified replacement. Now, just this morning, he has "received a Message from the House" announcing a new vexation. They write "that they were well satisfied in the Governor's nomination of Richard Hill & James Logan & wish'd it might suit their circumstances to attend the service, but that they had found upon some communication those two members declined the Journey." Really? Keith is going to have to issue some communications of his own.[5]

He will not be drawn into a quarrel over which of these men is to attend him. "All members being acceptable," he tells them smoothly, they must "agree amongst them who should be the persons that would accompany him." More important, he wants their aid in drafting his remarks to the leaders of the Five Nations. After so many diplomatic mistakes, he cannot afford another wrong move. Whether or not Logan wants to take a speaking part in person, Keith needs the man's words. And he is actually less worried about whether Logan participates than the council may think. Wherever and however Logan chooses to spend the month of August, Keith knows his secretary will be a step behind.[6]

BACK IN JULY, WILLIAM Keith filled three sheets to Hannah Penn in his easy slant. You can get the best quills in the spring, when the geese sprout strong new feathers. A right-handed man like William Keith will always prefer a flight feather from the left wing. That way, the long barbs flare off the shaft away from the writing hand.[7]

"Madam," Keith writes, "it is, I conceive, very proper you should know that Mr. Logan has at last put me under a necessity of differing very widely with him in many things relating to the affairs of your family here." Keith claims that Logan has been conniving with members of the Assembly to pass a law giving the legislature, not the proprietors, the right to confirm or deny property titles. Though the governor has to admit that no such law has actually been made, he is sure that Logan is already working on other stratagems to cheat the proprietors. Faced with the failure of his legislation, Keith complains, "nevertheless, Mr. Logan still goes on brightly and as no man living knows better how to puzzle the state of an account, perhaps it will be no easy matter to unravel." Logan's cheerfulness is all the proof Keith needs that he is out to skim from the Penn family. If Keith has seen the neat columns of Logan's account book, the creamy pages filled with

notations "Cash" and "Contra," it seems he lacks the skills to understand the art of double-entry bookkeeping.[8]

But both men think they know enough to recognize double-
crossing when they see it. "He is very angry that I should pretend to
see or take any notice of his management in Proprietary affairs," Keith
tells the Widow Penn, now discrediting Logan by describing him as
angry. Keith himself is nothing if not incensed by Logan and Norris's
treacherous letters of April, but he does *not* make any reference to that
correspondence now, even as he seeks to undercut it. Instead, he puts a
new spin on the matter of the mining rumors.[9]

"The extravagant humour which prevails here about mines," Keith
begins a new paragraph with an amused-sounding reference to the
craze for copper, "has considerably raised the value of lands, so that if
discreet measures are taken, the opportunity may be wisely improved
to the immediate advantage and great profit of this fine estate." In other
words, Keith intimates that while mineral wealth may be imaginary,
there is real money to be made for the Penn family by selling land to
foolish dreamers at a dramatic markup. He says nothing of certain recent
land acquisitions of his own—of the tip he took from a man accused

OPPOSITE: *An eighteenth-century man's signature communicates his social
position. William Keith signals his high status by signing his name in
tall letters (four to five times the height of the rest of his writing) and
underlining his name with a broad flourish. His polite use of the phrases
"your most obliged and most obedient humble servant" shows the feigned
humility fashionable among the upper sort. John Cartlidge signs his name
as suits his status as a middling man of substantial property who holds an
official position. His signature is of modest size, but he adds curlicues to his
letters and underlines his name with a thin stroke. Isaac Norris's quickly
initialed signature comes not from a letter that was sent and received but
rather from a copybook. As a gentleman of leisure, he has the time to make
personal copies of every letter he writes, which he keeps in a leather-bound
book for future reference. His abbreviated use of the phrase "Thy loving
friend" is in the simple Quaker style, refusing false claims of modesty.*

SIGNATURES OF JOHN CARTLIDGE, ISAAC NORRIS, JAMES LOGAN, AND WILLIAM KEITH,
AUTHOR'S PHOTOS FROM DOCUMENTS AT THE HISTORICAL SOCIETY OF PENNSYLVANIA.

of murder, of his swift and secret horseback rides with mapmakers, of his rum-punch-sweetened conversations with Native peoples—actions that might hint that he himself harbors glittering dreams. Were he aware of all that Logan and Norris know or guess about his actions, and of how many of these surmises they have shared in letters sent across the ocean, he might craft his words with more care.[10]

As it is, Keith affects an air of detachment about "these extravagant humours" as he writes to Hannah Penn. He signs himself her "most obliged and most obedient humble servant" and underlines his name with his usual bold stroke. A flick of the wrist and a sprinkle of the pounce pot will dry the ink and set his version of the story for the ages.[11]

IT COSTS KEITH LITTLE effort to meet Logan's latest failure of cooperation with studied indifference. Let the man go in the horse train to Albany or stay at home to tend his wife, Keith has covered all his angles. Now he needs only to be sure that his secretary's connivances won't extend to contesting the way he conducts himself at Albany. No, the full council must be made to consult and concur on his speech before he departs. Then they will rise or fall together.

Turning his attention away from the question of Logan's travel plans, the governor commands the council to draw up the talking points "they may think necessary or useful for the Service of the Government, to be Treated of at the ensuing Meeting with the Indians of the Five Nations at Albany." Asking them to consult amongst themselves, he tells them, "Draw up the Heads accordingly against three in the afternoon." Better to set a midafternoon deadline for their next appointment, since there is bound to be further debate once he has their agenda items in hand. But before he dismisses them, he wants their advice on one other pressing public matter.[12]

Three accused murderers besides the Cartlidge brothers are currently being held "under sentence of death" in the colony's various county jails. Of course, the unfortunate Eleanor Moore has already swung. What, Keith wants to know, would the council members have him do in these other cases? He has the right, as the colony's chief magistrate, to announce a stay of execution. But he can do little to stay the tongues of council members who may gossip that any mercy the governor shows grows only from a desire to court popularity with commoners at the expense of public order. The council members discuss the matter and decree that two of the newly accused may continue in jail until such time as the facts of their case have been fully established.[13]

The third prisoner fares far worse. As Logan records it, "upon consideration," the council members advise that "Wm. Battin, being Convicted of divers horrid complicated Crimes, be Executed & hung in Irons in the most public place, at such time as the Govr. shall appoint, & that the Warrant for the execution be issued before the Governor sets out for Albany." With the possibility of releasing the Cartlidges still very much on the table, the city's leading residents need a show of official severity now more than ever. They have agreed to defer the decision about whether to hold a trial for the Cartlidges until after the governor returns from Albany. But they cannot allow the governor to speed out of town with multiple other murderers just waiting a chance to slip their chains. Governor Keith responds that he is "pleased to agree." With that, the council members file out of the chamber in time for a midday meal and perhaps a saucer of Bohea tea.[14]

⌒

WHEN DEATH DONS A barrister's wig, he directs a noisy business. All night long, as the condemned lie sleepless in their cells, whispering prayers or whimpering sorrows, they can hear hammers pounding and saws whining, sounds of their scaffolds being erected. Custom-built furniture for the poor and forgotten, the luckless ones who till now have counted themselves lucky to meet with a stump or a box on which to perch their arses.[15]

Not that today's executioner, when he comes, cuts a fine figure. Those in the crowd at Chester this hot August morning, gathered to witness the final living moments of William Battin, must crane to get a look at the officiant manning the scaffold. A redheaded little hang-

man, he is only a youngster dressed in a poor cotton jacket and osnaburg shirt and breeches. Members of the throng shuffle their feet. They
have just enjoyed a fine recitation of William Battin's full confession.
Now they are impatient for the denouement of the day's spectacle, the
moment when his legs will twitch their last.[16]

The young man designated as the hand of the law is not precisely
a free person himself. Bound by a servant's indenture, he was pressed
into this job by a county sheriff who caught him attempting to run away
from his legal master. In the depths of December last year, the young
man chose to face a frozen wilderness rather than stay one more night
under his master's roof. But he didn't get far before crossing paths with
the New Castle sheriff. By rights, the lawman should have marched the
runaway servant straight back to his master and booked him with an
extra year of service as punishment for his short-lived escape. But the
sheriff had other ideas about the best way to occupy the young truant's
time. Before long, he had equipped him with a rope and remade him
as the hand of the law. With so many additional capital crimes to be
punished under the colony's new legal statutes, Pennsylvania's lawmen
must improvise. They hit on the solution of imposing hangman's duties
as an informal punishment on those, like the redheaded runaway, who
have been accused of lesser wrongs.[17]

Today's is the second death sentence the short little hangman has
been obliged to inflict this summer. Back in May, it was he who led
Eleanor Moore into eternity. The New Castle sheriff approved of his
work enough to pass him along to the Chester sheriff and now he has
been officially tasked with taking another life. If it comes to it, he
would rather feel the rough of the rope in his hands than on his neck.
But he has had enough of doing Death's bidding. He wants more than
anything to be free of the stern commands of the law, the greedy gaze
of the mob, the cries of the condemned. As he climbs up next to William Battin, he is near enough to feel him tremble, their bodies as close
as their fates.[18]

William, an indentured servant just like the young man now bound
to take his life, has just stood by while his official last words were read
aloud for the crowd. "The Speech of the Boy Hang'd at Chester"
is to feature in next week's edition of the *American Weekly Mercury*.

All across the English-speaking Atlantic, from London to Glasgow to Dublin, newspaper readers have come to enjoy a fashionable new literary form: the gallows speech. Alongside the satirical essays and comical tales created by literary lights from Daniel Defoe to Joseph Addison and Richard Steele, news rags have begun to feature true-crime stories. Execution sermons by pious ministers warning of sin appear often now in print along with scaffold-side speeches credited to convicts. This is the ugly side of belles lettres. Even as the men of Philadelphia's gentry class try their pens at producing polite verses, along the lines of Aquila Rose's poetic effusions, the common folk of the colony also participate in transatlantic literary culture. Pennsylvania has now attained such heights of civility that its people, too, can generate the kinds of convicts' confessions being enjoyed in other large mercantile centers across the British Empire.[19]

Newspaper readers cannot get enough of murder narratives voiced by members of the criminal classes. Like all literary forms, the confessions of the condemned have quickly developed genre conventions, those easily recognizable patterns and practices that distinguish artistic production. A good gallows speech always features a condemned person born of an honest father and mother who, after being dismissed from an apprenticeship, wallows in loose living with bad companions, slips into a sordid life of petty crime and sin, and then falls into committing a capital crime. Moral failings are best symbolized by sexual transgressions, so these tales usually contain a certain exciting element of titillation. Remorse is obligatory, as is a warning to other young people to shun temptation. You might think that the highly formulaic nature of confession narratives would lead some to question their authenticity. But to the contrary, successful adherence to literary standards is simply appreciated as a mark of cultural quality.[20]

William Battin's "Speech and Confession" did not disappoint today. The statement "read at the Gallows before his execution" began with the admission that he "dishonoured and rebelled against" his parents and "regarded not their care for me." There they were, the honest parents. Next, Battin said, "I gave myself up to serve the Devil." He began his life of crime with petty theft: a whalebone whip, a knife and fork, a row of pins. As time went on, he began to pilfer more costly items: a silk handkerchief, a silver watch, a beaver hat, a suit of clothes, and a shirt. Each theft was marked in turn with a whipping, a beating, a stay in prison, a lost apprenticeship. Still, he wanted to finger luxury materials like silver and silk, exotic ones like whalebone and beaver skin, a whole new world of goods out of reach suddenly within his grasp.[21]

Point by point his tale met every literary expectation. Finally, Battin said, "My father . . . ordered me to be brought over into this Province of *Pennsylvania*. About 7 or 8 days after the Ship . . . was safely arrived, I was sold." Though his father signed him over to the ship-master on the London dock, neither he nor his parents had the legal authority to dispose of his life from that point forward. Like tens if not hundreds of thousands of other "infortunates," he arrived as a so-called "exchanged servant" bound in England on no specific terms, then marketed to a new master from the ship deck when he arrived in the colonies. He signed no voluntary contract with his Pennsylvania master but simply "was sold" to him at profit. And so this young thief of Atlantic consumer goods himself became a trade item.[22]

Battin's alleged crime would make anyone shudder. He supposedly admitted to deliberately setting fire to his master's house while the man and his wife were absent, burning their three children, ages six, four, and two, to death in their beds. Down came the whole house in flames, staircase and all. As if working from a gallows-speech checklist, Battin added, "since then I have been guilty of that vile and abominable Sin of buggery with a Sow." But his most shocking confession was this: "Before my trial, at the Time of it, and afterwards, I continued in Obstinancy, and denied the Truth, which I had before confess'd." Was a false confession coerced and then recanted? Battin's official record contained this hint. Yet it ended by adhering closely to convention. Battin stated "my sins are so odious and so many, that I can hardly expect forgiveness" and closed by declaring, "I greatly desire all Youth may take Example by me, and have a Care how they disobey their Parents, which if I had not done, I should not be here this day." With admirable narrative instincts, he brought the tale full circle, just as the gallows speech genre would dictate.[23]

How did William Battin, thieving, murdering servant boy, achieve such literary heights? Battin's statement was recorded, perhaps worded, by one "William Davies, of Chester, schoolmaster" while he was being held in prison. As a teacher, Davies could be expected to know how to coax, command, and cajole a boy into talking. He could also be assumed to know well how to write with style. Once he had crafted the convict's statement to his requirements, Davies asked him to approve it; the young man "signed with the Mark of William Battin." Battin did not know his letters well enough to sign his own name. Could he actually have composed the polished crime account Davies prepared and asked him to sign? Though no schoolmaster ever taught him to read or write, one appeared by his side to pen his confession when he was accused of a capital crime. Hardly the master of his own life, Battin is credited nevertheless as the author of his own death.[24]

In short order, the young executioner finishes his work. Battin's body is left hoisted high in an iron gibbet, a cage where one and all can see his corpse as it begins to decompose. Later he may lay claim to the labors of one last carpenter. Perhaps his remains—that is, whatever is left of him after the birds have torn him piece by piece—will be placed in a plain pine box made by some joiner's apprentice. Then he can be buried in the "Stranger's Burying Ground." But not for Battin the "two fine chests of drawers, and Two Tables, one of Mahogany, the other of Spanish Elm" advertised in the same issue of the paper that reports his demise and prints his story.[25]

Like advertisements for exquisite furniture, the appearance of Battin's scaffold speech in the *Weekly Mercury* offers evidence of Pennsylvania's material and cultural advancement. Both mark the commercial maturity of a colony that now has men of property to protect as well as a reading public eager to follow the latest literary fashions and able to appreciate a well-told gallows confession. Coerced, compelled, or perhaps entirely created by the schoolmaster who played amanuensis, Battin's written account of his crimes connects him to the culture of letters. In this, it confirms his humanity, however fallen. No such niceties were offered to the "Negro man" who was executed last summer for housebreaking without ever even being recognized by name in print.

ON AUGUST 7, GOVERNOR Keith and his council gather together one last time before his scheduled departure for Albany. Having duly produced "a Rough Draught" of the remarks Keith is to make at the Albany conference on the afternoon of September third, they meet now to polish the plan. The council members have metal on their minds today. Iron is for prison chains; gold is for finger rings. Base for the base of society and precious for the precious few. They intend to make mention of both kinds of bands in the speech they are drafting for the governor to make to the Five Nations.[26]

The council members tell Keith "they humbly propose it as their opinion" that he begin by reminding leaders of the Five Nations of how William Penn had long ago entered "Leagues of friendship with them." They recommend that he then move on to mentioning a visit to Philadelphia last summer from "that wise and good man Ghesaont," one of the four leading members of the Haudenosaunee who ultimately lost his life under suspicious circumstances on his final journey to Virginia. His death, and the hole it has left in the community, has recently led the Five Nations to demand that the Native peoples of the Susquehanna join them in new captive-taking raids. Only if Native grief is assuaged may they choose peace over war, and so, the council tells Keith, he must describe the colonists' "great grief that good man died before he returned." Furthermore, Keith should remind the Five Nations' leaders that, during the meeting with Ghesaont, Indians and colonists "brightened the chain together," employing the Haudenosaunee metaphor for alliance that makes metal links the main symbol of ties between peoples.[27]

Remind the Indians, too, the council tells Keith, of "the Golden Medal and the presents they delivered." Last summer, they gave Ghesaont an embossed disc bearing an image of the British King. Diplomatic medals like this are meant to be impressive tokens of alliance. Council members hope that by mentioning last year's offerings alongside this year's grief they can begin to match Indian expectations for the pairing of words and gifts. Led by Logan, the council members make their best efforts to adhere to Native forms. Yet English settlers do not accept the substance of Indigenous ideas, that ritual presents and ceremonial words have spiritual meanings that help to create and

confirm communal relationships. The medal that the colonists presented to that leader of the Five Nations last summer was not made of
genuine gold. It was only *golden*, glimmering with an offer of friendship that may yet prove equally cheap.[28]

Next, the council tells Keith he ought to turn to discussing the crisis that is driving him to Albany, "a very unhappy accident which has
fallen out which has given us great Grief." Determined to shrink the
meaning of Sawantaeny's death, the council members suggest that the
governor recast it as a happenstance occurrence, not a deliberate act.
Still, they know by now how grave a mistake they committed in sending neither condolences nor compensation when news of the death first
emerged. They hasten to have the governor point out that since then
he has "sent some Tokens to the five Chiefs of the five Nations which
he hopes they have received with the Mourning Gold Ring from the
Govrs. own finger." If a brass medal was thought sufficient in 1721,
Sawantaeny's death has finally persuaded the governor that he had better gild his displays of respect with real gold.[29]

Still, the most important point, council members think, is to stress
again their commitment to good order and impartial justice. When
you get to Albany, they advise the governor, tell the leaders of the
Five Nations that "the men who did this were brought to Philadelphia,
committed to Prison, and put in Irons, and there remain to be tried
for their Lives according to our Laws, in the same manner as if they
had Killed an Englishman." Gone, suddenly, are the vacillations about
manslaughter versus murder, the careful efforts to minimize the crime
and mitigate the consequences. They are offering the Five Nations an
actual iron-clad guarantee that the perpetrators will be prosecuted on
pain of death.[30]

Satcheechoe might as well never have mentioned the Five Nation's
position that "they desire John Cartlidge may not die for this. They
would not have him killed." The colonists remain unwavering in their
insistence that they will continue to handle the case according their
own perspectives on crime and punishment. A proven killer belongs
swinging from a scaffold, not sitting beside a communal fire.[31]

Even by the standards of their own laws, Pennsylvania's leaders are
taking extreme measures. They claim they have had the Cartlidges

"put in irons." Holding a prisoner in iron shackles can only occur in exceptional circumstances. According to that recently published reference book on the correct general conduct of English justice, the *Conductor Generalis* so helpfully reprinted by Andrew Bradford, "No Prisoner shall be put in Irons but Traytors, or those taken for Felony or Trespass *in parcis et vivariis*." Applying this guideline to the Cartlidge case requires some effort. No matter the danger that their attack on Sawantaeny may pose to security in the colony, neither Cartlidge brother can be fairly accused of acting as a traitor by any standard meaning of the term. But they *have* been accused of committing a felony *in parcis et vivariis*—that is, in a park or preserve—on private property belonging to a lord. According to this interpretation of English common law, a crime committed on the manor grounds of a lord exposes the accused to harsher punishments than would the same action taken in the village square. If the Cartlidges had gotten into a drunken brawl and killed a man in a city tavern, they could still be taken to prison, but they could not be held there in irons, loaded with heavy shackles even as they sat behind bars. But because they assaulted and killed Sawantaeny on proprietary lands, they have committed a special category of crime.[32]

In parcis et vivariis. In other words, even as the governor and council present their harsh correction of the Cartlidge brothers as proof of their commitment to providing Indians with equal justice, the strict style of punishment they have chosen—putting the brothers in irons—actually constitutes another claim on Native ground. The Cartlidges can be kept in chains precisely because they committed their crime on land that colonists are claiming as Penn family property. With one move, colonists prosecute Sawantaeny's death and lay claim to his birthright. That takes brass.

⟜

LOGAN HAS RENDERED THE governor his services and his fellow council members have approved his request to be excused from official obligations at Albany. "Those of the Secretary's Family being considered, it was allowed that no man of humanity could desire him to absent himself from it at this time." These functionaries may clap men in cuffs or swing them in cages, but they never lose a chance to reassert their own humanity. Let Logan go and listen to his wife's groaning pains. There are plenty of other men ready to lend an ear to the governor's speeches at the Indian conference. "Richard Hill, Isaac, Norris & Andrew Hamilton were prevailed on to undertake the Journey." Once again, perfect balance will be preserved; two Quaker members of the government and two Anglican ones will go to Albany to promote the colony's interests and, not incidentally, their own. The Cartlidges' lives are on the line, but hardly weigh on the governor and his council.[33]

The council's parting advice to the diplomatic party is that the speech they have planned may be modified as needed, "varied as the circumstances of affairs, Time & Place, in the Judgement of the Gov.r and the members of Council who accompany him, may render it necessary." Perhaps they realize that not all of their claims will rest well with the Five Nations. Maybe they have a nagging sense that they ought to have followed Satcheechoe's recommendations regarding the fate of the Cartlidges more closely and not made unasked-for promises that the pair will pay with their lives for the loss of Sawantaeny. If so, they have permission to revise on the fly.[34]

Finally, and not incidentally, the governor informs the council that the Assembly has granted him the tidy sum of £130, to cover the costs of his journey to Albany and "those of the Gentlemen of the Council that are to accompany him thither." Assured that they will travel in style, the council members then learn that the Assembly has authorized a further £100 to be used to purchase trade goods to present as diplomatic gifts to the leaders of the Five Nations at Albany. One hundred pounds sterling. This is how much the colony is willing to spend to cover the death of Sawantaeny. While not a trivial sum, it is significantly less than the travel allowance being given to their own leaders. "Money and good men are scarce," warns this month's almanac prophesy.[35]

By August 12, the governor and his entourage will have trotted out of the city. By August 13, Logan's wife will be "safe delivered" of a baby daughter, "called Rachel after her only sister." By August 15, William Battin will have been put to death. And by August 23, Battin's hangman will himself be "committed to the Custody of John Hall, Esq., Sheriff of Bucks-County Pennsylvania." The advertisement declares, "he says he belongs to John Garner or Gardiner." Apparently, the runaway servant boy has decided he would prefer to name his former master and take his chances on returning to him than to continue life on the lam. The young executioner, his own name never recorded, nonetheless finds his story presented in the pages of the *Mercury*. "He says he left his said Master on the 27th of December last and has lived since with the Sheriff of New Castle, till he had hanged a Woman there, after which Service, he gave him a Pass, since which he came to Chester and hanged the Boy." This runaway servant escaped household labor only to find worse trouble in houses of correction.[36]

Having had the opportunity to take the full measure of English justice, the hangman himself is ready to throw down the rope. "This is to give Publick Notice to the said John Gardiner in order that he may have his said Servant again" finishes the ad. The notice appears a second time two weeks later, then never again, suggesting a successful reunion between the redheaded young man and his former master. Order is restored.[37]

Chapter 20

JAMES LE TORT

J AMES LE TORT HEAVES UP HIS LOAD OF HIDES AND HANDS the whole slippery bundle over to James Logan. Logan weighs it carefully and makes a mental note. Across the American colonies this August, fur traders are hooking huge bales of skins on iron steelyards, sliding the counterweight away from the fulcrum along the marked lines of the longer arm, making a few adjustments, finding the correct balance, and recording the weight. Few handle more pelts than James Logan. He leans over the smooth expanse of his wide wooden table and adds a new entry to the "Contra" column in the large ledger book where he records the charges made against him: "By James Le Tort p[ai]d for carriage of his skins &c." Bound books, boots and belts, rawhides or well-cured skins: The summer air fairly smokes with the layered scents of many leathers.[1]

James Le Tort may not seem like a man in urgent need of extra money. After all, the fur trader and translator has just been included among the "gentlemen" chosen to ride with Governor Keith to Albany, and the group has been handsomely supplied with travel funds by the colonial assembly. Nevertheless, on August 10, just two days before the delegation is to depart, Le Tort meets with Logan to trade deer coats. Logan compensates him precisely down to the last pence: £38, 3 crowns, 8 shillings, and 2 pence for the lot. Such a conveniently timed payment can only help ensure that Logan's interests will not be neglected even as the governor and his delegation leave him behind.[2]

James Le Tort, like James Logan, is a close associate of John Cartlidge. Le Tort has translated beside Cartlidge at diplomatic meetings held at Conestoga. He maintains a friendly rivalry with his fellow fur trader, each plying the same forests and vying with the other to reap the highest profits. Along with Peter Bezaillion and others, they range over the countryside, exchanging rum, cloth, and other manufactures for Indian furs and skins—deerskins, primarily, as well as rarer varieties of pelts: bears, martins, fishers. Whenever one of the smaller traders has a nice haul collected, he brings his bounty to Logan for cash or credit.[3]

Logan stands atop a fur-trade pyramid, his spyglass pointed out to sea. He awaits the regular arrival of the tall-mast ships that will carry his cargo to England, where merchants know the magic that can convert fur into gold. There is more than one way to mine the forest. Likewise, there is more than one way to keep tabs on Governor Keith. In Le Tort, Logan knows he has an extra set of eyes and ears.[4]

Much that passes between the two men that day goes unrecorded and perhaps unspoken. James Le Tort has complex personal investments in the crisis facing John Cartlidge and his brother Edmund. Of course, they are closely linked by trade. But Le Tort's connection to the case cuts even deeper than that. Sawantaeny's killing closely mirrors the untimely end of a member of Le Tort's own family. An uncle of Le Tort's was murdered decades ago by unknown Indians—and no one has ever been held accountable for the crime. As James Logan reminded the Native community at Conestoga this past February, "for near forty years past," colonists and Native peoples have lived together peacefully and "scarce any one Injury has been done, nor any one Complaint made on either side except for the Death of La Tour and his Company." Though Indians subjected a Euro-American man to a violent death, no official complaint was ever made against the perpetrators by the colonists.[5]

From the moment he first met Native people to discuss the case back in March, Logan believed that if the Native peoples of the river valleys could be made to recall the lenient colonial attitude after the killing of the man named Francis Le Tort, they might be willing to accept something less than the Cartlidges' execution as the cost of Sawantaeny's life. In the months since, Native messages have greatly strengthened his hopes for this. Still, the leaders of the Five Nations may need a direct reminder of those events. James Le Tort's personal attendance at the meeting can offer powerful evidence that there is precedent for allowing a cross-cultural homicide to go unremarked by the law. As the two Jameses lock eyes over the heap of furs, neither can have these facts far from mind.

PENNSYLVANIA COLONISTS HAVE CREATED only a murky record of the family of Le Torts who lived and died in their midst. Indeed, they refer to members interchangeably by the names Le Tort, le Tore, La Tour, and L. Tort, to name just some of the more frequent variations with which the English scrawl the French name. Jacques Le Tort, James's father, first gained notice in the official minutes of the province in 1689, when the colony's governor reported "a Letter he had rec[eive]d from one Capt Le Tort (a frenchman living up in the Country)." Le Tort had written to pass on "several Rumours of danger from ye French & Indians in conjunction with ye Papists." Le Tort was a Protestant, a Huguenot, and anxious to prove himself an asset to the new English owners of the territory he lived in. Yet the council declared immediately that "they did not see any reason to give heed unto" his letter. Despite the way they devalued the intelligence he supplied, five years later, in 1694, the council required "Capt Jacque Le Tort give . . . sureties that he shall acquaint the governor with all matters he can hear of or observe concerning the Natives & the enemies of the Countrie." In the early years of the century, when Anglo-Pennsylvanians thought about the Le Tort family at all, they did so with suspicion.[6]

Jacques's wife, Ann (who at some unspecified point in time became his widow), along with his son James came to the attention of the governing council of the colony on multiple occasions. Almost always, they were thrust into the record by Native peoples lodging protests about their behavior. In 1707, James got caught up in Peter Bezaillion's mining scheme and was ordered before the council to be reprimanded for squatting on Native lands. Like Bezaillion, he got off with a slap on the wrist, but this was but one of many unfortunate incidents. In 1709, members of the Conoy Nation "complained that some of the Traders, especially J Le Tort wrong'd them in the measure of their match coats which he sold them." Council members frowned once again. Traders like James pad profits by cutting corners when they measure cloth, a practice that only earns them the distrust and disgust of Indian hunters who know the true value of their wares.[7]

Meanwhile, Ann came into conflict with Native women on the Susquehanna when "the old Queen of Conguegoes represented that the said M[adame] L Tort did them great Damages by keeping of Hogs, and that twice she turned them into the Queen's Corn in her own sight." Half-feral pigs gouging the countryside and gorging on Indian produce represent some of the worst of colonial incursions into Native life. Local women, whether leaders like Conguegoes or more ordinary wives and mothers, plant, tend, and harvest the community's crops and own all the bounty they raise. The Le Tort pigs were stealing food from the mouths of Indian children and money from the hands of Indian women. Ann added insult to injury when she drove her hogs deliberately into Native fields.[8]

Yet in spite of these workaday conflicts with the Le Torts, it was members of the Native community at Conestoga—not one of the local colonists—who took the lead in pressing governing Pennsylvanians to address the matter of the violent Le Tort death in 1711. And when they did, their request came from an unexpected quarter. Their demand to resolve the matter came at the behest of the leaders of the Five Nations.

On May 28, 1711, Peter Bezaillion entered the council chamber in Philadelphia, where then governor Charles Gookin presided, to deliver a message from Conestoga that community leaders there were requesting an immediate visit from colonial Pennsylvania officials and "desired some end may be made with the Shawanon Indians about the Death of Le Tore." In this first Anglo-American record of the death of the French woodsman, Conestoga leaders implicated neighboring Shawnee people in the killing. Bezaillion continued, "the Reason of their pressing the Govr.s presence at this time, is . . . that some of the Chief of the Council of the five nations are there." Here was more diplomatic intrigue. As communities in the Susquehanna region began to reshape their alliances in the midst of a shattered world, leaders of the

Five Nations of the Haudenosaunee had begun providing advice and oversight to the Shawnees. As the originators of the mourning war complex (whereby lost community members were replaced by captive-taking) the Haudenosaunee had exerted tremendous pressure on outsider populations during the seventeenth century, even as they had offered ever-greater protections for peoples living within their orbit. Faced with this reality, alongside the compounding stresses of European colonialism, the Shawnees, like many in the Susquehanna valley, had opted for an alliance that made them tributaries of the Iroquois. All of this added up to a situation in which a murder of a French colonist by a Shawnee man within the bounds of an English colony became a Five Nations problem.[9]

Three weeks later, on June 18, 1711, the Pennsylvania governor did as requested and journeyed to Conestoga to discuss the state of current affairs with leaders of the Five Nations then visiting there. In an opening speech, the colonial magistrate made no reference to any murders that might have occurred, but rather spoke blandly of the "great Regard" and "mutual friendship" that bound Indigenous peoples and colonists. In response, a well-known Shawnee chief named Opessa, speaking on behalf of the "Senequois & Shawnois"—that is, of the Senecas and the Shawnees—broached the subject himself. "Were it possible for us, by presents or any other way, [to] atone to the Lives of those Men our young people unadvisedly slew, we would be," he promised, "willing to make satisfaction." Here was one of the Pennsylvania colonists' first introductions to the Native way of mending the social fabric when it was rent by murder. "Such a Condescension would be forever greatfully remembered and more nearly Engage us," Opessa said. According to the traditions of the Haudenosaunee, a murder could be the occasion for closer engagement rather than for further estrangement.[10]

To this, the governor, Charles Gookin, retorted, much as his successor, William Keith, would over a decade later, "that the Laws of England were such, that whosoever Kill'd a man must run the same fate." English justice required an eye for an eye and a tooth for a tooth. If one man murdered another, he, too, must be put to death. Despite the English bluster, the assertion had no immediate significance, since

Opessa declared and Gookin accepted that the men who killed Le Tort and his companions were themselves "all Dead, save one who is gone to Mississippi." The gathered diplomats simply agreed to disagree and not to let competing principles stand in the way of common practicalities.[11]

Just to be sure, Opessa felt compelled to explain the event, to extenuate the offense, to exonerate himself and his people. He was, he claimed, "solicited by Jno Hans Steelman . . . either to bring back or Kill ffrancis De le Tore and his Company." Opessa swore that he had refused the request and bore no responsibility for anyone who had respected it. Steelman, according to Opessa, degraded his intended targets as "his Slaves & Dogs (meaning le Tore & Company)." This Steelman could have been either the original John Hans Steelman of Maryland, early entrant into the lucrative regional fur trade or John Hans Steelman Jr., the very man who would later rush down the Susquehanna River to Maryland to implicate the Cartlidges in Sawantaeny's death. Either way, this means that, by 1722, these Swedish fur traders, father and son, have been within splashing distance of two different murder cases involving rival Euro-American traders. Wide as the green woods are, they are repeatedly crossed and crisscrossed by peoples with long memories and tangled ties.[12]

Whenever social bonds are broken, by whatever means, people struggle to take up the thread of their lives. At their 1711 meeting with the Pennsylvania colonists, the Native peoples gathered at Conestoga had one more point to make on this score: "the Senequois also acquainted the Govr. that Le Tore had taken a Boy from them and had sold him at New York, and Requested the Gov.r would Enquire after him, that they might have him again." Here then, almost in an offhand fashion, Opessa revealed the true reason for Le Tort's murder. His death was not due to incitement by a rival fur trader, but to a Native indictment of his role as a slave trader.[13]

As so often in these years, the European practice of slave-trading, seizing people to sell as products at the highest prices the market will bear, had bled into the Native practice of captive-taking— a ceremonial act meant to materially augment and spiritually renew grieving communities through the adoption of new members. Anglo-

Pennsylvanians participate as eagerly in this trade as any Frenchman (and with as little concern for Native objections). But they are apparently willing to accept Native retaliation quietly when the hated dealer is a Frenchman with a price on his own head.[14]

⌒

THESE ARE THE FAMILY stories that James Le Tort has to mull over as he and Logan dicker over deerskins in the second week of August 1722. As Logan inks his ledger, both men know that John Cartlidge's fate is even now hanging in the balance. The Le Tort precedent could play out in diametrically different ways for the Cartlidges. On the one hand, it provides a model moment when colonists reacted calmly and with clemency when Indians murdered a colonist. The brothers have some room to hope for reciprocal forbearance from Native peoples now. On the other hand, it can happen that Indians decide to avenge one loss with another with little objection from colonists. The Le Tort case shows that Anglo-American leaders can be more than willing to accept the demise of an unruly commoner as the cost of maintaining cross-cultural ties. If that's the lesson of Le Tort's death, then the Cartlidges have every reason to spend the hot summer shivering with dread.

Le Tort cannot help caring deeply about the destiny of these two men who have spent a lifetime tramping the woods with him. But in many ways, Le Tort's future is suspended as well. This assignment as the governor's translator marks a key opportunity. Like his fellow French trader and translator Peter Bezaillion, James Le Tort must take every chance he can to ingratiate himself with the colony's English leadership. Perhaps he can finally overcome the opprobrium that has followed his family ever since Francis Le Tort made himself so unpopular with both Indians and colonists that no one objected to his grisly death.[15]

James Le Tort's life on the Susquehanna—not the unfortunate end of his uncle Francis—sets the pattern for what the Cartlidge brothers can still hope for. In spite of the conjoined crises of slavery and murder that once threatened cross-cultural relations, James and his mother, Ann, have remained living among the Native peoples of the river valleys, trading and drinking with them, for all the decades since. Community webs can be rewoven even after being terribly torn.

As for Governor Keith, the man who has commanded James Le Tort's company for his journey, he knows that all the members of his entourage have closer ties to one another than any of them do to him. Many of them have been together, living and working, fighting and reconciling, for a generation or even two. Keith knows Le Tort has long been in Logan's pay—even if he doesn't know just how recently he received his latest payment. Still, Keith has figured out that, no matter how strained his loyalties, James Le Tort has his uses.

Chapter 21

A WORD TO THE WISE

AUGUST–SEPTEMBER 1722

A Word to the Wise is enough.
—Titan Leeds, Verses for September,
The American Almanack for 1722

"**I** SET OUT FOR ALBANY YE 12TH DAY. EXCEEDING HOT," Norris writes in the facing leaf of Titan Leeds's almanac page for the month of August 1722. Trees beard the face of the countryside. Colonists scratch their late-day stubble and dream of a good shave. Cleared of trees, towns present a civilized aspect to tired eyes. But the forests shelter beasts and nurture danger. Everyone knows that "in the month of August, the weather being excessively warm," travelers through Penn's Woods are "constrained to keep awake for fear of the Bears, which often roam about in the Night." Soon Isaac Norris and Richard Hill, along with an unexpected and rather unwelcome traveling companion, will reach Burlington, New Jersey, the best place to find a safe bed before the long push to New York City tomorrow.[1]

Norris has picked up his almanac journal and put it down again many times in the last few days. He likes to make regular notes on his daily doings. "Days shorter," is the observation the book offers for August 14. True, they are well past the turn of the year, past time to resolve this crisis with the Indians. Perhaps he should let Leeds rest at home and plan to summarize his journey in his book after his return.

But then again, in matters of importance, nothing is so valuable as having a contemporaneous record.[2]

He has had too many other matters on his mind while packing for Albany to pay great attention to Governor Keith's latest connivance. Still, the governor never misses a chance to disoblige. He has stymied Norris's plan to wring a neat profit from the Albany expedition. "Having acquainted the board . . . that the Assembly had made choice of him for buying the Presents to be given to the Indians at Albany and had given him an order on the Treasury for £100 for that use," Norris had planned to spend the sum in Philadelphia. He and friends such as James Logan could easily have supplied everything needed. Now that the Indians were to be given "presents," why should not the colony's leading Quaker merchants allow themselves to benefit too? But the governor convened an extra meeting of the board on August 7, when neither Norris nor Logan were present. He took the opportunity to declare—with the full support of new Anglican allies appointed in the wake of Jonathan Dickinson's death—"It is the opinion of this Board that such presents will be on this occasion more commodiously purchased at New York, and it is ordered that the said Isaac Norris do apply the said sum of £100 for the purchasing of such Presents at York for the Indians at Albany." Just like that, Keith has found a new way to thumb his nose at the Quakers.[3]

If only Jonathan Dickinson had not passed away at such an inconvenient moment, the governor would not have been free to pack the council with pliant new men. Still, this fresh annoyance from Keith is small compared to the nuisance now being created by Dickinson's son, Joseph. "I was that day at home at very short warning preparing to go to Albany," Norris tells a correspondent later, when word arrived that Jonathan's son was raising trouble, accusing Norris, Logan, and the other executors of the Dickinson estate of "using him like a dog." Joseph objected to their efforts to prevent him from seizing the entirety of his father's estate—his house with all its mahogany, his fortune in trade goods, even his "watch, Buttons, Seals, and such like"—to the exclusion of his siblings. Dickinson, who so long ago warned the reading public against "the cruelly devouring jaws" of "cannibal" Indians and lectured that "ingratitude . . . after signal favors received is, amongst all civilized people, looked upon with just detestation" has left behind a son who epitomizes all he professed to detest. With no time left to lose, Norris and his intended traveling companion, Richard Hill, have agreed to journey toward Burlington in Joseph's company, hoping to reach an understanding with the young man en route to the first stop on their long trip north.[4]

Warm winds froth up the forest leaves till the air fills with the sound of their simmering. Norris and Hill remonstrate with Joseph as they ride. Norris lectures Joseph, "treat us more civilly, if not for our sakes, yet for thy own, as thou bears the character of a Gentleman." Still, the lines of civility seem to be ever receding out of reach beyond the horizon. They part company without coming to any firm understanding. Norris can spare no further thought for the Dickinsons. He is days behind the governor's train and there is much left to do once they reach New York City: procure the offerings essential to Native condolence protocols, find a shipmaster willing to sell them passage to Albany, and continue reviewing drafts of the message the governor will deliver there.[5]

"Arrived at N. York ye 14," Norris records. New York City presents a fair prospect from the south. Ships school in its waters, barques and brigs and schooners, the boats ranked by their number of masts, three, two, one. These vessels fly their flags for the commerce that sorts the status of colonial men. Though the city has not been known as New Amsterdam for over half a century now, Dutch-style brick houses topped by tall gables with stepped edgings—reminders of an earlier empire—still stand sentinel against the sky. The city counts some 9,000 inhabitants, about 10 percent of them enslaved. Philadelphia is fast approaching New York on both counts, but still this city is a sight to see. Somewhere on those teeming wharves are the people who can help Norris to complete his commission.[6]

~

ACROSS IROQUOIA IN THESE late August days, members of the Haudenosaunee, the Five Nations Confederacy, gather in their hilltop longhouses and prepare for the journey to the place the English call

Albany. The Haudenosaunee call themselves the Ongwehonweh—that is, "the original people"—and they know this land as no one else does. They ground themselves in the earth with the very names of their nations. From east to west they live as the Mohawks, "The People of the Flint"; the Oneidas, "The People of the Standing Stone"; the Onondagas, "The People of the Hills"; the Cayugas, "The People of the Great Swamp"; and the Senecas, "The People of the Great Hill." Flint and stone, marsh and mountain: The land claims the people, not the other way around. Throughout this region, community members are meeting in councils, collecting wampum and words, food and gifts, for a great gathering of many nations, Native and newcomer.[7]

"Now Squashes and Pompions are come they will be able to travel," Satcheechoe has explained to the colonists. On the surface, his pronouncement simply offered seasonal information about the planned scheduling of the conference. Gourds like these ripen in late summer or early fall. But like a pumpkin weighted within by a mass of pulp and seeds, his words carry many more meanings than may at first appear.[8]

Among the Haudenosaunee, guessing riddles is a sacred game, tied to midwinter religious rites. A favorite one challenges: "What I desire and what I am seeking is that which bears a lake within itself." The answer to this puzzler is: "a pumpkin." Squashes and pumpkins can be dried to make rattles, essential for the music and dancing that mark all important ceremonies. They also make practical mobile meals, easy to carry and quick to roast or stew over an open fire when evening falls. Perhaps most important of all, baked pumpkins can be a sign of welcome, offered to travelers met in the woods on their way to visit a Haudenosaunee town. When squashes and pompions are come, travel rations, ceremonial music, and hospitality go with them. When Satcheechoe speaks of pumpkins, he thinks of peace between peoples.[9]

Iroquois towns are a women's world, where men in need of pumpkins must ask their mothers, aunts, wives, and sisters to provide them. Women work the soil and claim key community roles as one reward for their toil. Questions of war and peace are debated by councils of women who call out the confederacy's warriors when they deem it necessary. This harvest season, throughout Iroquoia, clan mothers support the need for condolence ceremonies to cement community. They advise the men to appeal to the colonists and persuade them to enter a stronger alliance.[10]

The "white way of peace" has allowed the Haudenosaunee to strengthen the reach of their influence among Native peoples. Nations who enter the confederacy or who, like the communities of the Susquehanna River valley, accept a greater or lesser degree of oversight from them, enjoy a measure of protection. But enemy groups can expect to meet parties of Iroquois warriors. Even as they have suffered ongoing pressures on their own land and people from centuries of European settling and slaving, arms and ailments, Haudenosaunee raiding and captive-taking have reshaped the lives of other Native peoples. For the last couple of decades, peace has prevailed to their north as well as to their east and west. But the Haudenosaunee have not stopped the practice of the mourning war completely. Deaths still need to be covered. Native nations to the south must still beware of captive-taking by the Haudenosaunee—which means that colonists living in the path of their war parties must also be ever on the alert.[11]

Now, at the behest of their senior women, leading men from each member nation of the Haudenosaunee gather around council fires to coordinate their position. They start by giving thanks to earth, wind, and sky, to animals and plants, to moon and sun, and to the Creator of all. Only slowly, deliberately, politely, do they turn to talk of war and peace, trade and alliance. First Mohawk leaders consult with the Senecas so that the nations situated geographically to the far east and far west of the confederacy frame the discussion from the outside in. This is the proper order of procedure for any significant joint decision by member nations of the Confederacy. This summer, with the murder of a Seneca man threatening regionwide peace efforts, Seneca views matter more than ever. Once the Mohawks and the Senecas reach consensus, they pass their conclusions on to the next two nations, the Cayuga and the Oneida, for their consideration. These two nations deliberate and concur, then send their joint counsel to the Onondagas, who occupy the territorial and ritual center of the Haudenosaunee world. The Onondagas are given the official role of "fire keepers," responsible for keeping the council coals glowing and communications flowing among all the member nations.[12]

As colonial horses pound toward Albany and colonial ships ripple the Hudson, the Onondagas agree with their confederates on a plan for the conference. They pass their decision back to the Mohawks, who complete the circle of consultation by giving their final approval. The leaders of the assembled nations then select one man to carry their torch and convey their message to the leaders of the British colonies: a speaker named Tanachaha.[13]

~

ARRIVING FROM THE SOUTH, Governor Keith and his companions cannot miss seeing the imposing mortar walls of Fort George, the star-shaped bastion that presides over the New York City harbor, flags flying the Union Jack and cannons pointing toward the water. Keith has traveled to meet New York's governor, William Burnet, unburdened by the company of any of his Quaker councilors. Col. James French (added late to the governor's entourage) and Attorney General Andrew Hamilton have made comparatively easy traveling companions. Any sense of ease fades quickly, however, because within hours Keith confronts fresh perplexities.[14]

No sooner does the Pennsylvania governor reach New York City than he learns that he has committed a potentially serious breach of courtesy. Virginia's governor, Col. Alexander Spotswood, sailed his ship only as far as Sandy Hook, New Jersey, before dropping anchor and sending ahead a letter to New York's governor to request permission to "treat with the Indians of the Five Nations at Albany." Keith has not considered that proper formality requires asking leave of colonial leaders in New York before paying a visit to Native peoples living in the vicinity. But Burnet, Keith realizes, "expected an application of the same kind on the part of this government." Keith seems to have offended the New York governor before ever making his acquaintance. He frets that he has violated the unwritten rules of politeness that regulate the conduct of gentlemen. His worries are well placed.[15]

The Crown has been taking an ever-closer interest in the regulation of the king's colonies, from overseeing the laws passed by colonial legislatures to taking control of the colony of New England away from

Puritans. This effort to standardize the meaning of "English law" created the pressures that have led to Pennsylvania's recent legal revisions. Meanwhile, the Board of Trade has been equally interested in unifying imperial Indian policy. Pennsylvania's Governor Keith has been trying to promote himself as the best man to direct such efforts. This explains his desire to publish written accounts of his treaty conferences as widely as possible while sending lengthy private reports to the Board of Trade to promote the potential profits of the fur trade. But if Logan has put up obstacles to Keith's schemes, New York's Governor Burnet is blocking his path completely.[16]

William Burnet maintains his own close correspondence with the British Lords of Trade and considers himself the best-positioned person to direct Indian affairs in the colonies. Whereas the French once dominated the fur trade, New York, conveniently located on the border of New France, has parlayed its good relations with the Five Nations into a prominent place in this lucrative Atlantic trade. British manufactures imported to the colony for use in the "Indian Trade" fetch duties as high as 10 percent, while the furs gained in exchange are the colony's main taxable export.[17]

Burnet is determined to prove his worth, both to leading men in his own colony and to members of the Board of Trade, by serving as host and director of this late-summer meeting, a cross-cultural conference that all agree is essential to safeguarding British security in North America. He has already outright refused to allow any representatives from New England to attend the Albany treaty session—because Boston leaders spurned his demand to pre-clear their speeches. Burnet informed the Board of Trade that it was impossible that "their Deputys should treat with the Five Nations unless the particulars were first regulated with the Government here." Because the "Government of Boston" refused this proposal, Burnet has simply barred those officials from participating in the meeting and declared that he will represent New England's interests himself.[18]

Meanwhile, Burnet has spent a year in negotiations with the governor of Virginia over the latter's need to meet leaders of the Five Nations in territory claimed by the colony of New York. Virginia has been acutely concerned about the Iroquois's "warlike expeditions to the Southward," as Burnet puts it circumspectly in his letter to the Board of Trade. But the leaders of the Five Nations have refused to alter their actions unless officials from Virginia appear in Iroquoia to negotiate in person. "I did propose that they not exceed certain bounds," Burnet complained to the board, but the people of the Five Nations refused to recognize his authority. To the contrary, they told him they "expected the Government of Virginia should send them some person of distinction to renew the Covenant Chain as they call it." Burnet sniffed, "that is to give them a few presents to refresh their Memorys" of previous treaty provisions. It is hard to say whether Burnet is more miffed that the leaders of the Five Nations are setting the terms of diplomacy or that, in so doing, they are interfering with his efforts to claim a supervisory role over Virginia.[19]

As the members of the Five Nations see it, they have every right to assuage the mourning of their people by seeking captives among Native nations of the south. If colonists wish to interrupt this action, they must find some other way to compensate the Five Nations for the many losses they have endured. That means engaging in rituals of alliance, paying honorary visits to Iroquoia, and arriving with ample material evidence of their peaceful intentions. Native diplomacy relies on face-to-face meetings and regular gift exchanges to maintain ties between peoples. The dominant party plays host whenever a meeting is to occur. Convening in the city of Albany offers some concession to the preferences of the colonists, but only a small one. The key point is that the Haudenosaunee don't trouble themselves to travel to Philadelphia or Williamsburg on this occasion. And as the Ongwehonweh, the original people of the region, the leaders of the Five Nations are united in their view they alone have the standing to issue invitations. So even as colonists are bickering with one another over who among them has the right to parlay, the Five Nations of the Haudenosaunee are weaving their beads together east to west and west to east until they are ready to speak with one voice from the Onondaga council fire.

GULLS SCREAM IN THE humid summer air as Sir William Keith and his companions pick their way past the walls of Fort George to present themselves to the governor of New York. In the harbor beyond, the great ships of empire bob and bow before the battlements, their golden painted lionheads roaring. Ever quick with his quill, Keith decided first thing yesterday morning that it might not be too late to dash off his own polite petition to Burnet.[20]

"I am now come, accompanied by some few members of my council," his letter explained, "to entreat that, with Your Excellency's permission and in your presence, I may be allowed to renew . . . at Albany, the leagues of friendship that have formerly been made between the Province of Pensilva. and the Five Nations." Keith has treaded carefully as can be, anxious to prove he does not mean to overstep his bounds. "The unhappy accident of an Indian being lately killed in the woods by some of our traders" necessitates this visit, Keith explained. And furthermore, he added, Pennsylvanian colonists hoped "to prevent, if possible, the Five Nations from going to war and making a path through our settlements upon the River Sasquahanna." He and his councilors did not have to wait long for Governor Burnet's answer that New York's magistrates would "think it a great Honor and Happiness to confer with them on the best measures to be taken with the Five Nations." And so Keith and company find themselves crossing the cobblestones to meet the governor in his fort.[21]

Once Keith has entered Burnet's chambers, the conversation proceeds with ease. Keith and Burnet take each other's measure, each man a looking glass for the other in their long, luxuriantly curled wigs. Heads straight, chins up, shoulders back and down. Hats doffed, hands tendered, compliments offered. Colonial Englishmen of the age know that, as the advice books say, "this is the respectful behavior which Civility exacts." Some years hence, when William Keith comes to write his own conduct book "for British Nobleman," he will declare: "a genteel air is properly to be acquired . . . by the Amusement of dancing." Both Keith and Burnet have long since mastered the intricate steps of the minuet.[22]

After exchanges of pleasantries, Keith declares that "the points on which he now came to Treat with the five Nations were already communicated to His Excellency and the Council by his Letter of yesterday." Nevertheless, he takes a new breath and begins to elaborate.[23]

"The death of an Indian was an accident that could have happened anywhere," Keith says. He does not want to leave anyone room to argue that the government of Pennsylvania has been guilty of culpable negligence. This small mishap, as Keith prefers to characterize it, will be easily set right.[24]

He assures Burnet that it will be "only necessary for him to satisfy the Indians that the Government of Pensilvania was very sorry for it and had caused the offenders to be put into the Hands of Justice." Despite his careful mastery of the finer points of European dance, the Pennsylvania baronet is now taking new and unfamiliar steps. He has tripped into acknowledging Native protocols, not simply emphasizing English norms. First he mentions the importance of presenting colonial sorrow and regret—emotions the Five Nations might recognize as condolence. Only then does he hasten to reemphasize the pursuit of justice as English colonists understand the term.[25]

"SET HENCE IN A hired sloop 17. Arrived at Albany, 20, Early," Isaac Norris writes. It took three days, but he found one man who could supply his many needs. From the deck of Captain Peter Winne's sloop on this Monday morning, Norris can watch the dawn streak across the blackwater of the upper Hudson to illuminate the wooden palisade that surrounds the city of Albany. Winne sails this river often, aided by free and enslaved sailors. Norris is fortunate to have met the able young man in the shipyards of New York City, someone who knows the woods as well as the waters of this colony. Besides his main business, skippering furs and other goods up and down the colony's main artery, Winne also serves on the Albany City Council and acts as a sometime Indian agent. He is just the sort of man to consult in this delicate moment, and Norris and his traveling companion, fellow Quaker council member Richard Hill, have had three days aboard to confer with him. As Winne directs the ship to drop anchor, early light floods the brick statehouse on Albany's Court Street.[26]

The Pennsylvanians extract a promise from Winne that he and his crew will wait for them as long as their business at Albany may take, and then they set off to explore the city. Known under Dutch rule as

Beverwijck—literally the beaver district—the fortress city remains defined by the Indian fur trade. There are six gates through which you can enter the city, with Court Street fronting the river.[27]

The old Stadthouse, the statehouse or courthouse, is one of the first buildings that you'll see on Court Street. It is "a strong and substantial house" that Dutch burghers built decades ago "of choice clinker brick," those kiln-hardened pale-colored blocks preferred over lumber, both because they are more firesafe and because they impart an essential air of solidity. In Albany as in Philadelphia, the courthouse commands the prison. Here the jail is located in the fieldstone basement of the state-house itself. Meanwhile, the grandees of the city—men like Peter Van Brugh, mayor, and Philip Livingston, his wealthy son-in-law, as well as Philip's still active father, Robert Livingston—all meet in the upper story of the building in wainscoted rooms designed to convey their standing atop the city's social and economic hierarchy. Wretched as Albany's prisoners may feel being held down there during the city's icy winters, on hot summer days like this one they can laugh at fortune.[28]

Not so up in the cockloft back in Philadelphia, where the Cartlidges remain confined. Trapped in the attic, John and Edmund are baking like bricks. Insects whine and bite. John is getting a sick headache and nothing that Edmund does helps. His brother's body has become a fur-nace, their situation more than ever like a fever dream.[29]

OVER THE NEXT FEW days, the Philadelphia governing council meets daily with their counterparts from New York and Albany learning the streets of the city and the lay of the land. Behind Court Street lies "Handlers Street," named for the merchants and traders whose buying and selling help make the city hum. Bells chime from stone churches set on either end of Market Square: They clang in Dutch on the east side and in English on the west. From bench seats set beside their doorways, people call to one another in many languages: French, German, and Swedish, as well as English and Dutch. Voices sound, too, in varied Iroquoian and Algonquian tones, along with a smattering of African languages and Atlantic sailors' pidgin tongues. By evening, cattle throng in the streets along with the people, lending their pungent stench to the summer night.³⁰

When the city surveyed its population a few years ago in 1714, the town claimed 1,023 white "inhabitants" and 117 "slaves." With more than 10 percent of the population held in perpetual bondage, leading members of Albany society can spare themselves the most onerous everyday tasks. Enslaved seamen serve on ships like Peter Winne's alongside free and indentured whites, picking up news and passing it on. Domestic service is in high demand, and enslaved women outnumber the men two to one. Enslaved cooks stir up coals in the courtyards while enslaved maids string up laundry in the alleyways. And enslaved women are bearing children at rates just slightly below that of white women, a hint at the very many ways in which they are forced to labor. Notably, no one mentions the origins of those people who are enslaved. Many may be of African origin or have been trans-shipped from Africa by way of the Caribbean. Still others are Native Americans, including many Iroquois, stolen, gifted, or traded as captives, only to be thrust into a twilight life of colonial enslavement.³¹

The visiting contingent from Philadelphia has plenty of time to mix with the city's people. Mayor Van Brugh hosts Governor Keith at his home and the rest of the Pennsylvania delegation, along with those from Virginia, are "spread over" the homes of other leading citizens. Robert Livingston joins them often for meals, including a feast of venison and fresh grapes his wife, Alida, has had sent to the city from their country manor "with which the Governor is very pleased for the foreigners' sake." These men of different regions in British America live so disconnected and distant from one another that a man from New York can refer to fellow colonists from Pennsylvania and Virginia as "foreigners."³²

They find they enjoy the chance to become acquainted. Livingston reports to his wife, "Those from Pennsylvania have come in order to reconcile the death of one of the Five Nations, who has been killed by one of their people," adding that they "are not eager to carry on any trade with the Five Nations." Keith has wisely kept his ambitions to direct a series of trading posts across the entire Ohio valley to himself. For New York colonists, this conference is a chance to renew standing commercial ties with their most important Native partners, and they see themselves as the directors and hosts. As long as Virginians confine themselves to talking peace and Pennsylvanians to containing the effects of an inconvenient killing, the grandees of Albany are happy to let them join the party. Indeed, Livingston tells his wife with satisfaction, "they are very civil gentlemen."[33]

Not for another week does a contingent of leaders and speakers from each of the Five Nations finally arrive at Albany and ready themselves for the conference, which opens on Monday, August 27. Still, even then, "things are going on very slowly," as Livingston complains, because "some of the principle Sakamakers [Native leaders, or sachems as the English call them] and others have not arrived yet." With one delay and another, it takes two more weeks before the Philadelphians have their turn at talking formally with the Haudenosaunee.[34]

NEW YORK'S GOVERNOR BURNET exercises his prerogatives to the fullest: opens the meeting, tarries for weeks, turns the proceedings over to representatives from Virginia, delaying Pennsylvanians day after day. Norris passes some idle moments with his almanac, noting in it the dates of his travel to Albany. When he turns the page to September, he can read that "a Word to the Wise is Enough." Keith and his council have ample opportunity to reconsider what they plan to say once they finally have their chance to speak formally with the leaders of the Five Nations.[35]

To Sir William's great gratification, "immediately after their arrival" in Albany, two chiefs of the Seneca Nation, Connisooa and Cajenquarahto, come to wait "on the Governor in his chamber and la[y] an Otter Skin at his feet." Already a rare and prized fur by 1700, this precious otter pelt is intended as a powerful symbol. The offering, and its formal ceremonial presentation, indicates how seriously the Seneca leaders take this diplomatic opening. As Sawantaeny's nearest kinsman, they are taking the lead in approaching the governor on behalf of the Five Nations. Connisooa then shows the governor "the Golden Medal sent him last summer," and the governor is pleased to see it "being hung from his neck." Cajenquarahto likewise "produce[s] the Mourning Ring the Governor had sent last Spring by Satcheechoe." By exchanging and displaying gifts, the Seneca leaders wish to communicate that they have come to establish a lasting peaceful relationship with Pennsylvanians. Keith and his councilors may neither fully comprehend nor completely agree with the Seneca leaders, but they do take in many ideas and attitudes of the Haudenosaunee and adjust their planned speech accordingly. Once they complete their revisions, the remarks drawn up by Logan back in Philadelphia will be scratched with cross-outs and scribbles. Hardly a word that Logan wrote remains unchanged.[36]

Only in the waning moments of the conference, on September 7, 1722, does Burnet finally allow Keith to do more than sit and observe. As recorded in the official minutes of the colony of Pennsylvania, the governor's address is "in the following words, interpreted by James Le Tort, and an Indian for Sasquehannah, called Captain Smith." Captain Smith has come to Albany after all, but not in the sole service of the governor. He is appearing "for Sasquehannah"—that is, on behalf of his own community—rather than at the behest of colonial leaders. Though his linguistic skills may well augment colonial treaty efforts, Captain Smith has traveled north on his own terms and for his own reasons, not least of which is communicating the content of the treaty proceedings to various speakers of Algonquian languages who might otherwise have been ignored by the colonists. Keith, meanwhile, has no one to rely on but a man whom colonists once deeply distrusted: the murdered colonist's nephew, James Le Tort.[37]

"Brethren," Governor Keith begins his address, "I have travelled a great way to see you and to hold some Discourse with you." This, as he now understands, marks an essential concession. Rather than waiting in state for Native leaders to call on him in Philadelphia, he has agreed to dance attendance on them at Albany. Now that he is here, he will choreograph his comments carefully.[38]

"Remember the first settlement of the Province of Pennsilvania by Wm. Penn," he says, prodding them to recall how "we became as one People." Keith has come to understand how much such declarations of unity count with the Haudenosaunee. "Since that time," he says, "a

very unhappy accident has fallen out." These words sound a conciliatory note.

Still, the governor does not budge on the claim that Sawantaeny
was threatening and emotionally out of control. He sums up the colonial view of the case by saying that "the Indian was angry & went
hastily & took his Gun to Kill the Englishman." This is key to the colonists' theory of the Cartlidge legal defense: that an Indian in thrall to
the violent anger known to characterize savage peoples left the Cartlidges no option but to try to protect themselves. Nowhere does Keith
mention that, to the contrary, Shawnee witnesses stated that it was
Sawantaeny who told John Cartlidge "he need not be angry." Instead,
Keith goes on to say, "they in defense of themselves Seized the Indian
& in struggling gave him some Blows and left him. We heard that our
Indian friend and Brother died ye next day." But in other ways, Keith
is ready to accept the Indian view of the case.[39]

Next Governor Keith is supposed to say: "The men who did this
were brought to Philadelphia, committed to Prison & put in Irons and
there remain to be tried for their Lives." But already he has come to
think that the leaders of the Five Nations will not respond well to the
idea of the Cartlidges being kept in chains at imminent risk of execution. He says, instead, "The men who did this were brought to Philadelphia and put in Prison and they will be tried according to our Laws
in the same manner as if they had Killed an Englishman." Gone are
the irons and the explicit threat to the Cartlidges' lives. Now they are
to be imagined simply as prisoners awaiting trial. Still, Keith clings to
the notion that offering equal justice under English law is the highest
compliment he can pay the assembled members of the Five Nations.[40]

Keith is ready to go much further in floating the possibility that
the Cartlidges may yet be freed. After reminding the Iroquois leaders,
as planned, "I sent some tokens to your Sachims which I hope they
received, with a Mourning Gold ring off my own finger," he inserts
an entirely new point of discussion never even contemplated back in
council in Philadelphia.

"Satcheechoe," Keith comments, "told me you desired John Cartlidge might be released out of Prison & ye injury done to your Kinsman might be forgot." He reproduces Satcheechoe's statement closely,

down to the early misunderstanding about whether John acted alone in the assault on Sawantaeny. He can't resist because, here it is, the tantalizing possibility that they can all agree to proceed as if the "unhappy accident" actually never happened at all.[41]

"But Satcheechoe brought no Belt nor any other Token to confirm his words," Keith qualifies, "& therefore I have brought him along with me, that you may know & tell me if he spoke Truth." Counting time to a pianoforte only he can hear, Keith can't resist doing a quick reverse, flipping events so that he appears to have brought Satcheechoe to Albany, not the other way around. He implies that the Cayuga man's veracity is open to question because he brought no wampum with him to their July meeting in Philadelphia. In reality, the leaders of the Five Nations withheld wampum deliberately on that occasion as a sign that they would not consider a diplomatic solution to the Cartlidge case unless Keith agreed to appear before them personally.[42]

Before his audience can object to his characterization, Keith pirouettes again to return to the themes of unity and community, grief and condolence his listeners anticipate: "You see I have left my family & people and have travelled a great way to take you by the hand to joyn Hearts." He rushes on to show that he has learned the importance of sealing his airy promises with solid offerings:

> I have brought with me these goods to bind my Words, viz: Five pieces of Strouds for Cloathing; five Casks of Powder and five hundred weight of Lead, to encourage your hunting that you may grow Rich & Strong; And I desire you may receive them as a Pledge of our Resolutions to live in perpetual peace and under the strongest ties of ffriendship with the five Nations.

Gone completely is Keith's claim, made to Satcheechoe back in May, that he could not possibly honor the "Custom amongst you, when an Indian happens to be Killed, that his Relations often demand & expect Money or Goods for satisfaction." Where once Keith insisted that "the Laws of our Great King will not suffer any such thing to be done amongst us," he now smoothly conforms to Iroquois expectations. He offers no explanation for his shift, but the letters of Robert Livingston

fill the gap. In the days before the Haudenosaunee joined the conference, Livingston reported that "all the Governors and their Councillors plus our Councillors" had gathered for an assembly "where public
affairs were deliberated upon." By the time Keith makes his speech, he
is working with the advice and direction of the leading magistrates of
three colonies.[43]

Keith has found his rhythm now. Logan's script called for Keith to
suggest that "the words that now pass may be recorded." Keith polishes
this line too, instead telling them that "the Covenant Chain which is
now brightened may be recorded in everlasting Remembrance." And
then he adds another key statement, this one entirely new, saying that,
"I also give you those two pieces of Blankets to wipe away and dry
up the Blood that has been spilt, and to cover it so as it may never be
seen and heard of any more." With this ceremonial gift, Keith once
again offers to ritually "cover" the body of the murdered man. Wherever Sawantaeny may actually lie—and Keith himself has carefully
avoided finding this out—at last colonists have paid him the proper
formal respects.[44]

Finally, Keith lays down two belts of wampum. He is improvis-
ing now. Back in Philadelphia, they had not known whether or when
they would be able to acquire some of these finely fabricated pieces.
But there is no denying the essential spiritual and political impact of
the personal presentation of woven shell beads. Somehow, Keith has
obtained a pair of belts, and he offers them as the grand finale to his
performance. One stands for "strength," he tells the assembled members of the Five Nations, the other for a "true heart." He is proposing
a firm and loyal alliance. The leaders of the Five Nations hear him out,
then indicate that they will need time to consider their reply. Their delegation retires to discuss matters and leaves the Pennsylvanians to idle
for another three days.[45]

⌒

AT LAST, ON SEPTEMBER 10, 1722, the chosen Iroquois spokesman,
Tanachaha, stands and readies himself to address Governor Keith and
company. No one ever records anything else about this man beyond his

name. His national ties, his family relationships, his age, his interests, all go unremarked and unrecorded. The colonists note only that he addresses them, "Tanachaha being Speaker." Perhaps there is something fitting in this. For Tanachaha speaks not for himself, but rather for the many nations of the Haudenosaunee. In a diplomatic setting such as this one, the Five Nations seek to bring more people under the Haudenosaunee tree of peace, to gather new groups into community. Tanachaha has been selected, not to tell any singular story of his own but for his ability to be a voice for his people as a whole.[46]

Tanachaha tells the Pennsylvanians, "We thankfully receive and approve all the Articles in your Proposition to us." Keith and company can let out a collective sigh of relief. Tanachaha continues by explaining, "We receive & approve of the same with our whole hearts, because we are not only made one people by the Covenant Chain, but we also are people united in one head & one Body & one heart, by the strongest ties of Love and friendship." Here again is the language of the single body, the key notion that animates Iroquoian ideas about diplomacy. They are not envisioning, as the colonists do on their best days, peaceful bilateral relations. Rather, they are seeking spiritual unification that will result in far-reaching provisions for mutual care and protection.[47]

Having assured the colonists that they need not be concerned about what Keith described to Burnet as "warlike expeditions to the Southward," Tanachaha delivers further welcome news: "As to the accident of one of our friends being Killed by some of your People, which has happen'd by misfortune and against you[r] will," he tells them, "we say, that we are all in Peace." Again, this is the essential point Sawantaeny made with his dying words, but that the colonists have been slow to grasp. He was killed by his "friends." And among the members of the Five Nations, it is wrong to seek revenge for the victims of an accident among allies. Rather, such deaths provide important emotional focal points for the ritual recommitment to communal bonds.[48]

Tanachaha goes a key step further to try to make the colonists understand Native ways in cases of crime: "We think it hard the persons who killed our friend & Brother should suffer, and we do in the name of all the five Nations forgive the offence & desire You will like-

wise forgive it." How can he make himself more plain? Native peoples
have learned certain things from these months of conversation with
the colonists. They now realize that two "persons," not one, attacked
Sawantaeny. But they do not see the infliction of new suffering as the
right response to even so stark a moment of social rupture as violent
death. Forgiveness dominates their approach to conflict resolution.[49]

Tanachaha has one more instruction: "that the men who did it may
be released from Prison and set at Liberty, to go wither they please."
Unlike colonists, who insist that freedom of movement is a privilege to
be reserved for propertied men—meaning that high-ranking women
cannot appear in public with propriety and that servants and enslaved
people require written passes in order to move about—Native peoples
believe that liberty begins with the body. Now Tanachaha is telling
Pennsylvania's leading men that if only they will release the Cartlidges
from prison, "we shall Esteem that as a mark of Regard and ffriendship
for the five Nations, and as a farther confirmation of this Treaty." Far
from threatening war because the Cartlidges killed Sawantaeny, they
are now demanding the brothers' liberty as the proof of alliance.[50]

All this is possible, Tanachaha makes clear, because, after a shaky
start, colonial officials have at last engaged in the rituals of emotional
consolation, spiritual renewal, and material restitution that Native
peoples regard as essential for resolving a murder crisis. "We are glad
you have wiped & covered the blood of our dead friend and Brother,
and we desire the same may be forgot, so as it may never be more mentioned or remembered." This tragic tale, which has been told and retold
among multiple nations for many long months, can at last be set aside.
With that, Tanachaha "lay down a few Beaver, Bear, & dressed Deer
skins, and so concluded." Beaver, bear, and deer, glossy gray, silky
brown, and supple tan, friendship, forgiveness, and freedom: These
are the Native gifts.[51]

Governor Keith is almost frozen with relief. No more tricky steps
to perform. He simply expresses "his Satisfaction with their Answer"
and gives his "thanks for their good will & love to him and the People
of Pensilvania."[52]

Tanachaha is not quite ready to retire for the day. He desires again
"to know of the Governor, if the men who were in prison for killing

their friend and Brother were Discharged?" If colonists have gained essential knowledge of Native protocols through the last months, it seems that members of the Haudenosaunee have likewise been studying colonial stratagems.[53]

Keith cannot help himself. He whips into a fouetté and turns the facts once more. "They were let out upon Bail," he says. Should a half-truth count as a lie? The Cartlidges were indeed let out on bail between March and April. But by June, they were back in prison and petitioning once more for release. Nothing in the records of the Pennsylvania government indicates that they were freed after that point. The draft speech for the Albany conference created in Philadelphia at the end of August claimed that the brothers were being "held in irons." Either that was a bald falsehood or else Keith's current claim is. Either way, he knows that the leaders of the Five Nations have no immediate way of verifying whatever he chooses to say.[54]

Still, Tanachaha conveys a note of Haudenosaunee skepticism, repeating again that if in fact the brothers were not yet at liberty, "they then desired that the men might be discharg'd." Everyone present supports this plan, and Keith answers that the moment he returns to Philadelphia, he will "give such order in that affair as should fully answer the request of the five Nations, in order to confirm the ffriendship that is so happily renewed & established by this Treaty." On that note, the day's official proceedings ended. New York officials examined Pennsylvania notes on the session and certified them as "a true Copy."[55]

꧁

IN SPITE OF THIS success, Richard Hill is feeling tired. He, Isaac Norris, and the other council members are all more than ready to hasten home. After passing nearly a month in Albany, they decide to depart that very night, leaving Governor Keith to make his own way in his own time. "Ye 13th 7ber abt. 11 at night, R.H., A.H., J.F. & myself embark at Albany on ye sloop we had hired and who waited on us, Peter Winne, Mr.," Norris writes in his Leeds notebook. Not only Isaac Norris and Richard Hill sail off on the ship but also Andrew Hamilton and John French. Norris records their arrival in New York

City at the "break of day" on the seventeenth and their subsequent departure for Burlington on the eighteenth. Fortuitously, they will be passing through Burlington at the very moment that the Quaker Yearly Meeting is being conducted there. Many of those attending that annual gathering will be keenly interested in hearing the outcome of the Albany conference. Still, Norris will tread carefully if he is paying any heed to the acerbic observation that Leeds has reserved for September 18: "He has a sharp wit but makes ill use of it." Perhaps the book knows, as Norris cannot, that Governor Keith has decided to engage in one more conversation with the Five Nations still in Albany—waiting until after all of his council members have sailed safely out of the picture.[56]

QUAKERS FROM AROUND THE region gather in the hexagon-shaped brick building on High Street in Burlington for the last day of the Yearly Meeting of the Society of Friends. With its high-domed roof topped by a small hexagonal cupola, the meetinghouse resembles nothing so much as a beehive, and the Quakers within are buzzing today. There are plans to release John and Edmund Cartlidge from jail permanently, without ever forcing them to face trial. Edmund, having broken with the Quakers long ago, is none of their concern. But John is another story. If the colony's governor won't subject him to justice, his co-religionists can. Back in June, at Cartlidge's local monthly meeting, the neighbors with whom John and Elizabeth usually worshiped recorded in their official business minutes that "the Fr[ien]ds Appointed Produced a Paper Against John Cartlidge w[hi]ch was aprov'd of & ordered to be read at the close of ye next first day's meeting." John has already been publicly denounced for his violence.[57]

But today in Burlington, members of the Society of Friends have decided a printed statement is in order. Samuel Preston, both a Quaker elder and a member of the Provincial Council, has offered no discernable comment on the case until today. Now he stings Cartlidge without ever mentioning him by name. "The practice of Selling Rum or other Strong Liquours to the *Indians*," he says, "*is a Thing displeasing to the*

Lord, A Dishonour to Truth and a Grief to all Good People." Preston
tells the pious assembly that Quakers first testified against the practice
decades ago, back in 1687, and that since then only "People prefer-
ring their filthy Lucre before the Common Good continued in this Evil
Practice." He laments that although official proscriptions against traf-
ficking in alcohol have been renewed almost yearly, "it is yet too noto-
rious that the same hath not been duly observed by some Persons."
Preston strikes once more. Anyone who violates this teaching, he says,
"let them be speedily dealt with and censured for such their Evil Practice." Whatever the legal system may have to say about Cartlidge's
case, his co-religionists determine that he should be held accountable
for breaking accepted norms.[58]

Still, the Quakers stop short of calling for John to be held liable for
his violence itself. Indeed, their statement asserts that Indians are apt to
become dangerous when inebriated. The original prohibition on alcohol sales to Indians came because "those People when they got Rum
or other strong Liquours set no Bounds to themselves but were apt to
be abusive." With these words, Preston and his fellow Quakers seem
to imply that Sawantaeny brought his fate on himself, that whatever
John Cartlidge's ample sins, he cannot be fairly charged with a crime.
Even the most critical colonists apparently accept that he must have
acted in self-defense against a drunken Indian. The group at Burlington decides to publish their consensus on these points in pamphlet form
so that their conclusions may become widely known. Samuel Preston
signs the open letter they call an "epistle" on behalf of the meeting, and
soon enough Andrew Bradford has it in press.[59]

Chapter 22

JAMES LOGAN

J AMES LOGAN PUTS DOWN THE PAPER HE HAS BEEN READING and makes a decision. Sarah came through childbirth last week without incident and he cannot stay tethered to her bedside for one more moment. With Governor Keith and key members of the council away at Albany, the weight of responsibility for the colony falls ever more surely to him.

Far from shrinking at the burden of directing Pennsylvania's government in Keith's absence, Logan squares his shoulders and puffs out his chest. As he complains in a letter to an English friend, "The Govr., Council & Assembly all agreed in naming me for one to go to Albany, but a weak fear in my wife then just ready to lie down, (which she did the night after the Gov.r sett out) that if I went she should not live to see me again, detained me at home." Well, he shall tarry no longer.[1]

Word has arrived that Surveyor Isaac Taylor—taken into custody last June by an overzealous Cecil County, Maryland, sheriff who claimed he was mapping on Maryland's land—has now been arraigned and ordered to appear at the Cecil County Courthouse. Before leaving for Albany, Sir William wrote an appeal to Lord Calvert, but the latter has roundly rejected it. Now, it seems, an in-person appeal must be tried. Whatever Logan may think of Taylor's conniving with Keith and Cartlidge to claim the region's copper deposits, he certainly sees no reason to leave the man rotting in the jail of a rival colony. Nor is Logan prepared to allow the young Lord Calvert to lay claim to resources that he believes should rightfully be held in the Penn family name. Logan concludes that he is "obliged to go to Maryland." Manly courage demands action.[2]

Yet back in his storeroom after his quick trip to Maryland, Logan regrets that he has been able to do little for Taylor and less for the proprietary family's claims to the contested border territory. All that Lord Calvert would agree was that Taylor "should be bound over to the provincial court at Annapolis." Taylor may well fare better in Maryland's capital than he would in a provincial county court, but only time will tell. Meanwhile, Logan is left to fume and finger lengths of imported cloth.[3]

LOGAN IS GROWING TIRED of political combat with Keith and weary of the problems created by the uncertain state of the proprietary family's claims on the colony. He is eager, as he will tell John Penn by letter later that autumn, to "retire from the whole" of public life, "having been long oppressed with contending for no advantage to myself and but little to others . . . I desire a Countrey Retirement for my Portion." Even now, he has hundreds of acres being cleared by servants, indentured white ones and enslaved Black ones. Logan has dreams of building a large stone manor house with a great paneled library, a place where he can devote his life to the study of moral philosophy and natural philosophy, to knowledge of the mind, the heart, and the world.[4]

Logan has begun gathering thoughts for a major treatise he will one day call "The Duties of Man," in which he hopes to outline his own American ideas on human nature. He intends to bring together his knowledge of classical and modern philosophy, integrating the writings of Aristotle and Socrates with the newer work of Hobbes and Locke, Shaftesbury and Hutcheson, into a magnum opus enriched by his unique vantage point—his perch on the edge of a vast continent unimagined by the ancient world. He believes he has "had some thoughts" on the subject of "the laws originally impressed into Man at his formation" that he has "not met with in the authors who have treated of it." Among his account books with their scrolling ranks of numerals and his correspondence books with their dated letterheads, he is accumulating page after undated page of philosophical musings.[5]

Struggling to describe universal human virtues while also defending variations in human value, he will offer his own innovative system of morals. "Human virtue, or the practice of it, turns on the affections," Logan believes. "All those we term social virtues are founded in the affections and constitute the moral sense, those affections implanted in our species at our formation." Decades of interaction with enslaved Africans and embattled Indians leave Logan clear in his understanding that love, the bedrock of Christianity and foundation of morality, is to be found in every people. His reference to the human "species" calls on the most sophisticated scientific terminology of his day, giving the sheen of empiricism to his assertions. By embedding virtue and morality in naturally occurring senses and emotions, he, like Enlightenment thinkers generally, makes all-encompassing claims for human potential.[6]

Yet Logan will also assert that non-Europeans can neither enact nor embody virtue as well as European-descended peoples do because, in his view, they are not as beautiful to look at. Logan will begin by citing Francis Hutcheson who proposes in his celebrated book, *Inquiry into Our Ideas of Beauty and Virtue*, that there is a "moral sense of beauty in actions and affections." According to Hutcheson, the same sensory perceptions that allow the appreciation of beauty facilitate the recognition of virtue. Moreover, good behavior and fine feelings excite pleasure so that virtue can be a source of deep enjoyment. Logan agrees wholeheartedly with Hutcheson's theory and cites it directly in his own philosophical writing. Yet he also has some new ideas to propose on the subject of the universality of beauty—that is, on the essential unity of aesthetic and moral perceptions across varied human societies.[7]

As Logan develops his argument, it will diverge increasingly from the far more circumspect case offered by Hutcheson. Logan's problem is to explain how people can look different from one another if there is only one divinely appointed standard of beauty.

For Logan, any expressed preference for non-European faces and bodies constitutes an error. In fact, Logan will insist, "if we inquire a little deeper we shall find it thus: that Negroes should prefer their own color and acquiesce in their own common shapes is natural enough, for so monkeys, baboons, and all other creatures by instinct prefer their own species to all others." Here Logan careens close to claiming that people of African origin are less human than animal. But he quickly veers away from this position in order to defend his views on the universality of the human faculty for observing morality and beauty. Despite Africans' differences in color, Logan says, "their eyes are made as ours, and . . . when they can choose for beauty they make nearly the same judgments that we do." He claims that when given the chance, Africans adhere to European ideas of beauty, explaining "that they esteem flat noses and blubber lips above others is not true." They only seem to favor people who look like themselves, Logan claims, because "few of them have opportunities of much choice." Having made his point, he takes care to extend the principle to the Native peoples of North America, claiming that the same preferences are "so among the savage nations." Logan believes that his colonial position allows him to contribute new evidence that all people, across the Atlantic, enjoy an invariable ability to perceive beauty and pursue virtue. Human beings, regardless of color or country, all share an innate moral sense. Yet he also tries hard to demonstrate that only those of European origin can achieve the finest forms of both.[8]

Far from being an objective observer, Logan is a merchant, slaveholder, fur trader, and self-declared member of the select group he describes as "men of study." His leisure to contemplate questions of moral philosophy results directly from the astounding wealth he is daily accumulating by appropriating the lives, labor, lands, and resources of enslaved Africans and colonized Native peoples. And yet he attributes his fortune solely to the virtuous use he makes of his natural moral and mental endowments. As William Keith has said in another context, "no man living knows better how to puzzle the state of an account."[9]

~

CARTS AND PACKS, BUNDLES and barrels, trader after trader trundles up to James Logan's door this September. They come for fancy goods like fine white linen "cambrick" or tightly braided gold and silver ribbons of "gallooms," or silk handkerchiefs. Logan pauses a moment over the silk. Sarah has been asking for a pair of silk stockings, which he does not have on hand; she will have to go to one of the women who deal in feminine sundries to find what she wants. But he does stock cloth of every weight and material; the deeply napped woolen "duffles," the coarser, cheaper "half-thicks," useful in the hotter months. Or he can offer the smoother heavy "druggets" woven of wool and silk or wool and linen, as well as the ever-popular blue striped "strouds." Autumn is the optimal time to deal in peltry.[10]

Satcheechoe has been stopping in regularly since his return from Albany, dropping off a bushel of skins here, picking up a load of goods there. "Sundry Acco[un]ts Supplied Satcheecho," Logan records in the new daybook he begins this month, a place for him to record as line items the details of transactions that appear only as totals in his main ledger book. The Cayuga man is prospering from closer ties to Indians and colonists—from Conestoga to Albany to Philadelphia—that he has been able to develop over the last many months. Peter Bezaillion has been by several times this September, as have a number of lesser brokers in Logan's pyramid. Still, Logan might once have expected to be even busier.[11]

He has been daily expecting James Le Tort, but no one knows where he is. Isaac Norris and Richard Hill return safely to town from Burlington on September 20, bearing tidings of a successful treaty meeting at Albany and bringing a letter from the governor announcing plans for a new joint conference with Virginia's governor to be held in October at Conestoga. The letter includes no mention of Keith's other initiative, his decision to hold one last tête-à-tête with leaders of the Five Nations at Albany the moment his council members sailed out of the way. It simply asks for interpretation services at the upcoming October gathering. As Logan dutifully records in the council minutes, Keith, "desires the Secretary to give Notice to James Le Tort, and Smith, the Ganawese Indians, to the Chiefs of the four Nations of Indians settled upon the Sasquehannah River, viz. the Mingoes or Conestogoe Indians, the Shawanese, the Ganawese & the Delawares, to be ready to meet." Fortunately, Keith cannot hear Logan laugh from as far away as Albany.[12]

Logan once again enjoys a blameless opportunity to disoblige the governor. He notes, "But James Le Tort, and Smith the Indian, not being returned from Albany as the Govr. expected, the said direction of the Govrs. is at present impracticable." He can hardly be accused of sitting on his hands when they are simply tied by circumstances. Still, he cannot resist adding an editorial comment: "And further, this Board is of opinion, that they cannot concur directing our Indians to meet the Govr. Of Virginia at Conestogoe until this Government is acquainted with the End & Design of the said meeting." Eager as he is to put the crisis of the last six months behind him and turn his efforts toward trade and philosophical treatises, Logan cannot let go of the contest with Keith. The Cartlidge case has thrown up dust in all directions— bringing into question the nature of justice, the basis of peace, the channels of governance—and Logan keeps coughing.[13]

John Cartlidge has also failed to arrive to offer furs to Logan. Unfortunately, he is in no shape to resume his work in the forest. Released at last from the attic cell on High Street, Cartlidge has traded his prison pallet for a bed in the front chamber of his solid house in Conestoga. There, he lies sweating and puking through these scorching September days.[14]

~~

EVERYONE IN PHILADELPHIA IS ill this September, it seems. No one can escape this infernal heat. No sooner do you mop a brow than you feel a new ticklish trickle dripping from the tip of your nose. Next your stomach clenches and the burning bile starts to rise. By month's end, the deaths start. "Richard Hill was seized with a feaver the day he got home upon his Return from Albany," Logan writes to John Penn. "After, his Daughter and only Child was taken ill and in two days died." Isaac Norris reports the same calamity with greater detail. "I have lately had a feaver," Norris confides, "that left me weakly." Still worse, Richard Hill, "who was with me at Albany [was] taken with a fever on coming home," a sickness which "continued dangerous for a long time" and led to an even more "sore affliction." His "only Child, Elizabeth, dy'd of a feaver & violent vomiting w'ch carried her off in

3 days . . . she died the 26th . . . aged about 17." She was the Hills' last living child, but not their first. Her sister, Hannah, died five years earlier in 1717 at the age of eleven.[15]

"*Philadelphia* was founded on a Conjunction of the two Superior Planets *Saturn* and Jupiter, &c. It has always been observed that great Changes and troubles have happened on the Conjunctions of the Superiors," intones Titan Leeds in the pages of his almanac. So many of his dire predictions for 1722 have already come to pass. Is it any wonder that troubles continue to mount even after regional peace has been announced? Coming on top of months spent negotiating the terms of colonial mourning and atonement for the death of a Native man who died at the hands of one of their own fellow Quakers, the loss of Hill's daughter puts his friends in a pensive frame of mind. Births are a sign of God's blessing on this colony, of the rightness of settlement in North America; untimely deaths signal divine judgment. Every loss of a child whose life was an emblem of the future is, in ways literal and figurative, *unsettling*.[16]

When Richard Hill's elder daughter, Hannah, passed away, she left her people with a blessing. As she lay dying, able to see through the veil between heaven and Earth, she cried to the Lord and called out prophesies. "It was Astonishing (in one of her Years) to see and hear, how Powerfully she was drawn forth at times on Various Subjects," recalled one witness, "to wit, *That GOD in Mercy would yet more abundantly shower down his blessings on* Philadelphia *and the Inhabitants of these parts of the World.*" What comfort she offered her family and friends. Her father, Richard Hill, rushed to preserve her naïve wisdom in print, publishing a pamphlet he called *A Legacy for Children, Being Some of the Last Expressions and Dying Sayings of Hannah Hill* that went through three Philadelphia editions by 1717.[17]

Magic and science, wonder and terror, hope and fear. Settler colonists can never decide if they are on the verge of finding a new Eden—a place where wealth comes almost without toil and all the lush country is theirs for the taking—or if they have ventured to the very gates of hell, to a land where labor is forced by lash and land is seized by musket, where each person has a price and the cost of success is the surrender of every Christian ideal. They will say and do anything to try to have everything. Of Hannah Hill, one witness says, she was "kind to Servants, both White and Black." Can anyone object to keeping the vast majority of the population in varying states of unfreedom, so long as the lower sort are held down gently? Hannah's admirer thinks not. He concludes, "I have seen some Children very Rude and Imperious to their Parents' Negroes, but I observed the contrary in her; and Doubtless, it is Great and Crying Sin, in either Old or Young to abuse poor Slaves." Hannah's soft courtesy redeems the institution of slavery. Thus can English civility encompass all.[18]

"ACCOUNT OF EXPENSES MY wife paid," Logan notes in his daily ledger for September 29, recording her expenditure of 17 shillings for "a pair of Silk Stockings." Scarcely six weeks after Sarah was brought to bed with a new daughter, she is up and about, shopping for hose. Logan jots down every penny spent. This is a man who likes to keep count. And this fall, there are still scores to settle.[19]

As he tallies the columns in his new daily expense book at the close of September, Logan cannot know the exact words of Governor Keith's July letter to Hannah Penn. But someone has been at Logan's elbow, whispering secrets into his ear, telling him that the governor has been actively maneuvering against him and the Quaker members of the council. "I am credibly informed by one who ought to know," Logan tells John Penn in his autumn letter, that Keith has been "endeavouring to strike at our Reputation in some letters to thy mother, but particularly at mine with charges and Insinuations." No interesting piece of intelligence sent east across the Atlantic can be kept secure, no matter how elaborate the wax seal set on the contents. To Springett Penn, John's nephew, Logan likewise complains, "I am credibly informed the Governour has taken some Liberties with my Character to thy Grandmother and perhaps to thee, which if the Acco[un]t be true shew a very ill heart." With the Cartlidge crisis seemingly resolved, Logan has more time than ever to concentrate on mounting problems with Keith.[20]

Of course, Logan does want to take a moment to savor the late summer's fruits. To John Penn, the Anglican son of Penn's second wife, Hannah, he says, "I send the enclosed with this our Treaty with ye Indians at Albany which from an unfortunate occasion proved very happy." In this version, unlucky happenstance leads to ultimate happiness, a thorny bush bearing sweet treasure. If he cannot deny that Keith has had some success, Logan knows well enough to claim some of the credit. "The particular state of my family at that time with much ado prevented me from making one of the company," he says by way of excusing his absence from Albany, "but the speech was prepared in Council here, before the Gov.r's Departure. It was very expensive to the Province yet I believe well worth the Money." Looked at this way, the colonists' capitulation to Native demands for reparations was well worth the opportunity to maintain comity. Left unspoken are the unceasing efforts they have made to contrive a way to free the Cartlidges while seeming to uphold accepted standards of English justice.[21]

Logan tries out a far darker rendition of the story in the letter he writes to Springett Penn—William Penn's Quaker grandson from his first wife, Gulielma Springett Penn—on the very same day he writes to John. To Springett, he also mentions the "very happy Treaty with Indians at Albany." But the September event merits only that single phrase. Logan spends far more time impugning Keith's motives for holding his own earlier Indian conference at Conestoga in April. "Our Gov.r being informed of a prospect of discovering a valuable Copper Mine beyond Sasquehannah, took as conceived, some very indiscrete measures in Ap[r]l last to possess himself of it," Logan reports. To this sly scheme, Logan attributes Keith's efforts to ingratiate himself with the Penn family by promoting peace with the Native peoples of the region. "Afterwards, he bent himself to recommend his conduct to you and more especially to thee by a Treaty with the Indians intended only to amuse by representing thy name so often in it, tho in other cases we well know he is not fond of mentioning the Proprietor." Logan claims here that Keith's efforts at achieving understanding with local Native peoples should be regarded as nothing more than a cynical ploy calculated to appeal especially to the pacifist sympathies of Penn's Quaker grandson—as a cover for his naked grabs of Native land, property that Logan believes belongs to the colony's proprietors.[22]

Logan can only hope that, if the extra treaty conference the governor is now attempting to call for October in Conestoga does come to pass, Keith's true colors will be revealed amidst the fall foliage. There, Captain Civility and his companions now comb the forest for furs while womenfolk fill their harvest baskets. There, even now that he is free from jail, John Cartlidge is still battling for his life.

Chapter 23

STIFF OBSTINACY

OCTOBER 3–5, 1722

Your Obstinacy's Ne'er so stiff,
As when 'tis in a wrong Belief.

—Titan Leeds, Verses for October,
The American Almanack for 1722

J OHN CARTLIDGE CANNOT SEEM TO SHAKE THE FEVER THAT crept up the stairs to the cockle loft and left him locked in a new set of irons. People call it "gaol distemper." Everyone knows that vice leads to disease. Across the Anglo-American world, prisons are feared as filthy places where moral pollution meets physical rot. Of course, pestilence cares little for decorum. Foul airs and miasmas float about freely, refusing to stay in their proper place. And yet, they do seem to linger longest wherever there are squalid and crowded conditions. If you are held behind bars, a bout of jail fever is only to be expected.[1]

Still, John must hope to recover. His wife, Elizabeth, keeps a couple of pewter basins in the chamber closest of the room where he rests at home in Conestoga. He can call for one anytime he feels that acid warning in his belly. Downstairs in the parlor, the clock ticks away in its case, measuring time. Outside, on his three hundred acres, metal rasps against stone as his two servant lads grub and weed their way across his grounds. They pass his store as they go about their work, the Indian goods piled there taunting him to get up and go trading.

How long has it been since he chose one of his horses to saddle—black, brown, or sorrel, bay, roan, or gray—and cantered deeper into the woods? His infant has turned toddler during his months of confinement and five of his colts can now be called yearlings. The farm place pulses with life as he lies and languishes, a prisoner now in the hell of his own hot body.[2]

JUST A FEW MILES off, among the peoples of four main Native nations living in the villages of Conestoga, the folks of the river valleys are busy from dawn to dusk with the business of the season. The Green Corn Ceremony has just passed, and the Harvest Festival will soon arrive. Women are bringing in beans and peas from their fields, along with squashes and pumpkins. They carry in ear after ear of corn, drying most against the cold months, but enjoying many boiled or roasted now. From their orchards, they shake down apples, pears, and peaches. They dig up "eating roots" like turnips, carrots, potatoes, and parsnips and, for, medicinal purposes, such "choice Phisical Roots, as Sassafras, Sarsaparilla, Black-Snake Root, Rattle-Snake Root, and Pokake-Root." They gather all sorts of wild "saladings," a great bounty of "Mustard, Rue, Sage, Mint, Tanzy, Wormwood, Penny-Royal and Purslain." Beneath the trees, they collect walnuts and chestnuts, filberts and hickory nuts in baskets they have woven from wild hemp. The men of the villages are helping with the harvest or already abroad hunting, taking as much "fat venison" and "good turkey" as they can carry. They shoot and trap, stockpiling for the winter trading season.[3]

Nowadays, men like John and Edmund Cartlidge are key to the forest economy. Native men exchange furs for matchcoats and all the other European wares they wish for. But the women processing pelts in the river valleys don't think of themselves as essential figures in the fur trade; they consider themselves key to the cloth trade. They look at the exchange from a perspective that exactly inverts the colonial view. As primary property holders among Native peoples, these women benefit directly from the wealth created by trading colonial textiles.[4]

The goods-distribution system established by the peoples of the river valleys depends on flowing waters and fluid populations. People prize freedom of movement above all else. As the Indians of Conestoga explain in a communication they send to Philadelphia this season, they deeply enjoy and greatly value "their free Liberty to Pass and Repass" through the woods as needed.[5]

At the Albany congress just concluded, representatives of the Five Nations and governors of the colonies took opposing views on mobility and liberty at every level, from the question of whether the Cartlidges should continue to be held in prison to the contentious issue of Native travel rights to the fundamental question of human bondage. Virginians were concerned primarily with reinforcing slavery. They wanted members of the Five Nations to aid them in recovering any runaway "Negroes" that might have escaped Virginia. To the proposition offered at Albany that they serve as slave catchers for the colonists, the leaders of the Five Nations settled on a diplomatic middle course: acquiescence without action. They offered a "promise that if any Runaway Negroes or slaves shall happen to fall in our hands we will carry them" back to Virginia. The phrase "Negroes" *or* "slaves" hints at the possibility that enslaved Native people may be swept up in such nets. Yet the Iroquois do not practice slavery as Virginia colonists understand it, and they have little intention of actually carrying out such policies. "As to those Negroes which you said we promised last year," they demurred, "they lye very much out of our way and may be had more easily by other Indians." Cleverly, they neither denied the Virginians' request nor complied with it.[6]

Everything came back to control of land and people. At Albany, Virginia magistrates also told representatives of the Five Nations that they wanted stronger boundaries around each English colony. They promised the people of the Haudenosaunee that if they would agree to remain northeast of Virginia, in return Virginia officials would strive to ensure that no Native peoples from the southern area ventured across the dividing lines. Virginia's leaders tried to tempt the Five Nations into cooperating more actively by promising them that, if any Virginia-area Indians did trespass over the new proposed boundary line, the Haudenosaunee "might use them" however they "saw fit," implying that they could be killed or captured at will.[7]

But the assembled leaders of the Five Nations rejected this proposal, saying, "We assure you if any of your Indians should happen in
our way, we will not hurt them, but treat them as friends and give them
victuals, so desirous are we of being at Peace with them." Native peoples do take captives in wartime raids and sometimes march them in
fetters. Some of these captives, mostly fighting men, are later subjected
to ritual death. But women and children so taken, once they arrive in
new villages, are welcomed as kin, not chained as laborers or sold at
profit. Through marriage and adoption, Native women and children
become channels for new connections between their nations of origin and their new relations. Iroquoian patterns of warfare emphasize
incorporating newcomers into the community, not commercializing
people as trade items. And nowadays, the Five Nations are pursuing
policies of peace.[8]

In order to ensure that this message is widely received, leaders of
the Five Nations took an opportunity at the Albany conference to create a new code for use in the river valleys, telling "Conestogoes" and
others "which live upon Susquehana," along with the members of ten
different Native nations to the south, that they have devised a system
for signaling amity. Whenever trekkers in the woods extinguish their
campfires, they should "lay a stone in them when they leave their quar-
ters and we will do ye same, which will be a sign to us both that our
friends have passed." Rather than limit the places where people can
journey, the Five Nations prefer to ensure that travelers go in peace.
By constantly exchanging visits from one village to another over hundreds of miles of well-worn pathways, they create cultural solidarity
among far-flung peoples, a geography of reciprocity.[9]

Wherever they happen to be, the Native peoples of North America
scan the land for the stories written upon it. Often, they see char marks
on the ground that show where other hunters, travelers, and warriors
have camped. And sometimes, by prearrangement, they leave rocks in
the ashes, a message that only those with the requisite knowledge will
understand. Such stones are signs chipped from a cultural bedrock that
stretches across Native North America: a common appreciation for
mobility as liberty. From the West Coast to the East Coast, Indigenous
societies cage neither animals nor people. Neither prison pen nor jail

nor gibbet has any Native equivalent. Furthermore, when Native peoples do draw maps, perhaps on bark or on deerskin, they use them to sketch networks of social connections, not plats of territorial claims.[10]

⌐⌐

WILLIAM KEITH CALLS HIS board to order for the first time in nearly two months on Wednesday, October 3. Philadelphia is still steaming under unrelenting heat, but the governor keeps cooler than ever. He has accomplished much at Albany, and now it will be his pleasure to inform his courtiers—that is, his council members—of the details of his magisterial performance. His council members have also been busy, since many serve as city elders as well as colonywide leaders. Isaac Norris, alderman, was just "chosen by a Majority of Votes" for city mayor, but he has declined the position. Naturally, the council has turned to his closest associate, James Logan, as their second choice, and Logan, ready to reassert himself, has accepted the post just this morning. Let Keith preen that he has played the key part in the climactic scene of the Cartlidge drama. Quakers have no use for theater anyway, for what the members of the Burlington Yearly Meeting scathingly refer to in their latest epistle as "*Romances, Play-Books*" and "other vain and idle" amusements "which tend to corrupt the minds of Youth."[11]

Keith, by contrast, loves a good show. He hopes this latest effort at Albany will seal his reputation—from the halls of the British Board of Trade to the cabins of the Pennsylvania countryside—as the colony's leading man. Italian-style "flats" are all the rage in London theaters nowadays, backdrops that can be slid soundlessly along grooves in the floor, used in combination to achieve an array of scenic settings. Pity there are none to be had in the courthouse here today. Keith will have to conjure his flats with his words.[12]

"This being the first meeting of the Council since the Govrs. Return from Albany," Logan notes, he "expressed his satisfaction in seeing the members of. His Council together at this time." Actually, not everyone is here, for Richard Hill is still recuperating, but Keith makes no mention of his illness or absence. Instead, he declares that he will make them all "acquainted" with the specifics of his conduct on his journey to New York. He recites in minute detail his dealings with New York's governor Burnet, their genteel exchange of letters, his successful appearance at Fort George. Logan dutifully records the governor's recital and accepts copies of Keith's correspondence for inclusion in the official records of the colony.[13]

When no applause is forthcoming, Keith begins sliding his flats, ready to describe the weeks of meetings in Albany. But Logan interrupts. As he describes it, "the Secretary informed the Governor, that Richard Hill & Isaac Norris ... had ... Communicated to the Council the next day after their arrival here, the Governour's Negotiation with the Indians at Albany during the sd. Gentleman's stay there." No need for Keith to ramble on; members of council have already received and reviewed all of the relevant records. But Keith refuses to step out of the spotlight. "Whereupon, the Governor said that he needed only take Notice to the Board of what Farther Conference he had had with the Indians after the said Gentleman's departure from Albany homewards." Sir William has a little encore prepared, a recital the council members won't have heard before.[14]

Keith announces that he has a new land agreement to report, reached with the Five Nations at Albany on September 14, one day *after* the rest of the council departed the city. There is nothing Logan or the others can do but sit still and listen. Logan consoles himself by refusing to record what the governor says in the moment. Instead, he demands a copy of the official notes taken at Albany on September 14 and dutifully goes to work preparing an official transcript of all the treaty proceedings. An event this momentous must be publicized, even if it pains him to cast so many flowers at Keith's feet. The council agrees that all the speeches made at the Albany conference ought to be published in pamphlet form by Andrew Bradford.[15]

⌐━

AT THE SIGN OF the Bible on Second Street, an apprentice rubs "good lampblack" into varnish on his ink block, the sooty pigment blending with the mixture of linseed oil and rosin until it reaches a "brisk and vivid black complexion." The sometime poet Aquila Rose is one of Andrew Bradford's hands in the print shop and today they have an important project in press. They have just received an order from the governor and his council to print the official record of *A Treaty of Peace and Friendship Made and Conducted between His Excellency Sir William Keith, Bart., Governor of the Province of Pennsylvania, For and on Behalf of the Said Province, AND THE Chiefs of the Indians of the Five Nations, At ALBANY in the Month of September, 1722.*[16]

This is one of the few pamphlet or book-length publications that Bradford will produce this year, and so he is glad to have the commission. He supplements his income by selling whatever else comes through the door of the shop. This month he will offer the extra lamp-black he does not need: "very good lamp-black . . . by wholesale and retail, very Reasonable." And he is also advertising that he has, just in, "A Very handsome Negroe Boy, between Twelve and Thirteen Years of Age to be Sold. Enquire of Andrew Bradford." Black complexions of many kinds promise the best profits at the moment. And indeed, printers' revenues come from inking advertisements for enslaved people, not just from publishing the news.[17]

Bradford describes the "Negroe Boy" as being "very handsome." Does this mean he sees beauty in this youngster whom he is marketing as merchandise, some loveliness of form unimaginable to those, like James Logan, who can find no "beauty" in "black faces"? Peeling back the layers of meaning in the word "handsome" suggests another possibility. "Handsome" derives from the root word "hand" and has long had associations with things that are "handy" or useful as well as those that are simple to "handle"—that is, easy to control. Bradford's advertisement attests less to this boy's aesthetic attractiveness than to his value as a worker and his vulnerability to a prospective master's power. Buyers of enslaved laborers prefer to purchase adult men; Bradford is simply pushing a less desirable product as best he can by emphasizing that an enslaved boy may be easier to control than a full-grown man. Beautiful as he must have been to his mother, this boy, sold alone, will almost certainly never see her again.[18]

Bradford's newspaper, one of the first to advance freedom of the press in the British colonies, flourishes by limiting the freedom of ordinary people. Beyond direct sales of humans as goods, Bradford earns many an extra shilling by featuring notices about the indentured and enslaved in his "Advertisements" column. The teeming masses of the city are posted for sale and then, if disgruntled indentured servants or desperate enslaved people seek to escape, they are listed again for recapture. Colonial leaders deny basic freedom of movement to all but the highest-ranking members of their community.[19]

One indentured servant in the city who survives his term of service, makes it into the ranks of freemen, and then manages the singular feat of writing and publishing his own story—without the interpolations of ministers or schoolmasters—sums up by saying: "the Condition of bought Servants is very hard." An unsuccessful runaway himself, this memoirist attests, "if they endeavor to escape, which is next to impossible . . . their Masters immediately issue out a Reward for the apprehending [of] them . . . Advertisements are set up against the Trees besides those in the News-Papers." And if prospects are bleak for those serving indentures, they look still worse for those enduring enslavement. The memoirist explains:

> The Condition of Negroes is very bad . . . It is vain to attempt an Escape, tho' they often endeavor it; for the Laws against them are so severe that being caught after running away, they are unmercifully whipped; and if they die under the Discipline, their Masters suffer no Punishment, there being no Law against murdering them.

For all the fine talk you hear over cups and tankards at coffeeshops and tavern counters—gossip about fortunes in golden wheat or in mineral ore—much of the wealth being built by colonists in this new country comes from keeping iron control over flesh and bone.[20]

First Bradford and his apprentices set the type, each letter and word put in backward, line by line, to appear the right way round when paper is smoothed against them. "The honourable Sir William Keith," reads the first line, "having upon the Report that an Indian of the Five Nations had lost his Life by Means of Some Traders of the Province, sent two Members of the Council, in March last, to Conestogoe." Next, an assistant with the title of "beater" uses a leather ball stuffed with wool to smear the ink mixture over the type and, and finally, sheets of dampened paper are pressed into print. This is how the colonists preserve their views for posterity.[21]

JAMES LOGAN PURCHASES EXTRA copies of the printed treaty to send to his contacts back in Britain. "The Inclosed printed Accot. Of the Treaty at Albany will shew the happy Event of that unfortunate business of the Indian's death," Logan tells one recipient. The fates take, but they also give. Logan counts Sawantaeny's loss as the colony's gain. He is determined to profit from events personally as well, whatever Keith's efforts to claim all the credit and win all the benefit. "Coll. Frnch and I were the two members first sent up to Conestogoe," Logan informs his correspondent, adding with transparently false modesty, "tho I forebore mentioning our names in ye Preamble." Logan is claiming authorship not only of Keith's speeches at Albany, as he does in his fall letters to the Penns, but also of the treaty pamphlet Bradford has just published. In reality, of course, he cannot be the sole author of that production because neither he nor any other member of the council was present for the governor's final Albany meeting with leaders of the Five Nations on September 14.[22]

The Bradford pamphlet reveals that Governor Keith received a final visit from a delegation of ten leaders of the Five Nations at Albany, two from each nation, who declared, "we now freely surrender to you all those Lands above Conestogoe which the Five Nations have claimed." In return, they asked the governor to work to enhance commercial and communal ties between the Five Nations and the Pennsylvania colonists, requesting "that if any of our People come to trade at Philadelphia, you will order that they be received like Brethren and have the Goods as cheap as possible." This is the context in which the Iroquois as well as the Shawnee and other peoples of the river valleys have urged forgiveness for the Cartlidges.[23]

Rather than seek violent revenge, Native people have again and again explained that the crisis caused by the killing of Sawantaeny can be the occasion of strengthening real and fictive ties of kinship, communal bonds created and conserved through exchanges of emotional comfort and material goods. "We say," the Haudenosaunee leaders told Keith at Albany and Andrew Bradford now commits to print, "that as we are all in Peace, we think it hard that the Persons who kill'd our Friend and Brother should suffer." From their perspective, it is obvious that the Cartlidges should be set free to return to the fur trade. John, especially, has the linguistic ability and commercial savvy to serve as an important link in the long chain connecting Natives and colonists as people of one community. They are ready to reintegrate him into exchange networks, knowing he will now work harder than ever in the service of such ties.[24]

But colonists in Pennsylvania have little idea of the role of the Indigenous exchange economy in the creation of civil society. Nothing in English legal theory allows for creating new communities by engaging in commerce. That nation's foremost political philosopher, John Locke, has recently declared in his master work, *Two Treatises of Government*, "Tis not every Compact that puts an end to the state of Nature between Men, but only this one of agreeing together mutually to enter into one Community and make one Body Politick." The creation of governments is the most important foundation of civility as the English understand it: "other Promises, and Compacts, Men may make with one another, and yet still be in the state of Nature." Locke positively denies that commercial ties can ever create civic bonds, and he has America in mind when he claims this. Of course, a bargain is a bargain and must be honored. But economic links do not make civil connections. "The Promises and Bargains for Truck, etc. . . . between a *Swiss* and an *Indian*, in the Woods of *America*, are binding to them, though they are perfectly in a State of Nature in reference to one another. For Truth and keeping of Faith belong to Men, as Men, and not as Members of Society." Native peoples can and should be honorbound to colonists through debt and dependence, but, in the view of England's most advanced theorists, such economic relations do not imply any sort of civic union. You will scarcely find a colonist who doesn't agree.[25]

For all that Native peoples make effective use of the very "one body" metaphor favored by Locke, they never imply a desire to be incorporated into a British-controlled empire in which political bonds would fix them in a subordinate role. To the contrary, they try throughout the Cartlidge case to educate colonists on the possibilities of a more flexible form of civil community, one continuously renewed and re-created through trade and diplomacy. They are alive to the possibilities of something like dual sovereignty, a system in which Native peoples could retain their rights even as they create civil connections with newcomers.[26]

Pennsylvanians only preserve the record of speeches at Albany on the beautifully printed pages of their pamphlets because they wish to promote two pieces of news. First, although they have followed the dictates of English justice so far as they are able, they simply cannot prosecute a murder when the purported victim's body is missing. Second, they are celebrating that the leaders of the Five Nations have freely offered them the lands around Conestoga without requesting anything more than the right to trade in Philadelphia. No matter that the Five Nations have neither the authority to give away Conestoga lands nor the intention to alienate Native property in perpetuity. No matter that their every action has been in service of enhancing ties, not fencing land. Colonists hear only what they want to hear, and they publish their version as fast as they can.

New York's colonists pay no more heed to Indian concerns than do Virginia's or Pennsylvania's. When New York's governor, William Burnet, writes his report on the Albany conference for the British Board of Trade, he will summarize the great summit between the Five Nations and the Pennsylvania colonists as follows:

> the Governor of Pennsylvania found it necessary to give these Indi-
> ans a meeting upon an unfortunate accident of an Indian of the five
> Nations being killed in Pennsylvania by a Christian, for whose death
> he [Governor Keith] had not sufficient evidence. The Offender con-
> tinued a Prisoner till the Indians desired his enlargement and declared
> themselves satisfied and this is the subject of the conference between
> Sir William Keith and the five Nations.

The letter says so little and omits so much. Nowhere does Burnet name either Sawantaeny or John Cartlidge. They are simply the "Indian" and the "Offender." Nowhere does he note the Iroquois values of liberty and comity. Instead, he explains the quiet end of the whole affair as the inevitable result of English legal procedures. English due process simply won't allow a murder charge to be tried on insufficient evidence.[27]

And *why* is there no evidence? Of course, Pennsylvania's magistrates have been clever in declining to make any attempt to locate Sawantaeny's remains. No corpse, no case. But there is still more to it. At the very moment Burnet describes the "offender" as a "Christian" and the victim as an "Indian," he establishes the impossibility of prosecution. Even had a body been found, Keith would still have lacked "sufficient evidence" to prosecute the crime. Burnet knows, as does Keith—who lectured justices of the peace in Pennsylvania on this very point in 1718—that English precedents say "the Law will not permit that any *Christian* shall incur the Penalty of his Life, except upon the full and plain Testimony of Men openly professing their Belief of the same Faith in our Blessed Saviour Christ." In other words, whatever other internecine squabbles divide the various English colonies, the New York and Pennsylvania governors are united in their belief that Native people have no standing to press charges in this case.[28]

Native witnesses cannot testify in the murder trial of a colonist because Indians do not follow the Christian Testament. "Indians" are not legally accepted as "Christians"—no matter what faith they may profess. When Keith and Burnet offer apparent cooperation with Native protocols for grief and reconciliation, they are actually masking an insult. They are operating on an exclusionary set of assumptions wholly at odds with the founding philosophy of the Haudenosaunee, that people should use moments of shared grief to forge new bonds of sympathy and strive for unity under the Great Tree of Peace.[29]

JAMES LE TORT SWINGS back up into the saddle, bound once more for Conestoga to do the bidding of British colonial leaders. Crisp weather greets him as he goes. The heat broke at last on Sunday, the seventh of October, when, as Isaac Norris notes approvingly, "a gust of thunder & much lightening changed and cooled ye air." As Le Tort's horse clatters over the stony trail, he has ample time to contemplate the forest. Here and there, trees have begun to shed, their natural foliage less firmly fixed than the leaves of paper nailed to their trunks by owners advertising for missing indentured or enslaved people who have dared to set themselves free.³⁰

Le Tort returned safely from Albany, to the governor's great relief. Governor Keith has been hoping to have his help at the conference he is planning to convene at Conestoga in the company of Virginia's governor, Alexander Spotswood. But Logan and council have stayed his hand. "The extraordinary proceeding of your council in this affair, I cannot but complain of," Spotswood grumbles to Keith as he boards his ship and sets sail for the south without being able to personally deliver his "demand" for "some Negroes belonging to Virginia . . . harbored among the Shuannoes and said to be set free and protected by those Indians." Once again, the secretary has managed to outmaneuver the governor. The council agrees on the importance of informing the peoples of the river valleys about the final moments of Keith's visit to Albany, but they have forced the Virginians to embark without participating in the conversation.³¹

Furthermore, the Pennsylvania council members see no reason to fund yet another formal conference at Conestoga. They think a simple statement, delivered by a messenger and not by any of the magistrates, will suffice. They prepare a speech to be delivered to the people of Conestoga summarizing the concluding negotiations at Albany. Determined to leave the controversy over last March's killing entirely behind them, they intend this new message only to address the issues of slavery and mobility raised in Keith's unscheduled extra meeting. When James Le Tort arrives alone and delivers his speech in the name of William Keith and council at Conestoga on October 18, 1722, he never so much as mentions Sawantaeny's death or John Cartlidge's redemption. Nor does he utter a word about the way the Five Nations have seemingly ceded lands on the Susquehanna, territory to which they have no actual title.³²

Instead, with stiff obstinacy, Le Tort kicks the rocks off the embers of Haudenosaunee peace efforts and grinds the campfire ashes into the ground with his rhetorical boot. Following the instructions of Keith and council, he directs all his comments to the twin issues of controlling "Negroes" and "Indians" in the Pennsylvania region. He informs those assembled that Virginia has made "a very strict law" declaring that if any "Southern Indians" ford the Potomac River or cross the Allegheny Mountains into Pennsylvania without carrying a written pass, "it shall be lawful . . . to put such Southern Indians to death." Conversely, he asserts, the Five Nations have agreed on behalf of themselves, the "Conestogoes," and "the Shawannese" that none of them may traverse those boundaries in the opposite direction "without having a Passport to produce the same." And if any of them violate this order and appear on the wrong side of the line, "such Indians shall be put to death for so being or be transported and sold for Slaves." Finally, he tells them, "you know the Negroes are slaves" and warns them that "to entertain our slaves is not only scandalous to the Indians but an injury to the English." With no mention whatsoever of the Iroquois plan to welcome friends with victuals or signal benevolence with well-placed stones, he simply announces a new policy restricting mobility and crimping liberty.[33]

Le Tort records the Native speaker's reply but does not bother to document who speaks. He does not mention the national affiliations, much less the given names, of those he meets with. He confines himself to reporting back on "the Indians Speech to his Excellency Sir William Keith" with no identifying details. Still, something of the color of the local response seeps through the paper Le Tort uses to parcel up their words. "We have heard a relation of the Governour's Proceedings at Albany," they say, "and also of the Governor of Virginia's proceedings, from which we have a small Dread upon us." The translation is an odd one. How often are "dreads," properly understood as extreme fears, "small" and negligible in size?[34]

"We are troubled in mind of being stop't for some evil Consequences to happen thereby," they tell Le Tort. This goes against every tradition they hold most sacred. "We were in hopes there should have been free Liberty to Pass & Repass, but as it's agreed otherwise, we will observe." A world of future conflict is contained in that statement. For the Five

Nations have influence, not final authority, over the lands and lives of the peoples of the river valleys. With no record at all of who spoke these words of acceptance or who gave witness to them, we have to assume that they were contentious even as they flowed from Le Tort's pen.[35]

As for the matter of "these Negroes Slaves," the "Shawanna King" adds his own separate statement to the Native speeches delivered that day in which he once again dodges and weaves around colonial demands. He claims he can do nothing to find them now because "they are abroad a Hunting," but promises that eventually "I will go my own self" to recapture them. Then he puts off action till the following spring, at the time "when the bark will run." Let the sap rise in the maples before he stirs to track anyone. By then, as he must know, these "well armed" groups often "exceeding the number ten" will have moved off still deeper into the forest, well beyond reach of pens, parchment, printer's ink, or paper.[36]

⌁

WHENEVER AQUILA ROSE CAN take time from his work in Bradford's printing office, he likes to compose "occasional poems" commenting on the social life of the colony. It was just a year ago, in better times, that he wrote his ode in thanks for John Cartlidge's hospitality at an earlier Indian conference, declaring that: "The 'Delphian town shall know how well we fare / Since we are sure to feed less sumptuous there." No one could then have imagined that the city magistrates of Philadelphia would soon have a much darker reason to think of John. In the months since Rose wrote his poem, the Cartlidge brothers' killing of a Native man has catalyzed a cascading series of crises. And yet, already, John's "spreading Name," as Rose called his once-growing fame, seems to be fading from view again, not so much as mentioned in the midst of renewed colonial efforts to control Native people and property.[37]

On the Cartlidge farm in Conestoga this fall, his two servant lads are plowing and harrowing the rich Pennsylvania loam and planting "12 acres of winter grain" in the fat black mold. But John meets the reaper before his wheat does. No one leaves any record of the date he draws his last breath, nor any description of his final hours. But James Logan, faithful chronicler of events in the colony, includes the news of John's passing in a lengthy letter he writes from Philadelphia on November 22. After giving his English correspondent the best account he can of the Albany conference, Logan comments, "Jno. Cartlidge one of the unhappy occasions of that trouble died at home a few dayes agoe of a fever, which took him in this town before he left it. He had been a very serviceable man in those posts among the Indians and I have suffered deeply by his Death." Logan's brief remarks offer a rare expression of feeling from a carefully contained man.[38]

And Logan does more: One week later, on November 29, the secretary travels once again to Cartlidge's "capacious" house (as Aquila Rose described it) to meet with his widow, Elizabeth, and his brother, Edmund, and to witness the probate inventory of John's earthly property. John has died a substantial man and left Elizabeth a well-to-do widow. To £80 of housewares, he adds more than £700 in land, livestock, trade items, and farm tools. He holds no enslaved people as property but does claim years of the lives of his two servant boys, valued at £24 for the pair. After all the legal debates and Indian appeals, after being carted off to jail, stripped of his public office, set free on bail, denounced by his fellow Quakers, seized a second time and never offered trial, but ultimately released on Iroquois orders, John has finally lost to fate.[39]

In the letter that Logan writes memorializing John, he remembers him as Sawantaeny himself might have wished his "friend" to be described—that is, as a man "very serviceable" in Indian trading posts. Still, James Logan does not grasp the full meaning of Sawantaeny's words. Even in death, the victimized man honored more than a personal connection with the Cartlidge brothers; he named them as valued allies whose trading activities helped to link the material interests of Native peoples and colonists. Accustomed to cereal-grain monoculture, such as John Cartlidge's field of winter wheat, colonists little appreciate Native ways. Mobility, liberty, and trade can work together to fix unity in the civic soil, like so many complementary crops of corn, beans, and squash.

Chapter 24

CIVILITY'S LAST WORD

FROM WHERE WILLIAM KEITH SITS CONFINED ON THE "master's side" of London's Fleet Prison, the section of the jail where gentlemen debtors are held for security, you can still smell the combined effluvia of the River Fleet and of the desperate prisoners penned beside it. "What adds to the dampness and stench of the place," notes one contemporary critic, "is its being built over the common shore, and adjoining to the sink and dunghill, where all the nastiness of the prison is cast." Little did Keith ever imagine, back when he was placing the cornerstone for the mansion he called Fountain Low on his lands in Pennsylvania early in 1723, that before 1730 he would slink back to London, indebted and disgraced, only to slither in and out of prison there according to the caprice of his many creditors. As he stares at the unplastered brick walls and metal grates that surround him, Keith has plenty of time to reconsider his position on the usefulness of prisons. In fact, if he so chooses, he can contemplate the arguments in favor of freedom advanced by Captain Civility on the occasion of their final conference.[1]

WHEN TAQUATARENSALY ARRIVES IN Philadelphia to request an audience with Governor Keith on May 18, 1723, neither can guess that this meeting will be their last. Governor Keith is at the pinnacle of his power in the colony, ready to throw James Logan back on his heels

once and for all. Taquatarensaly finds the courthouse area greatly
altered since his last visit to the city. William Pawlett, sweeper of the
cobblestones and keeper of the gates and bell tower, has been bang-
ing his iron crow for weeks, prying apart wooden market stalls. In
April, the city council "ordered that ye Middle Row of Stalls between
ye Court House and ye Prison be pull'd down, and William Pawlett is
appointed to See ye Same done." Meanwhile, the old brick prison itself
stands empty, its vacant chambers echoing with neglect.[2]

Just a couple of weeks earlier, on May 1, the jail was "publickly sold
to the highest bidder" with the lucky winner of the auction "obliged to
remove ye same without delay." It is not that city elders have decided
against caging people. But they now prefer to situate places of incarceration farther out of sight. A few streets over from the grand balcony
of the courthouse and the high-domed arches of the city market, they
have erected a new stone prison complex on High and Third Streets.
Now they have one building for debtors and a separate one for criminals, the two structures joined by a wall of roughhewn stone enclos-
ing a workyard. A year after the Cartlidges' initial arrest, the city has
doubled its carceral capacity.[3]

Down on the docks by the Delaware, merchants and sailors are
cursing the weather. Water courses through the streets, turning the
carefully cobbled avenues into raging streams. Mulberry Street, "from
ye East side of the Front Street to ye River," is in a condition described
as "very ruinous by reason of ye . . . Great Rains." Still, schooners and
sloops are regularly arriving and departing, their rigging streaming
with as much freshwater as salt, their cargoes moldering, and their passengers shivering. On the slippery decks of the *Shaw Philadelphia*, "a
parcel of choice Servant-Men, Women, and Boys" just "imported from
Bristol," England, awaits inspection by buyers willing to brave the wet.
They likewise have to submit to an examination from the colony's official "Chirugen," Patrick Baird, who is paid to "go on Board all vessels
arriving from Sea" and check the passengers for signs of "any pesti-
lential or Contagious Distemper." This week, there are "Trades-men,
Husbandmen and Dairy Maids to be seen on Board the said Ship in
the River Delaware." As Taquatarensaly walks the neighborhood near
these wharves, concerns about confinement shackle his thoughts.[4]

The peoples of Conestoga have taken the winter to consider further the speech that James Le Tort delivered on behalf of Governor
Keith and his councilors last October. Little in what he had to say then
pleased them. Many of the conclusions that colonists seem to have
drawn from the saga of Sawantaeny are directly at odds with those
of the Native community at Conestoga. Furthermore, whatever the
Five Nations may have to say about the killing and its consequences
for land policy in the colony, they cannot presume to speak for all of
the nations, Algonquian and Iroquoian, who live cooperatively on the
Susquehanna. Whiwhinjac, "King of the Ganawese Indians," requests
that Captain Civility accompany him on a new diplomatic trip to Philadelphia, to once more try to weave the worlds of Natives and newcomers together.[5]

At this May meeting at the courthouse, Civility tells Keith clearly,
"William Penn said, We must all be one half Indian & the other half
English, being as one Flesh & one Blood under one Head." Civility
summarily banishes all talk of Indians as "children" or Natives and
settlers as "brethren" brought together by "joining of hands." No.
Civility insists, "in all these Cases, accidents may happen to break or
weaken the tyes of Friendship." But the idea of unity with diversity
continues to elude Keith and company. No metaphor can ever reach
the colonial leaders, determined as they are to turn a deaf ear to Indian
teachings.[6]

As rain lashes the many mullioned windows of the courthouse
chamber, Civility presses on. "As the Governor went last year to
Albany to make a firm Peace with the Five Nations, and to bury the
Blood of an Indian that had been spilt by the English," Civility says,
Whiwhinjac has come in the name of "the Ganawese, Shawannoes,
Conestogoes, and Delawares to desire that the same Blood may not
only be buried but wash'd away as it were by a swift runnin Stream of
Water never more to be seen or heard of." One has only to look out at
the weather today to appreciate the purifying effects of rushing water.
Here Civility is making a point, in the most polite terms, that Gover-
nor Keith has been remiss in the performance of his diplomatic duties.
Traveling in person to Albany was a necessary step in resolving the
crisis created when Sawantaeny was killed. Yet Keith *still* has not paid

an official visit to the peoples of the Susquehanna to express condolences or make material offerings to those most immediately affected by the murder in their midst. Having accepted the need to acknowledge the power of the Five Nations, Keith now exaggerates it, neglecting the attentions also due to local leaders.[7]

The peoples of the river valleys object strenuously to the idea that the final resolution of Sawantaeny's loss lies in their relinquishing more land to settlers. As Civility explains, "they desire that the English may not be suffered to straiten the Ganawese or the Shawannoes to make them remove further off." Alluding obliquely to the land commitments offered to Keith at Albany by the leaders of the Five Nations, he says, "they have heard some words to this purpose which they do not care to mention." To the contrary, the Conestoga representatives explain yet again that their desired outcome is an arrangement with the English that extends to colonists the kind of relationship that links "all the four Nations that live upon the Susquehanna," a series of independent but interlocking villages in which distinct languages and cultures are respected even as countless moments of cooperation and consensus bring people together. If colonists could come to a full understanding of Native ways, they would not make ever-greater demands for Native ground but would focus instead on developing ritual relationships and continuing the exchange of trade items.[8]

Here Civility pauses in his speech to linger on a positive trend: "They are glad to find the English continue to send their young men with Goods among them," he remarks. Civility does not mention Edmund Cartlidge by name, but, in fact, Edmund has returned to the community and peacefully resumed his work of farming and trading. To wash away the blood of the murdered man is to cleanse the Cartlidges as well. Far from ostracizing Edmund and those of his ilk, Native peoples wish to maintain cross-cultural ties through material exchanges. Traders have both the goods and the words, the carts full of products and the command of tongues, to make this possible.[9]

"They acknowledge that the Traders are now very Civil & Kind to them," Captain Civility remarks next, "whereby they Eat their Victuals without Fear & have a True Relish of them." At last the peoples of the Susquehanna region can eat in peace. All along, English colonists have insisted that they alone can define the rules of civility and the meaning of justice. But only now, after months of work to resolve the crisis created by the death of Sawantaeny—the Seneca hunter whom Captain Civility admired as a "civil man"—is the Conestoga spokesman willing to apply the same label to the traders of Pennsylvania, describing them today as "Civil & Kind." He has not lost hope that colonists may yet be made to understand an idea that his people have lived by for generations, for at least as long as they have used the Susquehannock-language title that the English first translated with the word "civility." Those who share a body must regard themselves as a collective community. The trouble is, *this* meaning of civility has been lost to the English language for over a century.[10]

With a final flourish, "Whiwhinjac, in the name & on behalf of all the said Indians, makes a present to the Governor of 200 skins." Conestoga community members will have to wait two days before the governor delivers them any answer. Very few members of the council are present today, not enough to make up a quorum. Keith decides he cannot respond until he has apprised the board members of Captain Civility's speech and gained their assistance in preparing a reply.[11]

AFTER TAKING SUNDAY OFF, Keith climbs the steps to the courthouse on Monday, May 20, in high dudgeon. James Logan's letters of last autumn were the final straw for Keith. The council has not met for months, but now that it is back in session, Keith will endure no more of the Quaker man's efforts to undermine him in the eyes of the Penn family. Addressing Logan along with Messrs. Assheton, Preston, and Masters, he informs the board that "he had thought fit to appoint Patrick Baird, his Secretary, to be Clerk of the Council." Just like that, Keith throws Logan out of office, replacing him with his own private assistant, the colony's "chirugeon," who strides off the docks and squelches up the courthouse steps. Keith can only hope that Baird will be able to inoculate him against Logan's attacks. Next, Keith calls on Logan to hand over the lesser seal of the province, that essential tool of the colony's clerk. From now on, the governor alone will decide which documents can be stamped with the Penn family crest and the promise of "Mercy & Justice." Keith has taken the law in hand.[12]

Characteristically, Logan inserts no comment whatsoever about Keith's action to remove him from office in the official minutes of the council. However, he does carefully set down all of Civility's words of two days ago. Moreover, when further business comes before the council today, he refers to himself in the notes he is making as "Mr. Logan, the Secretary." That evening, they all agree, they will reconvene at the courthouse, where the governor will deliver his official response to the speech Civility made on behalf of Whiwhinjac. Recording it will be Logan's last official act as Pennsylvania's provincial secretary.[13]

A large assemblage of Indians and English waits within the courthouse to hear Keith's words this evening. Logan notes the presence of "sundry Gentleman & many other People" along with "Whiwhinjac, Civility, sundry Chiefs & other Indians." Quite likely the phrases "other people" and "other Indians" indicate the presence of women as well as common men in the audience. Logan does not bother to record any women's names, but it is just possible that Weenepeeweytah is in attendance. Her cousin is acknowledged as a Shawnee chief, which means she herself may be of high enough standing to be included in the large delegation. Alice Kirk, on the other hand, most certainly is not there to perform translation duties in tandem with Civility today. Instead, that office is being filled by a new interpreter, a substantial Chester County farmer named Ezekiel Harlan.[14]

Official diplomatic work is a masculine activity, as far as Pennsylvania's government leaders are concerned. They little credit how much Native peoples respect and rely on the exertions of colonial women who engage with them in the many small-scale transactions that can keep people connected. In fact, of course, Alice Kirk's husband, Samuel, owes his prosperous ferry and tavern to his wife's inheritance from her first husband, and Alice's efforts remain essential to running it. By 1726, Samuel will wind up being appointed a justice of the peace for New Castle County, not a bad rise for a man who was first recognized as a freeman in 1717 shortly before his marriage to a well-to-do widow.[15]

Elizabeth Cartlidge follows a path similar to Alice Kirk's. Just months after John's death she takes up with a local man named Andrew

Cornish, who marries John's duties as well as his widow. By 1726, Cornish is serving as justice of the peace for Chester County, issuing writs and collecting fees just as John used to do. By 1728 he is welcoming Indians and colonists to the home and store Elizabeth once shared with John for another treaty conference. No doubt the repast that Elizabeth provides is as sumptuous as ever. By 1729, Cornish is accompanying Isaac Taylor—finally released from Maryland's legal clutches after many public appeals—on surveying missions across the colony. You can take note of how simply Andrew takes John's place or you can peer closer and see that he partners with Elizabeth in work as in life, just as John did.[16]

Once everyone has at last gathered, dripping, in the courtroom, Keith takes to his feet to deliver his address. From the first moment, he betrays either complete incomprehension of or total disregard for Indian ideals.

"Brethren," he begins, "you Know that I came from William Penn to fulfill his kind words to the Indians, and to be as a Father to them now." He speaks as if the men gathered before him had not explicitly rejected colonial claims of fatherhood over Native peoples a mere two days before.[17]

Still he tries to define "brethren" in an appealing fashion by assuring them, "You Know the English to be a faithful good People who always keep their Treaties & Leagues punctually with the Indians, and you also know that our Laws make no distinction between our people & yours." Here it is again, Keith's offering of English justice as a gift to be prized above all others.[18]

Civility's ears swim as Keith natters on at length about bright chains between their peoples, about washing away Sawantaeny's blood "under the ground that it may never be seen or heard of," about his efforts now and always to "take care of you as if you were my own children." Civility does perk up a bit at the promise that "no English Settlements shall hereafter be made too near your Towns to disturb you." That, at least, seems to offer something Whiwhinjac and the others actually want to hear. When Keith finally wraps up by promising substantial "presents," to include "a Barrell of Powder, Twelve Gallons of Rum, 300lb of Biscuit, one Groce of Pipes, 20lb of Tobacco,

15 Strowd Match Coats, 15 Blankets, 5 pair of Shoes & Buckles, 5 pair of Stockings, 150 lb of Lead and Meat to the value of Twenty Shillings," Civility can comfort himself that Keith has at least practiced some basic principles of reciprocity.[19]

Still, Civility draws himself up and tries one more time to explain the most essential Indigenous ideals to the ever-ignorant governor. "The Indians well approve of all the Govr. had said except where he told them the English Law made no difference between the English and the Indians," Civility tells him. It comes back again, as always, to the question of freedom. "They should not like, upon the Indian's committing a fault, that he should be imprisoned as they had seen some Englishmen were." Finally, he concludes, "They looked upon it as a great Hardship for them to be confined from Hunting on the other side of the Patwomeck, for that in their neighboring Woods was but little Game." Indians have well developed theories about the connections between individual liberty and collective geographic mobility. People need to be able to move around at will. Only then are they able to create the manifold connections to one another that combine to structure communities strong enough to reintegrate even those who make dire mistakes.[20]

Keith sputters that he only means that "if any Englishman did injury to an Indian, he should suffer the same punishment as if he had done it to an Englishman." At this moment he cannot conceive that there is any reasonable objection or realistic alternative to imprisonment as punishment for crime. And as for the rights of Native peoples to move freely over the lands of the region, he insists that "the Five Nations by their Treaty with the Governr. of Virginia had agreed not only to forbear themselves, but also to restrain the Susquehanna Indians." With that final dodge he largely invalidates his smooth assurances that the English will not disturb their Indian neighbors.[21]

⁓

EDMUND CARTLIDGE BENEFITS DIRECTLY from both the Native theory of freedom and Keith's view of property. Living once again in the Conestoga area, by 1725, he decides to acquire a new farmstead and enters into an agreement with a Delaware representative named Wiggoneeheenah for what the latter describes as "a Certain piece of Ground, formerly my plantation lying in a turn of Conestoga Creek formerly called by the name of ye Indian point." The deed that Cartlidge signs with Wiggoneeheenah demonstrates his reabsorption into a community that still values him despite the violence he brought into it. It shows the power that Native communities attach to the reciprocities that bring people together. And yet it also exposes a fundamental divide between Native and colonial ways of imagining the world. Cartlidge views the sale as a one-time transfer in which land changes names and owners, "Indian Point" to become Cartlidge's place. But Wiggoneeheenah's language leaves no doubt that the Delawares view this transaction as just one of an endless series of exchanges meant to confirm old bonds between people—not to set new boundaries around property. For while Wiggoneeheenah acknowledges receipt of "diverse large presents given unto me," the deed says clearly that Wiggoneeheenah acts "in behalf of all ye Delaware Indians Concerned" and has agreed to the transfer "in Consideration of . . . great Love and Respect" for a "true and Loving friend Edmund Cartlidge." Wiggoneeheenah signs with a mark, a delicate sketch of a fox.[22]

In many ways, Civility has failed in his efforts to draw together peoples of many nations. However many hundreds of skins he delivers to the colonists, they will never understand or accept the twined principles of amity and autonomy that such offerings are meant to advance. Each time colonists meet in treaty sessions with their Native counterparts, they find new ways to take land from people trying to give friendship and gain unity. In the end, rather than draw people in, Civility will find himself cast out. Thirteen years hence, in 1736, his name will appear in the records of colonial Pennsylvania one final time.

At a treaty session held that year at Philadelphia with the Six Nations (who now refer to themselves as such, having incorporated the Tuscarora into the former Five Nations), the Haudenosaunee leaders visit the city to push their claim to control Native lands in the region. On this trip, they positively deny that Civility has any authority to speak for those living on Susquehanna-area lands. The colonists document being told "that if Civility at Connestogoe should attempt to

KNow all men by these pessont.
that Twiggoneeheenah Do In behalf of allye
Dollaware Indians Concerned for and In Consideration
of the Greatt Love and Respectt as well as for
divers Large presentts made unto mee by my true
and Loveing friend Edmund Cartlidge Do hereby
Give Grantt and Dispose unto ye sd Edmund Cartlidge
all the rightt Title Intriest Claim and Demand
of my Self and theresst concerned of In and to a
Certain peice of Ground formerly my plantation
Lyeing In a Turn of Conostogoe Creek Called by the
name of ye Indian point to bee held by my sd
Edmund Cartlidge his heirs and assigns forever from
mee and my heirs and all othere In peaceable quiett
possesion In wittness whereoff I have hereunto
sett my hand and seale Dated this Eighth day
of Aprile Annoq Domini 1725
sealed and Delivered
In the presence of

Andd A Cox
marke

make a sale of any Lands to us or any of our neighbors they must let us know that he hath no Power to do so & if he does anything of the kind, they, the Indians, will utterly disown him." This is a defining moment in the Native history of Pennsylvania. With the Six Nations committed to a policy of appeasing colonists by ceding lands on the Susquehanna, lands that are not actually theirs to give, they have every reason to disavow the careful efforts Civility has always made not only to link the peoples of the river valleys to those in colonial settlements but also to Native nations to the north. After that last mention, Civility is silenced in colonial records.[23]

THE MAY 1723 MEETING in Philadelphia marks not only the last encounter between Keith and Civility but also the final time that Logan will write down what Civility has to say. After recording Civility's denouncement of imprisonment, James Logan obeys Keith's orders and puts down his pen. From now on, he will continue attending coun-

OPPOSITE: *This land deed is written in a clear calligraphic script by a man who used his handwriting to convey his status as a gentleman and who showed his education by using traditional legal phrasing ("Know all ye Men by these Presents"). Nevertheless, it is voiced in the first person as if being spoken by a Delaware representative: "I Wiggoneeheenah . . . in behalf of all ye Delaware Indians." The document is witnessed by one person, Andrew Cox, closing with the declaration: "Sealed and Delivered in the presence of Andw Cox, A, his marke." Colonists signed with a mark when they were illiterate, having learned to write only a single letter of their name. In lieu of a signature from Wiggoneeheenah, the document contains a pictogram, an accomplished drawing of a fox. In sum, it appears likely that Edmund Cartlidge prepared this deed himself and that he then had it witnessed and signed only by people who could not read it, much less certify his version of the paper's meaning and significance.*

WIGGONEEHEENAH, "KNOW ALL MEN BY THESE PRESENTS . . ." APRIL 8, 1725, CATALOGUED AS "INDIAN DEED TO E. CARTLIDGE FOR LAND," LOGAN FAMILY PAPERS, VOLUME 11, BOX 11, FOLDER 10, AUTHOR'S PHOTO FROM DOCUMENT AT THE HISTORICAL SOCIETY OF PENNSYLVANIA.

cil meetings as a member of the board, but he will no longer have any standing to make official records of the proceedings. And future secretaries, like the "chirugen," won't take the same care, indeed any care, in recording which Indian is speaking at any given meeting.

Nothing, however, can stop Logan from continuing to inform on Keith in the copious letters he continues writing to the Penn family. They can hardly be surprised by news of this falling-out. Last November, Logan explained to John Penn that while "the first Important Breach" to occur between him and Keith came as a result of the latter's "taking up some Land in an unprecedented manner in his own Right for the sake of a Copper Mine," the problem ran far deeper than the vein of venality revealed by Keith's actions. As Logan explained it, the problems had actually begun much earlier, "not long after the Title of Knighthood fell to him by the Death of his father." Keith seemed to change after that, puffed up with notions of his own advantages and prerogatives. Logan said "he forgot as much as if his very fabric had been changed with his appellation." Much as Keith congratulates himself on his knowledge of the "genteel airs" of "British nobleman," Logan regards him as hopelessly swollen with pride.[24]

Although there are a few transplanted English aristocrats in America, men like William Keith with empty pockets and high positions, the British Crown never creates a new class of lords in the colonies. In sharp contrast to the French in Canada with their cavaliers, the British never establish an American aristocracy. The old order of noblesse oblige, in which merciful lords temper the law's severity in return for recognition of their liege, is long gone. But neither do the English in America adopt the values of Native peoples. The ideals repeatedly described by Captain Civility are communal ones in which the strength of societies is measured by the health of dynamic reciprocal relationships. Anglo-American colonists reject both the mutual obligations that bound feudal lords and peasants and the communal ethos that governs Native peoples. Instead, middling men of wide ambition, the Logans and the Norrises of Britain's American colonies, set out to establish relations of property and politics based entirely on contractual individualism, systems that stress personal accountability to such a degree they leave no room for emotional reconciliation or community restitution in cases of crime.[25]

Keith enjoys a few more rollicking good years in Pennsylvania. He builds a large home for himself and his family where he and his wife entertain lavishly with the help of some fifteen people they keep enslaved. But Keith fails to find copper or much of anything else of value. All his high living is financed on credit. By 1726, largely as a result of Logan's untiring efforts, he is ousted from his post as governor, replaced by a new man sent by the Penns. At that stage, Logan receives a full exoneration and even an invitation to resume his duties as secretary, an offer the Quaker grandee politely declines. Keith hangs on in Philadelphia and environs for a few more years, even running for a seat in the colonial assembly. Ultimately, however, he is forced to set sail for England, leaving his house in his wife's name and hoping one day to have the funds to return. Keith never gains them. Instead, he dies alone in London in 1749, still living in the neighborhood of the Fleet Prison in a quarter known as the "Old Bailey"—that is, in the district patrolled by bailiffs charged with keeping a close eye on those out on bail, such as overextended debtors who may be at any moment wanted back in jail.[26]

Logan goes from strength to strength, building a showcase stone mansion he calls Stenton, becoming chief justice of the colony, working on his philosophical writings, and collecting books until his library numbers over 2,600 volumes. He never does sire a son he finds worthy to argue philosophy with. As he confides to an English friend in 1734, "It sometimes gives me an uneasy thought, that my considerable collection of Greek and Roman authors, with others in various languages, will not find an heir in my family to use them as I have done." Though he has four children, they take no interest in his books, a preference he explains by claiming, "they generally take more after their mother than me." If he regrets the choice he made in 1724, after discovering that his daughter Sally could learn to recite the entire "34th Psalm in Hebrew . . . perfectly in less the two hours time" not "to give her that or any other learned language," he does not say so. Instead, he contents himself with tutoring Elizabeth Bartram Cartlidge Cornish's nephew, John Bartram, in Latin, aiding the young man in becoming a preeminent botanist.[27]

Ultimately, Logan donates his books to the nation's first public lending library, a little scheme cooked up by a young runaway apprentice by the name of Benjamin Franklin who flees Boston for Philadelphia in 1723 and becomes Logan's close confidant, Andrew Bradford's rival at the printing press, and, as the author of *Poor Richard's Almanack*, a sharp thorn in the side of Titan Leeds. In one celebrated prank, Franklin predicts an imminent death for Leeds, claiming tongue-in-cheek to have read his fate in the stars. While Franklin cannot kill Leeds, he does ruin his business.[28]

Of all Logan's many public actions, his support for Franklin's free library has long been celebrated as one of his finest contributions to American society. Despite his own snobbish belief, spelled out in detail in his never-published masterwork *The Duties of Man*, that "there are very few proofs to be found of any influence that reason has upon the general mass of mankind," his pride in his book collection leads him to donate this resource to the public. Almost by accident, support for an essential element of democracy, free access to advanced knowledge, becomes the most celebrated element of Logan's legacy.[29]

YET ONLY NOW, IN the twenty-first century, may we be ready to appreciate another less-noticed inheritance from Logan. He has left us much more than a mere collection of classical authors of the ancient world. He has given us a window into the complex culture of a place he and other Europeans considered a new world.

In the end, Logan served as Civility's scribe as much as the colony's clerk. Because Logan held on to his post as secretary long enough to provide careful transcriptions of Civility's many comments on the Cartlidge case, we have the opportunity to learn about Haudenosaunee philosophies at an unusual level of detail and in direct historical context. However little regard the English had for Indigenous ideas and values, Logan was far too punctilious to be satisfied with vague identifiers such as James Le Tort's lazy note of what "ye Indians" said.

Logan took the trouble to record Native names with care and to transcribe Civility's words as closely as he could. As a result, he preserved
for posterity key Native precepts that he himself neither grasped nor
granted.[30]

The Albany Treaty of 1722 has remained in effect right down to
today, the oldest continuously recognized Indigenous treaty in Anglo-
American law. It has stayed on the books for three hundred years for
the simple reason that it recorded new land cessions made by the Five
Nations in western Pennsylvania and New York, providing part of
the legal underpinning for those colonies' territorial claims and later
for the sovereign rights of the United States. But at the same time,
the treaty also memorialized the condolence ceremonies that colonists
engaged in to help the Haudenosaunee become reconciled to the loss of
Sawantaeny and the reparations payments they made under the guise
of giving the Indians "presents." It recorded a request for the liberation
of a pair of forgiven murderers. Kept for centuries as the record of a
property transfer, "The Great Treaty of 1722," as it came to be called,
also commemorates Indigenous principles of restorative justice embedded in balanced values of pluralism and communalism. Here is a part
of our national heritage ripe for reclamation. After centuries covered
with night, we may yet hope for a new dawn.[31]

ACKNOWLEDGMENTS

Contrasting claims of savagery and civility characterize a great deal of early modern European writing on imperialism. For this project, I was eager to find a way to write a history of encounter that would foreground Indigenous ideals and experiences as Native people confronted the ideas of settler colonists. The story of Sawantaeny's killing by the Cartlidge brothers and the long process of resolving the resulting crisis has long been almost entirely buried, occasionally mentioned in histories of Indian diplomacy but never excavated fully enough to show what the case reveals about Indigenous philosophy. When I found it, I knew I had an important new story to tell.

Catalyzed by the documented speeches of a Native man from Conestoga called "Captain Civility"—who responded to Sawantaeny's death by working to build community out of catastrophe—this project synthesizes extensive work by prior scholars. I've relied on a wide range of earlier studies, from Haudenosaunee informants who shared their histories with early twentieth-century ethnographers, to the newly invigorated and invigorating field of Native American and Indigenous studies. I have also been greatly influenced by work on social justice and criminal-justice reform, from the social historians of the 1970s, whose foundational work shaped my undergraduate formation, to the eloquent advocacy of today's social critics. Writing a new book at mid-career brings new joys: the opportunity to bring together disparate accumulated reading and the chance to draw on the revelations of countless conversations with students and colleagues. Again and again my fellow scholars have helped me appreciate how a strong understanding of the past can inform and embolden our efforts to address the problems and possibilities of the present.

When Toni Morrison, author and advocate for criminal justice reform, presented a lecture, "Goodness: Altruism and the Literary Imagination," at the Harvard University Divinity School on December 14, 2012, she began her discussion of the nature of "genuine 'goodness,'" by describing a remarkable instance of forgiveness for a murderer. She related the story of an Amish community in twenty-first-century Pennsylvania where people faced with a grisly mass murderer "forgave the killer, refused to seek justice, demand vengeance, or even to judge him." Viewing their attitude as "extraordinary," Morrison set out to understand what could lead people to offer forgiveness in such extreme cases. Perhaps she would have been intrigued to know that there was a centuries-old precedent originating from the same region, one created not by colonial forebears of the Amish, but rather by the Native peoples of the Susquehanna Valley.

Many thanks to the people and institutions whose collections have made this project possible, especially: the American Philosophical Society, the Historical Society of Pennsylvania, the Library Company of Philadelphia, the New York Public Library, and the Library of Congress. Great thanks to William L. Fenton and James N. Green at Library Company, where Jim brought his fifty years of archival experience to my aid. And thanks to the School of Arts and Sciences at NYU for providing the sabbatical leave that enabled a crucial uninterrupted year of writing.

Many thanks to the members of scholarly seminars who read and critiqued early versions of this work, including the City University of New York Early American Republic Seminar, where I was warmly welcomed by David Waldstreicher and his PhD student, seminar organizer Helena Yoo; the Columbia University Seminar on Early American History and Culture, where I was grateful to have the invitation of co-organizers Hannah Farber and Andrew Lipman; the McNeil Center for Early American Studies, where Laura Keenan Spiro, director of scholarly programming, and Daniel K. Richter, director, gathered an ideal group of interlocutors; and the Omohundro Institute of Early American History and Culture Colloquia Series, where I particularly appreciated director Karen Wulf's generous invitation to present and Joshua Piker's careful criticisms of my paper.

The history department at NYU acknowledges that we are located in Lenapehoking, the homelands of the Lenape ancestors who participated in the events chronicled in this book and whose descendants contribute in countless ways to life in New York today. Special thanks to my NYU Atlantic History Workshop faculty colleagues: Elizabeth Ellis, Rebecca Goetz, Karen Kupperman, Jennifer Morgan, and Susanah Romney. I am proud to count them all as key intellectual influences and as friends. Jennifer has been an essential partner in building the Atlantic Workshop Karen founded. Liz's enthusiasm for this project when it was still in its genesis along with her gifts of historical insight were especially crucial. The Atlantic Workshop is greatly enhanced by the involvement of leading faculty in allied programs, including Karl Appuhn, Ada Ferrer, Michael Gomez, Andrew Needham, John Shovelin, Sinclair Thomson, and Barbara Weinstein. Thanks as well to our students, past and present, especially: Nuala F. Caomhanach, Lila O' Leary Chambers, Emily Connolly, Erica Duncan, Juneisy Hawkins, Alejandro McGhee, Mairin Odle, Timo McGregor, Elise A. Mitchell, Hayley Negrin, Shavagne Scott, and Samantha Seeley. Extra thanks to the members of my Early American Literature of the Field graduate class who pitched in to help with final editing under deadline and offered keen critiques and insights in the process: Madison Bastress, Michael Greenberg, Xinyi Hu, Annabel Lamb and Dante Whittaker. Thanks also to my co-teachers in the American History PhD Program at NYU. The opportunity to co-teach key scholarship in early American history in partnership with Thomas Bender (now retired), Rachel St. John (now at UC Davis), Martha Hodes, and Elizabeth Ellis over four different semesters in the past decade has forever widened my perspective on early America. Finally, my thanks to department chair Edward Berenson, and to the staff in the NYU history department, whose efforts have aided me and my work immeasurably: Karin Burrell, Chelsea Rhodes, Maura Puscheck, Guerline Semexant, David Mendoza, and Jackie Menkel.

My deep gratitude goes to the mentors and longtime friends who provided detailed feedback on large portions of the book proposal and/or the manuscript, including: Patricia Bonomi, Kathleen M. Brown, Elaine Crane, John Demos, Richard S. Dunn, Sally Gordon, Martha

Hodes, Karen Ordahl Kupperman, Bill Nelson, Daniel K. Richter, John Smolenski, Fredrika J. Teute, Karim Tiro, and Michael Zuckerman. In the last few years as I worked on this book, I lost three dear friends who had played integral roles in my academic development over decades: Andrew R. L. Cayton, C. Dallett Hemphill, and Jan Ellen Lewis. I mourn the loss of their brilliance and generosity and take solace in the way they live on in their writing and in the lives of their many students and colleagues. Into the breach stepped three extraordinary scholars, historians whose dedication to the field can be the only explanation for their engagement with my work. I first came into contact with Eric Hinderaker early in the process of developing this project, and his wise council helped reshape the book in crucial ways. He returned to cheer my final progress and I am deeply grateful for his input and expertise. Likewise, Michael Oberg offered keen observations and a sharp editorial eye; I already owed him for steering his outstanding undergraduate student, Lila Chambers, to the history PhD program at NYU, and now I can add incisive manuscript critiques to the list of reasons I remain in his debt. Finally, Matthew Dennis took on the task of vetting the entire manuscript in detail. Matt's deep knowledge of Haudenosaunee history, combined with his flair for the written word, made him the ideal informal editor for this project. Through their exacting efforts, these three scholars of Native American history have improved this manuscript immeasurably; I hasten to add that all remaining shortcomings of style and substance are mine alone.

Publishing this project with Liveright/W. W. Norton has been a wonderful experience. If not for the intercession of Mia Bay, who turned a chance conversation at a conference dinner into an amazing and unexpected opportunity, I would never have approached the editors at Liveright. Mia, there is no way for me to convey how grateful I am for your active interest in the project, much less requite your kindness, and I can only hope you will feel at least partially repaid by the final product. At Liveright, I owe thanks to Marie Pantojan, former associate editor, who was instrumental in acquiring the book, and to Dan Gerstle, senior editor, who worked tirelessly with me to hone the manuscript. Dan, your numberless emails, full of trenchant comments and supportive asides, have kept me going throughout the revision process. May you feel as pleased with the book as I do with the editor and publisher!

I must thank the close friends who have lent a listening ear as I worked through ideas and questions about this project or who simply provided great alternative topics of conversation, especially: Carolyn Allen, Joan Bristol and Randolph Scully, Yenyen Chan, Lisa Duffy-Zeballos and Gonzalo Zeballos, Elizabeth and Nelson Fitts, Allison and Robert Gray, Fabienne Doucet-Gibson, Rachel Hartnett, Laura Ginsberg-Peltz, and Sara and Alex Schuh. Extra thanks to Lisa Duffy-Zeballos, PhD, who leveraged her ace research skills for my benefit.

Finally, thanks first, last, and always to my family. My parents, Tom and Cely Eustace, have always affirmed my deep desire to write history. I much appreciate your willingness to pick up your pencils and go over this manuscript. My devoted mother-in-law, Elizabeth Klancnik, performed similar service. Thank you, Betty! Readers can thank all three for eliminating awkward lines and confusing statements. I know that had he lived to read this book, my departed father-in-law, James M. Klancnik, Sr., would have enthusiastically covered it in Post-it notes just as as he did my first two. My brother Ned Eustace and his wife, Jeralyn Mastroianni Eustace, have overcome all manner of challenges in the years in which I was writing this book. You both inspire me every day. My nephew, Lachlan, and niece, Adeline, are super-hugging superheroes. I am so grateful for the good humor and great cooking of my extended Klancnik family: Maggie, Gordon, Jen, Amelia, Sara, and Will. Once again, Jaitrie Paul's work and care to keep the household running were critical in providing me with the time and peace of mind to write. Reading books with Jem and Lex is one of the best parts of my day. Lex, I love listening to you laugh out loud at the funny parts. Your smart comments and questions have made me a more careful reader and a better writer. You have such a strong sense of justice and sharp ear for history. Jem, you have grown up along with my writing career. Seeing my "scientist son" turn into a remarkable writer himself has been a great pleasure, and I can't wait to see all the ways you will use your energy and talent. Jay, if I could send my college self a postcard describing our lives today, I think she would just say, "I told you so." Somehow, we always knew all along.

NOTES

ABBREVIATIONS USED IN NOTES

PUBLISHED PRIMARY SOURCES

AWM   *The American Weekly Mercury*

CSP   Cecil Hedlam, ed., *Calendar of State Papers, Colonial America and West Indies: Volume 28, 1714–1715* (London: 1928)

CCQS   Chester County Quarter Sessions

DRNY   E. B. O'Callaghan, ed., *Documents Relative to the Colonial History of the State of New York, Vol. 5* (Albany: Weed, Parsons, & Co, 1855)

EJCCV   McIlwaine, H. R., ed., *Executive Journals of the Council of Colonial Virginia, V. IV, October 25, 1721–October 28, 1739* (Richmond: The Virginia State Library, 1930)

MCCP   *Minutes of the Common Council of the City of Philadelphia, 1704 to 1776* (Philadelphia: Chrissy & Markley, 1847)

MPCP, V. 1   *Minutes of the Provincial Council of Pennsylvania, Vol. 1, Containing the Proceedings of the Council from March 10, 1683 to November 27, 1700* (Philadelphia: Jo. Severns & Co, 1852)

MPCP, V. 2   *Minutes of the Provincial Council of Pennsylvania, Vol. 2, Containing the Proceedings of the Council from December 18, 1700 to May 16, 1717* (Philadelphia: Jo. Severns & Co, 1852)

MPCP, V. 3	*Minutes of the Provincial Council of Pennsylvania Vol. 3, Containing the Proceedings of the Council from May 31, 1717 to January 23, 1735–6* (Philadelphia: Jo. Severns & Co, 1852)
MPCP, V. 4	*Minutes of the Provincial Council of Pennsylvania, Vol. 4, Containing the Proceedings of the Council from February 7th 1735–6 to October 15, 1745, Both Days Included* (Philadelphia: Theo. Fenn & Co, 1852)
PCM	Archives of Maryland, *Proceedings of the Council of Maryland 1636–1667*, William Hand Browne, ed. (Baltimore: Maryland Historical Society, 1885)
PWP V. 1	Dunn, Richard S., and Mary Maples Dunn, eds., *The Papers of William Penn, Volume 1, 1644–1679* (Philadelphia: UPenn, 1981)
PWP, V. 2	Dunn, Richard S., and Mary Maples Dunn, eds., *The Papers of William Penn, Vol. 2, 1680–1684* (Philadelphia: UPenn, 1982)
PWP, V. 4	Dunn, Richard S., and Mary Maples Dunn, eds., *The Papers of William Penn, Vol. 4, 1701–1718* (Philadelphia: UPenn, 1987)

ARCHIVES

APS	American Philosophical Society
CCAR	Chester County Archives and Records Services, West Chester, Pennsylvania
HSP	Historical Society of Pennsylvania, Philadelphia, Pennsylvania
LCP	Library Company of Philadelphia, Philadelphia, Pennsylvania
LoC	Library of Congress, Washington, DC
MHS	Maryland Historical Society
NYPL	New York Public Library, New York, New York

MANUSCRIPT PRIMARY SOURCES

ASWK	"Address of Sir William Keith to Council," William Keith Personal Notes, April 16, 1722, Collection 966. F. 3, HSP

CCI   *Chester County Historic Resources Inventory, Appendix B*, CCAR, Battle of Brandywine 2009–2010, ABPP Study Area Historic Resources Atlas (West Chester, PA: Chester County Board of Commissioners, 2010), B-23

DSC   "Deposition of Witnesses," City and County of Philadelphia, March 10, 1722, in Indian Treaties, Du Simitière Collection, Box 3, HSP

FHL   Friends Historical Library, Swarthmore College, Swarthmore, Pennsylvania

JL/DL   Deborah Logan, "Selections from the Correspondence of the Honorable James Logan, Copied from the Original Letters and Papers by D. Logan, Stenton, 1823," LFP, HSP

INLB   Isaac Norris Letterbook, Collection #454, HSP

ITP   Isaac Taylor Papers, Collection # 651, HSP

JCI   "Inventory of the Lands and Tennements [*sic*] Good and Chattles of John Cartlidge late of Conestogoe In ye County of Chester and province of Pennsylvania," November 29, 1723, Wills and Administrations Index, 1714–1923, Chester County Archives and Records Department, West Chester, Pennsylvania

JLD   James Logan, Daybook (fragmentary), September 15, 1722–January 16, 1723, Vol. 2, LFP

JLL   James Logan Ledger, 1720–27, LFP, HSP

LFP   Logan Family Papers 1664–1871, Vol. 3, Collection # 379, HSP

LVFP   A.P.G. Jos van der Linde, trans., Livingston Family Papers, manuscript, Franklin D. Roosevelt Library, Hyde Park, New York

NIL   Isaac Norris, handwritten notes in Titan Leeds, *The American Almanack, 1722* (Philadelphia: Bradford, 1721), volume in the collections of HSP on deposit at LCP

PSWK   *Portrait of Sir William Keith*, painting in the collections of the Pennsylvania Capitol Preservation Committee, Historic Print Catalog, Print Catalog #132

PFP   Penn Family Papers, Official Correspondence,
          1683–1723, HSP

PPCM   "Pennsylvania Provincial Council Minutes, May 19,
          1712," Mss.974.8.P378, APS

SMC   Society Miscellaneous Collection, Box 11
          C, 1722, HSP

With a few exceptions for clarity, I have reproduced original spelling as it appeared in primary-source quotations. I have silently changed punctuation for clarity as needed. Please note that, in order to create an immersive experience for the reader, only statements made by historical subjects are placed in quotation marks in the main text, to function as dialog would in fiction. On occasion, I include key words or phrases from a secondary-source work in the main text *without* quotation marks. In those cases, the citation in the endnote clearly indicates that the material is a quotation and credits the author. This is a work of nonfiction. All of the details described are authentic and drawn directly from my sources. The footnotes offer a good guide to the research that supports this work.

INTRODUCTION

1. Leeds, *American Almanack*, n.p.
2. Leeds, *American Almanack*, n.p.

    For Norris's personal copy see Isaac Norris, "1722," custom-bound and dated copy of Leeds, *American Almanack*.

    On Titan Leeds and the slow-declining popularity of magic, see Eisenstadt, "Almanacs."

3. The University of Nebraska at Lincoln maintains a website listing federally recognized treaties with American Indian tribes and designates the "Great Treaty of 1722 Between the Five Nations, the Mahicans, and the Colonies of New York, Virginia, and Pennsylvania" as "Ratified Treaty #1." See Charles D. Bernholz et al., "Early Recognized Treaties with American Indian Nations," University of Nebraska Libraries, http://treatiesportal.unl.edu/earlytreaties/, accessed July 27, 2020.

    Some Native people embraced U.S. citizenship in 1924, while others had it thrust upon them unilaterally in what could be regarded as a U.S. challenge to Native sovereignty. See Deloria, Jr., and Wilkins, *Tribes, Treaties, and Constitutional Tribulations*.

4. Montesquieu published *The Spirit of Laws* in French in 1748, and it was first published in English in 1750. The edition quoted here is the revised

and expanded one published in English in 1770. As noted below, however, ideas about civility originated with classical philosophers. See Montesquieu, *The Spirit of Laws*, vol. 2, Book 19, Chapter 4, 111.

I employ the term "settler colonists" deliberately. While its use remains a matter of debate, and it applies more fully at some times and places in eighteenth-century North America than in others, I invoke it here in summary comments to underline how often Europeans and their descendants sought to destroy Indigenous populations in order to ensure a continuous supply of new land for trans-Atlantic migrants. For recent historians who argue the need for the term, see, for example, DeLucia, *Memory Lands*, 42, and Parsons, *A Not So New World*, 186.

5. "At a Council held at Conestogoe, the 14th day of March, 1721–2," *MPCP, V.3*, 147–56.

    Historians have long recognized that eighteenth-century Native Americans responded to the crime of killing with very different aims and assumptions than did Euro-Americans. See White, *Middle Ground*.

6. See Schutt, *Peoples of the River Valleys*. I employ Schutt's artful term for the collective Native peoples of the broader Pennsylvania region throughout this book.

    William N. Fenton dates the first recorded performance of a condolence ceremony by an Iroquois diplomat to New France in 1645. See Fenton, "Structure, Continuity, and Change in the Process of Iroquois Treaty Making," in Jennings, ed., *History and Culture of Iroquois Diplomacy*, 15.

    The metaphor of darkness was already prevalent among the Iroquois in 1722, and its use can be seen in the *Great Treaty of 1722*, as quoted below. However, the first specific mention of the traditional use of the precise phrasing quoted here came from early twentieth-century oral histories. See Parker, *Parker on the Iroquois*, 20.

    Iroquois condolence ceremonies "worked to reassert structures of affiliation between Iroquois people." See Parmenter, *Edge of the Woods*, xxvii.

7. As Alyssa Mt. Pleasant and her collaborators have recently pointed out, "Native peoples have always communicated and expressed themselves through a variety of media." Nevertheless, for too long mainstream historians have failed to adequately engage with Native ideas as transmitted in diverse modes of communication, much less to sufficiently appreciate the "analytic and interpretive work" done by "Native communities and their knowledge bearers." See Mt. Pleasant et al., "Forum," 220. See also: Wroth, "The Indian Treaty as Liter-

ature"; Brooks, *Common Pot*, 229; Rasmussen, *Queequeg's Coffin*, 76; Jeffrey Glover, "Introduction," in Cohen and Glover, eds., *Colonial Mediascapes*, 4; and DeLucia, *Memory Lands*, 14–18.

8. See Sleeper-Smith et al., eds., *Why You Can't Teach United States History without American Indians*.

　　"Indigenous forms of knowledge were embedded in deep and wide-ranging contexts of ritual practice and social and cultural authority." See Ramos and Yannakakis, eds., *Indigenous Intellectuals*, 1, 3, and 4.

9. See "William Blathwayt's Draft of the Charter of Pennsylvania," [24 February 1681], in Dunn and Dunn, eds., *PWP*, *V. 2*, 66.

10. Sir Thomas Smith, *Discourse of the Commonweal of this Realm of England*, as quoted in Armitage, *Ideological Origins*, 49–50. Adam Smith, "Of the Influence of Custom and Fashion upon Approbation," in Haakonssen, ed., *Adam Smith*, 239–40.

　　See Horning, *Ireland in the Virginia Sea*. See also: Pagden, *Ideologies of Empire*, and Elliot, *Empires of the Atlantic World*.

11. See Blackburn, *Making of New World*, 267.

12. See Johannes Campanius, "Vocabulary of the Minque Language," in Kolm, ed., *Description of the Province of New Sweden*, 158–59. And see Salvucci, ed., *A Vocabulary of Susquehannock*.

　　On Native practices of diplomatic gifting, see Hall, *Zamumo's Gifts*.

13. William Penn himself was eager to benefit from Atlantic slavery. See William Penn to James Harrison, London 25th 8 mo [October] 1685, *PWP*, *V. 2*, 66. See Nash, "Slaves and Slaveowners," and see Soderlund, "Black Importation."

　　On the multiple peoples regrouping on the Susquehanna around the turn of the eighteenth century, see Schutt, *Peoples of the River Valleys*. On alliances between the Lenape and the Susquehannocks, see Soderlund, *Lenape Country*.

14. On the increasing efforts of the British Crown to regulate its American colonies, see Edelson, *New Map of Empire*, and see Stanwood, *Empire Reformed*.

15. See *Laws of the Province of Pennsylvania*.

　　On Pennsylvania's adoption of a "reactionary Anglicized criminal code" in 1718, see Marietta and Rowe, *Troubled Experiment*, 7. See also Barnes, *Evolution of Penology*, 37–39, and Hayburn, "Who Should Die?," 23 (legal timeline on 14). On the overall importance of "the English system of law and liberty" to the British colonial self-image, see Jack P. Greene, "Empire and Identity from the Glorious Revolution to the American Revolution," in Marshall and Low, eds., *Oxford*

History, 222. See also William M. Offutt, "The Atlantic Rules: The Legalistic Turn in Colonial British America," in Mancke and Shammas, eds., *The Creation of the British Atlantic World*, 160–81.

16. See Oberg, *Head in Edward Nugent's Hand*; Cave, *Pequot War*; Lepore, *Name of War*; DeLucia, *Memory Lands;* Brooks, *Our Beloved Kin*; Webb *1676*; and Rice, *Tales from a Revolution*.

    On the Yamasee War, see Hahn, *Invention of the Creek Nation*, 116, and see Ramsey, *Yamasee War*, 205. See also Snyder, *Slavery in Indian Country*, 46–79, and Gallay, *Indian Slave Trade*, 331.

    On the connections between wrongful death and Indian wars, see Snyder, *Slavery in Indian Country*, 80.

17. On the French in North America, see Moogk, *La Nouvelle France*; Noel, ed., *Race and Gender*; and White, *Wild Frenchmen*.

18. On the Five Nations' new and growing influence in the Ohio valley beginning in the 1720s, see McDonnell, *Masters of Empire*, 127–28. Many authors emphasize that Pennsylvanians found it simpler to portray the Iroquois as all-powerful than to engage with the myriad smaller nations actually complicating Indigenous geopolitics. This was particularly true in regard to the community at Conestoga. See, for example, Lakomäki, *Gathering Together*, 38. On the Haudenosaunee strategy of balancing power with power by giving "a parallel paper claim" to North America to both the English and French, see Daniel Richter, "His Own, Their Own: Settler Colonialism, Native Peoples, and Imperial Balances of Power in Eastern North America, 1660–1715," in Gallup-Diaz, ed., *The World of Colonial America*, 222. See also Shannon, *Iroquois Diplomacy*, esp. 73–77.

19. Leeds, *American Almanack*, n.p.

    For the newer emphasis on diplomacy over warfare see Shannon, *Iroquois Diplomacy*. And on the Iroquois policy in the 1720s of striving to maintain "peace and balance" see Richter, *Ordeal of the Longhouse*, 237.

20. See "The Answer Made by the Indians of the Five Nations" in Keith, *Treaty of Peace and Friendship*, 7.

CHAPTER 1: TOMORROW'S DOOM

1. *MCCP*, 222 and 210; *MPCP, V.3*, 186 and 147.
2. *MCCP*, 177, 215, 101.
3. *MPCP, V.3*, 156.
4. *MPCP, V.3*.

5. *MPCP, V. 3*, 189. The ferry keeper's journey is conjecture; see note 33 below.

"The Five Nations of the Haudenosaunee" is the preferred modern term. I employ the term "Iroquois" to refer to the language and cultural group, which included peoples who were not formal members of the confederacy such as the Susquehannocks.

Scholarly opinion on whether the Five Nations of the Haudenosaunee can or should be classed as an imperial power remains sharply divided. Still, the influence and importance of the Iroquois across northeastern North America is not in dispute. For the claim that the Iroquois sought and claimed a degree of imperial power that they did not achieve, see Jennings, *The Ambiguous Iroquois Empire*, 297. See also Richter and Merrell, eds., *Beyond the Covenant Chain*, 6–7. For the related view that Iroquois power, though real, was in decline by the 1730s, see Richter, *Ordeal of the Longhouse*. For a contrary emphasis on Iroquois peacemaking, see Dennis, *Cultivating a Landscape of Peace*, 44 and 257–58. On the impact of Iroquois power, in spite of what he regards as the sometimes mythologized reach of their empire, see Aquila, *The Iroquois Restoration*. For the view that the Iroquois moved from claims of "vague authority" to attempts at suzerainty in the 1720s, see Hinderaker, *Elusive Empires*, 26–27. For an emphasis on diplomacy, not warfare, as the Iroquois "tool of choice," see Shannon, *Iroquois Diplomacy*. For a related argument on Iroquois use of spatial mobility as a political tool, see Parmenter, *Edge of the Woods*, 276–77.

Recent scholars have described Indian imperialism in a variety of settings. See McDonnell, *Masters of Empire*, and see Hämäläinen, *The Comanche Empire*.

6. On the perils of transmission errors in intercultural conversations, see Merrell, *Into the American Woods*, chapter 5.

7. *MPCP, V. 3*, 150.

8. See "1715 November 18 Council of Trade and Plantation to Mr. Secretary Stanhope [James Stanhope, Secretary of State]," in *CSP*; and see Keith, *A Collection of Papers*, 189.

9. *DRNY*, 655–57.

On the fur trade and tax revenues, see Bonomi, *A Factious People*, 79–80.

10. See Donehoo, *Indian Villages*, 67. On Conestoga cabins, see Kent, *Susquehanna's Indians*, 379–82.

On the "complex crosscutting claims" of the multiple peoples grouping and regrouping at Conestoga around 1720, see Schutt, *Peoples of the River Valleys*, 65–66.

On the Conestoga "legacy of resilience and adaptability," see Merrit, *At the Crossroads*, 23.

On Native America as a "mille feuille" (thousand layer) social space, see Witgen, *An Infinity of Nations*, 396.

11. "Web of . . . relationships," Witgen, *An Infinity of Nations*, 50.

On the successful survival strategies of small Native polities, see Ellis, "The Many Ties of the Petites Nations." And see also Elizabeth Ellis, "Dismantling the Dream of 'France's Peru': Indian and African Influence on the Development of Early Colonial Louisiana," in Gallup-Diaz, ed., *The World of Colonial America*, 357.

12. On alliances between the Lenape and the Susquehannocks, see Soderlund, *Lenape Country*, 141. On relations with the Shawnees, see Warren, *The Worlds the Shawnees Made*, 147–53.

13. For descriptions of Taquatarensaly's ethnicity, see, for example: *MPCP, V. 2, 565; MPCP, V. 3*, 133; and *MPCP, V. 4*, 53.

14. See Kimball and Henson, *Governor's Houses*, 347.

15. On Keith's biography, see Morris, *The History of Pennsylvania*, 46–53.

On fraught relations with Quakers, see Smolenski, *Friends and Strangers*, chapter 7.

16. On Pennsylvania's adoption of a "reactionary Anglicized criminal code" in 1718, see Marietta and Rowe, *Troubled Experiment*, 7. See also Barnes, *Evolution of Penology*, 37–39, and on the prohibition of "cards, dice, lotteries, or such like," 35.

17. On mines in Pennsylvania, see "Isaac Norris to Hannah Penn," INLB, April 1722, 310 and 311. Governor Keith reported later on these rumors. See William Keith to Hannah Penn, July 5, 1722, and on complaints over Keith's claims on copper mines, see James Logan to Henry Gouldney, April 8, 1723, both in PFP.

18. PSWK. On the Shippen house, see Westcott, *Historic Mansions and Buildings of Philadelphia*, 96. On Fountain Low, see Cotter et al., *The Buried Past*, 383–84.

19. John Smolenski argues that Indians wished to avoid English justice the better to deny English jurisdictional sovereignty over them. Smolenski, "The Death of Sawantaeny and the Problem of Justice on the Frontier," in Pencak and Richter, *Friends and Enemies in Penn's Woods*, 106.

20. List of trees from Bartram, *Observations*, 43, 48, 49, 50, 51.

On "trade, land, and power," see Richter, *Trade, Land, and Power*.

21. "Mouse . . . that ruffles the leaves," *MPCP, V. 2*, 512. The people of

Conestoga invoked this imaginary noise at the June 1710 meeting with colonists to dramatize their concern about enslavement. See Snyder, *Slavery in Indian Country*; Rushforth, *Bonds of Alliance*; and Newell, *Brethren by Nature*.

22. Barnes, *The Evolution of Penology*, 69.

23. "Public conveniences," quoted in Lloyd, "The Courts of Pennsylvania," 36; "scolds" in Barnes, "The Criminal Codes," 84.

   On "space and structures of control," see Fuentes, *Dispossessed Lives*, 13–45.

24. JCI, November 29, 1723.

25. On Pawlett, see *MCCP*, 137 and 144.

26. *MCCP*, 154; *MCCP*, 155; and *MCCP*, 163–64.

27. *MCCP*, 211.

28. On Indian paths, see Wallace, *Indian Paths*, 4 and 64.

   Taquatarensaly and Satcheechoe's route remains conjectural; we know only that the Great Minquas Path existed and that Satcheechoe stopped at Conestoga to get Taquatarensaly before proceeding to Philadelphia (see Note 5).

   While "Mingo" is now understood to refer primarily to Senecas of the Ohio region, contemporary Pennsylvanians referred to residents of Conestoga by this name. See, for example, *MPCP V. 3*, 21.

29. *MCCP*, 212.

   Paul Mapp notes that "empire and . . . geographic ignorance went hand in hand." See Mapp, *The Elusive*, 5.

30. On Native American mobility and flexibility, see Witgen, *An Infinity of Nations*, 42 and 123.

   On the connections between "paths and power" in Indian country, see Dubcovsky, *Informed Power*. On paths as a "central metaphor" for "friendship" among Indians, see Paulett, *Empire of Small Places*, 116–17. And see also Grandjean, *American Passage*.

31. Taquatarensaly enters the records of colonial Pennsylvania in "At a Council Held at Philadelphia, June 16, 1710." He is described as a "young Indian" and "One of the chiefs of Conestogo" on March 23, 1713, just less than a decade before the Cartlidge–Sawantaeny crisis of 1722. See *MPCP, V. 2*, 511 and 565.

32. On Alice Smith Vandever Kirk, see Craig, "Jacob & Catharina Van der Veer and their Vandever Descendants," 2 and 4, and Alison Duncan Hirsch, "Indian, *Métis*, and Euro-American Women on Multiple Frontiers," in Richter and Pencak, eds., *Friends and Enemies*.

   The idea that Taquatarensaly and Satcheechoe stopped on the

Brandywine to pick up Alice Kirk is speculative, based on her place of residence and business, the route of the Great Minquas Path, and her extensive interactions with Native people (implied by her linguistic competence).

33. On Francis Smith of Kennet, see Futhey and Cope, *History of Chester County*, 179.

On married English colonial women and property, see Wulf, *Not All Wives*, 3. For the colonial Dutch comparison, see Romney, *New Netherland Connections*, 61–62, and see Narrett, *Inheritance and Family Life*.

34. "Advertisements," *AWM*, May 12, 1720, 4, and "Advertisements," *AWM*, June 16, 1720, 3. On Samuel Kirk's admission as a freeman, see "At a Comon Council at Philada ye 29th April Ao 1717," in *MCCP*, 120.

35. "Advertisements," in *AWM*, August 2, 1722, 2.

36. *MPCP*, 189.

37. *MPCP*, 189.

38. *MPCP*, 190.

39. *MPCP*, 189.

40. See Wallace, *Death and Rebirth*, 94–98, and see Richter, *Ordeal of the Longhouse*, 236–39; Dennis, *Landscape of Peace*, 44; and Parmenter, *Edge of the Woods*, xliv.

41. The phrase "covered with night" was first recorded by early-twentieth-century ethnographers working with Haudenosaunee informants. Nevertheless, this evocative term comports closely with ceremonial traditions of grief and condolence already in widespread use among the Five Nations by 1722 and clearly recorded in written records of the period, and so I am making advised use of this vivid phrase. See Fenton, ed., *Parker on the Iroquois*, 20.

42. *MPCP*, 189.

43. *MPCP*, 189.

44. *MPCP*, 189.

Daniel Richter notes that Iroquois "mourning and burial customs" were "characteristics of a worldview utterly foreign to Europeans." See Richter, *Ordeal of the Longhouse*, 276.

Native peoples across the northern part of North America shared a common aversion to the idea of punishing murder with state killing. Yet this philosophical position could play out differently, depending on the relative power of the parties involved. Unlike White's Algonquians who sought to meet French colonists on a "middle ground," Pennsylvania's Indigenous peoples sought more to defend their "Native ground." See White, *Middle Ground*, 90–93.

In 1722, the Five Nations of the Haudenosaunee were still easily able to "maintain their own sovereign identity" and "make independent decisions." See Duval, *Native Ground*, 5. Philip J. Deloria emphasizes that White never intended the concept of the middle ground to apply broadly beyond the interactions of French and Algonquian peoples of the Great Lakes region. See Deloria, "What Is the Middle Ground Anyway?"

James Merrell argues that no people in colonial Pennsylvania lived as "denizens of some debatable land between Native and newcomer." See Merrell, *Into the American Woods*, 37. See also Barr, "Did Pennsylvania Have a Middle Ground?"

45. See Keith, *A Letter*, 6 and 8.

46. "Boston, July 23," in *AWM*, August 2nd, 1722, 1 and 2.

As late as 1911, Euro-American writers inverted the emotions and moral positions of the case's participants, insisting that Indians were angry while colonists were calm. See Morris, *History of Pennsylvania*, 47–48.

47. For example, see "Pennsylvania" in notes by James Logan, January 19, 1721, and "Pennsilvania" in notes by James Logan, May 22, 1722, in *MPCP*.

48. "Atackqua, *shoes*," in Holm, *Vocabulary of Susquehannock*, 19.

49. Isaac Norris, handwritten notes, July 1722, NIL. On the imposition of classical names on enslaved people, see Burnard, "Slave Naming Patterns," 335 and 336.

50. *PCM*, 486 and 518.

On "Onas," see Jane Merritt, "Metaphor, Meaning, and Misunderstanding," in Cayton and Teute, eds., *Contact Points*, 85, note.

Euro-Americans sought to position themselves as sovereign, Native peoples as servile. See Oberg, *Dominion and Civility*.

Merrell raises but rejects the possibility that the name recognized Taquatarensaly's "polished colonial manners." See Merrell, *Into the American Woods*, 59.

51. On the ritual torture and execution of some prisoners taken in seventeenth-century mourning wars among the Iroquois, see Wallace, *Death and Rebirth*, and see Richter, *Ordeal of the Longhouse*.

On European ideas of savagery, see Sayre, *Les Sauvages Américains*, and see Sheehan, *Savagism and Civility*.

52. *MPCP*, 190.

53. Early Americans came to view the imprisoned as having "a hardened 'criminal identity,' " as opposed to having committed a criminal action. See Manion, *Liberty's Prisoners*, 4.

54. *MPCP*, 190.
55. *MPCP*, 190.

   See Johnson, " 'Goods to Clothe Themselves,' " 124. And see Shannon, "Dressing for Success on the Mohawk Frontier."

56. *MPCP*, 190.
57. "the Cock-loft, which will serve for a prison," quoted in Barnes, *Evolution of Penology*, 69; "Cock-loft, n." and "Cockle, n. 5," *Oxford English Dictionary*; for "Two pence per day," *MCCP*, 279.
58. This alternate evidence will be discussed at length in later chapters.
59. *MPCP*, *V. 3*, 191.
60. *MPCP*, *V. 3*, 191.
61. *MPCP*, *V. 3*, 191.
62. *MPCP*, *V. 3*, 191.
63. *MPCP*, *V. 3*, 191.
64. *MPCP*, *V. 3*, 191.
65. *MPCP*, *V. 3*, 191. Reliance on a face-saving polite fiction to lessen the assertion of dominance by the Iroquois underscores that English and Indians found it "less useful to be clearly understood than to be creatively misunderstood." See Pekka Hämäläinen, "The Shapes of Power: Indians, Europeans, and North American Worlds from the Seventeenth to the Nineteenth Century," in Barr and Countryman, eds., *Contested Spaces*, 53–54.
66. *MPCP*, *V. 3*, 191.
67. *MPCP*, *V. 3*, 192.

   On strouds, see Braund, *Deerskins and Duffles*, 123. On Conestoga, specifically, see Johnson, "Goods to Clothe Themselves," 122–123 and 126.

CHAPTER 2: TAQUATARENSALY (CAPTAIN CIVILITY)

1. *MPCP*, *V. 3*, 45.
2. Descriptions and figures are compiled from city tax rolls. See *MCCP*, 118–35.
3. *MPCP*, *V. 3*, 45–46.
4. *MPCP*, *V. 3*, 46.
5. *MPCP*, *V. 2*, 553, 565, 603, and 613, and *MPCP*, *V. 3*, 15, 45, 80, and 310.
6. See Thomas Nairne, *Nairne's Muskhogean Journals: The 1708 Expedition to the Mississippi River*, as cited in Patricia Galloway, " 'The Chief Who Is Your Father,' " in Waselkov et al., eds., *Powhattan's Mantle*, 360–61.
7. On the Native practice of appointing "Squirrel Kings" beyond the

Choctaws and Chickasaws, see Piker, *Okfuskee*, 23 and 214 n. 14, and see St. John, "Inventing Guardianship," 366.

8. *PCM*, 518.

On another man named "Civility" in seventeenth-century Maryland, see Hanna, *Wilderness Trail*, 80–81. See also Kent, *Susquehanna's Indians*, 62. On "natives and newcomers," see Axtell, *Natives and Newcomers*; I use Axtell's artful phrase a number of times throughout this work.

9. "Civility, n.," in Oxford English Dictionary Online (hereafter cited as OED online). January 2018. Oxford University Press. http://www .oed.com.proxy.library.nyu.edu/view/Entry/33581?redirectedFrom= civility (accessed February 6, 2018).

10. *MPCP, V. 3*, 46, and see *MPCP, V. 2*, 516.

11. *MPCP, V. 3*, 46.

12. *MPCP, V. 3*, 46 and 47.

13. *MPCP, V. 3*, 48.

14. *MPCP, V. 3*, 50.

CHAPTER 3: WHEN THINGS GO ILL

1. Dialogue is reconstructed, based on Ayaquachan's testimony regarding Sawantaeny's words to Cartlidge: "the Sinnekae told him he need not be angry at him for asking more for he owed it to him." *MPCP, V. 3*, 150.

2. *MPCP, V. 3*, 150.

3. Testimony of "Ayaquachan, the Ganawese," Testimony of "Aquannachke, the Shawana," and "Testimony of Metheequeyta, the other Shawana Lad," *MPCP, V. 3*, 150 and 151.

4. Testimony of "Ayaquachan, the Ganawese," *MPCP, V. 3*, 150.

The steady price of deerskins and the fall in prices for beaver were both noted by Keith, *MPCP, V. 3*, 121. Logan noted many raccoons in his ledger in 1721. See JLL. Logan referred to himself as a "bearskin merchant" in a 1721 letter; see Wulf, *James Logan*, [n.p., 3] and 18.

5. Testimony of "Ayaquachan, the Ganawese," *MPCP, V. 3*, 150.

On Native women in the fur trade, see Sleeper-Smith, *Indigenous Prosperity*, 99–100.

6. Testimony of "Ayaquachan, the Ganawese," *MPCP, V. 3*, 150. On redware at Conestoga, see Barry C. Kent, "European Objects: European Ceramics," in Kent, *Susquehanna's Indians*, 264.

7. *MPCP, V. 3*, 124.

8. "John Cartliedge," November 1718, Docket 1710–1723, Chester County Quarter Sessions Papers Index, 1681–1870, CCAR.

9. Edmund Carledge, February 1718/19, John Cartledge, November 1719 and November 1719, February 1719/20, and May 1720, Chester County Quarter Sessions Papers Index, 1681–1870, CCAR.

10. *MPCP, V. 3*, 129.

Keith's permissive stance toward technically illegal alcohol sales was a common English colonial tactic for "insinuating empire into a distant continent." See Brett Rushforth, "Insinuating Empire: Indians, Smugglers, and the Imperial Geography of Eighteenth-Century Montreal," in Gitlin et al., eds., *Frontier Cities*, 64–65.

11. *MPCP, V. 3*, 149. Sawantaeny was identified as a Seneca chief in *PCM*, 379.

12. See Philemon Lloyd, "Patowmeck Above Ye Inhabitants," 1721, Manuscript Map, Calvert Papers 1621–1775, Special Collections Department, MHS. Iroquois leaders gained status by redistributing goods acquired through the fur trade; see Richter, *Ordeal of the Longhouse*, 91.

13. On Weenepeeweytah's family connections, see testimony of "Civility," *MPCP, V. 3*, 149.

On Native women's work in processing peltry, see Sleeper-Smith, *Indigenous Prosperity*, 6. On Native meanings of gift exchange, see Hall, *Zamumo's Gifts*, 13.

14. *MPCP, V. 3*, 362.

15. See "Correspondence, n." defined as "1., the action or fact of corresponding, or answering to each other in fitness or mutual adaptation, congruity, harmony, agreement" and definition "2a., relation of agreement, similarity, or analogy;" "3., Concordant or sympathetic response. *Obsolete*" (last citation dated 1680), and "4., Relation between persons or communities; usually qualified as *good, friendly, fair, ill, etc., Obsolete* (Very common in 17th c.)" in OED Online. January 2018. Oxford University Press. http://www.oed.com.

On Iroquois ritual diplomatic efforts to ensure "good correspondence and understanding between people," see Parmenter, *Edge of the Woods*, xlvii.

16. *MPCP, V. 3*, 556, and JLL.

On commodities versus gifts, see Hall, *Zamumo's Gifts*, 13. On the impact of the commodification of animals on economies, ecologies, and societies, see Cronon, *Changes in the Land*, 82–107.

17. *MPCP, V. 3*, 129.

18. "Ghesaont" of the "Sinnekaes Nation," *MPCP, V. 3*, 124–25. On ritual gift exchange and the resulting atmosphere of "an emotional climate of peace," see Richter, *Ordeal of the Longhouse*, 40.

19. *MPCP, V. 3*, 129.

20. James Logan, June 21, 1721, JLL. Logan paid Civility less than the usual value for deerskins. See *MPCP V. 2*, 553; *MPCP V. 2*, 601; and *MPCP V. 3*, 49.

   AWM periodically recorded current prices being paid for furs in Boston and New York but never those in Philadelphia. In June of 1720 (the closest date available), the paper noted "Buck and Doe Skins . . . in Indian Dress" were selling for "4 shillings 6 pence each at Boston," or nearly twice what Logan paid Civility. See "Prices Current at Boston," *AWM*, June 16, 1720, 3.

   Gail MacLeitch notes that by the mid-eighteenth century, the Iroquois "intermixed old and new economic tendencies." See MacLeitch, *Imperial Entanglements*, 85–86.

21. "His countenance . . . giving ym umbrage," Isaac Norris to Henry Gouldney, 9 Second Month [April] 1722, INLB.
   Testimony of "Weenepeeweytah," *MPCP, V. 3*, 151.

22. "Edmund a strong man did it," quoted from Isaac Norris to Henry Gouldney, 9 Second Month [April] 1722, INLB.

23. Testimony of "Ayaquachan, the Ganawese," *MPCP, V. 3*, 150.

24. Native witnesses were consistent in specific claims that Edmund broke Sawantaeny's gun over his head. See Testimony of "Ayaquachan, the Ganawese" and of "Weenepeeweytah," *MPCP, V. 3*, 150 and 151; *PCM*, 379–80.

25. On the archaeological evidence for nearly universal gun ownership among adult men at Conestoga, see Kent, *Susquehanna's Indians*, 257.

   On the cycle of captives, fur, and firearms that amounted to an "Indian arms race" in the Susquehanna valley see Silverman, *Thundersticks*, 35–48.

26. On guns and flints, see Kent, *Susquehanna's Indians*, 247–57.

27. "John Cartlidge stript off his Clothes," testimony of "Weenepeeweytah," *MPCP, V. 3*, 151.

28. Testimony of "Weenepeeweytah," *MPCP, V. 3*, 151.

29. Testimony of "Aquannachke, the Shawana," *MPCP, V. 3*, 151.
   On "Ash Wednesday," see Leeds, *American Almanack*, "February."

30. "Ghesaont, in the Name and on behalf of all the ffive Nations," *MPCP, V. 3*, 124.

31. Keith, *Particulars*, 7. The pamphlet was advertised in *AWM* on July 27, 1721.

32. On Edmund's departure from the Society of Friends and John's ten-

uous place within it, see Isaac Norris to Henry Gouldney, 9 Second Month [April] 1722, INLB. For John's Quaker style of address, see John Cartlidge to Isaac Taylor, 17 February 1721/22, ITP.

33. Keith, *Particulars*, 3. See also Keith, *Particulars* (Dublin, 1723).

34. According to the archaeological evidence, Native men could be buried with guns or gun parts. See Kent, *Susquehanna's Indians*, 248, 254.

35. Testimony of John Hans Steelman and his Indian companions, "John Bradford to Colonel Thomas Addison," February 17, 1721/22, *PCM*, 381–82, and Testimony of "Weenepeeweytah," *MPCP, V. 3*, 151.

I infer that Weenepeeweytah would have worked the bearskin based on Native women's traditional work. See Van Kirk, *Many Tender Ties*, 61.

36. John's land ambitions are documented in John Cartlidge to Isaac Taylor, 17 February 1721/22, ITP; on the relative success of the two brothers, see Isaac Norris to Henry Gouldney, 9 Second Month [April] 1722, INLB. On the Steelmans' fortunes, *PWP, V. 4*, 54, n.9, and 55, n.14.

37. On the Steelmans, see *PWP, V. 4*, 54, n.9, and 55, n.14.

38. "John Bradford to Thomas Addison," n.d., *PCM*, 379.

39. "John Bradford to Thomas Addison," n.d., *PCM*, 379.

40. "John Bradford to Colonel Thomas Addison," *PCM*, 381–82.

41. *MPCP, V. 4*, 53.

There are other well-known instances of Cayuga Indians living in the eighteenth-century Susquehannnah River valley taking the names of Pennsylvania colonists to whom they were not related by blood. See Sayre, *Indian Chief as Tragic Hero*, 181–82.

42. "John Bradford to Colonel Thomas Addison," *PCM*, 381–82.

"The objective of criminal law . . . was to give legal effect to the community's sense of sin, and to punish those who breached the community's taboos." See Marietta and Rowe, *Troubled Experiment*, 40.

43. Shecockkeneen, "A Chief of the Delawares, formerly on Brandywine, all at present Inhabitants on Susquehannah," *MPCP, V. 3*, 47.

44. "John Bradford to Thomas Addison," n.d., and "John Bradford to Colonel Thomas Addison," *PCM*, 379.

45. "The State House and State Circle," Maryland State House, 2007, accessed July 28, 2020, http://msa.maryland.gov/msa/mdstatehouse/html/archivesrm_stehouse.html.

On Annapolis, see Bushman, *Refinement of America*, 145–51. On dancing and fiddling, see Bushman, *Refinement of America*, passim.

46. "Charles Calvert to John Bradford," Annapolis, February 21, 1721, *PCM*, 380. See also Hoffman, *Princes of Ireland*, 79–80.

47. "Charles Calvert to John Bradford," Annapolis, February 21, 1721, *PCM*, 380.

48. "Charles Calvert to John Bradford," Annapolis, February 21, 1721, *PCM*, 380.

49. "Charles Calvert to John Bradford," Annapolis, February 21, 1721, *PCM*, 380.

CHAPTER 4: SAWANTAENY

1. Testimony of "Weenepeeweytah, the Squaw," *MPCP, V. 3*, 151.

2. Native informants shared these traditional stories in the early twentieth century. See Parker, ed., *Seneca Myths*, 19.

   On upstreaming as method, see Fenton, *Iroquois Journey*, 49 and 73. For a critical response, see Fred W. Voget, "Anthropological Theory and Iroquois Ethnography" in Foster et al., *Extending the Rafters*, 347–51.

3. Parker, ed., *Seneca Myths*, 65.

4. See Edward Cornplanter, "Origin of the Charmholder's Medicine Society" in Parker, ed., *Seneca Myths*, 386, 388, and 390.

5. On the smoky setting of Seneca children's stories, see Parker, ed., *Seneca Myths*, 50.

6. On bearskins, see "Philadelphia 8ber the 15th day," JLD, 5. On "Prices Currant at Philadelphia," see *AWM*, February 27, 1722, 3. Prices were listed in the paper only occasionally, making this date the most relevant available.

7. Isaac Norris to Henry Gouldney, 9 Second Month [April] 1722, INLB and *MPCP, V. 3*, 194.

   The assertion that "the said Indian would not buy of their Rum which they brought there to sell" was made by John Hans Steelman Jr. and his Native companions in their visit to Maryland. *PCM*, 380.

8. The claim that Sawantaeny told John Cartlidge that "he need not be angry" comes from the testimony of "Ayaquachan, the Ganawese," *MPCP, V. 3*, 150.

9. Alexander Spotswood, "Williamsburg, January 25th 1719/20," *MPCP, V. 3*, 87

10. Spelling is modernized in the main text. Compare the original in

Lydgate, *The Hystorye, Sege and Dystruccyon of Troy,* and see Lidgate, *The Beasts in Power.*

See "Wood, n.1," defined as "2. A collection of trees growing more or less thickly together" derived from "Old English *widu,*" and see "Wood, adj., *Obsolete,*" defined as "1, a. "out of one's mind, insane, lunatic . . . often expressing fury or violence," and as "3, b. "violently angry or irritated; enraged, furious," derived from "Old English *wód.*" All citations are from the OED Online. Accessed January 2018. Oxford University Press, http://www.oed.com

Early modern British readers derived from classical literature the cultural and linguistic connection between forest dwelling and violent fury.

11. Colonists feared the woods as "trackless wastes" where "one could "lose one's cultural bearings and lapse into . . . savagery." See Merrell, *Into the American Woods,* 22, and see Williams, *Wilderness and Paradise,* 4.

12. Testimony of "Weenepeeweytah," *MPCP, V.3,* 151.

13. The Seneca vested friendship "with an extraordinary degree of interest." See Wallace, *Death and Rebirth,* 78.

14. "Throughout Iroquoia . . . marriage . . . transformed political amalgamation into full social unity based on kinship." See Dennis, *Cultivating a Landscape of Peace,* 59.

On Native-made baskets in the Susquehanna region, including a bark basket with cordage, see Kent, *Susquehanna's Indians,* 184–85.

15. Richter, *Ordeal of the Longhouse,* 136–37.

16. The rise of Iroquois condolence rituals reflected a deepening commitment to resolving conflicts occurring within the group without violence. See Will Fenton, "Structure, Continuity and Change in the Process of Iroquois Treaty Making," in Jennings, ed., *History and Culture of Iroquois Diplomacy,* 14.

Richard White affirms that Native peoples only sought "blood revenge" when one of their people was killed by an enemy; in the case of death at the hands of an ally, they expected that the death would either be "covered" through the gifts and rituals of condolence, or else that the dead would be "raised" through the adoption of a captive to fill the dead person's place. See White, *The Middle Ground,* 79.

CHAPTER 5: SORROW WILL COME FAST

1. Leeds, "March," *American Almanack for 1722,* and "Philadelphia, March 10" in *AWM,* March 10, 1722, 2.

2. See "Philadelphia, March 10," in *AWM,* March 10, 1722, 2.

   Bradford published editions of his *Weekly Mercury* on a semiregular weekly basis. To maintain a weekly schedule, he should have been readying his press on March 6 to go to print on March 7. But in fact, he brought out the edition another three days later and dated it for a ten-day period instead of the more usual week. See "Philadelphia, March 10" in *AWM,* March 10, 1722, 2. And see "Advertisements" in *AWM,* March 1, 1722, 2, and March 10, 1722, 2.

   On printers' aprons, see Newman, "Benjamin Franklin and the Leather-Apron Men."

3. *MPCP, V. 3,* 146.

   On a court case from 1702 that saw "a butcher . . . indicted as a common swearer and drunkard," see Watson, *Annals,* 308.

4. *MPCP, V. 3,* 146. For the 1721 case of the butcher who "did . . . blow up the meat of his calf," see Watson, *Annals,* 309.

5. *MPCP, V. 3,* 146.

6. *MPCP, V. 3,* 146.

7. See "Casualties," *AWM,* March 1, 1722, 2.

   On population, see Nash, *Urban Crucible,* 65–66. And see Nash and Smith, "The Population of Eighteenth-Century Philadelphia," 366.

8. Peter Cooper, *The Southeast Prospect of the City of Philadelphia,* c. 1720, oil on canvas, LCP. For reproduction and discussion, see Wolf, 2nd, and Korey, eds., *Quarter of a Millennium,* entry #138. And see "A Curious View of Old Philadelphia" in Dean, *Historical Magazine,* 136–39, and Lindsey, "Colonial Philadelphia," 5.

9. *MPCP, V. 3,* 146.

   See "the way he murdered him" in "John Bradford to Colonel Thomas Addison," February 17, 1721/22, *PCM,* 379, and see "the Murderers are under the Pennsylvania Government" in "Charles Calvert to John Bradford," Annapolis, February 21, 1721, *PCM,* 380.

10. *MPCP, V. 3,* 146.

11. Keith, *Particulars.* Dozens of other colonists joined in the festivities surrounding the meeting including Aquila Rose, who wrote this poem. See Rose, "To J——n C——dge, Esq. on His Generous Entertainment of Sir William Keith, and his Company, at Conestogoe," in Rose,

26. Rose died in 1723, and Keith's only known visit to Conestoga to treat with Indians before this time occurred in 1721.

On Rose, Keith, and their literary set, see Shields, "The Wits and Poets of Pennsylvania," 104.

12. *MPCP, V. 3*, 146.

13. *MPCP, V. 3*, 146.

14. On "men of sense against the men of wit," a quotation from Daniel Defoe, see Shields, "Henry Brooke," 6.

The three Lloyd daughters were: Rachel Preston, Hannah Hill, and Mary Norris. See Watson, *Annals*, 519.

15. See Dickinson, *God's Protecting Providence*, Hill, *A Legacy for Children*, and Isaac Norris, personal copy, Shaftesbury's *Characteristicks, V. 3* (London, 1717), LCP. While Logan never published his manuscript, and continued to work on it at least through 1737, a portion of it is dated 1725, indicating that he would likely have begun thinking about it in this approximate period. See Valenti, ed., Logan, *Duties of Man*.

16. On the escapade with William Penn Jr., see Shields, "Henry Brooke," 5. Scandalous gossip about Hamilton's way with widows appears in *Life of a Strange He-Monster*. See also Walker, "Andrew Hamilton."

17. See Brooke, "The New Metamorphosis, or, the Fable of the Bald Eagle," Appendix, in Shields, "Henry Brooke," 20 and 21, lines 13–14 and 16.

18. *MPCP, V. 3*, 146.

19. *MPCP, V. 3*, 146.

20. *MPCP, V. 3*, 146.

21. *MPCP, V. 3*, 146.

22. On household goods, see Gillingham, "Estate of Jonathan Dickinson."

23. On the environmental and labor history of mahogany production as well as the social and racial symbolism of mahogany furniture's reflective qualities, see Anderson, *Mahogany*.

24. See Dickinson, *Gods Protecting Providence*.

From the moment that early European explorers reported their suspicions that leading religious figures among the Native peoples of the Americas occasionally engaged in the ritual consumption of small amounts of human flesh, Europeans used the claim to draw an impermeable line between themselves and the people they encountered in the Americas. Although the most sacred rite of Christianity rested on the communal consumption of Christ's body, a ceremony in which Catho-

lics accepted bread as the actual body of God, Europeans simultaneously regarded cannibalism as the single gravest transgression humans
could commit.

On European views of cannibalism, see Davies, *Renaissance Ethnography,* and see Walker, "From Alterity to Allegory."

25. Dickinson, *Gods Protecting Providence, i.*

See Greenblatt, *Marvelous Possessions,* Woodward, *Prospero's America,* and Rivett, *Science of the Soul.*

26. Dickinson, *Gods Protecting Providence,* 1.

27. Dickinson, *Gods Protecting Providence, 3.*

28. Society of Friends, *Exhortation,* 1.

29. On the history of the pamphlet's reception and rejection, see Gerbner,
"Antislavery," and see Brycchan Carey, " 'We are against the traffic of
men-body' Pennsylvania, 1688–1700," in Carey, *From Peace to Freedom,* 70–104.

Intellectual opposition to slavery emerged in tandem with the institution itself. See Greene, *Evaluating Empire.*

30. Society of Friends, *Exhortation,* 2. On the history of George Keith and
the Quaker elite, see Nash, *Quakers and Politics.*

31. Society of Friends, *Exhortation,* 1.

Dickinson's book was reprinted in Philadelphia in 1751, 1756, and
1791; in Germantown, Pennsylvania (in German) in 1756; in Dover, New
Hampshire, in 1792; in Stanford, New York, in 1803; and in Burlington, New Jersey, in 1811. The Pennsylvania printings during the Seven
Years' War period in the 1750s presaged the completion of genocidal
attacks on the Native peoples of Conestoga committed by the "Paxton
Boys" in 1763, while the 1811 printing presaged the significant further
seizure and control of Native lands carried out in the War of 1812.

32. For the phrase "peace came in the form of a woman" and discussion of
Native women's roles in diplomatic relations, see Barr, *Peace Came in
the Form of a Woman.*

33. *MPCP, V. 3,* 146.

34. *MPCP, V. 3,* 146.

Descriptions of the seal of the province of Pennsylvania are based
on examples in the Penn Papers at HSP. See also Pilcher, *Seal and Arms
of Pennsylvania,* 3–6.

CHAPTER 6: JOHN CARTLIDGE

1. Psalm 31:12 (King James Version).
2. JCI.
3. JCI.
4. "Advertisement, February 1, 1721[1722]," in *AWM*, February 20, 1722, 4.
5. See Anderson, *Creatures of Empire*.
6. *MPCP, V. 3*, 552.
7. "A failure to manure equaled barbarism." See Montaño, *Roots of English Colonialism*, 131. For comments on the "well manured farms" of Pennsylvania, c. 1729, see Moraley, *The Infortunate*, 52.
8. Sir Thomas Smith, *Discourse of the Commonweal*, as quoted in Montaño, *Roots of English Colonialism*, 148. See also Horning, *Ireland in the Virginia Sea*.
9. "At a Council held at Philadelphia, July the 20th, 1720," *MPCP, V. 3*.
   For in-depth discussion of go-betweens in colonial Pennsylvania, including John Cartlidge, see Merrell, *Into the American Woods*.
10. John Cartlidge to Isaac Taylor, February 17, 1721/22, ITP.
11. John Cartlidge to Isaac Taylor, February 17, 1721/22, ITP.
12. *MPCP, V. 3*, 146.

CHAPTER 7: WHAT CONTENT AND DECENCY REQUIRE

1. *MPCP, V. 3*, 148.
2. See Ashmead, *Historical Sketch of Chester*, 63–67 and 77–82.
3. *MPCP, V. 3*, 148–55.
   For biographical information on the Taylors, see "Taylor, Isaac" and "Taylor, John" in Smith, *History of Delaware County*, 506.
4. Logan and French Report, *MPCP, V. 3*, 148. On the Taylors' roadwork with John Cartlidge, see Futhey and Cope, *History of Chester County Pennsylvania*, 353.
5. Saltar Deposition and Rescarrick Deposition, DSC.
6. For George Rescarrick's father's will (with a note on the 1720 inventory), see "1714 March 21. Rescarrick, George," and for George Rescarrick's own will, proved by 1729, see "1728–29 Feb. 15, Rescarrick George," both in Nelson, ed., *Calendar of New Jersey Wills*, 381. On George Rescarrick's family trade, see https://www.east-windsor.nj.us/moodyfield.
   On Richard Saltar Jr.'s appearance in the will and inventory of his

wife Hannah Lawrence Saltar's father, Elisha Lawrence, see Nelson, ed., *Calendar of New Jersey Wills*, 284.

7. The uncorrected transcript reads: "present at A Councile held there by John & Edmd Cartlidge and other Xtians there on the one part and one Captain Sevility an Ingen man who appeared for himself and many other Ingens present on ye other" (first quotation) and "to Enquire into the Cause and manner of the Death of a Cartain Ingen man soposed to be killd by Edmond Carltidge etc" (second quotation). See Saltar Deposition, Philadelphia, March 10, 1722.

8. The uncorrected transcript reads: "he would have more Rum or yt he wou'd shoot them." When Sawantaeny "went for his Gun," Edmund followed, struggled to remove it from the Indian's hands, and, in so doing, became "intangled wth ye Indian." He "did strich until he had brok off the breech of ye said Gun . . . of which he died in A few Dayes." See Saltar Deposition, Philadelphia, March 10, 1722.

9. On colonial ventriloquism, see Chaplin, *Subject Matter*, 26–27.

10. On Pennsylvania's abundance and on conflict resolution, see Penn, *To the Free Society of Traders*, 4 and 7; Thomas, *Historical and Geographical Account*, 17; Moll, *British Empire*, 157; and Moll, *British Empire, 2nd Ed.*, 306.

11. The uncorrected transcript reads: "the sd Capt Sevillity on ye part and behalf of the Indians said, yt at the first Settlement of this Country by the Xtians the Indians and they were two people, but after at the coming of Willm Penn he made the Two people one flesh, and had soe Continued on the same Chaine of friendship Ever Since." See Saltar Deposition, Philadelphia, March 10, 1722.

12. "July the 12th 1720," in *MPCP, V. 3*, 93. Penn, "Articles of Agreement with the Susquehannah Indians," April 23, 1701, *PWP*, 49–55, 51.

13. The uncorrected transcript reads: "is a good and True Deposition as Reaches (if not the very words) the very Sence of the sd Councils, according to the interpretation as this Deponent understood." See Rescarrick Deposition, Philadelphia, March 10, 1722.

14. Vining had close business dealings with Aquila Rose, as revealed in "At a Comon Council held at Philada the 16th April A° 1722," in *MCCP*, 207. See also "Transcript from the Family Record of the Vinings of Delaware," in Boogher, *Miscellaneous Americana*, 20.

15. On the colonial practice of "absurd transcription" of Indian statements, see Chaplin, *Subject Matter*, 27–28.

16. On the "sham" quality of the trial, viewed from a Euro-American perspective, see Jennings, *Ambiguous Iroquois Empire*, 291, and Merrell,

Into the American Woods, 117. Smolenski rightly emphasizes Indian concerns for sovereignty. See Smolenski, "The Death of Sawantaeny and the Problem of Justice on the Frontier," in Pencak and Richter, *Friends and Enemies*, 118 and 121–22.

17. "Mortising posts and hewing rails," March 9, 1722, NIL.

18. For the descriptions of "woods," "air," "meadow," and "horses," and the list of berries, see Thomas, *Historical and Geographical Account*, 8, 9, 9, 8, and 17, respectively.

   On Native practices of forest management, including controlled or "swidden" burning, see Cronon, *Changes in the Land*, 50.

19. "Sow'd clover and trefoil mixt," March 10, 1722, NIL.

   Norris did not do this work personally; it was performed by a man identified as "Dick" (most likely enslaved), along with hired help from a neighboring man and his son. Norris's activities as a slaveholder will be discussed below.

20. *MPCP, V.3*, 35.

21. *MPCP, V.3*, 148, and "hair couch," JCI.

22. *MPCP, V.3*, 148. I infer that Logan and French boarded at Cartlidge's house during their stay in Conestoga both because this is where Philadelphia officials stayed the previous summer and because Logan notes at the close of his account of this trip that community members "came over to John Cartlidge's to see us at our Departure." See *MPCP, V.3*, 154.

23. "In ye Studdy . . . a p[ai]r of brass Scales," JCI.

24. *MPCP, V.3*, 148 and 149.

25. *MPCP, V.3*, 148, and "Minutes taken from Michael Bezaillion concerning . . . the Indians, 1ober 1718," LFP.

26. *MPCP, V.3*, 148.

27. "From in ye house . . . one walnut Table one hair Couch," JCI; *MPCP, V.3*, 148.

28. On James Logan and powdered wigs, see Watson, *Annals*, 525. On Great Lakes catlinite beads at Conestoga, see Kent, *Susquehanna's Indians*, 166–71.

29. Hazard, ed., "James Logan," 321–22, *MPCP, V.3*, 149.

30. *MPCP, V.3*, 149.

31. *MPCP, V.3*, 148.

32. *MPCP, V.3*, 149.

33. On the English tendency to conflate fatherhood with political authority and on their related practice of equating Indians with children, see Brewer, *By Birth or Consent*, 20 and 365.

34. Notes on a meeting conducted by James Logan on June 27, 1720, with "the Chiefs of the Mingoes or Conestogoe Indians, the Sachim or Chief of the Shawanese, the Chief of the Ganawese, with several of their People, and some of the Delawares . . . at John Cartlidges," *MPCP, V. 3*, 92. On the uses and abuses of familial metaphors in Anglo-American/Native American diplomacy, see Jane Merritt, "Metaphor, Meaning, and Misunderstanding: Language and Power on the Pennsylvania Frontier," in Cayton and Teute, eds., *Contact Points*, 60–87.

35. *MPCP, V. 3*, 149.

36. *MPCP, V. 3*, 149.

37. *MPCP, V. 3*, 149; *PWP, V. 2*, 128–29.

38. *MPCP, V. 3*, 149; Keith, *Letter*, 6.

   On emotion in native diplomacy, see Richter, *Ordeal of the Longhouse*, 40, and Rasmussen, *Queequeg's Coffin*, 68; see also Williams, *Linking Arms Together*, 54.

39. "At a Council held at Conestogoe, the 14th day of March, 1721–2," *MPCP, V. 3*, 150.

40. *MPCP, V. 3*, 150.

41. On William Penn's use of a wig, and consequent ridicule as one of the "Perriwig men," see George Fox to Henry Sidon, 25 Third Month [May] 1677, in *PWP, V. 1*, 376–77.

   On wigs as a sign of gentility, see Bushman, *Refinement of America*, 61–62.

42. On catlinite beads at Conestoga, see Kent, *Susquehanna's Indians*, 166–71.

43. "Indian concepts of justice . . . stressed the compensation of victims more than the punishment of offenders." See Richter, *Ordeal of the Longhouse*, 33, quotation 302, n. 6.

44. *MPCP, V. 3*, 152.

45. "Weenepeeweytah, the Squaw . . . then examined," *MPCP, V. 3*, 151.

46. *MPCP, V. 3*, 152.

47. *MPCP, V. 3*, 152.

CHAPTER 8: PETER BEZAILLION

1. *MPCP, V. 3*, 147–55, 152.

   On the history of "Old Peter's Road," see Wallace, *Indian Paths*, 118–19.

2. On the lives and looks of coureurs de bois versus voyageurs, see Slater, "Fur Traders," 107.

   On the outlines of Peter Bezaillion's biography, see Lancaster, *Historical Papers*, 155–61. This account notes his burial in a Church of England graveyard, key evidence of his Protestantism. And see also David H. Lands, "Conoy Indian Town and Peter Bezaillion," in Lancaster, *Papers Read*, 113–36.

3. On Logan's aid, see Lands, "Conoy Town," in Lancaster, *Papers Read*, 128, and on Logan's leverage over smaller traders, see Merrell, *Into the American Woods*, 96–97.

4. On payment and other issues, see Merrell, *Into the American* Woods, esp. 96–97.

5. On Nantes, and French migration more broadly, see Greer, *People of New France*, 14–15.

6. On the colonial impact of eighteenth-century Anglo-French wars, see Banks, *Chasing Empire*, 27–29. And on Iroquois success at gaining substantial "money and material" as a result of French and English competition for their support, see Parmenter, "After the Mourning Wars."

7. *MPCP, V. 1*, 396. On French maneuvers in North America, see Banks, *Chasing Empire*, 29.

8. *MPCP, V. 1*, 397 and 435; *MPCP, V. 2*, 100–1.

9. *MPCP, V. 2*, 403.

10. "Pennsylvania," in Moll, *Atlas Geographicus*, 724. On alchemy, see Woodward, *Prospero's America*, 20.

11. *MPCP, V. 2*, 404.

12. On "possessive curiosity," see Parish, *American Curiosity*, 236 and 239–40.

13. *MPCP, V. 2*, 404. On "Canatowa, Queen of the Mingoes," *MPCP, V. 3*, 81. Native women in the Susquehanna region, such as Canatowa, frequently took the lead in protesting abuses against land and people. See Fur, *A Nation of Women*, 41–42.

14. *MPCP, V. 2*, 404–6.

15. *MPCP, V. 2*, 565–66.

16. *MPCP, V. 3*, 19; "Minutes Taken from Michael Bizaillon concerning the Route from Canada to the Meshasippi & the Indians of those parts, 10br 1718," V. 11, Indian Affairs, Box 11, Folder 9, LFP; *MPCP, V. 3*, 92–98, 92, and 97.

CHAPTER 9: TWO HEADS ARE BETTER THAN ONE

1. *MPCP, V. 3*, 152.
2. Testimony of "Ayaquachan, the Ganawese" and testimony of "Aquan-nachke, the Shawana," *MPCP, V. 3*, 150 and 151. Peter Mancall notes that "a culture of violence appeared like a malignancy wherever traders took rum or brandy." See Mancall, *Deadly Medicine*, 95.
3. "In ye Front Chamber ... one Bedd and furniture four [Chairs?]" and "In ye Parlour Chamber ... one ordinary bed & furniture & Chest," JCI.
4. "Plate Carried to Pennsylvania," *PWP, V. 2*, 287–89.
   On colonial alcohol consumption, see Mancall, *Deadly Medicine*, 14.
5. See "Deed from the Delaware Indians, [15 July 1682]," *PWP, V. 2*, 261–66; and see *MPCP, V. 2*, 33. My thinking on this aspect of the case has been very much influenced by reading work-in-progress on "liquid diplomacy" by Lila Chambers, a PhD candidate at NYU currently completing a dissertation with the provisional title "Liquid Capital: Alcohol and the Making of the British Atlantic Empire, 1640–1751."
6. "William Penn to Gulielma Penn and Children," [4 August 1682], *PWP, V. 2*, 274.
7. *MPCP, V. 3*, 153.
8. *MPCP, V. 3*, 153.
9. *MPCP, V. 3*, 153.
   On Europeans being taught to "cover" Native dead, see Dennis, *Cultivating a Landscape of Peace*, 49.
10. *MPCP V. 2*, 546 and 48.
    Fenton dates the first recorded performance of a condolence ceremony by an Iroquois to New France in 1645. See Fenton, "Structure, Continuity, and Change in the Process of Iroquois Treaty Making," in Jennings, ed., *History and Culture of Iroquois Diplomacy*, 15.
    On Peter Bezaillion's biography, see Hanna, *The Wilderness Trail*, 168–70.
11. On the use of condolence rituals to create "an emotional climate" of "peace," see Richter, *Ordeal of the Longhouse*, 40.
12. *MPCP, V. 3*, 153.
13. *MPCP, V. 3*, 153.
14. *MCCP*, 207.
15. *MPCP, V. 3*, 153.
16. *MPCP, V. 3*, 153.

17. *MPCP, V. 3*, 153.

"Prices Currant at Philadelphia," *AWM*, 15, 1722, 4.

18. On Logan's trade order, see "James Patterson, Do. To Sundry Accots," under the page heading "Philadelphia, 1722, 7th mo. 22," JLD, 2. See "harping-iron, n." in OED Online.

19. *MPCP, V. 3*, 153.

20. *MPCP, V. 3*, 153.

21. *MPCP, V. 3*, 153.

On "material symbols of influence" and on gifts as "material proof" of "symbolic power" see Hall, *Zamumo's Gifts*, 71 and 92. On the sacred power of wampum and its importance in substantiating spoken statements, see Schutt, *Peoples of the River Valleys*, 10-12.

22. *MPCP, V. 3*, 153.

23. *MPCP, V. 3*, 153.

24. See Thomas Nairne, as cited in Patricia Galloway, " 'The Chief Who Is Your Father,' " Waselkov et al., eds., *Powhattan's Mantle*: 360–61.

25. *MPCP, V. 3*, 153.

26. "Philadelphia, July 13th," *AWM*, July 13, 1721, 4. Aquila Rose, "To J——n C——dge, Esq. on His Generous Entertainment of Sir William Keith, and his Company, at Conestogoe," in Rose, *Poems*, 26. "Arm chair" and "hair couch," JCI.

27. *MPCP, V. 3*, 154.

28. *MPCP, V. 3*, 154.

On the Covenant Chain, see Jennings, *Ambiguous Iroquois Empire*, *xvii–xviii*.

29. *MPCP, V. 3*, 154.

30. Native peoples often excused violent acts committed by people under the influence of alcohol. See Mancall, *Deadly Medicine*, 79.

31. "Philadelphia, July 13th," *AWM*, July 13, 1721, 4. The unnamed man, identified only by his race, enjoyed no "right of clergy." While no people of African origin are known to have been judicially executed in Pennsylvania before 1718, increasing numbers of "women, blacks, and youngsters" were subjected to the death penalty afterward. See Marietta and Rowe, *Troubled Experiment*, 75.

32. *MPCP, V. 3*, 154.

33. *MPCP, V. 3*, 154.

34. "Satisfaction, n.," OED Online. January 2018. Oxford University Press. http://www.oed.com.proxy.library.nyu.edu/view/Entry/1712 23?redirectedFrom=satisfaction (accessed February 6, 2018).

35. The exact timing of the formation of the League of the Haudenosaunee and the precise nature of its ceremonial and political functions remain contentious. For an overview, see Kuhn and Sempowski, "A New Approach."

36. "The next day, viz. the 15th of March," in *MPCP, V. 3*, 154.

37. "Prices Currant at Philadelphia," in *AWM*, March 15, 1722, 4.

38. On Native use of alcohol in "hospitality customs and mourning rituals," see Mancall, *Deadly Medicine*, 78–79. On Iroquois use of alcohol to gain access to the spiritual world, see Sallinger, *Taverns and Drinking*, 34. On the archaeological evidence for the ornamental use of wineglass stems at Conestoga, see Kent, *Susquehanna's Indians*, 227.

39. *MPCP, V. 2*, 33.
    Native peoples turned to "destructive drinking in the wake of destabilizing social and economic change"; see Mancall, *Deadly Medicine*, 8.

40. *MPCP, V. 3*, 154. Satcheechoe "hoped to be with the Sinnekaes in Eight Days, and to return in thirty," *MPCP, V. 3*, 155.

41. On the power conferred by Native information networks, see Dubcovsky, *Informed Power*.

42. *MPCP, V. 3*, 154.

CHAPTER 10: WEENEPEEWEYTAH AND ELIZABETH CARTLIDGE

1. *MPCP, V. 3*, 153.

2. *MPCP, V. 3*, 153.

3. *MPCP, V. 3*, 153.

4. "A Few Certificates and Marriages, 1684–1763," Darby Monthly Meeting, Quaker Meeting Records, Friends Historical Library, Swarthmore College.

5. *MPCP, V. 3*, 153.
   On the gendered nature of grief, including women's tears as a tactic of petitioning, see Eustace, *Passion Is the Gale*, 285–354.

6. *MPCP, V. 3*, 153.

7. See *The Descendants of John Bartram, The Botanist (1699–1777)*, digital publication on CD (Philadelphia: The John Bartram Association, 2001). See also West, "The Mystery of the Death of William Bartram." For landscape quotations, see Bartram, *Observations on the Inhabitants*, 9 and 10. The journey recounted occurred in 1743. On Elizabeth Bartram's books and clothing, see JCI.

8. On the comparative value of Elizabeth and John's worldly goods, see JCI.

   On "pseudo-widowhood," see Ulrich, *A Midwife's Tale*, 274–82, quotation on 282, and on "deputy husbands," see Ulrich, *Goodwives*, 35–50. On married colonial women's lack of civic, legal, and property rights, see Norton, *Founding Mothers and Fathers*, 83–89. See also Snyder, *Brabbling Women*, esp. chapter 5.

9. *MPCP*, 106.

10. On Haudenosaunee women in mourning wars, see Sarah M. S. Pearsall, "Recentering Indian Women in the American Revolution," in Sleeper-Smith et al., eds., *Why You Can't Teach*, 60. For an overview, see "Haudenosaunee Women," in Johansen, *Encyclopedia*, 124.

11. See Barr, *Peace Came in the Form of a Woman*.

12. "His Squaw, a Shannawese Woman, named Weynepreeueyta," *MPCP, V. 3*, 149–50.

   On parallels between Algonquian and Iroquois mourning and traditions of captive adoptions, see Warren, *Worlds the Shawnees Made*, 72.

13. "Weenepeeweytah, the Squaw," *MPCP, V. 3*, 149–51.

   On women's central role in the ritual resolution of death among the Shawnees, see Warren, *Worlds the Shawnees Made*, 72–73.

14. The Iroquois' member "moieties [were] responsible for restoring one another's emotional equilibrium and spiritual power," and the "Cayugas played a forward role in managing relations with Native peoples along the Susquenahhana." See Tiro, *People of the Standing Stone*, 3 and 4.

15. Testimony of "Passalty's wife and the Hermaphrodite," *MPCP, V. 3*, 152.

   A "mediating position" allowed third-gender people to play a special role in "conveying persons from life to death in burials." See Fur, *A Nation of Women*, 45 and 194. On the work of condolence in restoring the "mystic power or *orenda* of the group," see Dennis, *Cultivating a Landscape of Peace*, 79.

16. Testimony of "Passalty's wife and the Hermaphrodite," *MPCP, V. 3*, 152.

CHAPTER 11: FORGIVE ANYONE SOONER THAN THYSELF

1. Logan and French noted that they "brought . . . the Lad Jonathan" with them back to Philadelphia after arresting the Cartlidges, *MPCP, V. 3*, 155.

On "cookshops" and "bakehouses," see Thomas, *Historical and Geographical Account*, 40.

2. On Swindel's age, see "The Examination of Jonathan Swindel," March 21, 1722, SMC.

    On the composite details of Philadelphia street signs and the wares they announced for sale in 1722, see "Advertisements" in the *AWM*, June 28, 1722; March 29, 1722; September 26, 1722; May 5, 1720.

    I infer that Swindel could not sign his name because no signature was attached to his testimony. Testimony taken from his fellow servant, William, was signed "W, mark of Wm Wilkins" rather than with a full signature. Quite possibly, the eighteen-year-old Swindel (likely still a minor at the time his indentures were signed by an adult guardian) had not even learned to form the letter *S*. See "The Examination of Jonathan Swindel" and "William Wilkins, Servant . . . Saith," SMC.

3. On indentured servants in early Pennsylvania, see Tomlins, *Freedom Bound*, 291–95, and Wareing, *Indentured Migration*.

    On Swindel's valuation as one of "2 Servantt Lads" together assessed at £40, see JCI. On "course Osnabrigs," see Moraley, *The Infortunate*, 35.

4. On the Shippen garden, see Thomas, *Geographical Account*, 49–50. Based on the fact the clover was being sown ten days earlier on the Norris farm outside Philadelphia (see chapter 7) I infer that tulips would have been blooming by now in Philadelphia.

5. *MPCP, V. 3*, 147. Logan revealed much more about what he knew in James Logan to Hannah Penn, "Honored Mistress," April 12, 1722, PFP.

6. James Logan to William Penn, December 5, 1703, and the Dickinson-Masters marriage both in Armstrong, ed., *Correspondence*, 256, and n. 1, 423–24.

7. *MCCP*, 198–205, quote on 201. This account condenses and reorganizes a extensive commentary on the duel among the governor and the city's mayor and aldermen between October 3 and October 9, 1721.

8. See Douglas Hay, "Property, Authority, and the Criminal Law," in Hay et al., eds., *Albion's Fatal Tree*, 41–49.

9. "The Address of the Mayor, Aldermen, & Commonality of the City of Philadelphia in Answer to His [the Governor's] Speech of the 3rd Instant," *MCCP*, 198–205.

10. "Mayor's Speech of the 3rd Instant," *MCCP*, 198–205. On dueling and status, see Gorn, " 'Gouge and Bite,' " 18–43.

11. On anger and status, see Eustace, *Passion Is the Gale*, 151–200.

12. See William Keith to "Mr. Mayor," October 5, 1721, *MCCP*, 195–97.

13. "A Copy of a Speech the Governor Made, 8br 3d 1721" and "Mayor's Speech of the 3rd Instant," *MCCP*, 193–94 and 199.

14. *MPCP, V. 3*, 148–55.

15. *MPCP, V. 3*, 155.

16. *MPCP, V. 3*, 155.

17. *MPCP, V. 3*, 155.

18. On the percentile rank, in taxable wealth, of those who participated in criminal trials in Chester County, Pennsylvania, in 1718, see Marietta and Rowe, *Troubled Experiment*, 104.

19. *MPCP, V. 3*, 155.

20. William Penn, "To the Kings of the Indians," *PWP, V. 2*, 128–29.

21. See Keith, *Letter*, 9.

22. *MPCP, V. 3*, 155.

23. *MPCP, V. 3*, 155.

24. *MPCP, V. 3*, 156. Stretch was paid for "mending and Care of the Town Clock" in 1720. [See "At a Comon Council at Philada ye 4th July 1720," *MPCP, V. 3*, 177.] I have found no descriptions of this clock, but Charles Wilson Peal made an engraving that featured the later town clock built in 1753 by Peter's son Thomas Stretch. See James Trenchard, Engraver, and Charles Willson Peale, *A N.W. view of the state house in Philadelphia taken/C.W. Peale delin.; J.T. sculp* (Philadelphia, 1787). Photograph. Library of Congress, https://www.loc.gov/item/2004671521/.

    For information on the hundreds of clocks Peter and then Thomas Stretch produced for private purchasers, see Fennimore and Hohmann, *Stretch*.

25. See "Examination of Jonathan Swindel" in SMC.

26. "Examination of Swindel," SMC, 10.

27. "Examination of Swindel," SMC, 10. Compare the testimony of "Ayaquachan, the Ganawese," "Aquannachke, the Shawana," and "Weenepeeweytah, the Squaw," respectively, *MPCP, V. 3*, 149, 150, and 151.

28. "Advertisements . . . Philadelphia March 21, 1722," in *AWM*, March 22, 1722, 2.

29. "Examination of Swindel," SMC, 11. Swindel's options and opportunities were severely limited by his low status. Recent work has documented the structural privations of many Pennsylvania poor folk.

Compare Lemon, *The Best Poor Man's Country*, with Smith, *The "Lower Sort,"* and Kotowski, " 'The Best Poor Man's Country?' "

30. "Examination of Swindel," SMC, 11.

31. *MPCP, V. 3*, 156.

32. *MPCP, V. 3*, 156.

33. "Births, Burials, and Casualties in the City of Philadelphia for the Month of March," *AWM*, April 5, 1722, 2.

On the colonial theory of "hereditary heathenism" and its role in the creation of racial slavery, see Goetz, *Baptism of Early Virginia*, 3.

34. *MPCP, V. 3*, 156.

35. *MPCP, V. 3*, 156.

36. *MPCP, V. 3*, 156.

37. *MPCP, V. 3*, 156.

38. *MPCP, V. 3*, 156.

39. *MPCP, V. 3*, 156.

40. *MPCP, V. 3*, 156.

41. *MPCP, V. 3*, 156.

42. *MPCP, V. 3*, 156.

43. *MPCP, V. 3*, 156.

44. William Keith to Isaac Taylor, Philadelphia, March 26, 1722, ITP.

45. *MPCP, V. 3*, 157.

46. On stationery supplies, Thomas, *Explicatory Catechism*, back matter, 4 and Bradford, *Secretary's Guide*, i.

47. William Keith to Isaac Taylor, Philadelphia, March 26, 1722, ITP.

CHAPTER 12: ISAAC NORRIS

1. Isaac Norris Sr. to Isaac Norris Jr., "Fairhill, ye 10th 2nd Month 1722" (April 10, 1722), INLB, 299–304, 303. Reinberger and McLean, "Isaac Norris's Fairhill."

Landscape paintings were costly investments. See Lovell, *Art in a Season of Revolution*.

2. Isaac Norris to Henry Gouldney, "Pennsylvania ye 9th 2 mo., 1722" (April 9, 1722), INLB, 293.

3. James Logan to Hannah Penn, "Honored Mistress," April 12, 1722, PFP.

4. Isaac Norris, "2nd Month, 5th," NIL.

5. Isaac Norris to Henry Gouldney, "Pennsylvania ye 9th 2 mo., 1722," INLB, 293 and 94.

6. Isaac Norris to Henry Gouldney, "Pennsylvania ye 9th 2 mo., 1722," INLB, 294 and 296.

7. The labor theory of property rights originated with John Locke. See Yirush, *Settlers, Liberty, and Empire*, 101, 110, and 130, notes 84 and 85.

8. Isaac Norris, handwritten notes, March and April 1722, NIL; "Isaac Norris," Stephen, ed., *Dictionary of National Biography*, 127; Joyner, *Down by the Riverside*, 219; Rugemer, *Slave Law*, 41–42; "Bushel . . . oats," see Alexander J. Lindsey, "Bushels, Test Weights, and Calculations," Ohioline, December 26, 2018, Ohio State University, https://ohioline.osu.edu/factsheet/agf-503, accessed July 28, 2020.

9. Rugemer, *Slave Law*, 41–42 and 69–70.

10. Isaac Norris, handwritten notes, March 14, 1722, NIL.
    See "Blunder, n.," OED Online. June 2018. Oxford University Press.
    Unlike Norris, modern scholars interpret such "blunders" by enslaved people as deliberate acts of sabotage, what Stephanie Camp describes as "everyday resistance." See Camp, *Closer to Freedom*, 2, 3.

11. Isaac Norris to Henry Gouldney, "Pennsylvania ye 9th 2 mo., 1722," and Isaac Norris Sr. to Isaac Norris Jr., "Fairhill, ye 10th 2nd Month 1722," INLB 293 and 300.

12. Isaac Norris Sr. to Isaac Norris Jr., "Fairhill, ye 10th 2nd Month 1722," INLB, 302.

13. See Norris's bookplate with family crest in his copies of Shaftesbury, *Characteristicks*, LCP. See also the description in Crozier, *Crozier's General Armory*, 99.

14. See Norris's copy of Shaftesbury, *Characteristicks*, V.1, 271 and 272, LCP.
    On Shaftesbury, see Hayley, *First Earl of Shaftesbury*, and see Lesser, *South Carolina Begins*. On the selectivity with which Anglo-American slaveholders versed in moral philosophy applied it, see Chaplin, *Anxious Pursuit*, 65.

15. Isaac Norris Sr. to Isaac Norris Jr., "Fairhill, ye 10th 2nd Month 1722," INLB, 303.

16. Isaac Norris to Henry Gouldney, "Pennsylvania ye 9th 2 mo., 1722," INLB, 295.

17. Isaac Norris to Henry Gouldney, "Pennsylvania ye 9th 2 mo., 1722," INLB, 295.

18. Isaac Norris to Henry Gouldney, "Pennsylvania ye 9th 2 mo., 1722," INLB, 295.

CHAPTER 13: HE WILL GO TO LAW

1. War dances reported in William Keith, ASWK.

   On Iroquois war councils, see Parmenter, *Edge of the Woods*, 214. On seasonal rhythms of hunting, see Cronon, *Changes in the Land*, 48. On winter as the season for war, see Perdue, *Cherokee Women*, 87. On the ways in which Shawnee "men and women divided the year between hunting and farming," see Warren, *Worlds the Shawnees Made*, 25. On the complex relationship of Conestoga Indians to the Five Nations, see Smolenski, "Death of Sawantaeny," in Pencak and Richter, eds., *Friends and Enemies*, 124.

2. Thomas, *Historical and Geographical Account*, 13.

3. Schutt, *Peoples of the River Valleys*, esp. 66–72.

4. On the tradition of making antler combs at Conestoga, which enjoyed a "possible resurgence" in the eighteenth century, including the example of the finely carved comb featuring a "white man and what is apparently an Indian in a posture of hand-holding," see Kent, *Susquehanna's Indians*, 177 and 180, fig. 42.

5. ASWK.

6. ASWK.

7. ASWK.

8. "At a Council with the Indians held att Conestoga April 6th, 1722," ASWK. Note that according to Maryland reports, "Indians" wish to see "the murtherer is brought to Justice." See John Bradford to Thomas Addison, no date, as quoted in *PCM*, 379.

9. "At a Council with the Indians held att Conestoga April 6th, 1722," ASWK.

10. "Orocguae, *flesh*, meat," in Holm, *Vocabulary of Susquenhannock*, 21.

11. "At a Council with the Indians held att Conestoga April 6th, 1722," ASWK.

    On racial patriarchy, see Brewer, *By Birth or Consent*.

12. "At a Council held at Philadelphia, October the 16th, 1721," *MPCP*, V. 3, 140. On love and power, see Eustace, *Passion Is the Gale*.

13. Keith remarks on Native women's corn production. See "Conestoga April 7th Post Meridian, The Governor spoke again to the Indians," ASWK.

    April was corn-planting season in Pennsylvania. Moraley, *The Infortunate*, 52. On Native women's maize cultivation techniques, see

Schutt, *Peoples of the River Valleys*, 13–16. On the use of iron hoes among the Native peoples of the Susquehanna, see Kent, *Susquehanna's Indians*, 340.

14. "At a Council with the Indians held att Conestoga April 6th, 1722," ASWK.

15. "At a Council with the Indians held att Conestoga April 6th, 1722," ASWK.

16. "At a Council with the Indians held att Conestoga April 6th, 1722," ASWK.

17. *Laws of the Province of Pennsylvania*, 309–10, and "At a Council held at Philadelphia, March the 22nd, 1721 [1722]," *MPCP, V. 3*, 156. As late as August, members of the council would continue to describe the Cartlidges as being "tried for their Lives." See *MPCP, V. 3*, 194.

18. "Felony, n. 1," OED Online. June 2018. Oxford University Press.
    "Murder," in *Conductor Generalis (1722)*, 162. Compare with: *Conductor Generalis* (1674).

19. See the folder "Deposition of Witnesses," DSC.

20. "At a Council with the Indians held att Conestoga April 6th, 1722," ASWK.

21. "At a Council with the Indians held att Conestoga April 6th, 1722," ASWK.

22. Silverman, *Thundersticks*, 9.

23. "At a Council with the Indians held att Conestoga April 6th, 1722," ASWK.

24. *Psalms* 139:9 and 12 (King James Version).

25. "Conestoga, April 7th 1722, The Indians' Answer Spoken by Civility," ASWK.

26. *EJCCV*, 8.

27. *EJCCV*, 8.

28. *EJCCV*, 8, and "Conestoga, April 7th 1722, The Indians' Answer Spoken by Civility," ASWK.

29. "At a Council held at ye Capitol March 7th 1722," *EJCCV*, 8.

30. On use of the term "intermitting fever" to describe malaria, see Finger, *Dr. Franklin's Medicine*; on early modern views of disease, see Kupperman, "Fear of Hot Climates"; on Native explanations for disease, see Silver, *New Face*, 79–80; on Native uses of poison, see Parish, *American Curiosity*, 233; and on Native ideas about malaria specifically, see Kelton, "Avoiding the Smallpox Spirits," 48.

31. This summation is based on "Conestoga, April 7th 1722, The Indians' Answer Spoken by Civility," ASWK. On the trade goods at Conestoga, see Kent, *Susquehanna's Indians*, 203–95.

32. "Conestoga, April 7th 1722, The Indians' Answer Spoken by Civility," ASWK. See also Merrell, *Into the American Woods*, 362, n. 59.

33. On mirrors at Conestoga, see Kent, *Susquehanna's Indians*, 223.

34. "Conestoga, April 7th 1722, The Indians' Answer Spoken by Civility," ASWK.

35. "Conestoga, April 7th 1722, The Indians' Answer Spoken by Civility," ASWK.

36. "Conestoga, April 7th 1722, The Indians' Answer Spoken by Civility," ASWK.

37. "Conestoga, April 7th 1722, The Indians' Answer Spoken by Civility," ASWK.

    On the Covenant Chain, see Richter, *Ordeal of the Longhouse*, 141.

38. "Conestoga, April 7th 1722, The Indians' Answer Spoken by Civility," ASWK.

    On the mutual influence of Indians and colonists in early America, see Axtell, *Natives and Newcomers*.

39. Genesis 2:24, KJV.

    Keyword searching for the word "flesh" in the *Papers of William Penn*, the *Minutes of the Provincial Council of Pennsylvania*, *The Journal of the Common Council of Philadelphia*, and the *Acts of the General Assembly of Pennsylvania* reveals the rarity of discussions of the concept of "one flesh" among Anglo-Pennsylvanians. I have found just one other instance of the phrase in a court case discussed below, *MPCP*, V. 2, 11.

    Matthew Dennis has found related language in use by seventeenth-century Iroquois, suggesting an alternate source for Civility's concepts. See Dennis, *Cultivating a Landscape of Peace*, 235–41.

    Daniel Richter notes of the Five Nations that "people thrived not only through reciprocity but through the unity that came from alliances with the other sex." See Richter, *Ordeal of the Longhouse*, 25.

40. On Locke, marriage, and political philosophy, see Eustace, *Passion Is the Gale*, 148–49, and 527, n. 83.

41. "Conestoga, April 7th 1722, The Indians' Answer Spoken by Civility," ASWK.

42. "Conestoga, April 7th 1722, The Indians' Answer Spoken by Civility," ASWK.

43. "Conestoga, April 7th 1722, The Indians' Answer Spoken by Civility," ASWK.

44. Interjection by William Keith included under the heading "Conestoga, April 7th 1722, The Indians' Answer Spoken by Civility," ASWK.

45. "Conestoga April 7th Post Meridian, The Governor spoke again to the Indians," ASWK.

46. Plane, *Colonial Intimacies*.

    Uncles rather than fathers played the central role in the lives of Native children, making English patriarchy all the more distinctive— and cross-cultural relationships modeled on fatherhood all the more ambiguous. See Jane Merritt, "Metaphor, Meaning, and Misunderstanding" in Cayton and Teute, eds., *Contact Points*, 60–87.

47. "Conestoga April 7th Post Meridian, The Governor spoke again to the Indians," ASWK.

48. On Locke, see Eustace, *Passion Is the Gale*, 148–49, and 527, n. 83.

49. *MPCP, V. 2*, 11.

50. Moraley, *Infortunate*, 56.

CHAPTER 14: SATCHEECHOE

1. On Satcheechoe's birthplace, see *MPCP, V. 3*, 189. And see Wallace, *Indian Paths of Pennsylvania*.

2. "Dry, level, and direct," see Wallace, *Indian Paths of Pennsylvania*, 2. On the watercourses of Iroquoia, see Richter, *Ordeal of the Longhouse*, 11. On the Iroquois use of relay runners, see Grandjean, *American Passage*, 60. On paths and diplomacy, see Parmenter, *Edge of the Woods*, 13, xi, and on "Iroquois Internationlism," see Stevens, "The Historiography of New France," 148–49. On the travel time of war parties between Iroquois and the Cherokee, see Powell, *Nineteenth Annual Report*, 352.

3. On the "Iroquois Trail," see Grandjean, *American Passage*, 60.

4. Details on Satcheechoe's travel schedule, *MPCP, V. 3*, 155.

    The Iroquois followed a "practice of naming enduring groups of people rather than particular places." See Jordan, *The Seneca Restoration*, 98. And on space versus place in Native geography, see Greer, *Property and Dispossession*, 291.

5. On the gun, powder, and lead supplied for Satcheechoe's journey, see *MPCP, V. 3*, 153.

6. On Iroquois foodways, see Waugh, "Iroquois Food."

    On how the "landscape was alive with spiritual power," see Richter, *Ordeal of the Longhouse*, 24. On clan names, see Barbeau, "Iroquois Clans and Phratries," 393–94.

 On Susquehanna petroglyphs, see Paul Nevin, "Rock-Art Sites on the Susquehanna River," in Diaz-Granados and Duncan, eds., *Rock Art*, 239–57.

7. On the English use of surveying to mark boundaries and claim property (as well as their comparative lack of mathematical sophistication), see Seed, *Ceremonies of Possession*, 24.

8. See Evans, *Map of Pensilvania*.

 On "competing for empire and coping with geographic ignorance," see Mapp, *Elusive West*, 5.

9. See Evans, *Map of Pensilvania*. On European theories on "seashells in the Appalachians," see Winterer, *American Enlightenments*, 41.

10. *MPCP, V. 3*, 164.

11. For "Cheekaragoes," see statements attributed to Satcheechoe, *MPCP, V. 3*, 164.

 On the Iroquois strategy of balance, see Richter, *Ordeal of the Longhouse*, 206.

12. "Deed from the Delaware Indians" [July 15, 1682], in PWP, *V. 2*, 262, and Lewis Evans, *Map of Pensilvania*.

CHAPTER 15: STARK NAUGHT

1. The city council noted "Breeming of Ships and Vessells ... to the Southward of the Dock," *MPCP*, 206.

2. The Moore case was reported in "New Castle, April 24," *AWM*, April 26, 1722, 2.

 On "disorderly women" and sin, see Juster, *Disorderly Women*, and see Reis, *Damned Women*. Eighteenth-century Quakers enjoy a reputation for taking a more moderate attitude toward women than other Christian groups; nevertheless in 1717 Pennsylvanians singled out "the necessity of a ducking stool and house of correction, for the just punishment of scolding, drunken women." See Lloyd, "The Courts of Pennsylvania," 35 and 36.

3. *MPCP, V. 3*, 163.

4. The vast majority of accused criminals in Pennsylvania were poor transients. See Marietta and Rowe, *Troubled Experiment*, 90–91.

5. *Moll Flanders* was mentioned under the dateline "London, January 29," *AWM*, May 10, 1722, 1 and 2.

6. *MPCP*, *V. 3*, 160.

7. *MPCP*, *V. 3*, 160.

8. James Logan to Hannah Penn, "Honored Mistress," April 12, 1722, PFP.

9. *MPCP*, *V. 3*, 160.

10. *MPCP*, *V. 3*, 163.

11. *MPCP*, *V. 3*, 163.

12. *MPCP*, *V. 3*, 163.

13. *MPCP*, *V. 3*, 163.

   On Farmer's payment on behalf of John Cartlidge, *MPCP*, *V. 3*, 1157.

14. Dubcovsky, *Informed Power*, esp. chapter one, "Paths and Power."

   On the use of wire as hair ornament at Conestoga, see Kent, *Susquehanna's Indians*, 209.

15. *MPCP*, *V. 3*, 163.

16. *MPCP*, *V. 3*, 164.

   On the joining of word and gift in Iroquois ritual culture and on the sacred properties of wampum, see Richter, *Ordeal of the Longhouse*, 47–48.

17. *MPCP*, *V. 3*, 164.

18. *MPCP*, *V. 3*, 164.

19. On "the Faces of the Gods," see Wallace, *Death and Rebirth*, 78–80. On mortuary practices and on the inclusion of catlinite false faces in graves at Conestoga, see Kent, *Susquehanna's Indians*, 387–89 and 168–69.

20. *MPCP*, *V. 3*, 164.

21. *MPCP*, *V. 3*, 164.

22. *MPCP*, *V. 3*, 164.

23. *MPCP*, *V. 3*, 165. On the double meanings of "bonds of alliance" and on the use of beaded halters and strings in captive-taking, see Rushforth, *Bonds of Alliance*.

24. *MPCP*, *V. 3*, 164.

25. *MPCP*, *V. 3*, 165.

26. *MPCP*, *V. 3*, 165.

27. *MPCP*, *V. 3*, 165.

28. *MPCP*, *V. 3*, 165, and see "An Act for imposing a Duty on Persons convicted of heinous Crimes and imported into this Province as Servants or otherwise," in *Acts of the Province of Pennsylvania*, 36.

29. "Contra, 1722, 3. Mo., 2, 4, 4, & 9," JLL.

30. *MPCP*, *V. 3*, 167.

31. *MPCP, V. 3*, 167.

32. *MPCP, V. 3*, 167.

 On English reluctance to regard eighteenth-century trade between colonists and Indians as market transactions rather than as gift exchanges, see Stern, *Lives in Objects*.

33. "At a Council held at Philadelphia, May 9th, 1722," *MPCP, V. 3*, 167.

34. "New Castle, May 10, The Last Speech of Eleanor Moore at her Execution on Wednesday the 9th Day of May," in *AWM*, May 17, 1722, 3 and 4.

35. This Shaftesbury quotation is used to similar purpose in Hay, "Property, Authority, and the Criminal Law," in Hay et al., eds., *Albion's Fatal Tree*, 19.

36. *MPCP, V. 3*, 170 and 168.

 On Native American demands for costly fabrics, see Stern, *The Lives in Objects*, 130–34. On the English silk trade, see Eacott, *Selling Empire*, 82-85.

37. *MPCP, V. 3*, 168.

38. *MPCP, V. 3*, 168; PWP, *V. 2*, 128–29.

39. "2d. message to ye 5 Nations," as recorded in notes taken "At a Council held at Philadelphia, May 11th, 1722," *MPCP, V. 3*, 168.

40. *MPCP, V. 3*, 166–70.

41. On Pennsylvania's shifting legal code, Hayburn, "Who Should Die?," Table 1, 14–15. On ink, see Barrow, "Black Writing Ink."

42. *MPCP, V. 3*, 170.

43. *MPCP, V. 3*, 170. *Laws of the Province of Pennsylvania*, 309–10.

44. *MPCP, V. 3*, 150.

45. *MPCP, V. 3*, 169.

CHAPTER 16: WILLIAM KEITH

1. "The Speech of His Excellency Sir William Keith, Bart. . . . May the 22nd, 1722," *AWM*, May 24, 1722, 1. On the use of "shear steel" in eighteenth-century penknives, see Edmonson, *American Surgical Instruments*, 274. PSWK.

2. *MPCP, V. 3*, 168.

3. *MPCP, V. 3*, 168.

4. *MPCP, V. 3*, 168. See Keith, *Letter*, 8.

 Iroquois attention to grief and condolence "directed mourners' emotions into ritualized channels" in order to contain violence by restoring reason. See Richter, *Trade, Land, and Power*, 72.

5. On the political intrigue surrounding Keith's arrival as governor, see "Sir William Keith" in Horle, *Lawmaking and Legislators*, 561–88.

6. On Gookin's conflict with Quakers, see Hayburn, "Who Should Die?," 43–48; Smolenski, *Friends and Strangers*, 249–85; and Nash, *Quakers and Politics*, 315–18 and 331–33.

7. On William Penn's negotiations to sell his proprietorship back to the crown, see Murphy, *William Penn*, 350.

8. Keith, "Report . . . of the Indian Nations," Philadelphia, February 16, 1719, *CSP*. Keith subsequently published this letter as "The Report of the Honourable William Keith Esq.," in Keith, *Collection of Papers*, 185–99 ("four small forts" on 196).

9. Keith, *Collection of Papers*, 192–93 and 198.

10. James Logan, "My Letter and Observations to Coll. Keith on his Report to the Board of Trade, 8th 2d Mo. 1719," JL/DL, 59–64.

11. On humoral theory, see Parish, *American Curiosity*, 78–80. For a description of bloodletting with folding knife lancets, see Edward Shirter, "Primary Care," in Porter, ed., *Cambridge History of Medicine*, 108.

12. On varieties of lancet cases, see Edmonson, *American Surgical Instruments*, esp. 271–87.

13. Keith, "The Speech of His Excellency," *AWM*, May 24, 1722, 1.

14. Keith, "The Speech of His Excellency," *AWM*, May 24, 1722, 1.

15. Keith, "The Speech of His Excellency," *AWM*, May 24, 1722, 1.

   On Keith's strategy of allying himself with the assembly against the council—and using newspapers to reach the populace—see James N. Green, "English Books and Printing in the Age of Franklin," in Armory and Hall, eds., *Colonial Book Trade*, 248–313.

16. William Keith to the Council of Trade and Plantations, May 24, 1722, *CSP*.

17. "Advertisements," *AWM*, May 24, 1722, 2.

CHAPTER 17: TAKE HIM NOW

1. "Advertisements . . . A Pair of Globes," *AWM*, June 7, 1722, 4 and "To Be Sold . . . A Pair of Globes . . . ," *AWM* June 14, 1722, 2.

   Bradford's brief description of his globes is quoted in full. My further description is speculative, taken from Harris, *Astronomical Dialogues*, esp. *i–2* and 16–18. James Logan owned the 1719 edition of this book, and today the Logan copy can be found in the collections of LCP.

On celestial and terrestrial globes, see Thornton, "The 'Use of Globes.' " See also Sumira, *Art and History of Globes*.

2. See Leeds, *American Almanack*, n.p.

Astrology and astronomy were treated as linked sciences. See Stahlman, "Astrology in Colonial America." And see Tomlins, *Divinity for All Persuasions*, 29.

3. See *Conductor Generalis* (1722) and see "Advertisements," *AWM*, June 14, 1722, 2. Meriton, *Conductor Generalis* (1679). The Meriton version went through multiple London editions.

Some ten different books and pamphlets were printed in Philadelphia in the year 1722. Most were of only local interest, and only *Conductor Generalis* was a reprint of an English title. Generally, colonists ordered the volumes they wanted from London. Bradford's reprint was unusual, indicating the urgency of the need for this particular book. See Wolf, *Book Culture*, and see Armory and Hall, eds., *Colonial Book Trade*.

4. See "Advertisements," *AWM*, June 14, 1722, 2.

5. Keith noted suffering from fever in "Copy of the Governor of Pennsylvania's Letter to the Governor of Maryland . . . June 23rd, 1722," *MPCP, V. 3*, 184. We can hypothesize that the moon was visible in Philadelphia on June 18 because Isaac Norris noted that a "long drought" beginning on June 9 ended with "rain" on June 24, NIL. I have found no observations in Philadelphia sources about the eclipse. However, the British Royal Society recorded that an eclipse occurred on June 18, 1722 (one day later than Leeds had calculated). See "From an Observation of a lunar eclipse taken . . . in Jamaica the 18th of June 1722," in Reid and Gray, eds., *Philosophical Transactions*, 365.

Keith recounted his mid-June activities on the Susquehanna, including providing copies of correspondence and treaty minutes dated between June 15 and June 23, 1722, *MPCP, V. 3*, 178–87.

The activities of rival surveyors on the Maryland–Pennsylvania border throughout the spring and summer of 1722 are described in James Logan to Simon Clement, November 22, 1722, PFP.

6. For a summary of the Isaac Taylor case, see, *MPCP, V. 3*, 212.

7. See "Persons added to the Commissions of peace . . . For the County of Chester . . . John Cartledge, & Francis Worley," *MPCP, V. 3*, 50.

On Keith's whereabouts, see Keith, "From Francis Worley's near Conestoga, June 18th 1722," *MPCP*, *V. 3*, 178–79.

On the William Barns Inn, see Moss, *Historic Houses*, 216–17.

8. I infer that Keith was tormented by mosquitos because he recorded treating his fever with "bark"—that is, with quinine. British colonists learned about quinine from the Native peoples of South America via the Spanish, but did not understand the insect-vector nature of the "fevers" they suffered. See Crawford, *Andean Wonder Drug.*

On the trouble with mosquitos in Pennsylvania, including the tradition of keeping "fires before the houses in the evenings" and the unhealthy swamps near Maryland, see Moraley, ed., *The Infortunate*, 57–91.

9. William Keith, "To the Gentlemen of the Councell at Philadelphia," June 18, 1722, *MPCP*, *V. 3*, 178–79 & 181–82.

10. William Keith, "To the Gentlemen of the Councell at Philadelphia," June 18, 1722, *MPCP*, *V. 3*, 181–82.

11. *MPCP*, *V. 3*, 182–83.

12. On the Gunter's chain, see Greer, *Property and Dispossession*, 278.

13. See notes describing "Survey of the Mannor of Springets-Bury upon the River Susquehannah," *MPCP*, *V. 3*, 184–86.

14. See "Copy of the Governor of Pennsylvania's Letter to the Governor of Maryland . . . June 23rd, 1722," *MPCP*, *V. 3*, 183–84.

15. See "Copy of the Governor of Pennsylvania's Letter to the Governor of Maryland . . . June 23rd, 1722," *MPCP*, *V. 3*, 183–84. And see "malaria, n.," OED Online. December 2018. Oxford University Press.

16. Isaac Norris, handwritten notes recorded June 1722, NIL. On eclipse records, see above.

17. Isaac Norris Sr. to Isaac Norris Jr., "Pennsylvania ye 12th 4 mo. 1722" (June 4, 1722), INLB, 312–13, and notes recorded in June 1722, NIL.

"Births, Burials, and Casualties," *AWM*, July 5, 1722, 3.

18. On Jonathan Dickinson's household goods, see Gillingham, "Notes and Documents." Dickinson's account of his time in Florida is discussed in chapter 5.

19. George Keith's antislavery teachings were published by consensus as Society of Friends, *Exhortation.* On Keith's contributions to this pamphlet, see Gerbner, "Antislavery in Print." On Keith's life and career, see "George Keith," in Bowden, *Dictionary*, 287–88. Nash, *Quakers and Politics*, 145–60.

20. Keith, *Geography and Navigation*. No copies of this book are held today by LCP; since it was founded on the gift of James Logan's personal library it is safe to assume he did not own the book.

The quotation on comets is from Whitlocke, *History of England*, 297–98. James Logan's copy of this book remains at LCP.

21. Thomas, *Historical and Geographical Account*, 53.

22. JLL, 6.

23. JLL, 6

24. "Govrs. Letter to the Gentln. Of the Council . . . with the Councils answer to the same," *MPCP, V. 3*, 178–89.

25. *MPCP, V. 3*, 186.

26. *MPCP, V. 3*, 187.

27. *Conductor Generalis*, 130.

28. *Conductor Generalis*, 160.

29. See "An Abstract of one of CATO's Letters," *AWM*, June 7, 1722, 1 and 2, and "An Abstract of one of CATO's Letters," *AWM*, June 21, 1722, 1 and 2.

30. See Americo Britannus [pseud.], "To the Author of the AWM," *AWM*, June 21, 1722, 1, and see "An Abstract of one of CATO's Letters," *AWM*, June 21, 1722, 2.

Bradford's quotation is from Trenchard, *Fifth Collection*, 28, and see Logan, trans., *Cato's Moral Distiches*.

31. *MPCP, V. 3*, 187.

32. *MPCP, V. 3*, 187.

33. On the links between astronomy and imperialism, see Strang, *Frontiers of Science*, 129.

CHAPTER 18: OUSEWAYTEICHKS (SMITH THE GANAWESE)

1. Notes on events in Conoy town, *MPCP, V. 3*, 187–89. For the Conoy house description, see White, "Narrative of a Voyage," 117. On grief as metaphorical darkness and on the "tree of the great peace," see "The Dekanawida Legend," in Parker, "The Constitution of the Five Nations," 9–10 and 20.

2. On Conoy history, see Schutt, *Peoples of the River Valleys*, 65, quotation on page 71.

3. On Smith's linguistic "perfection," *MPCP, V. 3*, 93. On the diplomatic virtuosity of Algonquian nations, see Grandjean, *American Passages*.

4. This Captain Smith, "the Ganawese," appears about a half a dozen times in *MPCP*, beginning *MPCP, V. 3*, 93.

    On the Nanticoke request of Smith, see James Mitchell to William Keith, "From the Township of Donnegall, bounded by the Susquehanna, July 12th," in *MPCP, V. 3*, 187–88.

5. For these appearances in the record by Smith, see *MPCP, V. 3*, 148; *MPCP, V. 3*, 123; *MPCP, V. 3*, 182.

6. For the argument that "the land spoke Algonquian," see Grandjean, *American Passages*, 70. On Algonquian tree carvings, etc., and on Algonquian transmission of (dis)information, see Cohen, *Networked Wilderness*, 124 and 191, n. 5.

7. For Logan's notes on meeting the Conoy man named Smith, see *MPCP, V. 3*, 93.

8. *MPCP, V. 3*, 19.

    On Captain Christopher Smith's work as a surveyor, see Alexander, ed., *Journal*, 14; as a diplomat, see Aquila, *Iroquois Restoration*, 213. "Smith the Ganawese's" English name provides another instance, like that of "Jon Hans, the Cayuga," of a Native man taking a colonist's name. For more on the practice, see Sayre, *Indian Chief*, 181–82.

9. *MPCP, V. 3*, 182–83.

10. James Mitchell to William Keith, "From the Township of Donnegall, bounded by the Susquehanna, July 12th," in *MPCP, V. 3*, 188.

11. James Mitchell to William Keith, "From the Township of Donnegall, bounded by the Susquehanna, July 12th," in *MPCP, V. 3*, 188. And see *MPCP, V. 2*, 546 and 48.

    Specialists debate the nature of the relationship between the Lenapes and the Five Nations of the Haudenosaunee, particularly whether the Lenapes were equal allies or subordinate tributaries of the Five Nations. A recently rediscovered manuscript in the collections of the American Philosophical Society contains sketches of the thirty-two belts presented in 1712; that document clearly refers to "the Delaware . . . . many years ago being made Tributaries to the Mingoes or 5 Nations." Moreover, this 1722 delegation, including the Lenape, bearing the identical number of wampum belts, seems to signal, at the least, a regular and formal arrangement between peoples of the river valleys and the Haudenosaunee. For the claim that the Lenape were *not* subordinate, see Jennings, *Ambiguous Iroquois Empire*, 263. For the manuscript, see PPCM.

12. Arthur C. Parker, "The Constitution of the Five Nations," in Parker, *Parker on the Iroquois*, 20.

    "Condolence is based on the theory that the emotions must be addressed before politics," Wiseman, *Voice of the Dawn*, 81. On the manufacture and meanings of wampum, see Otto, "Wampum." And on wampum, Haudenosaunee spirituality, and state formation, see Rasmussen, *Queequeg's Coffin*, 72–73s and passim.

13. On the role of "presents" of wampum in making messages physically "present," see Richard Cullen Rath, "Hearing Wampum: The Senses, Mediation, and the Limits of Analogy," in Cohen and Glover, eds., *Colonial Mediascapes*, 290–324, esp. 303–5.

14. See "The Govrs. Letter to the Ganawese King," *MPCP, V. 3*, 188–89.

CHAPTER 19: MONEY AND GOOD MEN

1. James Logan to Simon Clement, 22 November 1722, PFP. On the month of August of 1722 as "exceeding hot," see NIL. For the phrase "the rising of the apron," see Knott, *Mother Is a Verb*, 56.

2. The standard biography of James Logan notes that he lost a son named James early in his marriage. See Tolles, *James Logan*. The most thorough information is from an online family genealogist, Horatio Connell Snyder. See http://www.pennock.ws/names108.html#LOGAN. Snyder gives the life and death dates as January 9, 1716–July 1, 1717, for this infant James Logan. The original records documenting the 1714 marriage date are at *Marriage Certificates, 1672–1759*, Quaker Meeting Records Collection, *MR Ph:359*, Swarthmore College, Swarthmore, Pennsylvania.

3. On the "stair-step children" born one to two years apart and conventionally depicted in height order in colonial family portraits, see Lines, *Visual History*, 15.

    Isaac Norris, handwritten notes recorded July 5, 1722, in NIL.

4. "Advertisements," *AWM*, July 5, 1722, 4, and "Advertisements," *AWM*, July 26, 1722, 4.

5. *MPCP, V. 3*, 192–93.

6. *MPCP, V. 3*, 192.

7. William Keith to Hannah Penn, July 5, 1722, PFP. On quills, see Finlay, *Western Writing*.

8. William Keith to Hannah Penn, July 5, 1722, PFP, and see JLL.

9. William Keith to Hannah Penn, July 5, 1722, PFP.

10. William Keith to Hannah Penn, July 5, 1722, PFP.

11. "To the Author of the *AWM*, July 18, 1722," in *AWM*, July 19, 1722, 1, and William Keith to Hannah Penn, July 5, 1722, Penn Manuscripts, HSP.

12. *MPCP, V. 3*, 192–93.

13. *MPCP, V. 3*, 192–93.

14. *MPCP, V. 3*, 193, and "Bohea Tea" in "Advertisements," *AWM*, August 23, 1722, 4.

15. On the condemned hearing the saws and hammers being used to build their scaffolds, see Linebaugh, *London Hanged*, 445. On the poor's use of boxes as seats in early America, see Demos, *Little Commonwealth*, 43.

16. The young executioner's mini-biography appeared when he was advertised as a runaway servant immediately following his work hanging William Battin. See "Advertisements," *AWM*, August 23, 1722, 4.

17. "Advertisements," *AWM*, August 23, 1722, 4.

18. "Advertisements," *AWM*, August 23, 1722, 4.

19. "The Speech of the Boy Hang'd at Chester," *AWM*, August 23, 1722, 2 and 3. On this literary history, see Shields, *Civil Tongues*. On the rise of the gallows speech as a popular genre, see Guthke, *Last Words*, 168, and see Schorb, "Review Essay." See also Cohen, *Pillars of Salt*; Halttunen, *Murder Most Foul*; and Seay, *Hanging Between Heaven and Earth*.

20. On the gallows speech as a literary genre following similar conventions across the eighteenth-century English-speaking world, see Kelly, *Gallows Speeches*.

21. "The Speech of the Boy Hang'd at Chester," *AWM*, August 23, 1722, 2 and 3. For the evocative phrase "new world of goods," see Norton, *A New World of Goods*.

22. Wareing, *Indentured Migration*, 45 and 60. Scholars estimate that more than half of eighteenth-century English migrants to British North America came as bound servants. See Moraley, *The Infortunate*, xvii.

23. "The Speech of the Boy Hang'd at Chester," *AWM*, Thursday, August 16 to Thursday, August 23, 1722, 2 and 3.

24. "The Speech of the Boy Hang'd at Chester," *AWM*, August 23, 1722, 2 and 3. On the lack of formal education for prisoners prior to the 1790s, see Schorb, *Reading Prisoners*.

25. "Advertisements," in *AWM*, August 23, 1722, 4. On the practices involved in being "hung in irons," see Banner, *Death Penalty*, 72–74.

26. *MPCP, V. 3*, 193.

27. *MPCP, V. 3*, 193, 194.

28. *MPCP, V. 3,* 194. Medals were considered an important element of diplomacy. See Greg O'Brien, "Supplying Our Wants: Choctaws and Chickasaws Reassess the Trade Relationship with Britain, 1771–72," in Brown, ed., *Transformation of the Gulf South,* 77 and 78, and see Shannon, "Dressing for Success."

29. *MPCP, V. 3,* 195.

30. *MPCP, V. 3,* 194.

31. *MPCP, V. 3,* 190.

32. "Of Prisons," in *Conductor Generalis,* 248.

33. *MPCP, V. 3,* 193.

34. *MPCP, V. 3,* 195.

35. *MPCP, V. 3,* 196.

36. "Advertisements," *AWM,* August 23, 1722, 4, and "Advertisements," *AWM,* September 6, 1722, 4.

37. "Advertisements," *AWM,* August 23, 1722, 4, and "Advertisements," *AWM,* September 6, 1722, 4.

CHAPTER 20: JAMES LE TORT

1. JLL, 6.

    Though Logan did not note the method by which he weighed Le Tort's skins, because he recorded payment down to the last penny, he must have precisely weighed them. Steelyards were standard equipment in the eighteenth-century fur trade. See James Merrell, " 'Our Bond of Peace': Patterns of Intercultural Exchange in the Carolina Piedmont, 1650–1750," in Waselkov et al., eds., *Powhattan's Mantle,* 285, and see Hazard, ed., *Register of Pennsylvania, V. 2,* 190.

    The large size and weight of Logan's ledger book means that he would necessarily have spread it open on a table in order to write in it.

2. "At a Council held at Philadelphia, August 7th, 1722," *MPCP, V. 3,* 196, and JLL, 6.

3. See, for example, "John Cartlidge and James Le Tort, Interpreters," "At a Council held at Conestogoe, July the 7th 1721," *MPCP, V. 3,* 123. On the close connections between the Le Torts and Bezaillion, see Hanna, *Wilderness Trail,* 169.

4. On Logan's fur-trade empire, see Hinderaker, *Elusive Empires,* 22–25.

5. "At a Council held at Conestogoe, the 14th day of March 1721–22," *MPCP, V. 3,* 149. It seems most probable that Francis was the brother

of Jacques and the uncle of James, the subject of this chapter. See Egle, *Notes and Queries*, 92.

6. "At a Council held at ye Govrs Lodging in Philadelphia ye 29th 6th Mo, 1689," and "At a Councill Held att philadelphia the sixt of February, 1693–94," *MPCP, V. I*, 299 and 436. See also Benson, "Huguenot Letorts."

7. "At a Council held at Philadia., the 26th of July 1709," *MPCP, V. 2*, 471.

8. "At a Council held at Philadia., the 23rd of July 1712," *MPCP, V. 2*, 554.

    The interactions of women such as these play a key part in the daily encounters that cumulatively define the terms of colonial contact, however little comment their lives gain in the records created by colonial men. See Anderson, *Creatures of Empire*.

9. See "At a Council held at Philadelphia, the 28th May, 1711," *MPCP, V. 2*, 531.

    On the population replacement motives for Iroquois captive-taking, see Robbie Ethridge, "Introduction," in Ethridge and Shuck-Hall, eds., *Mapping the Mississippian Shatter Zone*, 25 and 29–31. On the strategic tributary status taken by the Shawnees in relation to the Iroquois, see Warren, *Worlds the Shawnees Made*, esp. 151 and 181.

10. *MPCP, V. 2*, 533.

11. *MPCP, V. 2*, 533.

12. *MPCP, V. 2*, 534.

13. *MPCP, V. 2*, 534.

14. On the fraught history of Indian slavery and its uneven legal and economic development, see Newell, *Brethren by Nature*, 196.

15. "A petition from James Le Tort, prisoner in ye Common Goal of Philadia.," "Petition from ye Prison," of Peter Bezaillion and James Le Tort, *MPCP, V. 2*, 163 and 539.

CHAPTER 21: A WORD TO THE WISE

1. Isaac Norris, handwritten notes on the page facing "August," NIL. For "in the month of August . . . bears . . . ," see Moraley, *Infortunate*, 92. On deforestation as the mark of colonial civility, see Van Horn, *Power of Objects*, 54.

2. It is impossible to determine for certain whether Norris brought the book with him, but I believe he did. Based on a comparison of the handwriting, it seems clear that he made all four entries for August together at one time and all four entries for September together at another. It

may be that the August entries were made in Albany after he arrived, possibly as he waited for the conference to begin, and that the September ones were made after he had returned to Pennsylvania. See NIL.

3. *MPCP, V.* 3, 196.

4. Isaac Norris to Leonard Vassel, December 8, 1722, INLB, and Dickinson, *God's Protecting Providence, i.*

5. Norris to Vassell, December 8, 1722, INLB.

6. Isaac Norris, handwritten notes, "August," in NIL. On the comparative populations of New York City and Philadelphia, see Nash, *Urban Crucible,* 66.

7. For "Ongwehonweh," see Wilkins, ed., *Native American Political Development,* 30. On the land owning the people, see Greer, *Property and Dispossession,* 51.

   The common names now used to refer to the member nations of the Haudenosaunee Confederacy were not originally used by the people themselves and often do not even derive from Iroquois languages. Many modern Haudenosaunee peoples advocate for a return to the use of their original nation names: Mohawk (Kanienkahagen), the People of the Flint; Oneida (Onayotekaono), the People of the Upright Stone; Onondaga (Onundagaono), the People of the Hills; Cayuga (Guyohkohnyoh), the People of the Great Swamp; and Seneca (Onondowahgah), the People of the Great Hill. The Tuscarora gained recognition as the Sixth Nation. However, as of 1722, Euro-American settler colonists continued to refer to the Haudenosaunee as the Five Nations. For more information, see https://www.haudenosauneeconfederacy.com/.

8. "Now squashes," *MPCP, V. 3,* 190.

9. "What I desire . . . pumpkin," in Wallace, *Death and Rebirth,* 64–65; on pumpkin and squash rattles, see Speck, *Midwinter Rites,* 43 and 100–3, and on pumpkins as welcome gifts, see Richter, *Ordeal of the Longhouse,* 92.

10. Colonial record keepers seldom knew of, much less noted, the influence of Indigenous women on Native policies. I infer that Iroquois women must have offered this advance council because we now recognize that their role was to shape such policies. See Sarah M. S. Pearsall, "Recentering Indian Women in the American Revolution," in Sleeper-Smith et al., eds., *Why You Can't Teach,* 60. And see also Karim Tiro, "Iroquois Ways of War and Peace," in Dixon and Tiro, eds., *Cadwallader Colden, xxiv.*

11. On the Haudenosaunee Confederacy practice of captive-taking as a means of cultural self-preservation, see William A. Fox, "Events as

Seen from the North: The Iroquois and Colonial Slavery," in Eth-ridge and Shuck-Hall, eds., *Mapping the Mississippian Shatter Zone*, 72–74. And for the argument that captive-taking by members of the Five Nations engaged in "mourning wars" should be "understood as a response to massive population losses," see Tiro, "Iroquois Ways of War and Peace," *xxiv*. On the 1722 threats of the Five Nations against southern Native nations, see the details offered in chapter 13.

12. See "The Great Law of Peace" in Wilkins, ed., *Native American Political Development*, 16–18.

13. See "The Great Law of Peace" in Wilkins, ed., *Native American Political Development*, 16–18.

14. This description draws on details from John Harris, *A South Prospect of ye Flourishing City of New York in the Province of New York in America* in the Miriam and Ira D. Wallach Division of Art, Prints, and Photo-graphs: Print Collection, NYPL.

15. *MPCP, V.3*, 203.

16. See [Keith], *Particulars* [1721]. On the interest the Board of Trade took in creating a "unitary empire," see Steele, *Politics*, and on related royal efforts to streamline the Indian trade, see Yirush, *Settlers*, 183–89. Internal rivalries between the king's Privy Council and the Board of Trade eclipsed the latter's influence between 1724 and 1748, leading later historians to underestimate the earlier interest and influence of the Board of Trade. See Shannon, *Indians*, 77–82.

17. On the impact of the fur trade on the finances of colonial New York, see Bonomi, *Factious People*, 79–80.

18. William Burnet to the Council of Trade and Plantations, New York, November 21, 1722, *CSP*.

19. William Burnet to the Council of Trade, New York, November 21, 1722, *CSP*.

20. A contemporary engraving of New York City features seagulls and painted ships carved with lions. Carwitham, *A View of Fort George*. I. N. Phelps Stokes Collection of American Historical Prints, NYPL.

21. William Keith to William Burnet, New York, Augst 13, 1722, *MPCP, V.3*, 203 and 204.

22. *MPCP, V.3*, 204; *William Burnet*, painting c. 1726 by John Watson, in the Massachusetts State House Art Collection. For the conduct-book quote, see Bushman, *Refinement of America*, 65. And see Keith, *Essay*, 3.

23. *MPCP, V.3*, 204.

24. *MPCP, V.3*, 204.

25. *MPCP, V. 3*, 204.

26. Isaac Norris, handwritten notes, "August," NIL. On Peter Winne, see Stefan Bielinski, "River People in Early Albany 1686–1800," http://exhibitions.nysm.nysed.gov/albany/art/art-rpea.html#pw/.

27. Isaac Norris, handwritten notes, "August," NIL. On Albany's gates, see Venema, *Beverwijck*, 12.

28. Johannes La Montagne, "Memorandum, 1660," Gehring, ed., *Fort Orange Court*, xxvii. See also Van Laer, *Minutes of the Court of Fort Orange and Beverwyck*, 10 and 11.

29. On John Cartlidge's fever, see James Logan to Simon Clement, Philadelphia, November 22, 1722, PFP.

30. The description in this paragraph is based on two 1695 maps of Albany. See "Fig, 3, Albany" and "Fig. 4, The Fort of Albany," in Shea, ed., *Description*, 95 and 96. Further details are drawn from Kalm, *Travels*, 256–58. Kalm's account was written in 1749, however, I have no reason to believe that the conditions he described were significantly different twenty-five years earlier.

31. In Albany in 1714, forty "female slaves" over age sixteen were counted and eighteen "male slaves." There were fifty-five enslaved children under age sixteen. (The ratio of adult enslaved women to children was thus 1:1.4). There were 302 white female "inhabitants" over age sixteen and 256 white male "inhabitants" over sixteen, with 465 white children under age sixteen. (The ratio of adult white women to children was thus 1:1.5.) For raw data, see "A List of the Inhabitants and Slaves in the City & County of Albany, 1714," in O'Callaghan, ed., *Documentary History*, 905.

   On the enslavement of the Iroquois as part of the Albany-Montreal fur trade, see Rushforth, *Bonds of Alliance*, 317. On the ambiguous and vulnerable legal position of bound Indians under English law, see Newell, *Brethren by Nature*, 13–14. On information trading by free and enslaved Atlantic creoles in New York, see Berlin, *Many Thousands Gone*, 59. On enslaved women's reproductive work, see Morgan, *Laboring Women*.

32. Robert Livingston to Alida Livingston, August 25, 1722, and Robert Livingston to Alida Livingston, August 30, 1722, LVFP. Thanks to Professor Wayne Bodle, Indiana University of Pennsylvania, who provided me with his personal photocopies of these documents.

33. R Livingston to A Livingston, August 25, 1722, LVFP.

34. R Livingston to A Livingston, August 30, 1722, LVFP.

35. Pennsylvania's negotiations with the Five Nations began on September 7: *MPCP, V. 3,* 196. And see Verses for September 26 and 27 in Leeds, *American Almanack, 1722.*

36. The details of this meeting were recounted in Keith, *Treaty of Peace,* 2.
   On the rarity of otter pelts by 1700, see Wallace, *Death and Rebirth,* 59.

37. "The Govrs. Speech, to the Indians of the ffive Nations at Albany, the 7th instant," *MPCP, V. 3,* 196, and William Keith to William Burnet, New York, August 13, 1722, *MPCP, V. 3,* 205.

38. "The Govrs. Speech, to the Indians of the ffive Nations at Albany, the 7th instant," *MPCP, V. 3,* 197.

39. "The Govrs. Speech, to the Indians of the ffive Nations at Albany, the 7th instant," *MPCP, V. 3,* 198.
   For the Shawnee youth's testimony on Sawantaeny's words, see *MPCP, V. 3,* 150.

40. Compare the draft text with the final text: "At a Council held at Philadelphia, August 7th, 1722," *MPCP, V.3,* 194, with "The Govrs. Speech, to the Indians of the ffive Nations at Albany, the 7th instant," *MPCP, V. 3,* 198.

41. "The Govrs. Speech, to the Indians of the ffive Nations at Albany, the 7th instant," *MPCP, V. 3,* 198.

42. "The Govrs. Speech, to the Indians of the ffive Nations at Albany, the 7th instant," *MPCP, V. 3,* 198.

43. "The Govrs. Speech, to the Indians of the ffive Nations at Albany, the 7th instant," *MPCP, V.3,* 198. R. Livingston to A. Livingston, August 25, 1722, LVFP.
   To compare Keith's May remarks, see "Speech to the Conestogoes," "At a Council held at Philadelphia, May 11th, 1722," *MPCP, V.3,* 170.

44. Compare "At a Council held at Philadelphia, August 7th, 1722," *MPCP, V.3,* 194, with "The Govrs. Speech, to the Indians of the ffive Nations at Albany, the 7th instant," *MPCP, V. 3,* 198–99.

45. *MPCP, V.3,* 199.

46. *MPCP, V.3,* 199.

47. *MPCP, V.3,* 199.

48. See "The Answer made by the Indians of the Five Nations," *MPCP, V. 3,* 200.

49. *MPCP, V.3,* 200.

50. *MPCP, V.3,* 200.

51. *MPCP, V.3*, 201.

52. See "The Answer made by the Indians of the Five Nations," *MPCP, V.3*, 201.

53. See "The Answer made by the Indians of the Five Nations," *MPCP, V.3*, 201.

54. See "The Answer made by the Indians of the Five Nations," *MPCP, V.3*, 201.

55. See "The Answer made by the Indians of the Five Nations," *MPCP, V.3*, 201.

56. See Isaac Norris, handwritten notes, "October," NIL; Leeds, Verses for September 18, in Leeds, *American Almanack, 1722*; and Society of Friends, *Epistle*. See also "Albany the 10th day of Septr. Anno, 1722," *MPCP V.3*, 201.

57. See Minutes recorded at "Monthly Meeting held at ye 27 of ye 4th month 1722," Gwynedd Monthly Meeting Minutes 1714–1747, FHL.

On "The Friends Meeting House, Burlington," see Collins, *Reminiscences*, 16.

58. Society of Friends, *Epistle*, 4.

59. Society of Friends, *Epistle*, 4.

CHAPTER 22: JAMES LOGAN

1. James Logan to Simon Clement, November 22, 1722, PFP.

2. James Logan to Simon Clement, November 22, 1722, PFP and *MPCP, V.3*, 212-214.

3. *MPCP, V.3*, 212.

4. James Logan to John Penn, Philadelphia, 12 9ber [November] 1722, PFP. On Stenton, see Reinberger and McLean, *Philadelphia Country House*, 210–31.

5. See Logan, *Duties of Man*, 84.

Logan composed "The Duties of Man Deduced from Nature" over a twenty-year period from approximately 1722 to 1742. On its claim to fame as "the earliest purely philosophical treatise composed in America," see "Logan," in Shook, ed., *Dictionary*, 650. On Franklin's views of Logan's treatise, see Schactman, *Gentlemen Scientists*, 286.

6. Logan, *Duties of Man*, 323.

7. Logan, *Duties of Man*, 84. Hutcheson, *Inquiry*, xiv and xv. On Logan as a humanist and scientist, see Tolles, *James Logan*, 20–30.

8. Logan, *Duties of Man*, 274 and 275. For European philosophical context see Margit Pernau, "Civility and Barbarism: Emotions as Criteria of Difference," in Frevert et al., eds., *Emotional Lexicons*, 230–59.

The critical literature analyzing Enlightenment theories on race and beauty is vast; see Camp, "Black Is Beautiful," 679.

9. William Keith to Hannah Penn, 5 July 1722, PFP, and see JLL.

By embedding virtue and morality in naturally occurring senses and emotions, Logan, like Enlightenment thinkers generally, made all-encompassing claims for human potential. Yet Logan took care to demonstrate that non-Europeans could enact and encapsulate only lesser versions of virtue. Most of the globe's peoples somehow inhabited "zones of exception" within universalist paradigms. While everyone had the same moral obligations, only Europeans could reach the highest levels of moral achievement and, not incidentally, merit the greatest material rewards. On the concept of "zones of exception," see Lowe, *Intimacies*, 16.

10. Cloth listed in "29th Day 7th month 1722," and see the note on silk, "Philadelphia, 1722, 7th month ye 29th," JLD.

On the association of fashion with feminine frivolity, in spite of its economic centrality, see Haulman, *Politics of Fashion*.

11. "Satcheechoe," 27th 7th month 1722, "Peter Bizallion," 28th day 7th month 1722, "[Su]ndry Accots Supplied Satcheecho," 29th day 7th month 1722, JLD.

12. "The Secretary Communicated to Board a Letter he had received from the Gov.r of this Province, dated at Albany," *MPCP, V. 3*, 202.

13. *MPCP, V. 3*, 202.

14. James Logan to Samuel Clement, Philadelphia, 22 9ber, 1722, PFP. On the September heat, see Isaac Norris, handwritten notes "October," NIL.

15. James Logan to John Penn, Philadelphia 12th 9 Mo. [November] 1722, PFP. Isaac Norris to Charles Lloyd, Philadelphia, ye 3rd 9ber [November] 1722, INLB.

16. "Of the ECLIPSES," Leeds, *American Almanack, 1722*, n.p.

17. Hill, *Legacy for Children*, 15.

18. Hill, *Legacy for Children*, 31–32. See Ostler and Shoemaker, "Settler Colonialism."

19. Entry for 29th day 7th month 1722, JLD.

20. James Logan to John Penn, Philadelphia, 12 9ber [November] 1722,

and James Logan to Springett Penn, Philadelphia, 12 9ber [November] 1722, PFP.

21. James Logan to John Penn, Philadelphia, 12 9ber [November] 1722, PFP; "Summer fruits," Thomas, *Historical Account*, 33, 75, and 77.

22. James Logan to Springett Penn, Philadelphia, 12 9ber [November] 1722, PFP.

CHAPTER 23: STIFF OBSTINACY

1. On "gaol distemper"/"jail fever," see Siena, *Rotten Bodies*, chapter 3.
2. JCI.
3. On corn and harvest rituals, see Wallace, *Death and Rebirth*, 50–76. List of Native foodstuffs compiled from Thomas, *Historical Account*, 35, 36, 69, and 75.
4. On Native women's involvement in the fur trade qua "cloth trade," see Sleeper-Smith, *Indigenous Prosperity*, 6.
5. "The Indians Speech to his Excellency Sir William Keith," *MPCP*, V. 3, 215.

   On the defining importance of mobility in Iroquois culture, see Parmenter, *Edge of the Woods*.
6. See "Further Answer of Ye five Nations to His Excellency Alex[ander] Spotswood, Esq., Governor of Virginia in Albany 12 Septr. 1722," *DRNY*, 676.
7. See "Further Answer of Ye five Nations . . . 12 Septr. 1722," *DRNY*, 675.
8. See "Further Answer of Ye five Nations . . . 12 Septr. 1722," *DRNY*, 675–76. See Brooks, *Captives and Cousins*, and on Iroquois practices specifically, see Rushforth, *Bonds of Alliance*, 142. Though the Iroquois became increasingly embroiled in European-style commodification of captives over time, their priority remained "absorbing broken groups." See Snyder, *Slavery in Indian Country*, 117.
9. See "Further Answer of Ye five Nations . . . 12 Septr. 1722," *DRNY*, 676. On spatial consciousness and social reciprocity, see Parmenter, *Edge of the Woods*, x–xii.
10. On the lack of penal institutions among Indigenous peoples of the Los Angeles area prior to the arrival of the Spanish, see Hernández, *City of Inmates*; on Native maps of this period as reflections of geopolitical space, see Dubcovsky, *Informed Power*, 23–24.
11. *MCCP*, 216–18. And see Society of Friends, *Epistle*, 3.
12. Keith came under Quaker criticism for his love of a "risqué" show. See

Wendell, "Life and Writings of Sir William Keith," 95–96. On "flats," etc., see Canfield, ed., *Broadview Anthology*, xviii.

13. *MPCP, V. 3*, 203.

14. *MPCP, V. 3*, 203.

15. Later Logan adds to the record that "the same is N.B. inserted into the preceding minutes of Septr. 21st, as it was taken from the printed copy," *MPCP, V. 3*, 205.

16. "Advertisements," *AWM*, October 11, 1722, 4. On printer's ink, and the quotation praising ink of a "black complexion," see Wroth, *Colonial Printer*, 119. On the racial meanings of eighteenth-century commentary on complexions, see Block, *Colonial Complexions*.

    See Keith, *Treaty of Peace and Friendship*.

17. See "Advertisements," *AWM*, October 11, 1722, 4. A study of the *Pennsylvania Gazette* found that by the 1730s a single runaway ad could generate 70% of the revenue of a full year's newspaper subscription. See Waldstreicher, *Runaway America*, 24.

18. See "handsome, adj., adv., and n.," OED Online. June 2019. Oxford University Press.

    On the increased prevalence of sales of enslaved children in North American ports where slavers lacked the purchasing power to buy adult men, see O'Malley, *Final Passages*, 129–30.

19. On slavery, freedom, and the press, see Waldstreicher, *Runaway America*.

20. Moraley, *Infortunate*, 60–61 and 58.

21. See Keith, *Treaty of Peace and Friendship*, 2. On the work of "beaters," see Wroth, *Colonial Printer*, 81.

22. James Logan to Samuel Clement, Philadelphia 22 9ber [November] 1722, PFP.

23. See Keith, *Treaty of Peace and Friendship*, 8.

24. See Keith, *Treaty of Peace and Friendship*, 7.

25. Locke first published this work in 1690. The 1713 edition, published closest to the time of the Cartlidge case, is quoted; Locke, *Two Treatises*, 190.

26. On Indian concerns over sovereignty and justice, see John Smolenski, "The Death of Sawantaeny," in Pencak and Richter, *Friends and Enemies*, 118 and 121–22.

27. William Burnet to the Council of Trade and Plantations, New York, November 21, 1722, as transcribed in "America and West Indies: November 1722," *CSP*, 158–77.

28. Keith, *Letter*, 9–10.

29. On the Iroquois use of occasions of grief and condolence as opportunities for creating close connections through suffering; and on the "Tree of Peace" as an integral symbol in the founding epic of the Five Nations of the Haudenosaunee, see Williams, *Linking Arms Together*, 54 and 58–60.

30. *MPCP*, *V. 3*, 209. On the break in the heat, see Norris, handwritten notes, "October," NIL.

31. "Colonel Alexander Spotswood to Sir William Keith, Philadelphia, 8 October 1722," *MPCP*, *V. 3*, 206.

32. For Le Tort's October 18 meeting with "the Indians of Conestogoe" see *MPCP*, *V. 3*, 215. The speech he read was written in council on October 11.

33. "Message to the Indians," draft text, *MPCP*, *V. 3*, 210 and 212.

34. "Answer . . . received from Conestogoe" *MPCP*, *V. 3*, 215.

35. "Answer . . . received from Conestogoe," *MPCP*, *V. 3*, 215.

36. "From the Shawanna King to His Excellency Sir William Keith," *MPCP*, *V. 3*, 215. These escapees from Virginia were never again mentioned in *MPCP*, suggesting that they remained free.

37. Aquila Rose, "To J———n C———dge, Esq. on His Generous Entertainment of Sir William Keith, and his Company, at Conestogoe," in Rose, *Poems*, 26.

38. See Rose, "To J———n C———dge." See "Inventory of . . . John Cartlidge," and for descriptions of Pennsylvania soil see Moraley, *Infortunate*, 71. John's death is discussed in James Logan to Simon Clement, 22 November 1722, PFP.

39. Elizabeth Carthedge [Cartlidge], "Admin Bond fil'd the 29th 9th 1722," Wills and Administrations Index, 1714–1923, CCAR.

CHAPTER 24: CIVILITY'S LAST WORD

1. British prison records note: "William Keith, for an action of debt . . . Sir Wm stands charged now in Execution in the Fleet Prison." See Entry 1409, Sir Wm Keith Bart, December 30, 1735, *London, England, King's Bench and Fleet Prison Discharge Books and Prisoner Lists, 1734–1862*, Series PRIS 10. The National Archives, Kew, England.

   For the prison description, see *Report . . . Relating to the Fleet Street Prison*.

2. Civility's visit on May 18 is recorded in *MPCP*, *V. 3*, 262. Prison details, *MCCP*, 206 and 229.

3. Barnes, *Evolution of Penology*, 68–70.

4. "Ye late Great Rains," *MCCP*, 230. On the *Shaw* and its human cargo, see "Advertisements," *AWM*, May 23, 1723, 4; "An Act to prevent Sickly vessels arriving in in this Province," *MPCP*, *V. 3*, 112.

5. On Whiwhinjac, see *MPCP*, *V. 3*, 216–18.

6. See "Speech of Whiwhinjac, King of the Ganawese Indians, delivered to the Governor . . . by Civility," *MPCP*, *V. 3*, 217.

   On Indian goals as "unity with diversity" see Schutt, *Peoples of the River Valleys*, 150.

7. "Speech of Whiwhinjac," *MPCP*, *V. 3*, 217. Knowing that there were "great rains" around the time of Civility's visit and noting that he uses the metaphor of "streams of water" suggests that Civility was inspired by actual rain on the courthouse windows.

8. "Speech of Whiwhinjac," *MPCP*, *V. 3*, 217–18.

9. "Speech of Whiwhinjac," *MPCP*, *V. 3*, 218.

10. "Speech of Whiwhinjac," *MPCP*, *V. 3*, 218.

11. "Speech of Whiwhinjac," *MPCP*, *V. 3*, 218.

12. *MPCP*, *V. 3*, 216. For the subsequent debate over whether to "restore the Lesser Seal into the Custody of Mr. Logan, as Secretary of the Government" see *MPCP*, *V. 3*, 252.

13. *MPCP*, *V. 3*, 218.

14. *MPCP*, *V. 3*, 219. Whiwhinjac attended Logan's March inquiry at Conestoga along with Savannah and "a Shawanese Woman, named Weynepreeueyta [an alternate spelling of Weenepeeweytah], Cousin to Savannah, Chief of that Nation." *MPCP*, *V. 3*, 150. Information on Harlan appears in Harlan, *History and Genealogy*, 11–12.

15. On Kirk's appointment as a justice, *MPCP*, *V. 3*, 254.

    On diplomatic work as women's work among the Native peoples of Pennsylvania, see Fur, *Nation of Women*.

16. On the marriage of Elizabeth Bartram Cartlidge and Andrew Cornish, including their residence in John and Elizabeth's former house, see "John Cartledge, The King's First Magistrate," in *Historical Papers . . . of . . . Lancaster*, 164. On Cornish's rise, see *MPCP*, *V. 3*, 256, 309, and 345.

17. *MPCP*, *V. 3*, 219.

18. *MPCP*, *V. 3*, 220.

19. *MPCP*, *V. 3*, 218 and 220–21.

20. *MPCP*, *V. 3*, 221.

21. *MPCP*, *V. 3*, 221. On how Native property was "embedded in social relations," see Greer, *Property and Dispossession*, 62.

22. Wiggoneeheenah, "Know all men by these presents . . ." April 8, 1725, catalogued as "Indian Deed to E. Cartlidge for Land," LFP.

23. *MPCP, V. 4, 93*

24. See James Logan to John Penn, 12 November 1722, PFP.

25. William Penn requested the right to confer honors and titles within his colony when first designing his charter, but the request was denied by the crown. See PWP, *V. 2*, 62. On the French "chevalier" class in New France, see Crouch, *Nobility Lost*, 29. See also Greer, *Property and Dispossession*.

26. On Keith's life and death, see Keith, "Sir William Keith"; Horle et al., *Lawmaking and Legislators*, 561–89; and see Spencer, ed., *Bloomsbury Encyclopedia*, 606–9. On Fountain Low, see Reinberger and McLean, *Philadelphia Country House*, 205–9.

On Logan's invitation to return to (and decline of) the office of secretary, see *MPCP, V. 3, 252*.

27. James Logan to Thomas Story, "Philadelphia, 25th 8ber, 1724" and "Philadelphia, 16th of 9th Month, 1734," as quoted in Armistead, ed., *Memoirs of James Logan*, 96 and 113.

On Stenton, see "Establishing an Architectural Norm: Stenton and Its Property," in Reinberger and McLean, *Philadelphia Country House*, 210–31.

See Tolles, *James Logan*. For more recent critical commentary on Logan's activities as a colonial fur trader and land speculator, see Richter, *Trade, Land, Power*, 160–61, and see Soderlund, *Lenape Country*, 175. For current commentary on his activities as a slaveholder, see Soderlund, *Quakers and Slavery*, 169.

28. On Franklin's prank on Titan Leeds, see Isaacson, *Benjamin Franklin*, 96.

29. See Logan in Valenti, ed., *Of the Duties of Man*, 311. On Logan, Franklin, and the Free Library, see Tolles, *James Logan*, 213–17.

30. Civility's story challenges persistent claims that Indians were culturally backward in comparison to Europeans. See O'Brien, *Firsting and Lasting*, xi–xxvi.

31. The treaty is officially identified as "The Great Treaty of 1722 between the Five Nations, the Mahicans, and the Colonies of New York, Virginia, and Pennsylvania," in Fassbender et al., eds., *Oxford Handbook*, 796.

BIBLIOGRAPHY

PRIMARY SOURCES

Alexander, Edward Port, ed. *The Journal of John Fontaine*. Williamsburg: The Colonial Williamsburg Foundation, 1972.

Armstrong, Edward, ed. *Correspondence between William Penn and James Logan . . . and Others . . .* with Notes by the Late Mrs. Deborah Logan, V. 2. Philadelphia: J. B. Lippincott and Co., 1872.

Bartram, John. *Observations on the Inhabitants, Climate, Soil, Rivers, Productions, Animals, and Other Matters Worthy of Notice Made by Mr. John Bartram in his Travels from Pensilvania . . .* London: Whiston and White, 1751.

Bradford, William. *The Secretary's Guide*. New York: Bradford, 1729.

Carwitham, J. "A View of Fort George with the city of New York, from the SW." London: Carington Bowles, [1740].

Conductor Generalis: The Office, Duty, and Authority of Justices of the Peace. Philadelphia: Andrew Bradford, 1722.

Dickinson, Jonathan. *Gods Protecting Providence Man's Surest Help and Defence in the Times of the Greatest Difficulty and Most Imminent Danger; Evidenced in the Remarkable Deliverance of Divers Persons, from the Devouring Waves of the Sea, amongst which They Suffered Shipwrack. And also from the More Cruelly Devouring Jawes of the Inhuman Canibals of Florida*. Philadelphia: Reinier Jansen, 1699.

Evans, Lewis. *A Map of Pensilvania, New-Jersey, New-York, and the Three Delaware Counties*. Philadelphia, 1749. Map, Geography and Map Division, Library of Congress.

Gehring, Charles T., ed. *Fort Orange Court Minutes, 1652–1660*. Syracuse: Syracuse University, 1990.

Harris, John. *Astronomical Dialogues between a Gentleman and a Lady.* London: Printed by T. Wood for Benj Cowse, 1719.

———. "A South Prospect of ye Flourishing City of New York in the Province of New York in America." London: William Burgis, 1719.

Hill, Hannah. *A Legacy for Children, Being Some of the Last Exions and Dying Sayings of Hannah Hill, Junr.* Philadelphia: Andrew Bradford, 1717.

Holm, Thomas Companius. *A Vocabulary of Susquehannock.* Translated by Peter Stephen Duponceau. Merchantville, New Jersey: Evolution, 2007.

Hutcheson, Francis. *An Inquiry into the Original of our Ideas of Beauty and Virtue, 3rd. ed.* London: J. & J. Knapton, 1729.

Kalm, Peter. *Travels into North America.* Translated by John Reinhold Foster. London: T. Lowndes, 1771.

Keith, George. *Geography and Navigation Compleated: Being a New Theory and Method Whereby the True Longitude of Any Place in the World May be Found.* London: B. Aylmer, 1709.

Keith, William. *A Collection of Papers and Other Tracts.* London: Printed by and for J. Mechell at the King's Arms, 1740.

———. *An Essay on the Education of a Young British Nobleman.* London: A. Millar, 1730.

———. *A Letter to His Majesty's Justices of the Peace for the County of Chester, with the Governor's speech from the Bench at a Court of Oyer and Terminer, held at Chester the 15th Day of April, 1718.* Philadelphia: Andrew Bradford, 1718.

———. *The Particulars of an Indian Treaty at Conestogoe, between his Excellency Sir William Keith, Bart. Governor of Pennsylvania, and the Deputies of the Five Nations. Published at the Request of the Gentlemen who Were Present and Waited upon the Governor in His Journey.* Philadelphia: Andrew Bradford, [1721].

———. *The Particulars of an Indian Treaty at Conestogoe, between his Excellency Sir William Keith, Bart. Governor of Pennsylvania, and the Deputies of the Five Nations. Published at the Request of the Gentlemen who Were Present and Waited upon the Governor in His Journey.* London: Printed from the Copy Published in Philadelphia by A. Bradford; sold at the Pennsylvania Coffee House [1722].

———. *The Particulars of an Indian Treaty at Conestogoe, between his Excellency Sir William Keith, Bart. Governor of Pennsylvania, and the Deputies of the Five Nations. Published at the Request of the Gentlemen who Were Present and Waited upon the Governor in His Journey.* Dublin: Reprinted by Elizabeth Sadler, for Samuel Fuller, at the Globe and Scales in Meath Street, 1723.

————. *A Treaty of Peace and Friendship Made . . . at Albany in the Month of September, 1722.* Philadelphia: Andrew Bradford, 1722.

Leeds, Titan. *The American Almanack for the Year of Christian Account 1722.* Philadelphia: Bradford, [1721].

Lidgate, John. *The Beasts in Power, or Robin's song with an Old Cat's Prophesy.* London: n.p., 1709.

Life and Character of a Strange He-Monster, Lately Arriv'd in London from an English Colony in America. London: n.p., [1726].

Locke, John. *Two Treatises of Government.* London: John Churchill, 1713.

Logan, James. *Of the Duties of Man as They May Be Deduced from Nature.* Edited by Philip Valenti. Philadelphia: Printed for the Editor, 2013.

Logan, James, trans. *Cato's Moral Distiches Englished in Couplets.* Philadelphia: Printed and sold by B. Franklin, 1735.

Lydgate, John. *The Hystorye, Sege and Dystruccyon of Troye.* London: Printed by Richard Pynson, 1513.

Meriton, George. *Conductor Generalis.* London: Printed for Geo. Sawbridge, A. Crook, W. Leak, A. Roper, F. Tyton, J. Place, W. Place, J. Starkey, T. Basset, R. Pawlet, and S. Heyrick . . . , 1674.

Moll, Herman. *The British Empire in America.* London: John Nicholson, 1708.

————. *Atlas Geographicus; Or A Compleat Ssytem of Geography, Ancient and Modern, Volume 5.* [London]: John Knutt [1711].

————. *The British Empire in America, 2nd Ed. Corrected.* London: J. Brotherton, 1741.

Montesquieu, Charles de Secondat, Baron de. *The Spirit of Laws. Translated from the French of M. de Secondat, Baron de Montesquieu. A new translation. In three volumes. . . .* Berwick, England: R. Taylor, 1770.

Moraley, William. *The Infortunate: The Voyage and Adventures of William Moraley, An Indentured Servant, 2d. ed.* Edited by Susan E. Klepp and Billy G. Smith. University Park: Penn State University, 2005.

Nelson, William, ed. *Documents Relating to the Colonial History of the State of New Jersey, Volume 23, Calendar of New Jersey Wills, Volume 1 1670–1730.* Paterson: Printing and Publishing co., 1901.

Penn, William. *A Letter from William Penn to the Free Society of Traders.* London: Andrew Sowle, 1683.

Province of Pennsylvania. *The Laws of the Province of Pennsylvania, Passed by the Governour and General Assemblies of Said Province, Held at Philadelphia in the years 1715, 1717 and 1718.* Philadelphia: Bradford, [1718].

————. *Acts of the Province of Pennsylvania pass'd in the General Assembly held at Philadelphia* (Philadelphia: Bradford, 1722).

Reid, Andrew, and John Gray, eds. *The Philosophical Transactions (from the Year 1720 to the Year 1732)*. London: William Innys and Richard Manby, Printers to the Royal Society, 1733.

A Report from the Committee Appointed to Enquire into the State of the Goals of this Kingdom: Relating to the Fleet Prison. London: Robert Knaplock, 1729.

Rose, Aquila. *Poems on Several Occasions*. Philadelphia: Collected and Published by His Son, Joseph Rose and Printed at the New Printing Office, 1740.

Salvucci, Claudio R., ed. *A Vocabulary of Susquehannock, Thomas Campanius Holm*. Merchantville, New Jersey: Evolution Publishing, 2007.

Shaftesbury, Anthony, Earl of. *Characteristicks of Men, Manners, Opinions, Times, in Three Volumes, the 2nd Ed. Corrected*. London: John Darby, 1714.

Society of Friends. *An Exhortation and Caution to Friends Concerning Buying or Keeping of Negroes*. New York: Printed by William Bradford, 1693.

————. *An Epistle from Our Yearly Meeting in Burlington . . . from the 15th to the 19th of the Seventh Month 1722*. Philadelphia: Bradford, 1722.

Smith, Adam. *Adam Smith: The Theory of Moral Sentiments*. Edited by Knud Haakonssen. Cambridge: Cambridge University, 2002.

Thomas, Gabriel. *An Historical and Geographical Account of the Province and Country of Pennsylvania*. London: A Baldwin, 1698.

Thomas, Vincent. *An Explicatory Catechism*. Boston: reprinted by John Allen for Nicholas Boone, 1711.

Trenchard, John. *The Fifth Collection of Cato's Political Letters in the London Journal*. London: J. Peele [1721].

Whitlocke, Bulstrode. *History of England*. London: Curll & Pemberton, 1713.

SECONDARY SOURCES

Anderson, Jennifer L. *Mahogany: The Costs of Luxury in Early America*. Cambridge: Harvard University, 2012.

Anderson, Virginia DeJohn. *Creatures of Empire: How Domestic Animals Transformed Early America*. Oxford: Oxford University, 2004.

Armitage, David. *The Ideological Origins of the British Empire*. Cambridge: Cambridge University, 2000.

Armory, Hugh, and David D. Hall, eds. *The Colonial Book Trade in the Atlantic World*. Chapel Hill: University of North Carolina, 2006.

Ashmead, Henry Graham. *Historical Sketch of Chester on Delaware*. Chester: Republican Steam Printing House, 1883.

Aquila, Richard. *The Iroquois Restoration: Iroquois Diplomacy on the Colonial Frontier, 1701–1754.* Lincoln: University of Nebraska, 1997.

Axtell, James. *Natives and Newcomers: The Cultural Origins of North America.* New York: Oxford University, 2000.

Banks, Kenneth J. *Chasing Empire Across the Sea: Communications and the State in the French Atlantic, 1713–1763.* Montreal: McGill-Queen's University, 2002.

Banner, Stuart. *The Death Penalty: An American History.* Cambridge: Harvard University, 2009.

Barbeau, C. M. "Iroquois Clans and Phratries." *American Anthropologist* 19 (1917): 392–402.

Barnes, Harry Elmer. "The Criminal Codes and Penal Institutions of Colonial Pennsylvania." *Bulletin of Friends' Historical Society of Philadelphia* 11, no. 2 (Autumn 1922), 68–84.

————. *The Evolution of Penology in Pennsylvania: A Study in American Social History.* Indianapolis: Bobbs-Merrill Co., 1927.

Barr, Daniel P. "Did Pennsylvania Have a Middle Ground? Examining Indian-White Relations in the Eighteenth-Century Pennsylvania Frontier." *Pennsylvania Magazine of History and Biography* 136, no. 4 (October 2012): 337–63.

Barr, Juliana. *Peace Came in the Form of a Woman: Indians and Spaniards in the Texas Borderlands.* Chapel Hill: UNC, 2007.

Barr, Juliana, and Edward Countryman, eds. *Contested Spaces of Early America.* Philadelphia: University of Pennsylvania, 2014.

Barrow, William J. "Black Writing Ink of the Colonial Period." *The American Archivist* 11, no. 4 (October 1948): 291–307.

Benson, Evelyn A. "The Huguenot Letorts, First Christian Family on the Conestoga." *Journal of the Lancaster County Historical Society* 65, no. 2 (1961): 92–105.

Berlin, Ira. *Many Thousands Gone: The First Two Centuries of Slavery in North America.* Cambridge: Harvard University, 1998.

Blackburn, Robin. *The Making of New World Slavery.* New York: Verso, 1998.

Block, Sharon. *Colonial Complexions: Race and Bodies in Eighteenth-Century America.* Philadelphia: UPenn, 2018.

Boogher, William F. *Miscellaneous Americana: A Collection of History, Biography, and Genealogy.* Philadelphia: Dando Printing and Publishing, 1895.

Bonomi, Patricia U. *A Factious People: Politics and Society in Colonial New York.* Ithaca: Cornell University, 2014.

Bowden, Henry Warner. *Dictionary of American Religious Biography*, 2nd ed. Westport, CT: Greenwood, 1993.

Braund, Katherine E. Holland. *Deerskins and Duffles: The Creek Indian Trade with Anglo America, 1685–1815*. Lincoln: University of Nebraska, 2008.

Brewer, Holly. *By Birth or Consent: Children, Law, and the Anglo-American Revolution in Authority*. Chapel Hill: OIEAHC/UNC, 2005.

Brooks, Lisa Tanya. *The Common Pot: The Recovery of Native Space in the Northeast*. Minneapolis: University of Minnesota, 2008.

Brooks, James F. *Captives and Cousins: Slavery, Kinship, and Community in the Southwest Borderlands*. Chapel Hill: OIEAHC/UNC, 2002.

———. *Our Beloved Kin: A New History of King Philip's War*. New Haven: Yale University, 2019.

Brown, Richard F., ed. *The Transformation of the Gulf South in the Seventeenth Century*. Lincoln: University of Nebraska, 2007.

Burnard, Trevor. "Slave Naming Patterns: Onomastics and the Taxonomy of Race in Eighteenth-Century Jamaica." *The Journal of Interdisciplinary History* 31, no. 3 (Winter, 2001): 325–46.

Bushman, Richard L. *The Refinement of America: Persons, Houses, Cities*. New York: Vintage, 1992.

Camp, Stephanie M. H. "Black Is Beautiful: An American History." *The Journal of Southern History* 81, no. 3 (2015): 675–90.

———. *Closer to Freedom: Enslaved Women & Everyday Resistance in the Plantation South*. Chapel Hill: UNC, 2005.

Canfield, J. Douglas, ed. *The Broadview Anthology of Restoration and Early Eighteenth-Century Drama*. Toronto: Broadview, 2001.

Carey, Brycchan. *From Peace to Freedom: Quaker Rhetoric and the Birth of American Antislavery, 1657–1761*. New Haven: Yale University, 2012.

Cave, Alfred A. *The Pequot War*. Amherst: University of Massachusetts, 1996.

Cayton, Andrew R. L., and Fredrika J. Teute, eds. *Contact Points: American Frontiers from the Mohawk Valley to the Mississippi, 1750–1830*. Chapel Hill, UNC, 1998.

Chaplin, Joyce E. *An Anxious Pursuit: Agricultural Innovation and Modernity in the Lower South, 1730–1815*. Chapel Hill: OIEAHC/UNC, 1993.

———. *Subject Matter: Technology, the Body, and Science on the Anglo-American Frontier, 1500–1676*. Cambridge: Harvard University, 2009.

Cohen, Daniel. *Pillars of Salt, Monuments of Grace: New England Crime Literature and the Origins of American Popular Culture, 1674–1860*. New York: Oxford, 1993.

Cohen, Matt. *The Networked Wilderness: Communicating in Early New England*. Minneapolis: University of Minnesota, 2010.

Cohen, Matt, and Jeffrey Glover, eds. *Colonial Mediascapes: Sensory Worlds of the Early Americas*. Lincoln: University of Nebraska, 2014.

Collins, John. *Reminiscences of Isaac and Rachael (Budd) Collins*. Philadelphia: J. B. Lippincott, 1893.

Cotter, John L., et al. *The Buried Past, An Archeological History of Philadelphia*. Philadelphia: UPenn, 1992.

Craig, Peter S. "Jacob & Catharina Van der Veer and their Vandever Descendants." *Swedish Colonial News* 3, no. 10 (Spring, 2009).

Crawford, Matthew James. *The Andean Wonder Drug Cinchona Bark and Imperial Science in the Spanish Atlantic, 1630–1800*. Pittsburgh: University of Pittsburgh, 2016.

Cronon, William. *Changes in the Land: Indians, Colonists, and the Ecology of New England*. New York: Hill and Wang, 2003.

Crosby, Alfred W. Jr. *The Columbian Exchange: Biological and Cultural Consequences of 1492*, 30th Anniversary ed. Westport, CT: Greenwood Publishing, 2003.

Crouch, Christian. *Nobility Lost: French and Canadian Martial Cultures, Indians, and the End of New France*. Ithaca: Cornell University, 2004.

Crozier, William Armstrong. *Crozier's General Armory: A Registry of American Families Entitled to Coat Armor*. Baltimore: Genealogical Publishing Company, 1972.

Davies, Surekha. *Renaissance Ethnography and the Invention of the Human: New Worlds, Maps and Monsters*. Cambridge: Cambridge University, 2016.

Dean, John Ward, ed. *The Historical Magazine and Notes and Queries Concerning the Antiquities, History and Biography of America, Volume 1*. Boston: C. Benjamin Richardson, 1857.

Deloria, Philip J. "What Is the Middle Ground Anyway?" *William and Mary Quarterly* 63, no. 1 (January 2006): 15–22.

Deloria, Vine Jr. and David E. Wilkins. *Tribes, Treaties, and Constitutional Tribulations*. Austin: University of Texas Press, 1999.

DeLucia, Christine M. *Memory Lands: King Philip's War and the Place of Violence in the Northeast*. New Haven: Yale University, 2018.

Demos, John. *A Little Commonwealth: Family Life in Plymouth Colony*. New York: Oxford University, 2000.

Dennis, Matthew. *Cultivating a Landscape of Peace: Iroquois European Encounters in Seventeenth-Century America*. Ithaca: Cornell University, 1995.

Diaz-Granados, Carol, and James R. Duncan, eds. *The Rock Art of Eastern North America: Capturing Images and Insight.* Tuscaloosa: University of Alabama, 2004.

Dixon, John M., and Karim M. Tiro, eds. *Cadwallader Colden, The History of the Five Indian Nations Depending on the Province of New-York in America: A Critical Edition.* Ithaca: Cornell University, 2017.

Donehoo, George P. *Indian Villages and Place Names in Pennsylvania.* Harrisburg: Telegraph, 1928.

Dubcovsky, Alejandra. *Informed Power: Communication in the Early American South.* Cambridge: Harvard University, 2016.

Duval, Kathleen. *The Native Ground: Indians and Colonists in the Heart of the Continent.* Philadelphia: UPenn, 2011.

Eacott, Jonathan. *Selling Empire: India in the Making of Britain and America, 1600–1830.* Chapel Hill: OIEAHC/UNC, 2016.

Edelson, S. Max. *The New Map of Empire: How Britain Imagined America Before Independence.* Cambridge: Harvard University, 2017.

Edmonson, James M. *American Surgical Instruments: The History of Their Manufacture.* San Francisco: Norman Publishing, 1997.

Egle, William Henry. *Notes and Queries: Historical, Biographical, and Genealogical, Chiefly Relating to Interior Pennsylvania, Volume 2.* Harrisburg: Harrisburg Publishing Company, 1895.

Eisenstadt, Peter. "Almanacs and the Disenchantment of Early America." *Pennsylvania History* 65, no. 2 (Spring 1998): 143–69.

Elliot, J. H. *Empires of the Atlantic World: Britain and Spain in America, 1492–1830.* New Haven: Yale University, 2006.

Ellis, Elizabeth. "The Many Ties of the Petites Nations: Relationships, Power, and Diplomacy in the Lower Mississippi Valley, 1685–1785." PhD Dissertation, University of North Carolina, 2015.

Ethridge, Robbie, and Sheri M. Shuck-Hall, eds. *Mapping the Mississippian Shatter Zone: The Colonial Indian Slave Trade and Regional Instability in the American South.* Lincoln: University of Nebraska, 2009.

Eustace, Nicole. *Passion Is the Gale: Emotion, Power, and the Coming of the American Revolution.* Chapel Hill: OIEAHC/UNC, 2008.

Fassbender, Bardo, et al., eds. *The Oxford Handbook of the History of International Law.* Oxford: Oxford University, 2012.

Fennimore, Donald L., and Frank L. Hohmann Jr. *Stretch: America's First Family of Clockmakers.* Winterthur : Winterthur Museum, 2013.

Fenton, William. *Iroquois Journey: An Anthropologist Remembers.* Lincoln: University of Nebraska, 2007.

Fenton, William, ed. *Parker on the Iroquois . . . The Constitution of the Five Nations*. New York: Syracuse University, 1981.

Finger, Stanley. *Dr. Franklin's Medicine*. Philadelphia: UPenn, 2012.

Finlay, Michael. *Western Writing Implements in the Age of the Quill Pen*. New York: Plains Books, 1990.

Foster, Michael K., Jack Campisis, and Marianne Mithun, eds. *Extending the Rafters: Interdisciplinary Approaches to Iroquoian Studies*. Albany: SUNY, 1984.

Frevert, Ute, et al., eds. *Emotional Lexicons: Continuity and Change in the Vocabulary of Feeling, 1700–2000*. Oxford: Oxford University, 2014.

Fuentes, Marisa. *Dispossessed Lives: Enslaved Women, Violence, and the Archive*. Philadelphia: UPenn, 2016.

Fur, Gunlög. *A Nation of Women: Gender and Colonial Encounters Among the Delaware Indians*. Philadelphia: UPenn, 2012.

Futhey, J. Smith, and Gilbert Cope. *History of Chester County, Pennsylvania, with Geological and Biographical Sketches*. Philadelphia: Loui H. Everts, 1881.

Gallay, Alan. *The Indian Slave Trade: The Rise of the English Empire in the American South*. New Haven: Yale University, 2008.

Gallup-Diaz, Igancio, ed., *The World of Colonial America: An Atlantic Handbook*. New York: Routledge, 2017.

Gerbner, Katherine. "Antislavery in Print: The Germantown Protests, the 'Exhortation,' and the Seventeenth-Century Quaker Debate on Slavery." *Early American Studies* 9, no. 3 (Fall 2011): 552–75.

Gillingham, Harrold E. "Notes and Documents: The Estate of Jonathan Dickinson (1663–1722)." *The Pennsylvania Magazine of History and Biography* 59, no. 4 (October 1935): 420–29.

Gitlin, Jay, Barbara Berglund, and Adam Areson, eds. *Frontier Cities: Encounters at the Crossroads of Empire*. Philadelphia: UPenn, 2013.

Goetz, Rebecca. *The Baptism of Early Virginia: How Christianity Created Race*. Baltimore: Johns Hopkins University, 2012.

Gorn, Elliott J. " 'Gouge and Bite, Pull Hair and Scratch' ": The Social Significance of Fighting in the Southern Backcountry." *American Historical Review* 40 (1985), 18–43.

Grandjean, Katherine. *American Passage: The Communications Frontier in Early New England*. Cambridge: Harvard University, 2015.

Greenblatt, Stephen. *Marvelous Possessions: The Wonder of the New World*. Chicago: University of Chicago, 1991, 2017.

Greene, Jack P. *Evaluating Empire and Confronting Colonialism in Eighteenth-Century Britain*. Cambridge: Cambridge University, 2013.

Greer, Allan. *The People of New France.* Toronto: University of Toronto, 1997.

———. *Property and Dispossession: Natives, Empires, and Land in Early Modern North America.* Cambridge: Cambridge University, 2018.

Guthke, Karl S. *Last Words: Variations on a Theme in Cultural History.* Princeton: Princeton University, 1992.

Hahn, Steven C. *The Invention of the Creek Nation.* Lincoln: University of Nebraska, 2004.

Hall, Joseph M. Jr. *Zamumo's Gifts: Indo-European Exchange in the Colonial Southeast.* Philadelphia: UPenn, 2009.

Halttunen, Karen. *Murder Most Foul: The Killer and the American Gothic Imagination.* Cambridge: Harvard University, 1998.

Hämäläinen, Pekka. *The Comanche Empire.* New Haven: Yale University, 2009.

Hanna, Mark. *The Wilderness Trail or the Ventures and Adventures of Pennsylvania Traders on the Allegheny Path.* New York: G. P. Putnam's, Sons, 1911.

Harlan, Alpheus H. *History and Genealogy of the Harlan Family.* Baltimore: Lord Baltimore, 1941.

Haulman, Kate. *The Politics of Fashion in Eighteenth-Century America.* Chapel Hill: UNC, 2011.

Hay, Douglas, et al., eds. *Albion's Fatal Tree: Crime and Society in Eighteenth-Century England.* New York: Verso, revised edition 2011.

Hayburn, Timothy. "Who Should Die?: The Evolution of Capital Punishment in Pennsylvania, 1681–1794." PhD dissertation, Lehigh University, 2011.

Hayley, K.H.D. *The First Earl of Shaftesbury.* Oxford: Clarendon, 1968.

Hazard, Samuel, ed. Samuel *The Register of Pennsylvania, Volume 2.* Philadelphia: W. F. Geddes, 1828.

———. *The Historical Register of Pennsylvania* 5, no. 21. Philadelphia: n.p., 1830, 321–22.

Hernández, Kelly. *City of Inmates: Conquest, Rebellion and the Rise of Human Caging in Los Angeles, 1771–1965.* Chapel Hill: UNC, 2017.

Hinderaker, Eric. *Elusive Empires: Constructing Colonialism in the Ohio Valley, 1673–1800.* Cambridge: Cambridge University, 1997.

Hoffman, Ronald. *Princes of Ireland, Planters of Maryland: A Carroll Saga, 1500–1782.* Chapel Hill: OIEAHC/UNC, 2002.

Horle, Craig W. *Lawmaking and Legislators in Pennsylvania: 1710–1756.* Philadelphia: UPenn, 1997.

Horning, Audrey J. *Ireland in the Virginia Sea: Colonialism in the British Atlantic.* Chapel Hill: OIEAHC/UNC, 2013.

Isaacson, Walter. *Benjamin Franklin: An American Life*. New York: Simon & Schuster, 2004.

Jennings, Francis. *The Ambiguous Iroquois Empire: The Covenant Chain Confederation of Indian Tribes with English Colonies*. New York: Norton, 1984.

————. *The History and Culture of Iroquois Diplomacy: An Interdisciplinary Guide to the Treaties of the Six Nations and Their League*. Syracuse: Syracuse University, 1985.

————. "The Indian Trade of the Susquehanna Valley." *Proceedings of the American Philosophical Society* 110, no. 6 (December 16, 1966): 406–24.

Johansen, Bruce E. *The Encyclopedia of Native American Legal Tradition*. Westport, CT: Greenwood, 1998.

Johnson, Laura E. " 'Goods to Clothe Themselves': Native Consumers and Native Images on the Pennsylvania Trading Frontier, 1712–1760." *Winterthur Portfolio* 43, no. 1 (Spring 2009): 115–40.

Jordan, Kurt A. *The Seneca Restoration, 1715–1754: An Iroquois Local Political Economy*. Gainesville: University of Florida, 2008.

Juster, Susan. *Disorderly Women: Sexual Politics and Evangelicalism in Revolutionary New England*. Ithaca: Cornell University, 1996.

Kent, Barry C. *Susquehanna's Indians*. Harrisburg: Pennsylvania Historical and Museum Commission, 1993.

Keith, Charles P. "Sir William Keith." *The Pennsylvania Magazine of History and Biography* 12, no. 1 (1888): 1–33.

Kelly, James. *Gallows Speeches from Eighteenth-Century Ireland*. Dublin: Four Courts, 2001.

Kelton, Paul. "Avoiding the Smallpox Spirits: Colonial Epidemics and Southeastern Indian Survival," *Ethnohistory*, 51 no. 1 (Winter 2004): 45–71.

Kimball, Hope P., and Bruce Henson. *Governor's Houses and State Houses of British Colonial America, 1607–1783: An Historical, Architectural, and Archeological Survey*. Jefferson, North Carolina: McFarland & Co., 2017.

Knott, Sarah. *Mother Is a Verb: An Unconventional History*. New York: Farrar, Straus & Giroux, 2019.

Kotowski, Peter B. " 'The Best Poor Man's Country?': William Penn, Quakers, and Unfree Labor in Atlantic Pennsylvania." PhD Dissertation, Chicago: Loyola University, 2016.

Kuhn, Robert D., and Martha L. Sempowski. "A New Approach to Dating the League of the Iroquois." *American Antiquity* 66, no. 2 (April 2001): 301–14.

Kupperman, Karen Ordahl. "Fear of Hot Climates in the Anglo-American

Colonial Experience." *William and Mary Quarterly* 41, no 2 (April 1994): 213–40.

Lakomäki, Sami. *Gathering Together: The Shawnee People Through Diaspora and Nationhood, 1600–1870*. New Haven: Yale University, 2014.

Lancaster, County of. *Historical Papers and Addresses of the Lancaster County Historical Society, Volume XII*. Lancaster, PA: Lancaster County Historical Society, 1908.

———. *Historical Papers and Addresses of the Lancaster County Historical Society, Volume XXI*. Lancaster, PA: Lancaster County Historical Society, 1917.

———. *Papers Read before the Lancaster County Historical Society, Volume XXXVII*. Lancaster, PA: Lancaster County Historical Society, 1933.

Lemon, James T. *The Best Poor Man's Country: A Geographical Study of Southeastern Pennsylvania*. New York: Norton, 1976.

Lepore, Jill. *The Name of War: King Philip's War and the Origins of American Identity*. New York: Vintage, 2009.

Lesser, Charles H. *South Carolina Begins: The Records of the Proprietary Colony, 1663–1721*. Columbia: South Carolina Department of Archives and History, 1995.

Lindsey, Jack L. "Colonial Philadelphia and the Cadwalader Family." *Philadelphia Museum of Art Bulletin 91, no. 384/385* (Autumn 1996): 5–9.

Linebaugh, Peter. *The London Hanged: Crime and Civil Society in the Eighteenth Century*. London: Verso, 2006.

Lines, Ruth. *The Visual History of the American Family*. Flint: University of Michigan, 1987.

Lloyd, William H. Jr. "The Courts of Pennsylvania in the Eighteenth Century Prior to the Revolution." *UPenn Law Review and American Law Register* 56, No. 1, Volume 47 New Series (January 1908): 28–51, 36.

Lowe, Lisa. *The Intimacies of Four Continents*. Durham: Duke University, 2015.

Lovell, Margareta M. *Art in a Season of Revolution: Painters, Artisans, and Patrons in Early America*. Philadelphia: UPenn, 2007.

MacLeitch, Gail. *Imperial Entanglements: Iroquois Change and Persistence on the Frontiers of Empire*. Philadelphia: UPenn, 2011.

Mancall, Peter C. *Deadly Medicine: Indians and Alcohol in Early America*. Ithaca: Cornell University, 1997.

Mancke, Elizabeth, and Carle Shammas, eds. *The Creation of the British Atlantic World*. Baltimore: Johns Hopkins University, 2005.

Manion, Jen. *Liberty's Prisoners: Carceral Culture in Early America*. Philadelphia: UPenn, 2015.

Mapp, Paul. *The Elusive West and the Contest for Empire, 1713–1763*. Chapel Hill: UNC, 2013.

Marietta, Jack D., and G. S. Rowe. *Troubled Experiment: Crime and Justice in Pennsylvania, 1682–1800*. Philadelphia: UPenn, 2006.

Marshall, P. J., and Alaine Low, eds. *The Oxford History of the British Empire: Volume II: The Eighteenth Century*. Oxford: Oxford University, 1998.

McDonnell, Michael A. *Masters of Empire: Great Lakes Indians and the Making of America*. New York: Hill and Wang, 2015.

Merrell, James. *Into the American Woods: Negotiators on the Pennsylvania Frontier*. New York: Norton, 1999.

Merrit, Jane. *At the Crossroads: Indians and Empires on a Mid-Atlantic Frontier, 1700–1763*. Charlottesville: UNC, 2002.

Moogk, Peter N. *La Nouvelle France: The Making of French Canada, A Cultural History*. Michigan State University, 2000.

Montaño, John Patrick. *The Roots of English Colonialism in Ireland*. Cambridge: Cambridge University, 2001.

Morgan, Jennifer L. *Laboring Women: Reproduction and Gender in New World Slavery*. Philadelphia: UPenn, 2004.

Morris, Charles. *The History of Pennsylvania*. Philadelphia: Lippincott, 1913.

Moss, Roger W. *Historic Houses of Philadelphia*. Philadelphia: UPenn, 1998.

Murphy, Andrew R. *William Penn: A Life*. Oxford: Oxford University, 2019.

Mt. Pleasant, Alyssa, Caroline Wiggington, and Kelly Wisecup. "Forum: Materials and Methods in Indigenous Studies: Completing the Turn." *William & Mary Quarterly* 75, no. 2 (2018): 207–36.

Narrett, David E. *Inheritance and Family Life in Colonial New York City*. Ithaca: Cornell University, 2011.

Nash, Gary B. *Quakers and Politics: Pennsylvania, 1681–1726*. Princeton: Princeton University, 1968.

———. "Slaves and Slaveowners in Colonial Philadelphia." *The William & Mary Quarterly* 30, no. 2 (April 1973): 223–56.

———. *The Urban Crucible: The Northern Seaports and the Origins of the American Revolution, Abridged Ed.*. Cambridge: Harvard University, 1986.

Nash, Gary B., and Billy G. Smith. "The Population of Eighteenth-Century Philadelphia." *Pennsylvania Magazine of History and Biography* 99, no. 3 (1975): 362–68.

Newell, Margaret. *Brethren by Nature: New England Indians, Colonists, and the Origins of American Slavery*. Ithaca: Cornell University, 2015.

Newman, Simon P. "Benjamin Franklin and the Leather-Apron Men: The

Politics of Class in Eighteenth-Century Philadelphia." *Journal of American Studies* 43, no. 2 (2009): 161–75.

Noel, Jan, ed. *Race and Gender in the Northern Colonies*. Toronto: Canadian Scholars, 2001.

Norton, Marcy. *A New World of Goods: A History of Tobacco and Chocolate in the Spanish Empire 1492–1700*. Berkeley: University of California, 2000.

Norton, Mary Beth. "The Law of Marital Subordination." In Norton *Founding Mothers and Fathers: Gendered Power and the Forming of American Society*. New York: Vintage, 1997.

O'Brien, Jean. *Firsting and Lasting: Writing Indians Out of Existence in New England*. Minneapolis: University of Minnesota, 2010.

O'Callaghan, E. B., MD, ed. *The Documentary History of the State of New York*. Albany: Weed, Parsons, & Co., 1850.

Oberg, Michael Leroy. *Dominion and Civility: English Imperialism, Native America, and the First Americans Frontiers, 1585–1685*. Ithaca: Cornell University, 1999.

―――. *The Head in Edward Nugent's Hand: Roanoke's Forgotten Indians*. Philadelphia: UPenn, 2008.

O'Malley, Gregory E. *Final Passages: The Intercolonial Slave Trade of British America, 1619–1807*. Chapel Hill: UNC/OIEAHC, 2014.

Ostler, Jeffrey, and Nancy Shoemaker. "Settler Colonialism in Early American History: Introduction." *The William & Mary Quarterly* 76, no. 3 (July 2019): 361–68.

Otto, Paul. "Wampum, Tawagonshi, and the Two Row Belt." *Journal of Early American History* 3, no. 1 (2013): 110–25.

Pagden, Anthony. *Ideologies of Empire in Spain, Britain, and France c. 1500–c. 1800*. New Haven: Yale University, 1995.

Parish, Susan Scott. *American Curiosity: Cultures of Natural History in the Colonial British Atlantic World*. Chapel Hill: OIEAHC/UNC, 2012.

Parker, Arthur C. "The Constitution of the Five Nations or the Iroquois Book of the Great Law." *New York State Museum Bulletin* 184 (April 1, 1916): 7–118.

―――. *Parker on the Iroquois: Iroquois Uses of Maize and Other Food Plants; The Code of Handsome Lake, the Seneca Prophet; The Constitution of Five Nations*. Syracuse: Syracuse University, 1981.

Parker, Arthur C., ed. *Seneca Myths and Folk Tales*. New York: Buffalo Historical Society, 1923.

Parmenter, Jon. "After the Mourning Wars: The Iroquois as Allies in Colonial North American Campaigns, 1676–1760." *The William & Mary Quarterly*, Third Series, 64, no. 1 (January 2007): 39–76.

————. *The Edge of the Woods: Iroquoia, 1534–1701*. East Lansing: Michigan State University, 2010, 276–77.

Parsons, Christopher. *A Not So New World: Empire and Environment in French Colonial North America*. Philadelphia: University of Pennsylvania Press, 2018.

Paulett, Robert. *An Empire of Small Places: Mapping the Southeastern Anglo-Indian Trade, 1732–1795*. Athens: University of Georgia, 2012.

Pencak, William A., and Daniel K. Richter. *Friends and Enemies in Penn's Woods: Indians, Colonists, and the Racial Construction of Pennsylvania*. University Park: Penn State University, 2004.

Perdue, Theda. *Cherokee Women: Gender and Culture Change, 1700–1835*. Lincoln: University of Nebraska, 1999.

Piker, Joshua Aaron. *Okfuskee: A Creek Town in Colonial America*. Cambridge: Harvard University, 2009.

Pilcher, James Evelyn, L.H.D. *The Seal and Arms of Pennsylvania*. Harrisburg: W. H. Stanley, State Printer, 1902.

Plane, Ann Marie. *Colonial Intimacies: Indian Marriage in Early New England*. Ithaca: Cornell University, 2000.

Porter, Roy, ed. *The Cambridge History of Medicine*. Cambridge: Cambridge University, 2006.

Powell, J. W. *Nineteenth Annual Report of the Bureau of American Ethnology*. Washington, DC: Government Printing Office, 1900.

Ramos, Gabriela, and Yanna Yannakakis. "Introduction." In Ramos and Yannakakis, eds., *Indigenous Intellectuals: Knowledge, Power, and Colonial Culture in Mexico and the Andes*. Durham: Duke University, 2014.

Ramsey, William L. *The Yamasee War: A Study of Culture, Economy, and Conflict in the Colonial South*. Lincoln: University of Nebraska, 2010.

Rasmussen, Brigit Brander. *Queequeg's Coffin: Indigenous Literacies and Early American Literature*. Durham: Duke University, 2012.

Reinberger, Mark, and Elizabeth McLean. "Isaac Norris's Fairhill: Architecture, Landscape, and Quaker Ideals in a Philadelphia Colonial Country Seat." *Winterthur Portfolio* (Winter 1997): 243–74.

Reis, Elizabeth. *Damned Women: Sinners and Witches in Early New England*. Ithaca: Cornell University, 1999.

Rice, James D. *Tales from a Revolution: Bacon's Rebellion and the Transformation of Early America*. Oxford: Oxford University, 2013.

Richter, Daniel K. *Ordeal of the Longhouse: The Peoples of the Iroquois League in the Era of European Colonization.* Chapel Hill: UNC, 1992.

———. *Trade, Land, and Power: The Struggle for Eastern North America.* Philadelphia: UPenn, 2013.

Richter, Daniel K., and James Merrell, eds. *Beyond the Covenant Chain: The Iroquois and their Neighbors in Indian North America, 1600–1800.* Syracuse: Syracuse University, 1987.

Rivett, Sarah. *The Science of the Soul in Colonial New England.* Chapel Hill: UNC, 2012.

Romney, Susanah Shaw. *New Netherland Connections: Intimate Networks and Atlantic Ties in Seventeenth-Century America.* Chapel Hill: UNC, 2014.

Royster, Charles. *Down by the Riverside: A South Carolina Slave Community,* 2d ed. Urbana: University of Illinois, 2009.

Rugemer, Edward B. *Slave Law and the Politics of Resistance in the Early Atlantic World.* Cambridge: Harvard University, 2018.

Rushforth, Brett. *Bonds of Alliance: Indigenous and Atlantic Slaveries in New France.* Chapel Hill: UNC, 2012.

St. John, Wendy B. "Inventing Guardianship: The Mohegan Indians and Their 'Protectors.' " *The New England Quarterly* 72, no. 3 (1999): 362–87.

Sallinger, Sharon V. *Taverns and Drinking in Early America.* Baltimore: Johns Hopkins University, 2004.

Sayre, Gordon M. *The Indian Chief as Tragic Hero: Native Resistance and the Literature of America from Moctezuma to Tecumseh.* Chapel Hill, UNC, 2006.

———. *Les Sauvages Américains: Representations of Native Americans in French and English Colonial Literature.* Chapel Hill: UNC, 1997.

Schactman, Tom. *Gentlemen Scientists and Revolutionaries: The Founding Fathers in the Age of Enlightenment.* New York: St. Martin's, 2014.

Schorb, Jodi. *Reading Prisoners: Literature, Literacy, and the Transformation of American Punishment, 1700–1845.* New Brunswick: Rutgers University, 2014.

———. "Review Essay: Punishment's Prisms, Execution and Eighteenth-Century Print Culture." *Early American Literature* 47, no. 2 (2012): 461–76.

Schutt, Amy C. *Peoples of the River Valleys: The Odyssey of the Delaware Indians.* Philadelphia: UPenn, 2007.

Seay, Scott D. *Hanging Between Heaven and Earth: Capital Crime, Execution Preaching, and Theology in Early New England.* DeKalb: Northern Illinois University, 2009.

Seed, Patricia. *Ceremonies of Possession in Europe's Conquest of the New World, 1492–1640.* Cambridge: Cambridge University, 1995.

Shannon, Timothy. "Dressing for Success on the Mohawk Frontier: Hendrick, William Johnson, and the Indian Fashion." *William & Mary Quarterly* 53, no. 1 (January 1996): 13–42.

———. *Indians and Colonists at the Crossroads of Empire: The Albany Congress of 1754.* Ithaca: Cornell University, 2000.

———. *Iroquois Diplomacy on the Early American Frontier.* New York: Viking, 2008.

Shea, John Gilmary, ed. *A Description of the Province and City of New York: with Plans of the City and Several Forts as They Existed in the Year 1695 by John Miller.* New York: William Gowans, 1862.

Sheehan, Bernard. *Savagism and Civility: Indians and Englishmen in Colonial Virginia.* Cambridge: Cambridge University, 1980.

Shields, David S. *Civil Tongues and Polite Letters in British America.* Chapel Hill: UNC, 1997.

———. "Henry Brooke and the Situation of the First Belletrists in British America." *Early American Literature* 32 (1988): 4–27.

———. "The Wits and Poets of Pennsylvania: New Light on the Rise of Belles Lettres in Provincial Philadelphia, 1720–1740." *The Pennsylvania Magazine of History and Biography* (April 1985): 99–143.

Shook, John R., ed. *The Dictionary of Early American Philosophers.* New York: Bloomsbury, 2012.

Siena, Kevin. *Rotten Bodies: Class & Contagion in 18th-Century Britain.* New Haven: Yale University, 2019.

Silver, Timothy. *A New Face on the Countryside: Indians, Colonists, and Slaves in South Atlantic Forests, 1500–1800.* Cambridge: Cambridge University, 1990.

Silverman, David J. *Thundersticks: Firearms and the Violent Transformation of Native America.* Cambridge: Harvard University, 2016.

Slater, Sandra. "Fur Traders, Voyageurs, and Coureurs des Bois: Economic Masculinities in French Canadian Fur Trade Society, 1635–1754." *Masculinities: A Journal of Identity and Culture* 1 (February–August 2014), 92–119.

Sleeper-Smith, Susan. *Indigenous Prosperity and American Conquest: Indian Women of the Ohio River Valley, 1690–1792.* Chapel Hill: UNC/OIEAHC, 2018.

Sleeper-Smith, Susan, Juliana Barr, Jean M. O'Brien, Nancy Shoemaker, and Scott Manning Stevens, eds. *Why You Can't Teach United States History Without American Indians.* Chapel Hill: UNC, 2015.

Smith, Billy G. *The "Lower Sort": Philadelphia's Laboring People, 1750–1800.* Ithaca: Cornell University, 1990.

Smith, George, MD. *History of Delaware County, Pennsylvania*. Philadelphia: Henry B. Ashmead, 1862.

Smolenski, John. *Friends and Strangers: The Making of Creole Culture in Pennsylvania*. Philadelphia: UPenn, 2011.

Snyder, Christina. *Slavery in Indian Country: The Changing Face of Captivity in Early America*. Cambridge: Harvard University, 2010.

Snyder, Terri L. *Brabbling Women: Disorderly Speech and the Law in Early Virginia*. Ithaca: Cornell University, 2003.

Soderlund, Jean R. "Black Importation and Migration into Southeastern Pennsylvania, 1682–1810." In *Proceedings of the American Philosophical Society* 133, no. 2 (June 1989): 144–53.

————. *Lenape Country: Delaware Valley Society before William Penn*. Philadelphia: UPenn, 2015.

————. *Quakers and Slavery: A Divided Spirit*. Princeton: Princeton University, 2014.

Speck, Frank G. *Midwinter Rites of the Cayuga Longhouse*. Lincoln: University of Nebraska, 1995.

Spencer, Mark G., ed. *The Bloomsbury Encyclopedia of the American Enlightenment*. New York: Bloomsbury, 2015.

Stahlman, William D. "Astrology in Colonial America: An Extended Query." *The William & Mary Quarterly* 13, no. 4 (October 1956): 551–63.

Stanwood, Owen. *The Empire Reformed: English America in the Age of the Glorious Revolution*. Philadelphia: UPenn, 2011.

Steele, Ian K. *Politics of Colonial Policy: The Board of Trade in Colonial Administration*. Oxford: Clarendon, 1968.

Stephen, Leslie, ed. *Dictionary of National Biography, Volume 41*. New York: Macmillan, 1895.

Stern, Jessica Yirush. *The Lives in Objects: Native Americans, British Colonists, and Cultures of Labor and Exchange in the Southeast*. Chapel Hill: UNC, 2017.

Stevens, Scott Manning. "The Historiography of New France and the Legacy of Iroquois Internationalism." *Comparative American Studies* 11 (2013): 148–56.

Strang, Cameron B. *Frontiers of Science: Imperialism and Natural Knowledge in the Gulf South Borderlands, 1500–1850*. Chapel Hill: OIEAHC/UNC, 2018.

Sumira, Sylvia. *The Art and History of Globes*. London: British Library Publishing, 2014.

Thornton, Tamara Plakins. "The 'Use of Globes': Mathematical Geography, the Mercantile Imagination, and Global Commerce in Postrevolutionary America." Paper presented to the Sixteenth Annual Conference of the Program in Early American Economy and Society, Library Company of Philadelphia, October 6–7, 2016, accessed at: http://librarycompany .org/Economics/2016conference/pdfs/PEAES%20--%202016%20 Conf%20--%20Thornton%20ppr.pdf.

Tiro, Karim. *People of the Standing Stone: The Oneida Nation from the Revolution Through the Era of Removal.* Amherst: University of Massachusetts, 2011.

Tolles, Frederick. *James Logan and the Culture of Provincial America.* New York: Little, Brown, 1957.

Tomlins, Christopher. *Freedom Bound: Law, Labor, and Civic Identity in Colonizing English America, 1580–1865.* Cambridge: Cambridge University, 2010.

Tomlins, T. J. *A Divinity for All Persuasions: Almanacs and Early American Religious Life.* Oxford: Oxford University, 2014.

Ulrich, Laurel Thatcher. *Goodwives Image and Reality in the Lives of Women in Northern New England, 1650–1750.* New York: Vintage, 1991.

———. *A Midwife's Tale: The Life of Martha Ballard Based on Her Diary, 1785–1812.* New York: Knopf, 2010.

Van Horn, Jennifer. *The Power of Objects in Eighteenth-Century British America.* Chapel Hill: UNC, 2017.

Van Kirk, Sylvia. *Many Tender Ties: Women in Fur Trade Society.* Norman: University of Oklahoma Press, 1983.

Van Laer, A.J.F. "Preface." In *Minutes of the Court of Fort Orange and Beverwyck, Volume 1.* Albany: University of the State of New York, 1920.

Venema, Janny. *Beverwijck: A Dutch Village on the American Frontier, 1652–1664.* Albany: State University of New York, 2003.

Walker, James. "From Alterity to Allegory: Depictions of Cannibalism on Early European Maps of the New World." In *The Occasional Papers: A Philip Lee Phillips Map Society Publication.* Washington, DC: Library of Congress Geography and Map Division, 2015.

Walker, Lewis. "Andrew Hamilton and the He-Monster." *The William & Mary Quarterly* 38, no. 2 (1981): 268–94.

Wallace, Anthony F. C. *The Death and Rebirth of the Seneca.* New York: Vintage, 1969.

Wallace, Paul A. W. *Indian Paths of Pennsylvania.* Harrisburg: Pennsylvania Historical and Museum Commission, 2005.

Waldstreicher, David. *Runaway America: Benjamin Franklin, Slavery, and the American Revolution.* New York: Macmillan, 2005.

Wareing, John. *Indentured Migration and the Servant Trade from London to America, 1618–1718: "There is Great Want of Servants."* New York: Oxford University, 2017.

Warren, Stephen. *The Worlds the Shawnees Made, Migration and Violence in Early America.* Chapel Hill: UNC, 2014.

Waselkov, Gregory A., Peter H. Wood, and Tom Hatley, eds. *Powhattan's Mantle: Indians in the Colonial Southeast.* University of Nebraska, 2006.

Watson, John F. *Annals of Philadelphia and Pennsylvania in Olde Time.* Philadelphia: Published for the Author, 1850.

Waugh, F. W. *Iroquois Foods and Food Preparation.* Anthropological Series, 12. The Canadian Geological Survey (Ottawa: Government Printing Bureau, 1916.)

Webb, Stephen Saunders. *1676: The End of American Independence.* New York: Syracuse University, 1995.

Wendell, Thomas H. "The Life and Writings of Sir William Keith." PhD Dissertation, University of Washington, 1964.

West, Francis D. "The Mystery of the Death of William Bartram, Father of John Bartram the Botanist." *Pennsylvania Genealogical Magazine* 20, no. 3 (1957): 253–55.

Westcott, Thompson. *The Historic Mansions and Buildings of Philadelphia: With Some Notice of Their Owners and Occupants.* Philadelphia: Porter and Coates, 1877.

White, Father Andrew. "Narrative of a Voyage to Maryland, April 1634." Maryland Historical Society, Fund Publication No. 7. Baltimore, 1874.

White, Richard. *The Middle Ground: Indians, Empires, and Republics in the Great Lakes Region, 1650–1815.* Cambridge: Cambridge University, 1991.

White, Sophie. *Wild Frenchmen and Frenchified Indians: Material Culture and Race in Colonial Louisiana.* Philadelphia: UPenn, 2013.

Wilkins, David E., ed. *Documents of Native American Political Development, 1500's–1933.* Oxford: Oxford University, 2009.

Williams, George H. *Wilderness and Paradise in Christian Thought.* New York: Harper, 1962.

Williams, Robert A. *Linking Arms Together: American Indian Treaty Visions of Law and Peace, 1600–1800.* New York: Routledge, 1999.

Winterer, Caroline. *American Enlightenments: Pursuing Happiness in the Age of Reason.* New Haven: Yale University, 2016.

Wiseman, Frederick Matthew. *The Voice of the Dawn: An Autohistory of the Abenaki Nation.* Hanover: University of New England, 2001.

Witgen, Michael. *An Infinity of Nations: How the Native New World Shaped Early North America.* Philadelphia: UPenn, 2011.

Wolf, Edwin. *The Book Culture of a Colonial American City: Philadelphia Books, Bookmen, and Booksellers.* Oxford: Oxford University, 1988.

———. *James Logan, 1674–51, Bookman Extraordinary.* Philadelphia: Library Company of Philadelphia, 1971, [n.p., 3] & 18.

Wolf, Edwin, 2nd, and Marie Elena Korey, eds. *Quarter of a Millennium.* Philadelphia: The Library Company of Philadelphia, 1981.

Woodward, Walter. *Prospero's America: John Winthrop, Jr., Alchemy, and the Creation of New England Culture, 1606–1676.* Chapel Hill; UNC, 2011.

Wroth, Lawrence C. "The Indian Treaty as Literature." *Yale Review.* 1928.

———. *The Colonial Printer.* New York: Grolier Club, 1931: 749–66.

Wulf, Karin. *Not All Wives: Women of Colonial Philadelphia.* Philadelphia: UPenn, 2005.

Yirush, Craig. *Settlers, Liberty, and Empire: The Roots of Early American Political Theory.* Cambridge: Cambridge University, 2011.

INDEX

Page numbers in *italics* refer to illustrations. Page numbers after 344 refer to notes.